Accession no.

D0301328

Divergent paths

Manchester University Press

Divergent paths

Family histories of Irish emigrants in Britain, 1820–1920

John Herson

LIS LIBRARY

Date | Fund
20-3-15 | i-che

Order No
2583781

University of Chester

WITHDRAWN

Manchester University Press

Copyright © John Herson 2015

The right of John Herson to be identified as the author of this work has been asserted by him in accordance with the Copyright, Designs and Patents Act 1988.

Published by Manchester University Press
Altrincham Street, Manchester M1 7JA
www.manchesteruniversitypress.co.uk

British Library Cataloguing-in-Publication Data
A catalogue record for this book is available from the British Library

Library of Congress Cataloging-in-Publication Data applied for

ISBN 978 0 7190 9063 9 hardback

First published 2015

The publisher has no responsibility for the persistence or accuracy of URLs for any external or third-party internet websites referred to in this book, and does not guarantee that any content on such websites is, or will remain, accurate or appropriate.

Typeset by Out of House Publishing
Printed in Great Britain by
CPI Group (UK) Ltd, Croydon, CR0 4YY

Contents

Figures

Tables

With the exception of Table 1.1 the data in all tables in the book is taken from the author's database of the Stafford Irish families, as outlined in Chapter 1. The structure and contents of the database are described in the Bibliography.

Acknowledgements

This book has been a very long time in gestation. Back in the 1980s I lived in my mother's home town of Stafford and whilst there reconstructed her family tree. I discovered an apparent Irish ancestor and was surprised to find that many Irish people were living in Stafford in the mid-nineteenth century. I must therefore thank long-dead Mary Corcoran from Co. Roscommon for stimulating my interest in the experiences of the Irish, their families and descendants. Dr Eddie Hunt at the London School of Economics gave early encouragement and rigorous guidance whilst initial development of my digital capability owed much to Val O'Hanlon at what was then Liverpool Polytechnic. Professor Roger Swift at the University of Chester also offered great support. Recent development of the work has owed much to the encouragement and criticisms of colleagues at Liverpool John Moores University, particularly Sam Davies, Helen Rogers and Jack Williams. Paul O'Leary of Aberystwyth University and Andy Gritt of the University of Central Lancashire have also provided me with much stimulating comment. Steve Lawler and Phil Rothwell have helped on issues of IT, and Phil Cubbin prepared two digital maps that are included in the final text.

I owe a great debt of gratitude to the staff at the William Salt Library and the Staffordshire Record Office in Stafford, at the Birmingham Archdiocesan Archives, at the National Archives and National Library of Ireland in Dublin, and at the Public Record Office of Northern Ireland in Belfast, particularly as they struggle to keep services going in the face of financial cuts that are undermining our status as civilised nations.

The work has gained immeasurably from the interest shown and help given by descendants of Stafford's Irish immigrants in the town itself, elsewhere in Britain and also overseas. This has been through correspondence, email, interviews and other face-to-face meetings. I cannot name all the people who contributed but, where appropriate, specific information is acknowledged in the textual notes. Some enduring friendships have resulted from the research. I am indebted to a number of people for permission to use photographs in their possession: Simon and Mary Godwin (Figure 5.4), Kathleen Boult (Figures 5.5 and 5.6), Sally Ann Harrison (Figures 7.3 and 7.4) and Mary Mitchell (Figure 10.3). May Galvin, Sheila Leslie-Miller and Michael Harrison have also been immensely helpful. It is sad that Joe Galvin, Roy Mitchell and Peter Godwin did not live to see the final result. The photograph of Martin Mitchell (Figure 6.5) is reproduced by courtesy of the Staffordshire County Museums Service. Figure 8.1 is derived from a commercial postcard in the author's possession that was published by the London and North Western Railway in the 1900s. Figures 8.2 and 10.2 are derived from photographs contained in Bernard Malley, *Solihull and the Catholic Faith*, privately published in 1939, a copy of which is in this author's possession. Despite diligent efforts it has not proved possible to identify the current copyright holder for this work.

Despite the availability of online information, reconstructing the genealogies of families is still an art subject to data ambiguities, gaps in the record and personal judgement. Every effort has been made to produce robust genealogies of the families discussed in the book but any inaccuracies remain the responsibility of the author. He will esteem it a favour if specific and proven errors of fact are brought to his attention.

Tony Mason and the staff at Manchester University Press have been unfailingly helpful and supportive during the production process. It has been a pleasure working with them.

Finally I would like to thank my wife Anne Boran and our son David for their help. That has not just been the natural support offered by one's loving family but has also been in more specific contributions to the project. Anne and her family in Co. Kilkenny and elsewhere in Ireland have offered many subtle and valuable insights into Irish life, attitudes and history that might not otherwise be apparent to an English outsider. David, on the other hand, has grown up as a mixed-ethnicity descendant in England and he has been able to offer me perspectives on the issues of identity and loyalty that result. His support for the England cricket team, the Ireland rugby team, Liverpool FC and the Kilkenny GAA hurling team says it all.

Abbreviations

BAA	Birmingham Archdiocesan Archives
BC	Borough Council
CC&S	Craft, clerical and service (families)
LNWR	London and North Western Railway
MOH	Medical Officer of Health
NA	National Archives, Kew
NAI	National Archives of Ireland
NLI	National Library of Ireland
PP	Parliamentary Papers
PRONI	Public Record Office of Northern Ireland
PTSD	Post-traumatic stress disorder
RC	Roman Catholic
RC Poorer Classes	*Royal Commission on the Condition of the Poorer Classes in Ireland* (1836)
RD	Registration District
SA	*Staffordshire Advertiser*
SBC	Stafford Borough Council
SRO	Staffordshire Record Office
TAB	Tithe Applotment Books (NLI)
VCH	*Victoria County History* (with relevant volume)

A note on citations

This study inherently makes great use of data from census enumeration returns that are now easily available from online sources and are also contained in the author's database described in Chapter 1. It is not practicable or useful to give the reference for every piece of data taken from the enumeration returns, and where the text contains evidence that specifically refers to a date in the census years – 1841, 1851, 1861 etc. – the reader should assume the source was the relevant enumeration return unless stated otherwise. In the citation of birth, marriage and death registration details the Registration District is abbreviated as RD, as in 'Stafford RD'. Similarly, unless stated otherwise, birth, marriage and death data have been taken from the Indices of Births, Marriages and Deaths in England and Wales, 1835–1915 and 1915–2000, published on the *Ancestry* database (www.ancestry.co.uk).

1

Irish emigrants and family history: a new approach

ALLEGED MANSLAUGHTER BY AN IRISHMAN.
An inquest was held on the death of Patrick Mannion, 61, who died from injuries received in a disturbance in his house in Snow's Yard on Saturday night. Shortly before midnight his son, John Mannion, and a labourer, Patrick Power, who was lodging there, had a quarrel. Patrick Mannion went upstairs to quieten them. Power struck him in the face and knocked him down. Mrs Mannion fell downstairs and hurt her face badly. A youth, Henry Ferneyhough, saw Power kick Patrick Mannion in the stomach in the back kitchen. Power then put on his boots and left the house ... John Raftery, living in Greyfriars, said Power aroused him early on Sunday morning ... Power said 'Jack, I've done it – I've crippled old Mannion. I've crushed his bones for him.' The witness told him it was not creditable to hurt an old man who had reared a big family.[1]

DEATH OF MR BARTHOLOMEW CORCORAN.
Mr Corcoran died on Wednesday at 24 North Street where only two days previously he had taken up residence. He was 77 years of age. Mr Corcoran came to Stafford about 50 years ago and carried on a business as a plumber and decorator for about 30 years in Foregate Street, retiring about ten years ago. Mr Corcoran took a keen interest in public affairs and served as a member of the Town Council from 1894 to 1903, whilst from April 1895 to 1901 he represented the East Ward on the Board of Guardians. As a member of the Catholic community, the deceased was a liberal benefactor to St Patrick's Church and Schools, and as a memorial to his first wife he presented the Stations of the Cross to St Patrick's Church. He was manager of the day schools and for many years was president of the St Vincent de Paul Society. The deceased, who was twice married, has eight children living.[2]

Patrick Mannion and Bartholomew Corcoran were Irish. They had left Ireland in the 1850s and settled in Stafford, a small town in the English West Midlands. They were just two individuals in the great wave of emigration that by 1900 meant more Irish people lived outside Ireland than in the country itself. Irish emigrants and their descendants were to be found in most parts of Britain, the United States, Australia, New Zealand, South America, South Africa and elsewhere.

Patrick Mannion was killed in 1899 whilst Bartholomew Corcoran died in 1908. Mannion died in Snow's Yard, one of Stafford's slum courts. Its squalid circumstances illustrate a common image of Irish immigrants struggling to survive in poverty, insecurity, drink and violence. His story could be repeated almost anywhere the Irish settled in Britain. Bartholomew Corcoran's life shows a different side of the Irish experience. He started off in another Stafford slum, Plant's Square, but died a prosperous and respected man. His success demonstrates how the paths of Irish immigrants could diverge from the common picture of misery and suffering. Corcoran's story could also be replicated amongst the Irish in other towns and cities.

A family-history approach to Irish emigrants

The press reports about Patrick Mannion and Bartholomew Corcoran contain some other evidence of a type generally ignored by historians of the Irish. These men were not isolated individuals. Both stories mention the family relationships of the deceased. They were, in other words, members of wider families. During their lives they had lived in various sorts of family situation and their actions had been influenced by other people, both related and unrelated. These simple facts define the target of this book. It tests a new approach to the study of Irish migrants by focusing on their *families* and on what happened to them. It charts the history of a representative sample of families and individuals settled in Stafford. It documents the lives they led and what happened to their descendants, and shows the ways by which many families, though by no means all, became integrated into English society. The aim is to show what their lives were like in a small town during the Industrial Revolution, and to extend our understanding of the variety and complexity of the Irish experience in nineteenth-century England.

The family is a core social institution. Sociologists debate the precise definition and significance of the family as a social phenomenon, but earlier research on Stafford demonstrated in practical terms both the importance and the persistence of family units amongst its Irish population.[3] This might seem a statement of the blindingly obvious, yet very few historians have looked at the family dimension to Irish immigration. Lynn Hollen Lees' study of the Irish in London discusses families generally both before and after migration, but she only occasionally mentions the experiences of specific families.[4] Bruce Elliott's book on Protestant Irish families in Canada was a pioneering work that includes some genealogies and limited family histories, but its approach is more diffuse than this book since it tracks families from their origin in Ireland to a multiplicity of places in Canada. His work has not been emulated for Britain.[5]

Some historians have documented family ties across the Irish diaspora using the evidence of letters and other sources. David Fitzpatrick's book of personal accounts of Irish migration to Australia offers fascinating insights, as does Kerby Miller and partners' work on early Irish immigrants to America. The letters of the Reynolds family in Manchester are rare evidence of life in a migrant family spread between Britain and America. There are a number of studies of localities in Ireland that trace emigrant families into the Irish diaspora.[6] These works provide some evidence of family structures and forces. Even so, their sources are inherently scattered in geographical terms and they do not record the long-term history of a sample of families in a specific location. They also deal almost exclusively with the perceptions of the emigrants themselves, not those of succeeding generations. Furthermore, we learn nothing of 'ordinary' families who left no documentary material.

Most historians of the Irish in Britain have ignored or glossed over the family dimension. There has been some work on family structures that includes the Irish. In 1971 Michael Anderson published his book on family structure in nineteenth-century Preston. This remains a seminal work that incidentally has a lot to say about the Irish. In 1994 Marguerite Dupree looked at a similar topic in the Staffordshire Potteries, an area close to, but very different from, Stafford town. She unfortunately had little to say about the Irish. Neither author looked at the long-term trajectories of specific families, however.[7] Carl Chinn's study of the Irish in Birmingham has selected family information and reminiscence but is not a comprehensive study of Irish families in the city.[8] Studies that document Irish *households* in the census enumeration returns have the problem that the census just provides a snapshot at one moment. Unless individuals and families are traced from one census to the next such studies cannot follow peoples' lives and experiences over time. They are forced to paint an aggregate picture of change in the Irish population, a process that can produce crude generalisations. It cannot document the variation in the immigrants' life trajectories and, more particularly, those of succeeding generations. As a result, the majority of long-term studies of the Irish in Britain tend to rely on associational evidence of people in workplaces, churches, political organisations, clubs and so on, or on instances of petty criminality and conflict documented by the State and in the press. Such an approach sees the Irish either as *individuals* operating in various social contexts or as *a mass* with a range of assumed identities and loyalties. Both fail to encapsulate the variations to be found in the total Irish population and do not reveal the family, kin

and social connections they may have had over time. This book originated, therefore, in dissatisfaction with these conventional approaches
to Irish immigrants.

No previous attempt has been made to explore how the evidence provided by family history can be used to explore the story of Irish migrants
in Britain. This book intends to do that. It argues that a focus on families
rather than on individuals or the mass offers a fruitful and sensitive way
of understanding the Irish experience. The picture that emerges is complex. It challenges simplistic interpretations of the relationship between
the Irish and the host population, and particularly the notion that there
was inherent tension or conflict between them. It shows the ways, often
problematic, by which Irish immigrants and their descendants became
integrated into the evolving society of England. In doing this it is a counterweight to the common view of Irish emigration with its emphasis on
exile and victimhood. The processes of identity formation and social
interaction bound up with family life in practice led to many different
outcomes.

The Irish experience and family history

By focusing on families this book provides new evidence on seven issues
concerning the Irish migrant experience. The first is that of timescale.
It is important to take the *long-term view* of a migrant population and
its descendants. Popular perceptions of the Irish naturally focus on the
Famine and the massive emigration it provoked. The process of emigration and settlement was inevitably stressful, and there is copious evidence of the uncertainties and sufferings that the migrant generation had
to endure. Modern research has increasingly tried to take a longer view,
however. What happened to the Irish and their descendants in the decades up to and beyond the Great War? The answers to this question are
often rather generalised or focus on those people whose Irishness was still
identifiable. The Irish inevitably fanned out in different directions, however, as generation succeeded generation. The family-history approach
can track this process. Family trajectories could change radically over
time through both generational succession and a changing environment.
The time of immigration and settlement was profoundly important, but
study of an extended period can reveal how its significance decayed.

The second issue is the basic one of defining who 'the Irish' were –
the question of *ethnicity*. Catholic and arguably 'Celtic' Irish people
formed the largest group of Irish emigrants in the nineteenth century.
Many studies have concentrated on these people and their experiences.
The fact is, however, that by the nineteenth century the population of
Ireland was a complex mix of ethnic groups resulting from centuries of

social, political, economic and religious action in the geographical space of the country. The ethnic identities of those groups were partly defined by their conflict with 'others' but they were also dynamic and subject to change.[9] The family-history approach has to define specific individuals and families as 'Irish', not just deal with a generalised body of people. The way this is done is discussed later. Studies of defined ethnic groups such as the Irish also run the risk of assuming that ethnicity was the dominant factor determining peoples' identity and life chances. This cannot be taken for granted. A focus on family history can show whether ethnicity was truly dominant or not.

Consideration of the family inevitably raises a third issue, that of *gender*. Traditional work on the public face of Irish migrants inherently tended to highlight men's activities. In 1979 Lees considered changes to the woman's role in the family economy of migrants in London, but her discussion was at a high level of generality.[10] Since then there has been some continuing interest in Irish women but work has tended to focus on specific issues in the public role of women, for example women and the Catholic Church, women in (paid) employment or the public role of women in running networks of mutual aid.[11] Paul O'Leary has more sensitively identified the interdependence between public and private life in discussing the significance of gender roles in the cult of Victorian respectability amongst the Irish.[12] This link is important, and what is needed is more evidence about the 'private' role of women. Adopting a family approach inherently highlights these more private gender relationships and roles whilst not ignoring the public interactions of both sexes. It considers the extent to which women as well as men contributed to family income generation but also whether women essentially defined the nature of the family and home environment. Was their role the prime determinant of how families developed over the long term? A study of family history also exposes the impact of domination by, or absence of, significant male or female individuals. This tests the extent to which, across different families, 'traditional' gender roles were entrenched, or in practice were more fluid.

The fourth issue, the *identity or identities* of Irish migrants and their descendants, has been discussed in many studies. Earlier work often argued that the 'Irish', again, normally the Catholic Celtic Irish, retained their identity as a defence against the hostile society into which they had moved. This involved some vision of their collective identity. Research over the past twenty years has produced a more nuanced picture but it still tends to focus on groups of Irish and their leaders rather than on ordinary individuals and their families.[13] The key problem is the interplay amongst individual, family and collective identities. Individual identity was affected by a person's diverse circumstances and the policies and practices of institutions with which he or she came into contact.

The family was one of those institutions. Family relationships were the main conduit down which memories, legends, attitudes and identity were transmitted. The family was, in other words, a key force moulding the impact of Irish collective identity on individuals. If, on the one hand, the ethnic group continued to be defined by reference to a hostile 'other' society, then its collective identity would continue to be formed by a struggle that had meaning to families and individuals. If, on the other hand, families and individuals perceived little value in adhering to the collective vision and took steps to engage with the 'other', the collective identity would tend to fade away.[14] It has been suggested that the Irish in fact demonstrated 'mutative ethnicity' depending on the circumstances of the places where they settled. Ethnic identity could only be maintained as an active force when it continued to distribute meaningful benefits such as employment or housing through ethnically structured channels. If these failed to exist because the numbers of Irish were too few or if intermarriage diluted ethnic distinctiveness and segregation, then ethnic identity would decline as a social force.[15]

Writers on the Irish have to account for the apparent mutation of identities over time, but almost all discussion of this phenomenon is at a general level, illustrated by evidence of ethnic associations and examples of specific individuals. The role of the family in the process of identity formation has been almost totally ignored. This study of Stafford will investigate the phenomenon. It will question whether ethnic identity trumped other factors in determining how people saw themselves and the outside world. It will look at the working-class Catholic and Celtic Irish but also at the higher-status and Protestant families who have been less studied but generally seen as less problematic. It will consider the significance or otherwise of religion and spirituality, both Catholic and Protestant, in moulding the ethos and identity of families. This involves considering the nature of the religious beliefs they brought from Ireland, the influence of organised religion in England, and the extent to which there was 'leakage' from the churches over time and down the generations.

The fifth issue revolves around the *origins and attitudes* of the emigrant Irish and how these affected their lives overseas. This arises particularly in relation to the 'Catholic Celtic' Irish. Many writers implicitly assume that this group formed an 'ethnie' – that they were defined by a myth of common ancestry, shared historical memories, a common culture, links with the homeland and a sense of solidarity.[16] In 1985 Kerby Miller articulated this perspective in emphasising that the migrant Irish were victims of exile and banishment. This 'exile motif' was the result of the culture and politics of Ireland itself as well as of the immigrants' appalling experiences in the slums of urban America.[17] Miller argued that:

> millions of Irishmen and [Irish]-women, whatever their objective reasons for emigration, approached their departures and their experiences

in North America with an outlook which characterized emigration as exile. Rooted in ancient culture and tradition, shaped by historical circumstances, and adapted to 'explain' the impersonal workings of the market economy, the Irish worldview crossed the ocean to confront the most modern of all societies. From the standpoint of the emigrants' ability to adjust and prosper overseas, the consequent tensions between past and present, ideology and reality, may have had mixed results. However, both the exile motif and the worldview that sustained it ensured the survival of Irish identity and nationalism in the New World.[18]

Miller's perspective has been very influential. It is, however, uncertain to what degree the exile motif is applicable to the Irish who settled in Britain. On the one hand it can be argued that many of those who settled in the land of the colonial oppressor were people, particularly amongst the Famine refugees, who were forced to take the cheapest, easiest option, whatever its economic and cultural drawbacks. From this perspective Britain remained a hated place of exile, and Irish identity, culture and memories would be transmitted to the succeeding generation(s). On the other hand, it can be suggested that settlement in Britain was adopted by those less burdened by a baggage of Irish cultural, religious and political identities. Their prime objective was to achieve individual and family advancement in the new society.

Donald Akenson has argued, indeed, that the exile motif and what he calls the 'Gaelic-Catholic disability variable' present a misleading paradigm for explaining the actual Irish emigrant experience down the generations. He suggests it was the specific nature of the environment facing the Irish immigrants that affected their success or otherwise.[19] The implication of this is that, whatever the traumatic circumstances surrounding an emigrant's departure from Ireland, a more fruitful perspective for investigating the Irish immigrant's experience is to see them as potential opportunists, entrepreneurs and colonisers rather than as helpless exiles and victims. This perspective has received powerful, though much criticised, support from Malcolm Campbell's more recent comparative study of the Irish in the USA and Australia.[20] Little attempt has been made, however, to explore the long-term history of specific Irish immigrants and families in Britain to see whether exile and banishment or settlement and opportunity – or a mixture of the two forces – left the greater permanent imprint on their attitudes, behaviour and relationships. The family-history approach can be used to show the range of trajectories followed by the Irish and the extent to which they might support the 'exile' or 'opportunist' explanations of the migrant experience.

This question is in turn affected by a sixth issue, namely how the immigrants' actual experiences were influenced by the *specific localities* in which they lived. It cannot be gainsaid that the migrants had to endure a change that was inherently traumatic. Most, though not all, had to cross a frontier that was not merely geographic but could involve a shift from rural to urban living within an environment that might be hostile in cultural, religious and social terms. Immigrants and their families therefore had to make a new start in circumstances that were only partly of their own choosing. The extent to which they experienced prejudice and hostility has been widely documented, particularly in Britain and America. The problem is that anti-Irish hostility and violence, by their nature, leave evidence in the form of newspaper reports, pamphlets, court proceedings and the like. Indifference to or acceptance of the Irish were more passive forms of behaviour that are harder to document. Furthermore, the environment within which relationships between the Irish and the various fractions of the host society developed was itself dynamic. Political relationships between Britain and Ireland, between the State and the Catholic Church, as well as the politics of class and social reform, changed substantially during the nineteenth century. These changes influenced the behaviour and identity of the immigrants, their descendants and the host society, but they were always mediated by the character of the specific places where the Irish settled. The local environment of an area of settlement might be either a constraining or an enabling influence on the Irish. There have been many local studies of the Irish but the vast majority conceptualise the key relationship as that between the individual, the mass and the place mediated by various forms of association or power brokers. Family history can, however, reveal much about how groups experienced and responded to a locality over time and down the generations. Were Irish families and individuals 'outcasts' and did they remain so?

The final issue relates to the *Irish Diaspora*. Irish emigrants were part of a worldwide pattern of movement. Their identities could therefore be influenced by wider geographical consciousness as well as by the local environment. The term 'diaspora' has been applied increasingly to this scattering of the Irish. In recent years the term 'transnational' has become popular to emphasise active, on-going linkages amongst dispersed diasporic communities.[21] Cohen suggests that diasporic peoples will normally exhibit a number of features. They will have suffered traumatic dispersal and have a collective memory, myth and idealisation about the homeland which sustains a strong ethnic consciousness over a long period of time, with a shared sense of solidarity with co-ethnic members in other countries. This may result in a troubled relationship with the host society although the migrants' distinctive culture may also enrich life in tolerant host countries.[22] Historians of Irish migration would mostly agree that these features apply to the Irish Diaspora. The problem is that such criteria are often seen as applying *generally* to people throughout the Diaspora whereas Cohen's criteria could be used at the local level to test the actual significance of diasporic consciousness amongst migrants and their descendant families. There was inevitably tension between a possible diasporic identity and the experience of life in a specific place of settlement. Family attitudes were a key mediating force influencing inter-marriage and dilution of ethnic purity down the generations, as well as the socialisation or incorporation processes of Church, school, State and other institutions. Family histories can throw some light on the changing balance amongst diasporic consciousness, transnational links and the forces undermining them. Differences amongst families in terms of long-term transience or permanent settlement may well have reflected variations in the continuing strength of transnational links.

Questions and concepts

This study of Irish families in Stafford seeks to throw light on the seven issues just outlined. This process requires a conceptual framework to help understand the workings of migrant families within their new environment. The 'family' is a problematic concept. Much early research on the family was concerned with the supposed rise of the nuclear family in industrial society – a unit composed merely of parents and their resident children. Such an obsolete perspective would be of little use in studying the Irish. Modern approaches have steadily widened the definition of the 'family' to include all manner of kin, a process undoubtedly bolstered by the growth of popular genealogy. There is also recognition of the significance of other 'quasi-familial' relationships. The definition of a 'family' for this study is therefore broad, but it centres on distinct individuals or groupings of kin identifiable partly by a common name or names but also by their revealed relationships.

Analysis of the history of Stafford's Irish families requires answers to three interrelated questions:

1. How did the families operate and evolve as social entities? This question explores the nature of their day-to-day life.
2. How was family life affected by the specific experience of emigration and settlement? This question explores the impact of migration.
3. How did the families interact with the wider social and economic environment? This question deals with the family in its context.

Answering these questions requires the use of concepts of family behaviour not normally within the purview of specialist historians of the Irish. Sociologists, historians and others have nevertheless developed concepts of the 'family' as a human phenomenon that can be used to investigate the Irish family experience in Stafford.

Each of the three questions can be enlightened by a specific body of theory, and this means the conceptual approach adopted here is rather eclectic. Some theories focus on the *actual behaviour* of families and the individuals within them. They are essentially 'bottom-up' perspectives that are particularly useful in dealing with the first question, that of how Stafford's Irish families operated and evolved. Other approaches are concerned with the family's role as an *institution* within the wider social and economic system. These 'top-down' theories start with the social and economic system and locate families within it. They offer some help in answering the third question, family interaction with the wider social and economic environment. The second research question, the impact of migration on families, is more specific and can be informed by modern work on population movement and settlement. The following discussion outlines these concepts in more detail.

Day-to-day life

A substantial body of literature has examined the internal behaviour of families, but there are three distinct perspectives. These can be summarised as the 'individualisation', 'family strategy' and 'relationships' approaches. The first emphasises the relationship between the individual and the family. It sees family members as actors who use their family instrumentally in pursuit of their individual goals, primarily those of economic survival and security. Anderson's study of Preston exemplifies this approach. His basic premise is that the individual lives his or her life in pursuit of personal goals within an environment where the options are likely to be limited. The pursuit of these goals will be influenced by society's values and norms, presumably inculcated partly through family upbringing, but the individual will essentially seek to use the family and its members to assist in the solving of life's problems. In doing this reciprocal support may be offered to others, but the individual actor will seek a 'psychic profit' in the outcome of instrumental relationships.[23]

Anderson's approach does focus on the detailed lives of individuals and their families and it can reveal some of the variation of response in a particular population. Even so, his view that family life was dominated by a 'short-run instrumental orientation to kin' offers a very one-dimensional view of human existence and the family.[24] It was not supported in the interview evidence collected by Tamara Hareven in her study of French-Canadian families in Manchester, New Hampshire.[25] The history of families in Stafford does not sustain the perspective either, and it is rejected for this study.

The family group could itself be seen to act as if it were an individual, maximising its security and economic or social returns through mutual support and the setting of goals for its members. In other words, a family might adopt an identifiable 'family strategy' and this is the second

behavioural approach to family life.[26] The strategy would be determined
by the circumstances in which the family found itself and foresaw in
the future. Any historical analysis of a particular family's strategy therefore has to place it within its wider economic and social context. This
is a strength of the concept in that it avoids the danger of the seeing
the family purely as an island of internal relationships independent of its
environment.

The idea of family strategy is particularly appropriate to the history
of migrants. In Ireland they were faced with major problems, above all
the Famine, that provoked decisions to emigrate. Those who ended up
in places like Stafford then had to make a new start in a difficult, potentially hostile, environment where economic and social survival would
be precarious. Families that could hold together and adopt attainable
goals would maximise their prospects for success in their new situation.
They could, for example, seek advantageous marriages for their children,
either in terms of strengthening their links in the Irish 'community' or,
conversely, by 'marrying out' into aspirant and secure families from the
host community.

The concept of family strategy is, nevertheless, problematic and
needs to be used critically. Explicit evidence on a family's goals is usually sketchy, and the historian is forced to infer them from observed patterns of behaviour. Such outcomes might either reflect a lack of strategy
or be the result of conflicting or inconsistent strategies.[27] The objectives
of family strategy might be primarily economic – ensuring a family's
economic survival and security. They could, however, encompass wider
values concerning lifestyle, morality, belief and identity. From this perspective a family strategy might be more a system of implicit principles
that were felt, understood and used by family members in their debates
about strategic and tactical decisions.[28]

If evidence suggests a distinct family strategy there is the question
of how, and by whom, that strategy was formulated. Some critics argue
that in practice Victorian 'family strategies' were largely determined by
the dominant male(s) and reinforced the subordinate position of women
within families.[29] Such a proposition is, however, amenable to empirical
investigation. Given the common male breadwinner role, women were
often left to control or dominate the home, the base of family life. In
doing so they could profoundly influence the ethos and even the objectives of the family. Elizabeth Roberts has stressed the significance of
women as both the financial managers and moral guides of working-class
families.[30]

In the 1960s and 1970s the so-called 'sentiments school' developed a
fundamentally different approach to the family. It was more concerned
to explore the affective world of the nuclear family and whether modern
assumptions about the importance of feelings and emotions had played a

significant role in the past.[31] This 'relational' approach inherently involves research into the *meaning* of family life as it was perceived by historical actors, a problematic enterprise because of the lack of sources on ordinary peoples' feelings and motivations. Nevertheless, by seeing the family as a *process – a lived system of relationships*, this approach stimulates the researcher to explore the actual workings of families and networks.[32] Such an approach has great potential value in examining the experience of Irish families in Stafford and is the one mainly used to structure the family histories in this book.

The relationships approach emphasises the need to be aware of the flexibility and variability of family, kinship and 'quasi-family' relationships.[33] Family boundaries were porous.[34] Groups of blood-related individuals might change over time as individuals and sub-groups entered or left active involvement in a geographically dispersed kinship network.[35] Furthermore, in the nineteenth century many related individuals lived in households containing other unrelated people – friends, landlords, lodgers, servants and 'visitors', as well as the families and associates of these people. There was not necessarily a clear distinction between the 'family' and the 'household' since the latter might function in a quasi-familial way and not be a set of purely mercenary bargains. Associations beyond the immediate physical space of a family and household extended and complicated the pattern of personal relationships. They might even form a kind of 'home away from home'.[36] The division commonly drawn between the 'public' and the 'private' sphere might in practice be blurred. Functioning families were also not necessarily restricted to geographical proximity. Improvements in transport and communications meant that meaningful family and quasi-family relationships could occur on a national or transnational basis, a feature clearly demonstrated by the diasporic Irish. Above all, from this perspective relationships were more than a set of interpersonal bargains aimed at ensuring individual support and survival. Emotions such as love, hate, anxiety, jealousy, distrust and so on were central to personal and family life, and the researcher has to explore how they influenced attitudes and behaviour.[37]

In their book *The Family Story* Leonora Davidoff and her co-workers suggest that the concepts of *blood*, *contract* and *intimacy* can illuminate the meaning and significance of relationships.[38] The concept of blood forces a consideration of the significance or otherwise of both blood and non-blood relationships (like marriage partners) in the family. The concept of contract carries echoes of individualisation thesis in highlighting the significance of contractual arrangements and financial reciprocity that may underlie many familial and quasi-familial activities. The concept of intimacy provides a countervailing insight into the 'private physical, sexual and emotional aspects of relationships, based on trust and loyalty. It also incorporates the seemingly oppositional characteristics of power and control.'[39] These ideas form a powerful set of criteria by which to consider the multi-layered ties that influenced immigrant families.

Davidoff and her colleagues also suggest a second set of concepts to structure the actual investigation of the history of a family. These are *self, kinship, home/household* and *identity*.[40] This structure can be used to build a multi-dimensional picture of the Irish experience and it is necessary to examine the four concepts in a little more depth. *Self* covers the consciousness of the individual and how this affected his or her relationship with the family and other social networks, as well as politics and the economy. An individual's potential capacity to act was motivated by their own objectives, but also by the meanings they attached to the world and their part in it. These will have been influenced by their upbringing and their family context. In the case of most Irish-born immigrants, their sense of self will have been determined largely by the social and family environment they had experienced in Ireland. The influence, or otherwise, of Christianity – both Catholic and Protestant – may have been an influence on an individual's beliefs, self-awareness and conduct, but its role is likely to have been enhanced or diminished by the family's spiritual ethos or the lack of it. The individual will also have been profoundly influenced by gender assumptions and roles, themselves partly determined by Christianity but also by legal institutions and common assumptions of gender superiority and inferiority.[41] Roles in the family were influenced partly by how men and women defined both themselves and others in gender terms. Experiences in childhood were seminal in determining an individual's sense of self, but so too were experiences in later life. In practice, the personal boundaries of self might be blurred by perceived links to the family group and ancestors.[42]

A family can be seen as an amalgam of genetic position and cultural construct.[43] The notion of *kinship* emphasises the potential significance of *meaningful* blood ties between related individuals. Clearly, individuals in complex societies such as Ireland and Britain had a multiplicity of blood ties (both collateral and amongst predecessors). The modern craze for genealogy exposes the breadth and complexity of such links. Whether these ties were significant for individuals and families in the past depended partly on ethnicity, partly on social traditions or culture, but also on the specific circumstances in which particular groups of related individuals found themselves.[44] The notion of kinship reinforces the need to look beyond the nuclear family or household when considering meaningful family relationships. Sibling and cousin relationships were significant amongst the migrant Irish for the support, companionship and even marriage opportunities they might offer in a potentially hostile world.[45] More generally, kinship could impose obligations to offer accommodation, financial support or practical support to kin. These obligations could be derived from family norms but also from legal requirements, for example from the Poor Laws. The extent to which such obligations were honoured, and reciprocal help delivered, determined the value or otherwise of kinship relations.[46]

People lived their lives in a local spatial world in which a focal point was the place or places they used for eating, sleeping and other domestic activities. The *household* was not just an economic unit but also a focus of meaningful family and social relationships. It could be *home*, a word that carried, and carries, a whole baggage of meanings. It has been argued that the Victorians invented the idea of 'making' a home.[47] John Gillis suggests that home came to have a sacred quality, an attempt to make a little heaven on earth. The same writer also asserted that 'Catholics were somewhat slower to attribute a sacred quality to domestic space ... the presence of pictures of the Blessed Mary and souvenirs of pilgrimages taken in the name of the faith were meant to remind them that true sanctity lay elsewhere.'[48] Stafford's Catholic migrants offer an opportunity to test this somewhat tendentious comment. The meaning they attached to 'home' could be complicated by whether 'home' still meant the place where they grew up and where family connections probably still remained.

In practice, many of the migrant Irish were too poor to have much chance of making the idealised Victorian 'home' in the squalid and overcrowded slums in which they had to live. Even so, the first thing most people with some security did was to find somewhere better. For some this was bound up with a search for respectability, evidence for which may survive in their social, political and religious activities as well as the quality of the neighbourhood in which they lived. Conversely, such evidence can indicate families and households demonstrably in the 'rough' category or experiencing status decline, as well as those somewhere in between. Historians have tended to neglect the home as a social phenomenon, and feminists argue this is also to neglect the primary role of women as home-makers.[49] Home was the centre of family power relations. The classic view is that women did the housework and organised the family space but husbands or other men were the 'masters of the house'. Family-history evidence can, however, suggest more varied and ambiguous gender roles.

Davidoff's final concept is *identity*. The importance of identity in Irish migrant studies has been discussed already, but here we emphasise that the family was crucial to the formation of individual and group identity.[50] The values and norms present in the family – immediate and extended – would carry major messages about desirable identity that would influence the individual. That person's response was not, however, pre-determined. It might be complete acceptance, total rejection or, more likely, something in between. Furthermore, the cultural environment of the family was itself always in a process of flux, particularly for migrant families. On the one hand the family was the repository of its own cultural heritage transmitted through memories, myths and naming practices as well as by more concrete traditions such as religion or political affiliation. On the other hand, the children had to be prepared for the future. They had to be offered a workable accommodation with the world in which they were actually growing up.

In this study, the core of that world was Stafford. We have to consider its culture and meaning as a place to the social groups who lived there. Continuing strongly expressed ethnic identity might be functional in this environment but, equally, it might be valueless or even dangerous. Children could not be out of place in the world they were entering. They might have to move across cultural boundaries and make fundamental changes to their identity. Their lives would always be in tension between their imposed cultural heritage and the practical choices to be made in the real world.[51] It was not an 'all or nothing' decision. People could have multiple identities, each expressed in response to the different worlds in which they operated. The descendants of Irish immigrants, even those from ethnically 'mixed' marriages, might still have a proud heritage of family connections and identify with their place (or places) of origin. This did not mean, however, that they necessarily expressed 'Irishness' in terms of adherence to nationalist causes, social activities or even the Catholic (or Protestant) religion.[52] Finally, we must always question how conscious people were of their identity when, for many, the simple struggle for existence dominated their lives.

The impact of migration

The concepts of self, kinship, home/household and identity will be used to structure the analysis of the history of Stafford's Irish families, but evidence for distinct family strategies will also assessed where it appears relevant. By definition, all Stafford's Irish families were united by at least one member's life-course event of emigration from Ireland and settlement in a strange town in a different country. The number of people directly affected could vary. At one extreme whole family units and extended groups moved en bloc or through a process of chain migration. All these Irish-born people directly experienced the effects of emigration. At the other extreme single individuals emigrated and either remained within the Irish milieu or entered relationships with British people. The families of the latter were immediately 'mixed' in ethnic terms, and the impact of migration and settlement will have been more restricted. Whatever the variation, we need to look for ways in which subsequent family life may have been affected by the specific experience of migration.

The rapid growth of international migration in the late twentieth century has provoked research into its impact on families. These insights provide some guidance on what to look for amongst Stafford's Irish families.

There are four interrelated themes. The first is the psychological stress, confusion and trauma caused by migration. Here it must be remembered that people's *existing* stressful conditions may themselves have provoked them to leave.[53] Emigration was a drastic way to escape existing stress and it could impose new burdens. Individuals and families could suffer disorientation and isolation when they settled in a new and unfamiliar place. Peoples' day-to-day outlook might be confused over whether the move was permanent or temporary. A generational conflict might develop between parents and children, the parents perhaps clinging to the belief their move was temporary – the myth of return – whilst the children became committed to the place where they were growing up. This conflict could be expressed in identity differences over time and between generations. More family stress would result from the economic insecurity and squalid living conditions that were the lot of many immigrants. For men, being forced to take any job could provoke a loss of self-worth and status in the family. For women, the poverty and drudgery of menial paid jobs, housework and child-rearing in foreign surroundings could equally bring them to the end of their tether. These problems would be exacerbated if drink was the short-term antidote to misery.[54] Previous studies of poor Irish immigrants have often documented the symptoms of these problems, but a family approach allows some estimate to be made of how widespread they were, what variations existed and why.

We also have to consider whether some people, particularly during and after the Famine, suffered not just stress but genuine trauma with on-going effects. In the past thirty years post-traumatic stress disorder (PTSD) has been identified as a specific emotional reaction that may be experienced by people exposed to an event causing loss of physical integrity, or risk of serious injury or death to self or others. The response involves intense fear, horror or helplessness and over the longer term may produce symptoms such as sleep disorders, anger or hyper-vigilance with significant impairment of ability in social relations or work.[55] It is doubtful whether day-to-day suffering during the Famine, bad as it was, would have been the event – the 'bolt from the blue' – that would trigger PTSD.[56] This is not, however, to deny that particular individuals experienced sudden and powerful events during the Famine that were trauma-inducing: for example, violent eviction, gruesome death, exposure to violence and squalor, or terrible conditions on the voyage to Britain.[57] The physical suffering of the Famine immigrants to Britain has been widely documented, but we cannot discount the possibility that some of them were also suffering symptoms that would now be diagnosed as PTSD. The violence, drunkenness and alienated behaviour frequently observed amongst the Irish could, in some individuals, be the only record we now have of deeper trauma. It would, of course, have had a direct and long-term impact on other family members and associates.

Secondly, migration could disrupt life-course events. Families could be broken apart by death or by dispersal. Marriages were deferred or abandoned because of uncertainty. Existing marriages became stressed or were even sundered by insecurity and poverty. Children could be orphaned or left with just one overworked parent.[58] But migration could also be constructive. Settlement in a new place offered opportunities to meet new partners and form new family units. The immediate result might be a wave of births. New kinship contacts and obligations might be stimulated.

Thirdly, migration might have an impact on a family's power relations. Modern critics debate whether or not migration reinforces male dominance in the family by bolstering men's control of employment and income. In this view women are 'tied migrants', 'trailing' behind their partners. They are forced to take any paid job, or to carry out unpaid housework, in an unfavourable location not of their choosing.[59] This issue links to the wider question of who takes the decision to move and the choices or constraints of migrants. The Irish have traditionally been seen as enforced emigrants with little choice, but whatever the 'push' forces, people had to decide where to settle. Historians have shown little interest in *why* Irish people settled in particular places – the causes are assumed to be self-evident. When a family's history is examined the actual choices made have to be analysed. The relative roles of men and women as dominant forces in this family decision-making can then be assessed through patterns of revealed behaviour.

Finally, there is the impact of migration on children and their role within the family. The results might be negative. Children were ripped from the only social world they had known back home and dumped in what might be a lonely and hostile environment. Their parents might also be struggling to cope and consequently neglect their children or give them little emotional support. Such children could grow up shy, angry, alienated and unable to integrate into the host society. By contrast, the results could be positive. Children are potentially resilient and flexible – they learn and adapt. They may be less bound by existing family and social rules. Migration might open up opportunities and the path to integration might be easier than for their parents. Indeed, it has been suggested that migrant children can play an essential role as 'culture brokers', demonstrating practically the workings of the host society to their parents and helping the family integration process.[60]

The family in context

A criticism of the approaches discussed so far is that they can over-emphasise internal family relationships and neglect the external forces acting on families. It is important to counterbalance these tendencies by locating families within their wider context and being aware of changes in that context. There are two aspects to this. The first is how the family related to the wider 'community' and the second is how it was affected by, and responded to, the structural forces of the economic and political system.

The fact that the families examined in this book all originated with people born in Ireland does not imply they necessarily formed a 'community' of people united by their place of birth. Similarly, focus on the geographical entity of Stafford does not necessarily imply the town formed a simple 'community' of which the Irish needed to become members. Sociologists and historians have debated the nature of 'community' extensively, but we can identify some of its defining features. They are, firstly, obligations – that people should have a network of active commitments to each other and they should also have organisation – a more or less formal system of institutions that express the commitments. The institutions and groups of individuals should perform actions that support each other and therefore express communal life actively. There is likely to be a network of relationships enfolding people generally and these are likely to be helped by geographical closeness in a defined location. Simple geographical proximity might, however, be replaced partly by networks running across a wider or transnational realm defined by ethnic or class identity, professional status and so on. A community should exhibit some stability in order to build up its obligations and institutions but the process of community definition is also dynamic. It develops in response to changes in the wider environment and the impact of other communities. Its cohesion will be partly defined by its relation to authority, particularly through conflict, and with powerful 'others' in society. This process will generate symbols and a rhetoric used consciously to identify the community and include or exclude members. Members of a community should have a consciously shared identity and a sense of belonging. Even so, they may not be members of just one community but of a number composed of competing forces.[61] Such ideas are particularly appropriate in looking at the Irish during their settlement in nineteenth-century Britain.

The tide of Irish emigration in the nineteenth century took place during industrial capitalism's transformation of the world economy. Indeed, that emigration was substantially a consequence of the uneven development of international capitalism and the laissez-faire ideology of its ruling class in Britain. The cyclical boom-and-depression pattern of development in the British economy demanded a reserve army of mobile and flexible labour, not just from the labouring poor but also from the trades and professions as well. The underdevelopment and deindustrialisation of Ireland provided such a reserve of labour. It is essential, therefore, to see the fate of Irish families in Britain within this overall structural context.

They shaped their own family histories but in circumstances usually not of their own choosing and to which they had to react.

Structural-functionalists and Marxists developed complementary perspectives on the family. The functionalists accepted the inevitability of industrial capitalism and argued that it had needed the 'modernisation' of the family, particularly through the supposed emergence of the nuclear family.[62] This institution was socially and geographically mobile and able to respond to the needs of a capitalist economy. It ensured that members of society were socialised into the values, norms and disciplines essential to sustain an orderly but competitive free enterprise system. The older extended family typified by the rural Irish was seen as suffused by pre-industrial values. Migrants from such backgrounds had to adopt the new structures in order to compete effectively. It was assumed that a rigid division emerged between home and work, the former a predominantly male environment, the latter predominantly female. From a hostile perspective, Marx also saw the family as moulded by capitalism's requirements but with the result that family ties were torn and children transformed into articles of commerce and instruments of labour.[63] Engels argued that, in the transitional industrial capitalist state, the family had replicated the system's class relationships, with the husband as the bourgeoisie and the wife as the exploited proletariat.[64]

The functionalist and Marxist perspectives emphasise the need to consider how industrial and finance capitalism and, in particular, its class and gender conflicts, impacted on families. Building on this, Marxist feminists argue that the 'family' has to be seen as an ideological construct whose historical role was to keep people functioning despite the stresses caused by outside economic processes. It was a key element in the process of social reproduction, but it also had contradictions. Families were always being threatened with disruption and break-up by the market system but they also might be the foci of resistance to pure market relationships and be the instigators of collective rather than individualistic values.[65] This approach emphasises the need to see a family's members within their various household contexts operating in the local economy. It suggests the importance of examining gender and class roles, as well as the changing position of people of various ages within the family and household.

Why study Stafford?

Concepts of the family and family life therefore offer a tool to investigate the experiences of the migrant Irish in the town of Stafford. It is, however, necessary at this point to pose the question: Why study Stafford? Many other places could have been picked for this study, and Stafford might at first sight seem an idiosyncratic choice. The author admits that the town was not selected after a review of possible places guided by rigorous research criteria. The real answer is that his mother and her family came from Stafford and initial interest in its Irish inhabitants was provoked by research into the author's genealogy. There seemed to be an Irish ancestor – Mary Corcoran from Castlerea, Co. Roscommon. In 1866 she married the author's great-great-grandfather, James Clewlow.[66] It was apparent that Mary Corcoran was not alone in Stafford. The census enumeration returns for 1851 and 1861 revealed a striking number of Irish-born people living there. Until then the writer had tacitly accepted the common view that the Irish had settled mainly in the industrial areas and big city slums, especially Liverpool. Yet here were significant numbers living in this obscure town in the west Midlands. It seemed to be worth looking at these people in more depth to find out when and why they had arrived in Stafford and what their experiences were in the town. Early work therefore concentrated on the Famine and its aftermath, and was a modest addition to the numerous studies covering that period that appeared in the late twentieth century.[67]

Despite the serendipitous origin of its selection, Stafford's value as a case-study location became more apparent as time went on. Its advantages are its location, economy, social character and size. These combine to offer an environment that contrasts with many of the previously studied locations whilst having features common to other locations. Stafford was a small town. In 1871 its population was 16,082 and Irish-born people numbered just 403, or 2.55 per cent of the total. This was a proportion very close to that in England and Wales as a whole. At that time the towns and cities of northern England had the largest concentrations of Irish but only a small number of places had more than 10 per cent Irish-born. Many more had between 4 and 10 per cent and most were again in the north. It is important to emphasise, therefore, that the Irish-born were a minority even in the areas of densest settlement. Stafford fell within a large group of settlements having between 2 and 4 per cent of Irish-born. These were geographically widely distributed and included London and a range of both large and small towns. The *absolute number* of Irish people in a settlement influenced their ability to form a definable 'community', and the possibilities in Stafford were different from those, for example, in Birmingham, which had almost the same *proportion* of Irish as Stafford but over 9,000 actual people. Even so, Stafford's position within this middling band of towns means it can be used to study phenomena inherently more difficult to examine in the larger settlements. It is feasible to cover the *whole* of the Irish population in detail and to trace the lives of its families down the generations. It also allows more light to be thrown on the Irish who did settle in the smaller towns, a neglected group in the literature. Over 7 per cent of the

Table 1.1 Estimated distribution of Irish-born in different types of settlement, England and Wales, 1871

Settlement type	Estimated Irish-born	% of total Irish-born
London boroughs	78,422	13.84
Liverpool	76,761	13.55
Manchester	34,066	6.01
Other cities (> 100,000) (11)	62,639	11.06
Large towns (50,000–99,999) (20)	48,576	8.57
Medium towns (30,000–49,999) (33)	33,705	5.95
Small towns (< 30,000) (189)	42,178	7.45
Non-municipal settlements	190,193	33.57
Total	**566,540**	**100.00**

Source: see n. 68.

Irish settled in towns with a population under 30,000 (Table 1.1).[68] They are directly comparable with Stafford. Furthermore, over one-third of the Irish lived in various types of non-municipal settlement. These included small towns and villages in rural districts, unincorporated settlements in industrial areas and suburbs beyond the boundaries of bigger towns and cities. Many of these places may have been analogous to Stafford but more local studies are needed to complete a comprehensive picture of the varied experiences of the Irish. Malcolm Smith and Don MacRaild have suggested that 'Herson's Stafford becomes more important as an example of a common experience as the Irish scattered into similar small towns (a process which was well in train by the 1870s), but even then, the small size of the Irish populace in that town still raises a question about typicality.'[69] This double-edged comment assumes there was a 'typical' environment that the majority of Irish people experienced. Similar thinking imbues the main writer on Liverpool's Irish when he emphasises that city's 'exceptionalism.'[70] But were Stafford and Liverpool 'exceptional' to some vision of the 'typical'? What place was 'typical'? This author believes every settlement had its 'exceptional' or specific aspects. Stafford's specific character will be described in Chapter 2. The task of the historical researcher is to identify the special circumstances that affected people's lives, but above all to make well-founded generalisations that others can test in comparative studies elsewhere. That is a major aim of this study of Stafford's Irish families.

The method

This study of ordinary families works in the tradition of 'history from below' or 'public history'.[71] It identifies the total population of settled Irish families and examines in depth a representative selection. The analysis is structured by the concepts of the family discussed earlier. The overall method can best be described as collective family biography or 'family prosopography'. The potential of this approach has been acknowledged in Irish migration studies, but the work done so far has been limited and almost none relates to the Irish in Britain.[72] Collective biography, or prosopography, investigates the characteristics of groups of historical actors by generalising from individual biographies of their lives.[73] The approach has normally been used to investigate *individuals* united by some common characteristic, for example Members of Parliament, but it is also appropriate to use collective biography to study the behaviour of families with apparently common characteristics. The strength of the prosopographic method is that it not only gives detailed information about individual cases but provides strong impressionistic evidence of the mass of ordinary people in their time and place. This is something that has often proved difficult in Irish migrant studies.

Chapter 3 describes the types of Irish families who settled in Stafford in the nineteenth century. Three definitions are needed to identify them. What defines a 'family', what was an 'Irish family' and what was a 'settled' family? Earlier discussion in this chapter has defined a 'family' as a distinct group of kin identifiable by a common name or names and a pattern of revealed relationships. Families could range from apparently lone individuals through nuclear units to groupings including all manner of kin. They were not, of course, isolated units but had overlapping boundaries and interconnections with other families. Even so, it was possible to identify distinct families over long periods of time.

What defined an 'Irish family'? The answer was any identifiable family that contained an 'Irish' person, meaning an individual born in Ireland. This study looks, therefore, at *all* the people and their families who claimed birth in Ireland, whatever their apparent background in that country. It exposes the full ethnic mix of the emigrants and the range of social structures in which they lived. There is no other way to encompass the range of 'Irish' people and avoid stereotypes of Irish ethnicity.[74]

What was a 'settled' family? The term 'settling down' is used commonly to imply a degree of long-term stability and commitment to a place. The extent to which people and families ever 'settle down' is affected by both circumstances and attitudes. Some families never 'settle' even after many years in a place, whereas others can show apparently deep stability and commitment after a short period of time. Nevertheless, the study had to adopt a practical and objective definition of 'settlement', and it was when a family was present for *at least ten years* – that is, it was identifiable in at least two censuses or there was evidence from other sources that indicated a similar time span.

These criteria identified 206 settled Irish families living in Stafford between the 1820s and 1901. The research documents their histories to around 1920. This cut-off date was chosen because it brings the narrative beyond the Great War and tests the nature of their commitment to living in British society by the early twentieth century. It also avoids discussing the adult behaviour of people who might still be alive today. The main chapters of the book present the histories of the selected families and discuss the factors that determined the character and fate of each. They provide insights into the lives of ordinary families and document the diversity of family outcomes. This provides a more subtle picture of the experience of migrant families in the long term and avoids the dangers of ethnic generalisation and stereotyping.

Academic historians have tended to underestimate the potential for cross-fertilisation between genealogy and professional social history.[75] The family histories presented here attempt to fuse profitably the sources and techniques of traditional 'academic' historians with those of digital historians and genealogists. The research would have been impossible without digital information technology. At its heart lies a Microsoft Access® relational database of material about Stafford's Irish families. This initially just captured from the census returns details of every household in Stafford containing at least one Irish-born person (or known descendants) between 1841 and 1901. The process of family identification was not always straightforward since there were many data discrepancies such as in the spelling of surnames, the use of forenames and the estimated ages of individuals. Families sometimes emerged through a fog of uncertain data, a fact demonstrating that the effective use of historical sources needs to combine information technology and critical human judgement. Despite this, the overall reliability and value of the census returns as a source was manifest. They are a tribute to the conscientiousness and, indeed, bravery of the enumerators in performing their task amidst the rookeries of Victorian towns and cities.

The database was later expanded to include linked classificatory tables on the nature of households and dwellings, together with data from burial records, marriage registers, poll books, Poor Law records, military information and other sources. Searching the database continually threw up evidence of meaningful connections that not only helped clarify the structure and interrelations of families but also suggested likely character, motivations and identities. It also enabled a picture to emerge of where families lived over time, of their neighbours and associates, and the neighbourhoods they and their descendants frequented.

The local newspaper, the *Staffordshire Advertiser*, was trawled from 1826 to 1922 for evidence concerning identifiable Irish people and also on the wider economic, social and political context. The original copies of the newspaper could be used in the William Salt Library, Stafford – a huge advantage over digital copies (not in any case available) in that evidence could be picked out easily in its context rather than by using predetermined word searches or scanning the text on a microfiche reader. It is another example of the benefits of marrying traditional with digital historical methods. A summary of each 'incident' was added to the database, classified by its type and date, and, where possible, cross-referenced to individuals from the census returns. This emphasises how databases not only aggregate large amounts of data but can also be used to identify individual cases and unexpected connections amidst a superficially inchoate mass of information. They help the researcher produce 'history with a human face'.[76]

Information from descendants of the Stafford Irish was solicited by means of a newspaper article in Stafford itself, but mainly through a website, *Diaspora Connections*. This brought 180 responses from around the world, of which 93 provided useful information on 60 distinct Stafford families.[77] During the 2000s the work was increasingly aided by the explosion of online data such as digitised newspapers, family history sites like *Ancestry* and other sources. Such digitised data are, however, far from perfect, and use of the genealogy sites revealed numerous cases of mistranscribed names and missing records. These instances reinforce the need to adopt a critical approach to the digital record and, indeed, to avoid total reliance on it.[78]

The process of writing each family's history began by reconstructing its genealogy using the census data from 1841 to 1911 and other sources.[79] This provided the skeleton on which to hang the family's history. Other data were then added to explore its evolving character using the conceptual frameworks discussed above. Many types of evidence were used in this process. The most priceless would have been surviving testimony in the shape of letters, diaries and publicly reported statements. Historians of the Irish in Australia and the USA have used such sources profitably, but historians in Britain have had a leaner time of it. This study is no exception. No surviving letters, diaries or similar sources came to light from the Stafford Irish and their descendants. There were a modest number of photographs and a reasonable number of reported statements in the press. That was all.

The second-best source for attitudes and identities was the knowledge that has come down to descendants. Here the picture was better. Through contacts by post, email and the website, information was offered by descendants on the past history and character of some families. This evidence was followed up by interviews with twenty of the descendants.[80]

Even so, the work inevitably had to use surviving documentary sources to build up a coherent picture. Information suggesting both life experiences and possible identities came in many forms. Apparent attitudes to Irish origins could be expressed in overt pride, associational activity or, on the other hand, behaviour suggesting a desire to obscure Irishness, such as changing a surname or place of birth. More generally, evidence could document behaviour and experiences: religious adherence or the lack of it, social involvements, pubs frequented, voting patterns, political activity, work-related activities, living conditions and dealings with public agencies. All of these could suggest attitudes and possible identities. Such information could, however, only intermittently and imperfectly pick up evidence of transnational links. This mainly occurred when members of a family emigrated from Britain. Lack of surviving correspondence and oral history data meant that the diasporic world of the families, both at 'home' in Ireland and elsewhere overseas, often remained obscure or unknown.

Enda Delaney has used oral history to present the 'inner history' of the post-war Irish in Britain. He cautions against over-reliance on traditional documentary sources that may tend to emphasise the Irish as a 'problem' and give little insight into how the Irish saw things themselves.[81] The historian of the nineteenth-century Irish is forced to use such sources – albeit critically – linking them, where possible, to the knowledge and opinions of descendants alive today. In the Stafford case the amount of data was never enough to write day-by-day family chronologies except in relation to specific reported incidents. This book does not try to pad out the historical record by writing fiction or even 'faction', but confines itself to presenting the known historical facts and discussing what can reasonably be inferred from them. Even so, across each family and over time evidence of its behaviour became available that enabled a plausible picture of its character and ethos to be painted. Information that specifically demonstrated family relationships and attitudes was inevitably more nuanced but not negligible. Evidence of domestic interactions between husbands and wives, parents and children or with other relatives and associates could suggest whether family relations were close, loving and supportive; or negligent, hostile and abusive; or somewhere in between. In some cases obituaries and death reports in the press could provide priceless evidence about the lives, careers, attitudes and family circumstances of individuals and of how they were regarded in the host community, though such reports were inevitably biased towards those who had either achieved some local prestige or whose death was particularly tragic or notorious.[82] The trajectories of children in terms of their school experiences and record, the jobs they took and the degree of social mobility they demonstrated suggested the attitudes and aspirations present in the family and even whether there was a 'family strategy'.

The totality of this evidence offers new perspectives on how immigrant families developed in the long term.

Notes

1 *Staffordshire Advertiser (SA)*, 22 July 1899.
2 *Ibid.*, 6 June 1908.
3 J. D. Herson, 'Migration, "community" or integration? Irish families in Victorian Stafford' in R. Swift and S. Gilley (eds), *The Irish in Victorian Britain: The Local Dimension* (Dublin: Four Courts Press, 1999), pp. 156–89.
4 L. H. Lees, *Exiles of Erin: Irish Migrants in Victorian London* (Manchester: Manchester University Press, 1979).
5 B. S. Elliott, *Irish Migrants in the Canadas: A New Approach* (Kingston, ON: McGill-Queen's University Press, 1988).
6 P. O'Farrell, *Letters from Irish Australia, 1825–1925* (Sydney: New South Wales University Press, 1989); D. Fitzpatrick, *Oceans of Consolation: Personal Accounts of Irish Migration to Australia* (Cork: Cork University Press, 1994); K. A. Miller, D. N. Doyle, B. Boling and A. Schrier, *Irish Immigrants in the Land of Canaan: Letters and Memoirs from Colonial and Revolutionary America, 1675–1815* (Oxford: Oxford University Press, 2003); L. W. McBride (ed.), *The Reynolds Letters: An Irish Emigrant Family in Late Victorian Manchester* (Cork: Cork University Press, 1999); D. Dunnigan, *A South Roscommon Emigrant: Emigration and Return, 1890–1920*, Maynooth Studies in Local History, 73 (Dublin: Four Courts Press, 2007); W. J. Bradley, *Gallon: The History of Three Townlands in County Tyrone from the Earliest Times to the Present Day* (Derry: Guildhall Press, 2000). For a brief review of other work on Ireland see P. Fitzgerald and B. Lambkin, *Migration in Irish History, 1607–2007* (Basingstoke: Palgrave Macmillan, 2008), pp. 270–7.
7 M. Anderson, *Family Structure in 19th Century Lancashire* (Cambridge: Cambridge University Press, 1971); M. W. Dupree, *Family Structure in the Staffordshire Potteries, 1840–1880* (Oxford: Clarendon Press, 1995).
8 C. Chinn, *Birmingham Irish: Making Our Mark*, (Birmingham: Birmingham Library Services, 2003).
9 R. Jenkins, *Rethinking Ethnicity: Arguments and Explanations* (London: Sage, 1997), esp. pp. 165–70.
10 Lees, *Exiles of Erin*, pp. 108–15.
11 For example, M. Kanya-Forstner, 'Defining womanhood: Irish women and the Catholic Church in Victorian Liverpool' in D. MacRaild (ed.), *The Great Famine and Beyond: Irish Migrants in Britain in the Nineteenth and Twentieth Centuries* (Dublin: Irish Academic Press, 2000), pp. 168–88; J. Belchem, *Irish, Catholic and Scouse: The History of the Liverpool Irish, 1800–1939* (Liverpool: Liverpool University Press, 2007), pp. 95–6. A notable exception is L. Letford, 'Irish and non-Irish women living in their households in nineteenth-century Liverpool: Issues of class, gender, religion and birthplace' (Ph.D. thesis, University of Lancaster, 1999).
12 P. O'Leary, 'Networking respectability: Class, gender and ethnicity among the Irish in South Wales, 1845–1914', *Immigrants and Minorities*, 23:2/3 (July/ November 2005), pp. 255–75.

13 Reviewed in R. Swift, 'Identifying the Irish in Victorian Britain: Recent trends in historiography', *Immigrants and Minorities*, 27:2/3 (July/November 2009), pp. 134–51.

14 J. Solomos, 'Beyond racism and multiculturalism', *Patterns of Prejudice*, 32:4 (1998), pp. 45–62.

15 A. O'Day, 'A conundrum of Irish diasporic identity: Mutative ethnicity', *Immigrants and Minorities*, 27:2/3 (July/November 2009), pp. 317–39.

16 J. Hutchinson and A. D. Smith, *Ethnicity* (Oxford: Oxford University Press, 1996), pp. 6–7.

17 K. Kenny, 'Diaspora and comparison: The global Irish as a case study', *Journal of American History*, 90:1 (June 2003), pp. 134–62 (p. 137).

18 K. Miller, *Emigrants and Exiles: Ireland and the Irish Exodus to North America* (New York: Oxford University Press, 1985), p. 8.

19 D. H. Akenson, 'The historiography of the Irish in the United States of America', in. P. O'Sullivan (ed.), *The Irish World Wide*, Vol. 2: *The Irish in the New Communities* (Leicester: Leicester University Press, 1992), pp. 115–21; D. H. Akenson, *The Irish Diaspora: A Primer* (Toronto: P. D. Meany, 1993), pp. 237–8. A useful summary of arguments is contained in Kenny, 'Diaspora and comparison', pp. 137–9.

20 M. Campbell, *Ireland's New Worlds: Immigrants, Politics and Society in the United States and Australia, 1815–1922* (Madison: University of Wisconsin Press, 2008).

21 A. Bielenberg (ed.), *The Irish Diaspora* (Harlow: Pearson Education, 2000); S. Vertovec, 'Conceiving and researching transnationalism', *Ethnic and Racial Studies*, 22:2, pp. 447–62; E. Kofman, 'Family-related migration: A critical review of European studies', *Journal of Ethnic and Migration Studies*, 30:2 (March 2004), pp. 243–62; J. D. Trew, 'Reluctant diasporas of Northern Ireland: Migrant narratives of home, conflict, difference', *Journal of Ethnic and Migration Studies*, 36:4 (April 2010), pp. 541–60.

22 R. Cohen, *Global Diasporas* (London: University College London Press, 1997).

23 Anderson, *Family Structure*, Chapter 2.

24 *Ibid.*, Chapter 12 (quotation on p. 177).

25 T. Hareven, *Family Time and Industrial Time: The Relationship between Family and Work in a Planned Corporation Town, 1900–1924* (Cambridge: Cambridge University Press, 1982), pp. 107–12.

26 M. Anderson, *Approaches to the History of the Western Family, 1500–1914* (London: Macmillan, 1980), p. 78.

27 D. S. Smith, 'Family strategy: More than a metaphor?', *Historical Methods*, 20:3 (Summer 1987), pp. 118–20 (p. 119).

28 L. A. Tilly, 'Beyond family strategies, what?', *Historical Methods*, 20:3 (Summer 1987), pp. 123–5 (p. 124).

29 Dupree, *Family Structure*, p. 31; D. H. J. Morgan, *Family Connections: An Introduction to Family Studies* (Cambridge: Polity Press, 1996), pp. 25–6.

30 E. Roberts, *A Woman's Place: An Oral History of Working-Class Women, 1890–1940* (Oxford: Basil Blackwell, 1984), esp. Chapter 8.

31 P. Ariès, *Centuries of Childhood: A Social History of Family Life* (New York: Jonathan Cape, 1962); L. Stone, *Family, Sex and Marriage in England,*

1500–1800 (London: Weidenfeld and Nicolson, 1977); E. Shorter, *The Making of the Modern Family* (New York: Basic Books, 1975). For a fairly sceptical review of the earlier work, see Anderson, *Approaches*, pp. 39–64.

32 L. Davidoff, *Thicker than Water: Siblings and Their Relations, 1780–1920* (Oxford: Oxford University Press, 2012), p. 16.

33 R. Parkin, *Kinship: An Introduction to the Basic Concepts* (Oxford: Blackwell, 1997), esp. Chapter 3.

34 R. Finnegan and M. Drake (eds), *From Family Tree to Family History* (Cambridge: Cambridge University Press, 1994), pp. 113–16.

35 Hareven, *Family Time and Industrial Time*, pp. 114–16.

36 J. R. Gillis, *A World of Their Own Making: Myth, Ritual and the Quest for Family Values* (Cambridge, MA: Harvard University Press, 1996), p. 33.

37 C. Smart, *Personal Life: New Directions in Sociological Thinking* (Cambridge: Polity Press, 2007), pp. 58 and 133–8.

38 L. Davidoff, M. Doolittle, J. Fink and K. Holden, *The Family Story: Blood, Contract and Intimacy, 1830–1960* (Harlow: Addison Wesley, Longman, 1999), p. 4.

39 *Ibid*, pp. 4–5.

40 *Ibid.*, pp. 52–5.

41 *Ibid.*, pp. 53–76.

42 M. Chamberlain, *Family Love in the Diaspora: Migration and the Anglo-Caribbean Experience* (London: Transaction, 2006), p. 9.

43 Davidoff, *Thicker than Water*, p. 4.

44 Parkin, *Kinship*, pp. 3–12.

45 L. Davidoff, 'Kinship as a categorical concept: A case study of nineteenth century English siblings', *Journal of Social History*, 39:2 (Winter 2005), pp. 411–13; and *Thicker than Water, passim*.

46 J. Finch, *Family Obligations and Social Change* (Cambridge: Polity Press, 1989), pp. 52–6, 115–35.

47 Gillis, *World of Their Own Making*, pp. 109–29.

48 *Ibid.*, p. 126.

49 Davidoff *et al.*, *Family Story*, pp. 83–7; Smart, *Personal Life*, pp. 159–66.

50 Davidoff *et al.*, *Family Story*, p. 90.

51 Smart, *Personal Life*, pp. 80–107.

52 See also J. D. Herson, 'Family history and memory in Irish immigrant families' in K. Burrell and P. Panayi (eds), *Histories and Memories: Migrants and Their History in Britain* (London: Tauris Academic Studies, 2006), pp. 210–33.

53 V. S. Khan, 'Migration and social stress: Mirpuris in Bradford' in Khan (ed.), *Minority Families in Britain: Support and Stress* (London: Macmillan, 1979), pp. 36–57.

54 E. Accampo, *Industrialization, Family Life and Class Relations: Saint Chamond, 1815–1914* (Berkeley: University of California Press, 1989), esp. Chapters 3 and 4; S. Vertovec, 'Transnationalism and identity', *Journal of Ethnic and Migration Studies*, 27:4 (October 2001), pp. 573–82; C. Brettell, 'Migration' in D. I. Kertzer and M. Barbagli (eds), *Family Life in the Long Nineteenth Century* (New Haven: Yale University Press, 2002), Chapter 7; G. Leavey, S. Sembhi and G. Livingston, 'Older Irish migrants living in London: Identity, loss and return', *Journal of Ethnic and Migration Studies*, 30:4 (July

2004), pp. 763–79; Trew, 'Reluctant diasporas'; M. J. Hickman, 'Census ethnic categories and second-generation identities: A study of the Irish in England and Wales', *Journal of Ethnic and Migration Studies*, 37:1 (January 2011), pp. 79–97.

55 Definition in American Psychiatric Association, *Diagnostic and Statistical Manual of Mental Disorders IV (Text Revision)*, 4th edn (Washington, DC, American Psychiatric Publishing, 2011) (normally abbreviated to *DSM-IV-TR*), which is often taken for medical and legal purposes as the agreed formulation of symptoms. The validity and reliability of the *DSM* approach to diagnoses is subject to criticism, an issue beyond the scope of this book.

56 G. Turnbull, *Trauma* (London: Bantam Press, 2011), pp. 56–7, 289–96.

57 Documented vividly by Frank Neal: F. Neal, *Black '47: Britain and the Famine Irish* (Liverpool: Newsham Press, 2003), Chapter 3.

58 Kofman, 'Family-related migration'; G. F. de Jong and D. R. Graefe, 'Family life course transitions and the economic consequences of internal migration', *Population, Space and Place*, 14 (2008), pp. 267–82; T. J. Cooke, 'Migration in a family way', *Population, Space and Place*, 14 (2008), pp. 255–65; L. Ryan, R. Sales, M. Tilki and B. Siara, 'Family strategies and transnational migration: Recent Polish migrants in London', *Journal of Ethnic and Migration Studies*, 35:1 (January 2009), pp. 61–77.

59 K. H. Halfacree, 'Household migration and the structuration of patriarchy: Evidence from the USA', *Progress in Human Geography*, 19:2 (2005), pp. 159–82; D. P. Smith, 'An "untied" research agenda for family migration: Loosening the "shackles" of the past', *Journal of Ethnic and Migration Studies*, 30:2 (March 2004), pp. 263–82.

60 S. M. Myers, 'Childhood migration and social integration in adulthood', *Journal of Marriage and the Family*, 61 (August 1999), pp. 774–89; C. Hafford, 'Sibling caretaking in immigrant families: Understanding cultural practices to inform child welfare practice and evaluation', *Evaluation and Program Planning*, 33 (2010), pp. 294–302.

61 C. J. Calhoun, 'Community: Toward a variable conceptualisation for comparative research', *Social History*, 5:1 (January 1980), pp. 105–29; B. Deacon and M. Donald, 'In search of community history', *Family and Community History*, 7:1 (May 2004), pp. 13–18; M. Drake (ed.), *Time, Family and Community: Perspectives on Family and Community History* (Oxford: Blackwell, 1994), esp. Chapters 10 and 13; W.T. R. Pryce (ed.), *From Family History to Community History* (Cambridge: Cambridge University Press, 1994), esp. Chapter 9; R. Frankenberg, *Communities in Britain: Social Life in Town and Country* (Harmondsworth: Penguin, 1966), esp. p. 238.

62 For an outline discussion of theories of the family, see Davidoff *et al.*, *Family Story*, Chapter 2. The most influential attempt to apply structural-functionalist ideas to a historical issue was N. Smelser, *Social Change in the Industrial Revolution: An Application of Theory in the Lancashire Cotton Industry, 1770–1840* (London: Routledge and Kegan Paul, 1959).

63 K. Marx, *Capital*, Vol. 1 (London: Lawrence and Wishart, 1974), pp. 459–60; K. Marx and F. Engels, *The Manifesto of the Communist Party* (London: CRW, 2004), pp. 43–4.

64 F. Engels, *The Origin of the Family, Private Property and the State* (London: Lawrence and Wishart, 1977), p. 72; Davidoff *et al.*, *Family Story*, pp. 23–4.

65 R. Rapp, E. Ross and R. Bridenthal, 'Examining family history' in J. L. Newton, M. P. Ryan and J. R. Walkowitz (eds), *Sex and Class in Women's History* (London: Routledge and Kegan Paul, 1983), pp. 232–58.

66 Subsequent research in fact disproved the link because Mary Corcoran was James Clewlow's second wife. The author is descended from Clara Clewlow, the final child of James's first wife, Mary Hodge, who died in 1864. Clara did, nevertheless, grow up with her stepmother, Mary Corcoran.

67 J. Herson, 'Why the Irish went to Stafford: A case study of Irish settlement in England, 1830–71', *Liverpool Polytechnic Papers in Social Studies*, 1 (April 1988); John Herson, 'Irish migration and settlement in Victorian Britain: A small-town perspective' in R. Swift and S. Gilley (eds), *The Irish in Britain, 1815–1939* (London: Pinter Press, 1989), pp. 84–103.

68 The 1871 Census only gives birthplace data for a limited number of towns. Table 1.1 estimates the distribution of Irish-born by using data for the 'principal towns' for which birthplace evidence is given. The known proportion of Irish-born in the towns of various size categories was then projected on to all towns in the same category listed in General Table VIII (*Census, 1871: Tables of Birthplaces of the People in Principal Towns in England and Wales. General Table VIII: Population of Cities and Boroughs Having Defined Municipal or Parliamentary Limits*). This allows an estimate to be made of the total Irish-born in each category (middle column of Table 1.1) and thence the distribution of Irish-born in different sizes and types of settlement. The residue of Irish-born not accounted for in this way therefore comprised those living in various types of non-municipal settlement.

69 M. T. Smith and D. M. MacRaild, 'Paddy and Biddy no more: An evolutionary analysis of the decline in Irish Catholic forenames among descendants of 19th century Irish migrants to Britain', *Annals of Human Biology*, 36:5 (September/October 2009), pp. 595–608 (p. 606).

70 J. Belchem, *Merseypride: Essays in Liverpool Exceptionalism* (Liverpool: Liverpool University Press, 2000), esp. Part 2, 'Irish Liverpool'.

71 H. Keen, P. Martin and S. J. Morgan, *Seeing History: Public History in Britain Now* (London, Francis Boutle, 2000), esp. essay by T. Brennan, 'History, family, history', pp. 37–50.

72 Fitzgerald and Lambkin, *Migration in Irish History*, pp. 264–5.

73 L. Stone, 'Prosopography', *Daedalus*, 100:1 (Winter 1971), pp. 46–79 (p. 46); L. B. Namier, *The Structure of Politics at the Accession of George III* (London: Macmillan, 1927); R. Syme, *The Roman Revolution* (Oxford: Clarendon Press, 1939).

74 Akenson, *Irish Diaspora*, p. 7.

75 A. Gritt, 'Introduction' and 'The value of family history' in A. Gritt (ed.), *Family History in Lancashire: Issues and Approaches* (Newcastle-upon-Tyne: Cambridge Scholars Publishing, 2009), pp. 3–4 and 5–13.

76 R. Crone and K. Halsey, 'On collecting, cataloguing and collating the evidence of reading: The "RED movement" and its implications for digital scholarship' in T. Weller (ed.), *History in the Digital Age* (Abingdon: Routledge, 2013), pp 95–110; N. Bulst, 'Prosopography and the computer: problems

and possibilities' in P. Denley, S. Fogelvik and C. Harvey (eds), *History and Computing II* (Manchester: Manchester University Press, 1989), pp. 12–18.

77　www.staff.ljmu.ac.uk/socjhers/stafford/index.html.

78　D. Thomas and V. Johnson, 'New universe or black holes? Does digital change anything?' in Weller, *History in the Digital Age*, pp. 173–93.

79　The 1911 enumeration returns only became available during the final stage of this work, too late to be included in the database. Data from 1911 were, however, used in the reconstruction of specific Irish families.

80　The nature of this evidence is discussed in Herson, 'Family history and memory'.

81　E. Delaney, *The Irish in Post-War Britain* (Oxford: Oxford University Press, 2007), pp. 7–8.

82　Most reports came from the local English press and contrasted with the inevitably eulogistic obituaries explored by Máirtín Ó Catháin in the Irish national and Catholic *Glasgow Observer*. M. Ó Catháin, '"Dying Irish": Eulogising the Irish in Scotland in *Glasgow Observer* obituaries', *The Innes Review*, 61:1 (2010), pp. 76–91.

2

The context: Irish emigration and Stafford

The Irish people and families who settled in nineteenth-century Stafford arrived in the town by three main routes. The largest numbers were impoverished Catholics from Connacht. By no means all of Stafford's Irish were 'pauper Catholic Celts', however. The second group of in-migrants were a mixed bag of unskilled workers, artisans, middle-class and even professional people who came from various parts of Ireland and sometimes via other places in Britain. A significant number were Protestants of various denominations. Finally, some of Stafford's Irish had served in the British military and arrived in Stafford either through a posting to the militia barracks or for other reasons after they were pensioned off. In this chapter we examine the reasons why these people left Ireland. We need to consider how their family backgrounds influenced their sense of self, their kinship patterns, and the identity they expressed in Ireland and later on during their migrant paths to Stafford. We also look at the nature of the town to which they came.

In his study of 'The End of Hidden Ireland' in Ballykilcline Robert Scally found it increasingly difficult to trace what happened to individuals and families as they moved farther away from Co. Roscommon.[1] This study suffers the same problem in reverse. It is often difficult to trace individuals and families back to specific places of origin in Ireland. Not impossible, however. Sometimes the census enumerators in Stafford recorded a county of origin. Added together over the censuses from 1851 to 1901 this scatter of evidence has helped to identify the likely county of origin of two-thirds of the 206 Irish families who settled long term in Stafford (Figure 2.1). Over half definitely came from Connacht, and it is likely this underestimates the true proportion since there were others probably from the same area for whom specific evidence is lacking. Although the Connacht families clearly formed the majority of Stafford's Irish, the other three provinces contributed a significant minority. Stafford's Irish population was by no means monochrome.

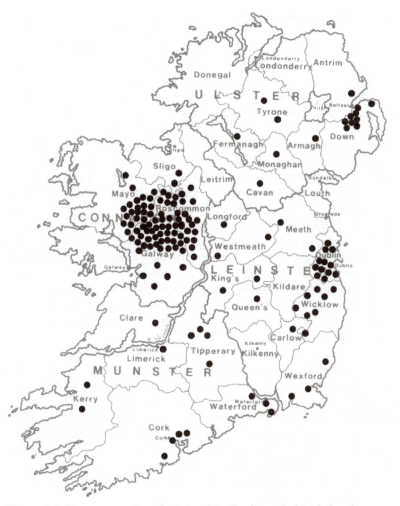

Figure 2.1 Known counties of origin of Stafford's settled Irish families

In some instances census enumerators noted the actual names of townlands or villages in Ireland in which people were born. Even when such evidence was lacking, it sometimes proved possible to identify a likely locality or localities of origin from the Tithe Applotment Surveys of the 1820s and 1830s and the Griffith's Valuations of the 1840s and 1850s. These sources yielded the precise origin of sixty, or just under 30 per cent, of Stafford's Irish families. We now need to look at the sources from which they came.

The Castlerea connection

The small town of Castlerea, Co. Roscommon, is about thirty-two miles north-west of Athlone and forty miles north-east of Galway city. It lies near the intersection of Cos Roscommon, Galway and Mayo. Twelve miles to the north-west lies the small town of Ballaghadereen, and the same distance to the west is Ballyhaunis, Co. Mayo. To the south-west, and sixteen miles distant, the village of Dunmore, Co. Galway, stands on the road to Tuam and Galway city. Ballymoe, Glennamaddy and Mount Bellew Bridge are in Co. Galway to the south of Castlerea, whilst to the north-east the hamlet of Frenchpark is about eight miles away on the road to Boyle. Today the district is quiet, remote and thinly populated, but it was not always so. In the first half of the nineteenth century the Castlerea district was densely peopled by thousands of poverty-stricken families. It was from this area that most of Stafford's Connacht Catholic settlers came (Figure 2.1). That is not surprising. It was one of three main sources of migrant labour in Ireland.[2]

The key to this situation was the land system. By the early nineteenth century land in the Castlerea district was owned by a wide variety of families, both Catholic and Protestant. Most landlords cared little about what was happening on their land as long as rents continued to roll in. This was not necessarily because they were absentees, although most were.[3] Where landlords were absent the management of their estates was usually in the hands of agents or the land was rented out on long leases to middlemen. The middleman system intrinsically meant a hierarchy of tenants with each layer paying the profits of the layer above. This worked as long as farm output, prices and labourers' wages rose as they had done in the Napoleonic Wars. After 1815 the Castlerea district, in common with much of rural Ireland, entered a period of acute economic and social crisis. The link between this part of Ireland and Stafford was one of the direct results of that crisis.

There was a dual economy – as Joel Mokyr says: two Irelands 'living alongside each other, intertwined and mutually dependent, though utterly different in their degrees of commercialisation, economic attitudes, agricultural techniques and so on.'[4] On one extreme there was a relatively small number – perhaps 2,000 – of commercial farmers whose fortunes were determined by the market economy of Britain and Ireland.[5] They occupied about one-fifth of the land. At the other extreme vast numbers of people – about 250,000 – lived in a broadly subsistence economy. They needed land on which to grow basic foodstuffs, above all potatoes. The two areas of the dual economy nevertheless interacted. The farmers and landowners needed the labour power of the subsistence peasants whilst the latter needed wages or labour service to pay rents and tithes, and for goods and services. Barred from the best land, they had to compete for the poor land, bog margins and bogs not occupied by the commercial farmers.

The subsistence sector was by no means monolithic, however. In the competitive struggle for land there was a hierarchy of tenants. Some were middlemen who had emerged with the resources to rent more substantial holdings between 20 and 100 acres. These families were local power brokers and this meant the immediate landlord of most Catholic sub-tenants was usually a fellow Catholic. Others were 'companies' of tenants who were part of the clachan-and-rundale system of communal farming settlements that had expanded in the west of Ireland since the seventeenth century. In the pre-Famine period clachans were particularly numerous in Kiltullagh and the southern part of Kilkeevin parish, Co. Roscommon, as well as in the parishes of north-east Galway.[6] The system was a response to, but also helped sustain, the massive population growth, since it allowed dense occupation of marginal land based on the intensive production of the potato for food, and turf from the bogs for fuel. As the population rose land-holdings in the clachans were divided and divided again, and new clachans established on even more marginal areas. In the eighteenth century many landlords allowed the system of co-partnership to expand since it was a way of extracting maximum rent from marginal land. In the decades before the Famine landlords began to break up the system and replace it with direct leases to individual small-holders.[7] Co-partnerships could be of minute size – just one-fifth of an acre – and were not restricted to full clachan-and-rundale settlements.[8]

The growth of population sustained by potato farming on marginal land together with the shift from communal land-holding to market-driven individual tenancies produced an army of effectively landless cottiers and conacre holders. Cottiers rented the land on which their cabins were built but had little or no cultivable land attached, whereas conacre plots were rented annually purely for tillage and normally had no permanent dwelling. These families were at the bottom of the economic hierarchy. The big estates and grazing farms needed labour available on demand and the landless families provided it. There was, however, never enough paid work to sustain even a fraction of the available labourers. Only about one in ten had any sort of regular employment and 8 pence a day was the maximum they could expect to earn.[9] Such people and their families needed land on which to grow the potatoes essential to survival, and by the pre-Famine period the landless were so desperate for conacre plots that landlords and middlemen routinely charged exorbitant rents for them.[10] The rent spiral was compounded because there was no open system of conacre land valuation. It was merely let to the highest bidder.

The three decades from 1815 to the outbreak of the Famine were crisis years for the mass of people living in the Castlerea district. The agricultural depression meant prices tumbled in the livestock and produce markets, and tenants of all classes, but especially the poorest, could no longer afford the high rents.[11] Rent arrears spiralled and this undermined the financial basis of many of the landlords, particularly those who had mortgaged their estates to support profligate expenditure on the basis of future income. The response of more vigorous landlords was to take direct control of tenancies, break up co-partnerships and combine small farms into larger holdings. Small tenants lost their land and in 1845 Joseph Sandford of Derry Lodge near Lough Glynn (Tibohine parish) described the process in more detail: 'They [the landlord or agent] generally pick the best tenant; and if there is waste to the farm, or any thing of that kind, they put those they cannot accommodate on the waste land, and give them the edges of bogs and so on. The country people term it transporting them; they are banished to some corner of the bog.'[12] Population growth drastically worsened prospects. The population of the Castlerea area rose by one-third from 186,538 in 1821 to 246,434 in 1841. Living conditions for the mass of people were appalling.[13] William Bourke, parish priest of Templetogher and Boyounagh reported that the housing was:

> most wretched, built of sods or sometimes mud, of stone very rarely; furnished? oh! Bedsteads, such as they are, very rarely enumerated, or to be found amidst the cabin furniture; a damp floor, a wad of straw or undried rushes, perhaps a sheet and a thing that was once a blanket, surmounted by the rags worn in the day, form the couch of the cabin's inmates.[14]

In forty parishes out of fifty-two in the region the poverty of the people worsened between 1815 and 1836, and in only three was some improvement reported.[15]

People and families could try to alleviate their poverty in a number of ways. The first, emigration, was the least popular option before the Famine, and local reports suggest few left the Castlerea district for destinations overseas.[16] The poorest Catholic, often Irish-speaking, people were reluctant to leave. Emigrants came disproportionately from the relatively better-off Catholic sub-tenants, farmers, artisans and small gentry, as well as Protestants. It accords with the picture painted more widely in Ireland's three southern provinces by S. H. Cousens and Kerby Miller.[17]

The second way people could supplement their incomes was by working in local manufactures, handicrafts or services. There was, however, no industrialised manufacturing in the area. Work in the domestic linen trade would have been an option as late as 1820, but by the 1830s the flax and linen trade was dead.[18] It was an example of the deindustrialisation that hit Ireland after the 1800 Act of Union. Another way off the land into some sort of job security was to join the army or the police.[19] Service in the army or police meant, however, breaking with close-knit family ties in the land economy. Recruits were forced to enter the 'modern' world of state organisation and control, and they had to make a radical shift in basic attitudes and identities in the process.[20]

The main way to make money to pay the rent was by going elsewhere to get seasonal work, particularly in Britain. That was how the connections were made that ultimately led to permanent emigration before, during and after the Famine. Seasonal migration developed after 1815 over a good deal of north-west and north-central Ireland, but particularly in the overpopulated parishes of north-west Roscommon and adjacent parts of Mayo and Galway. By the 1830s it had become very widespread, though not universal.[21] Perhaps the clearest picture was painted in the parish of Kiltullagh where Thomas Feeny, the Catholic priest, reported in 1835 that 'there are 1,320 families in this parish; I may say all of them poor. One and sometimes two men out of each of the most of these families go periodically to England or to Leinster, but more frequently to England, to obtain employment.'[22] These were men like Michael Byrne, Dominick Dooley or John Gallagher who, in the summer of 1841, were lodging in stables, barns and poultry houses in the Stafford area. Having planted their potatoes they set off in time to be in England for the hay and grain harvests. Staffordshire was an attractive destination since it was relatively close to Liverpool and the connection with people from the Castlerea area became particularly strong.

A final reaction to the problems people faced was through direct and violent action. In the first half of the nineteenth century the Castlerea district saw a lot of rural 'outrages' against landlords and magistrates.[23] There were direct links between this activity and seasonal migrants to Britain who could make contact with English radicals and sources of arms. In September 1845, for example, five harvest workers from near Williamstown (Boyounagh parish) in Co. Galway were arrested at Athleague, Co. Roscommon. They had been working in Staffordshire and were carrying 'guns and pistols as perfect as if [they were] out of a military barrack'.[24] One of those arrested and interrogated was Patrick Concagh, or Concar, who subsequently settled in Stafford and established a family still resident in the area.[25]

In sum, the Castlerea district before the Famine was a land of burgeoning poverty and misery. The desperate need to earn enough to survive forced many individuals and some families to leave the area for seasonal work and many went to the Stafford area. Some then settled permanently in the town. The contacts built up there were invaluable when the Famine disaster struck.

Family life in the Castlerea area

The crisis in the economic base of the Castlerea area between 1815 and 1845 began to have an impact on the nature of family life. At the beginning of the period the mass of families conformed to Young and Willmott's Stage 1 pre-industrial family.[26] They were largely self-sufficient units of production that existed within a strong communal structure and in which kinship ties and reciprocal obligations were strong. Partible inheritance of land allowed the creation of many separate child households within a sustaining extended family network. This pattern gave women, as wives, mothers and co-producers, substantial status in the family. Although husbands were the nominal family heads, it has been argued that wives and mothers wielded the real power. They controlled household management and frequently earned the only significant cash income through spinning, knitting and other forms of domestic production.[27] Men's activities, by contrast, were controlled by the annual cycles of subsistence farmwork that, it has been suggested, led to periods of idleness and uselessness that undermined male patriarchy and status.[28] This environment of relative gender equality favoured romantic attachment, free marital choice and early marriage. Its practical democracy also encouraged challenges to male authority in the home that might result in domestic brawls in which the women were as likely to 'win' as the men.[29] We shall see residual evidence of these pre-industrial characteristics in the behaviour of some of the families that settled in Stafford.

The destruction of communal tenure in favour of individual tenancies for the favoured, and landlessness for the poorest, increasingly undermined the traditional family pattern. This was accentuated by the demise of domestic goods production through 'deindustrialisation'. Seasonal work in England, mostly done by men, now became essential to sustain the family economy. These forces tended to shift the family power balance back towards men. The trend was accentuated after the Famine by the growth of impartible inheritance, which transmitted tenancy to a single, normally male, child with the rest of the children being forced to find alternative work, usually abroad. The so-called 'devotional revolution' of the Church imposed its stricter religious discipline mainly through women, but at the same time emphasised biblical teachings on women's subordination.[30]

Another factor undermining pre-industrial family and community life was the declining use of the Irish language. By the 1830s the advancing tide of English speech was sweeping over the Castlerea area and by 1851 it was only the poorest people who were monoglot Irish speakers. They had suffered disproportionate death rates during the Famine. The vast majority of people spoke at least some English and most of those who came to Stafford could, therefore, function in an English-speaking environment and culture. Their initial identity was at root Catholic Irish and influenced by communal memories of the Protestant plantations, the Penal Laws and the depredations of absentee landlords. Their experiences in the pre-Famine crisis economy, the Famine and the difficult post-Famine years bolstered these attitudes. It remains to be seen, however, to what extent families transferred and sustained these elements of identity after their settlement in Stafford. The nature of the Catholic identity that families brought to England was also complex. Pre-Famine seasonal workers and Famine emigrants grew up in the period before the 'devotional revolution'. The spiralling population in the Castlerea area meant priests were spread thinly, and they and the Church could be resented for the fees charged to poor parishioners for the life-events of christening, marriage and burial. Attendance at Mass was by no means universal or regular, and religious belief varied in doctrine and commitment. A general commitment to Catholicism hid wide variation in actual practice, characteristics that were to be visible amongst the families who settled in Stafford.

Before the Famine the family life of seasonal workers and emigrants from the Castlerea area to Stafford was, therefore, already in a state of flux. Specific families manifested these changes in their varied characteristics and patterns of behaviour. This, along with status differences in the local tenure hierarchy, meant that migrant families and individuals were far from the monochrome mass they are often portrayed to be.

Famine and post-Famine emigration from the Castlerea area

The existing links between Castlerea and Stafford proved vital for some of the Famine's victims. The population of the district fell from an estimated 255,779 in 1845 to 186,063 in 1851 – more than a quarter of the entire population had disappeared in just six years. Many died from starvation, privation and disease, but between 20,000 and 30,000 people emigrated from the Castlerea district to many parts of Britain and North America.[31] Some settled in Stafford whilst others stopped there for a time on their way to other places.

The general picture is clear, but the details are often hazy. It is easy to assume that the Famine was such a manifest disaster that the timing and reasoning behind people's emigration is obvious and not worth studying. The Famine Irish might superficially appear as an undifferentiated mass whose arrival was chaotic and mainly concentrated in the crisis year of 1847. The actual picture was more complicated. There were five factors that led people to emigrate during the Famine. Although they were often interrelated, and people may well have moved through a combination of causes, the operation of these factors differed in their timing and the people who were most affected.

The first driver to emigrate was the most direct impact of the Famine – people's starvation, destitution and inability to pay rent. On 20 October 1845 a constabulary report from Ballaghadereen, Co. Roscommon, said that 'incipient disease of the potato crop has shown itself in a partial way in this district within the last few days'.[32] The deadly potato blight, *Phytophthora infestans*, had arrived in the district. The Government of Sir Robert Peel introduced measures to alleviate the crisis but during the summer of 1846 the potato disease struck the new crop even more virulently than the previous year.[33] At the same time the new Whig Government ordered the winding-up of the Public Works programme, and by the autumn of 1846 the Castlerea district was in the grip of destitution caused by the failure of the potato crop and the rundown of the Public Works. The local Famine Relief Committees reported harrowing, and increasing, starvation and death.[34]

By the beginning of 1847 newspapers and other sources were commenting on the rising tide of emigration. The direct emigration to America from ports such as Galway city most impressed local commentators, but it was the route eastwards that was taken by the people who ended up in Stafford.[35] The evidence from the town shows these emigrants were already a mixed body of people, but the more or less destitute labourers and conacre-holders were above all those forced to emigrate purely as a means of survival.

A second force for emigration was eviction. The collapse of food supplies and the inability of many tenants to pay rents provided landlords with a golden opportunity to get rid of small-holders and conacre plots. Famine evictions started early in the Castlerea district, and the area was the scene of one of the most notorious 'exterminations' to take place in Ireland during these years. This was from the Gerrard land at Ballinlass in Ballinakill parish near Mount Bellew, Co. Galway.[36] On the morning of Friday 13 March 1846 the townland's inhabitants were evicted en masse. In all, 270 people in 61 families were violently thrown out and left to fend for themselves.[37] Most of the people were forced to huddle in the ditches along the road to Mount Bellew, and after that were forced into the workhouses, often to die there. A luckier few went to England for the seasonal work they had done in the past. Four of the evicted families were headed by Patrick Mannion, James Monahan, John Walsh and James Egan.[38] Men with these names turned up later in Stafford and although these names were widespread in east Galway they may have been survivors of Ballinlass eviction.

The third force driving people to emigrate was the impact of the Poor Laws on small land-holders, a factor that became more devastating in the late 1840s and early 1850s. Many families were victims of the clause in the Irish Poor Law Act that stipulated that landlords were responsible for paying the poor rates of tenancies valued at under £4 a year. Landlords had every incentive to clear their properties of such people and others were forced out by the Gregory clause, which denied poor relief to any tenant who held more than a quarter of an acre of land. Landlords forced tenants to give up their land or, if they went to the workhouse, tumbled their houses and rendered them totally destitute whilst they were away.[39] Massive evictions went on beyond the normally accepted end of the

Famine around 1850. Landlords continued to clear their properties of small tenants into the 1850s and that meant people continued to arrive in Stafford from the Castlerea district during the 1850s. The Poor Laws stimulated emigration during the Famine years in a different but equally important way. If tenants held more than four acres they were directly liable for poor rates, and the poor rates rose dramatically as thousands of destitute and starving people sought relief from the Poor Law. Many ratepayers were in no position to pay. Most of the tenants who emigrated because of rising poor rates decided to go to America but some went to England either by choice or through force of circumstances.

A fourth element of emigration was that many people in secondary and tertiary occupations, such as carpenters, builders and traders, found their incomes disappearing as the Famine depressed the economy and demand for their goods and services dwindled. We shall see examples of these people in Stafford. Finally, the 'push' factors for emigration were increasingly complemented by the 'pull' of people who had already emigrated and sent money, information and prospects of help to those left behind. Families had to tear themselves apart ruthlessly. In March 1848 the Castlerea Vice-Guardians reported that numbers of wives had been 'deserted' by their husbands who had gone to England or America. The wives and children were obtaining relief to survive before money arrived from abroad.[40] Patrick Mannion, one of the possible victims of the Gerrard eviction, went alone to Stafford. His wife had died in the Famine but he became the pathfinder for his daughter and two sons who followed him to Stafford in the 1850s. This phenomenon of family chain migration was common amongst Irish emigrants, but nuclear family units – man, wife and children – also moved lock, stock and barrel, and in Stafford's case nearly 30 per cent of the Irish families who settled long-term in the town appear to have arrived in that way.[41]

Emigrants from other parts of Ireland

Figure 2.1 shows that, although the majority of Stafford's emigrants came from the Castlerea area, a significant minority originated from many other parts of Ireland. Only six counties failed to provide a family that settled long-term in Stafford. Some of these emigrants were essentially similar to those from Castlerea and were forced out of other counties, particularly in the west, for the same reasons. Why they ended up in Stafford is often less clear, however; other geographically dispersed emigrants came from quite different backgrounds. The case studies will give some of the flavour of this variety. A significant number were Protestants and most of these were, of course, descended from immigrants planted in Ireland from Britain or went there for other reasons. They spoke English, were generally literate and their privileged background meant that they were unlikely to be caught in the poverty trap that afflicted Catholics from the west.[42] Many were, nevertheless, under economic pressure to leave Ireland. Deindustrialisation meant that workers in basic crafts like shoemaking and tailoring suffered from British competition and a lack of paying customers in an economy where spending on manufactured goods was inherently limited.[43] They could potentially make more money by coming to Britain and seeking jobs in the new economy. Others were from the professional classes and various levels of the Anglo-Irish Ascendancy.

The destination: Stafford

Stafford has not been short of critics. In 1787 a visitor described it as 'a dull, idle place'.[44] A barrister attending the Assize Court in 1819 averred it was the 'dullest and vilest town in England', and in 1852 Charles Dickens found it 'by no means a lively town. In fact, it is as dull and dead a town as any one could desire not to see'.[45] The theme of 'dullness' and contemptuous dismissal in these comments shows how Stafford had little appeal to literate outsiders. It seemed a grubby, unremarkable place with few social graces or people of distinction. Lichfield, fifteen miles to the south-east, with its beautiful cathedral, 'good conversation and good company', was far more attractive to the upper classes of Hanoverian England.[46] Even so, at the start of the nineteenth century Stafford was no decayed survival from medieval times. Its economy, and that of the surrounding area, was changing and growing.

Stafford lay in a strategic location between two dynamic industrial areas, the Potteries and the Birmingham/Black Country conurbation. Liverpool was over 60 miles to the north-west and London about 130 miles to the south-east (Figure 2.2). The main road and canal routes from the north-west to the Midlands passed through or close to the town. In 1837 Stafford's strategic location was enhanced by the opening of the Grand Junction Railway from Birmingham to Liverpool and Manchester. Although the town and its surroundings superficially looked bucolic in comparison with the heartlands of the Industrial Revolution, they were being affected by it, and the area was one of significant growth. This made it attractive to workers from outside seeking jobs, including the Irish.

Supposedly founded in the eighth century as a hermitage, Stafford lay on a small area of raised ground almost entirely surrounded by marshes through which the sluggish River Sow and its tributaries flow (Figure 2.3). The drainage and topography divided the town into four distinct areas: Foregate, the town centre and Forebridge in a line north to south and Castletown out to the west.

Figure 2.2 The location of Stafford (P. Cubbin, Liverpool John Moores University)

Stafford was the market town for the surrounding area and its labour-market influence extended beyond its boundaries. Many Irish workers in Stafford worked on farms in the countryside and this emphasises the close relationship between the town and its local hinterland. The trade for which Stafford became famous, boot- and shoemaking, grew rapidly in the late eighteenth century as is described in Chapter 8. Despite the growth of the shoe trade, in the first forty years of the nineteenth century Stafford's social and political affairs were largely in the hands of the town's traditional groups. Shopkeepers, craft producers and related

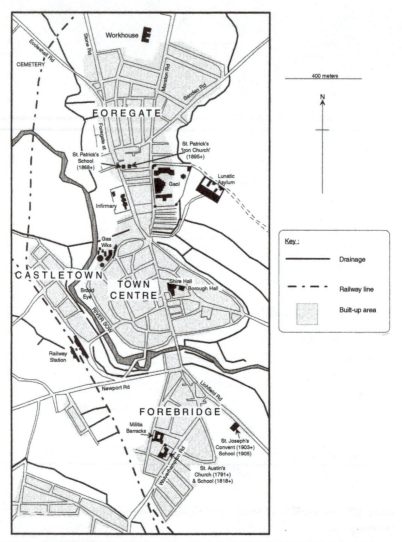

Figure 2.3 Stafford in the nineteenth century (P. Cubbin, Liverpool John Moores University)

traders, along with lawyers, bankers, gentry and some of the clergy, controlled local politics and social life. There was an elite of perhaps 150 families, about 10 per cent of the town's population.[47] The borough corporation was a closed oligarchy in which 'favouritism was rife and family connection was influential in a body many of whose members were related by blood or marriage'.[48] Shoe manufacturers already dominated the local economy and labour market, but they had not yet forced their way into the upper reaches of the local power structure. They were, nevertheless, significant in electoral politics since they had influence amongst the hundreds of boot and shoe workers dependent on them for work.

Stafford's charter of 1206 recognised its status as a free borough governed by its burgesses. The status of burgess, or freeman, was valuable because it gave the right to vote in municipal and parliamentary elections.[49] The attraction of this was not any idealistic belief in the virtues of democracy – far from it. Stafford's electoral politics were massively corrupt – 'no Cornish borough is more venal' was Josiah Wedgwood's opinion in 1780.[50] Every freeman's vote had its price, and electors had to be individually treated or bribed by candidates wishing to receive their votes.[51] Even after the Municipal Reform Act of 1835 a good part of the local electorate continued to be working-class freemen – 'bare-breeched burgesses ... in rags'– and they showed a sturdy lack of deference that reflected the well-known radicalism of shoemakers in the nineteenth century.[52] It was no coincidence that in 1874 the voters of Stafford elected the first working man to enter Parliament, the miners' leader Alexander McDonald. Politics in Stafford were often orchestrated in the clubs and residences of the town's elite but they spilled out into the streets and pubs of the working classes. Stafford's parliamentary and municipal politics offered opportunities to its Irish inhabitants.

If Stafford's politics were lively and often corrupt, its religious character is best described as diverse but generally tolerant. Although Anglicans were numerically dominant, both the town and the district had a Dissenting presence that became stronger and more varied during the nineteenth century. More importantly for this study, the district had a tradition of Catholic recusancy. By 1754 there was a Mass centre in Stafford itself and by 1811 there were around 127 English Catholics in Stafford. By 1831 the total had nearly doubled, partly because more people openly proclaimed their faith after Catholic Emancipation in 1829.[53] The fact that the faith had survived through the influence of local landowners meant that Catholicism was ensconced in part of the local elite and spread to elements in the professional, commercial and working classes. The result was that there was little mileage in sectarian conflict in Stafford. The town's elite and middle class were largely unmoved by active anti-Catholicism, and a general religious truce was in force.[54] There were no anti-Catholic mobs to be mobilised in Stafford.

The strength of native Catholicism had implications for Irish Catholics who settled. They had access to a chapel and a priest to minister to their needs. Catholic employers could offer them jobs. In the longer term, the secure Church offered routes to upward social mobility for the immigrants and their descendants. It was a sheltering umbrella in a new world.

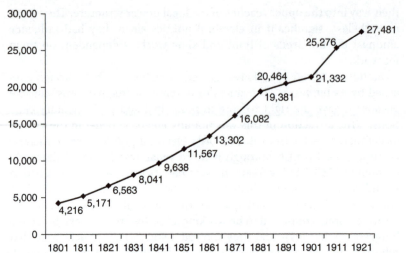

Figure 2.4 Stafford's population, 1801–1921

The sheer strength of local Catholicism meant, however, that the Irish had to accept the Church as they found it, dominated by its substantial, respectable and often wealthy native congregation. Catholicism in nineteenth century Stafford was never a purely Irish phenomenon as was often the case in other areas of Irish settlement.

Stafford was a dynamic town in the nineteenth century. Figure 2.4 shows how the population grew at an increasing rate from 1801 to 1881, by which time it had more than quadrupled. Slower growth occurred in the last two decades of the century as the shoe industry started to decline, but there was another surge in Edwardian times as the economy diversified, particularly into engineering. By 1911 the population was six times that in 1801.[55] Figure 2.5 shows how Stafford's economic performance, as reflected by its population growth, was well above the average for England and Wales as a whole. Shrewsbury, thirty miles to the west, performed miserably in the nineteenth century and Chester's growth was also mediocre compared to that of Stafford. Lichfield, the superior social centre of Staffordshire, was effectively marginalised and stagnant.[56] Stone, Stafford's sister shoe town seven miles to the north, could not ultimately compete. Stafford did not match the explosive growth of the key industrial and port cities – here, for example, Stoke-on-Trent, Wolverhampton or Liverpool – but its strongly expanding economy put it in the class of ancient towns that adapted successfully to the industrial age. This process meant that, generally, more workers were attracted to the town than left it. What was the character of the town to which they came?

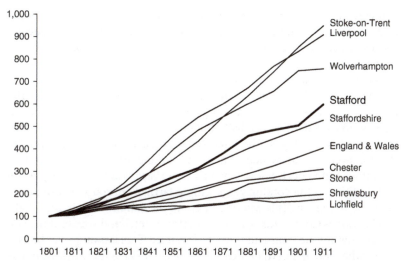

Figure 2.5 Comparative population indices for Stafford and selected areas, 1801–1911 (1801 = 100)

A vision of Stafford

Imagine it is May 1841. You are James O'Connor, a young man of twenty from Co. Roscommon. For the first time you are coming to England for harvest work. You have already had to tramp all the way across Ireland and had a sickening passage amidst the filth of a packet boat to Liverpool. Your colleagues James McGrath and John O'Neill have been to England before and they have picked up that Stafford would be a good place to try. For you it is all new. Already tired out, you set out to walk to Stafford either via Warrington and Newcastle-under-Lyme or through Chester and Nantwich.[57] The two routes join at Meaford near Stone and now you have to do the final eight miles to Stafford. Climbing out of the Trent valley, you have a depressing trudge up Yarlet Bank but at the top the road begins to slope gently downwards. Soon, if it is a quiet day, you will see the smoke of Stafford rising from its hollow two miles away. Going on past Tillington House you finally reach the Waggon and Horses pub at the junction with the Eccleshall Road. This is the northern edge of Stafford. It is time to look for lodgings.

Coming in from the Stone Road you have reached the Foregate, or Forehead, in popular parlance the 'north end' of Stafford (Figure 2.3).[58] This is the fastest-growing part of the town and rapidly becoming the focus of the shoe trade.[59] You are walking down a broad road – Grey Friars – along which a straggle of cottages and houses has been recently built. Lurking to the left is Plant's Square, a squalid court of nine tiny cottages. It will become Stafford's nearest approach to an Irish 'ghetto' in the 1850s and 1860s. New Street runs parallel to North Street beyond Plant's Square. A street of mean houses, it is, nevertheless, a bit better than Plant's Square, and is a place where many Irish families will settle as they become established in Stafford.

The town really begins at the junction with Browning's Lane. The main road, at this point called Foregate Street, is an odd mixture of open sites, grand residences, old half-timbered dwellings and new but often mean workers' cottages. The tatty Red Cow beer house stands opposite the junction with Browning's Lane, and lurking down an alley beside it is another slum court, Snow's, or Red Cow, Yard. Many Irish people will end up there in the coming years. Going farther on, you see Sash Street going off to the left. This will be a haunt of the Famine Irish in the 1850s. Just beyond is County Road, a rather better street, but the main thing you notice now are the walls and towers of Stafford Gaol looming over houses at the other end of the street. Beyond is the County Lunatic Asylum, newly built in 1818. In front of the Gaol, and parallel with Foregate Street, runs Gaol Road. Most of it is still undeveloped but amidst the heaps of refuse in the despoiled fields between the two streets you see Middle Row, a line of decrepit cottages also to become a refuge of the Famine Irish. Continuing down Foregate Street, you go past the Staffordshire General Infirmary. Given the current state of medical knowledge, it is a place to be avoided except in dire necessity. Beyond the hospital the street narrows and kinks to left and right and arrives at Gaol Square.

Gaol Square is the focal point for the streets in this part of town but all you see is an untidy mix of miserable buildings around a featureless expanse of road. It marks the entrance to Stafford's ancient town centre, however, and the main route goes straight ahead up Gaolgate Street. The stench is the first thing to strike you. Stafford's low-lying site means the drainage is poor and the surrounding streams and ditches are filled up with refuse and reeking effluent. Sewage pours down the streets in open channels. Try not to drink the water. It comes from wells contaminated by leaky cess pits and middens. Not for nothing will an assize court judge in 1870 describe Stafford as 'the most stinking town I was ever in in my life'.[60] If it is a fair day you will have to pick your way through pools of cow dung and urine because Gaolgate Street is the site of the main cattle market.

Despite the smell your walk up Gaolgate Street passes through part of the town's commercial heart. Shops line the street and there are seven pubs within 150 yards. Many of the buildings are half-timbered and thatched, dating back to the seventeenth century. At the top of the street you come to the real centre of Stafford, Market Square. Unlike Gaol Square, this is a civic space worthy of the town. It is dominated by the Shire Hall, an elegant classical building completed in 1798 to house the courts, the county justices and a hall much used for civic functions. The square is also the site of the town's Saturday market. That makes it a lively place with stall-holders and customers coming in from the surrounding districts. The other sides of the square are lined with generally impressive buildings occupied by some of the town's leading citizens, as well as by shops, public houses and banks.

Continuing south out of Market Square, the main street, now called Greengate Street, is lined with shops, pubs and other commercial premises. They look distinctly better than those in Gaolgate Street. This is where the prosperous farmers, squires and the middle classes gather on their trips to town. Most striking is the Ancient High House, a massive four-storey Elizabethan town house on the west side of the street. There is a wealth of other impressive half-timbered buildings to be seen, along with brick and rendered structures dating from the eighteenth century. Notable amongst these is the Swan Hotel, a massive coaching inn. It is just going into steep decline. At the height of its opulence it had derived much of its trade from the main post-road from Manchester and Ireland to London, but the new railway is rapidly destroying its trade. In eleven years time it will be so mournful and decayed that Charles Dickens will christen it 'the Dodo'.[61]

Greengate Street terminates at the bridge over the River Sow. It takes no more than ten minutes to walk from Gaol Square to the bridge but this is the length of the medieval town centre. You, however, need cheap lodgings and there is nothing for you on the main street. Look down the side streets. Within a few yards you will find the cramped, damp and bug-ridden cottages of the poor. Try the narrow and dingy street that goes off left at the bottom of Gaolgate Street. This is Back Walls North. As its name suggests, it is built along the line of the old town walls and is right next to the polluted marshes surrounding this part of town. It wanders off towards the Eastgate and is lined with decrepit old cottages. One hundred years later it will still be 'a slum, with sacking over the broken windows of dilapidated terraced houses, half-naked children sitting on the doorsteps, no shoes on their feet and scabs of malnutrition on their pallid little faces'.[62] Lurking in the smoky gloom are Allen's and Clarke's Courts and the little alley of Malt Mill Lane. Just past the site of the old Eastgate the street swings sharply to the right and heads back towards the main street as Back Walls South. There are gaps between the houses here but the open spaces are strewn with rubbish and filth dumped by both the slum dwellers and the servants from richer houses in Eastgate Street.[63] Halfway along Back Walls South is a tannery whose smells, rats, flies and nauseous effluent are the residents' constant neighbours.

The Back Walls are the worst areas of housing to the east of the town centre, but you come across huddled slums elsewhere, for instance in St Chad's Place, Hall's Passage and Appleyard Court. Things are much the same on the other side of the main street. Directly opposite the end of Back Walls South you see the entrance to Mill Bank, another narrow street lined with small cottages and in a dank spot close to the river. Stafford's slums are a mix of decaying half-timbered structures dating back to the seventeenth century and jerry-built cottages thrown up since the 1770s to profit from the rising population. Looming over these squalid surroundings is the tower of St Mary's Church, 'dilapidated and decayed'.[64] It is an eye-catching landmark visible from many parts of the town.

As you walk up Mill Bank you come to the town mill whose weir sometimes causes the River Sow to back up and flood this low-lying part of the town. At this point the street becomes Tenterbanks. It is another straggle of miserable dwellings that follow the course of the River Sow to the Broad Eye. Here a tangle of streets and courts lies around the site of the old west gate. It is dominated by a large stone windmill, but otherwise you see little that is pleasant. In many of the houses here – and all over town – you see and hear shoemakers at their work. For hours they are huddled over their trade in cramped and stuffy rooms. When it is dark they, like everyone else, struggle on in a gloom barely lightened by cheap, guttering candles. The scourge of tuberculosis debilitates many and will carry them off before their time. Another smell assaults your nostrils here. It is from the new gas works that will come to dominate the area and be an environmental eyesore for more than a century. You see that one of the streets running off Broad Eye is Talbot Lane, soon to be renamed Cherry Street. Despite its rustic name, Cherry Street is already a mean area that, like Broad Eye, will be home to many Irish families in the coming years. You continue walking down Gas Lane (later renamed Chell Road) past the gas works. A good place to look for cheap lodging will be either Dottell Street or Wilson's Court. The other option is to wander up Bull Hill, a narrow track that takes you back into Gaol Square.

The old town centre stopped at the Green Bridge over the River Sow, but you may have noticed that the built-up area extends beyond the bridge. This is Forebridge, the third part of the town's structure. The roads to the south and west – to Lichfield, Wolverhampton and Newport – converge here and you see a great mixture of housing. There are substantial villas and elegant residences, particularly along the Lichfield Road. It is the most desirable part of town. Even so, there are places to look for lodgings amongst the grimy houses in Plant's Court and Bailey Street. Irish people are already settled here and more will come during the Famine. That will be your last chance for somewhere cheap to stay in these parts, however. The built-up area soon fades away, but walk up the Wolverhampton Road and you will come to St Austin's Catholic Chapel. It is a relatively modest building, partly hidden behind an impressive but secular-looking presbytery. The chapel's location at the southern edge of town is fine for its respectable English congregation but a hefty walk from where most of the Catholic Irish will live.

As you have arrived in 1841 you will come across another part of Stafford. The Grand Junction Railway, opened in 1837, has already spawned a new suburb, Castletown, between the River Sow and the railway (Figure 2.3). Its houses are fairly small and will often be enveloped in a pall of smoke from the engine shed but they mostly have back yards or small gardens. They are distinctly better than the workers' housing in other parts of Stafford but are, of course, particularly home to railway families. The area is becoming a relatively respectable working-class suburb. You will not find accommodation here. Luckily you meet some other Irish labourers and they direct you back up Foregate Street to the Waggon and Horses pub. There the road to Eccleshall forks left along Brook Street – you missed it when you walked into town. Down there the Kearns family from Co. Roscommon run a lodging house that has room for you to stay. You and your comrades James McGrath and John O'Neill are there in time to be listed by an 1841 census enumerator. We shall meet the Kearns family again in Chapter 4.

You have seen the awful slums of Liverpool where many of your compatriots have ended up. Superficially Stafford looks more attractive than that, but you have now found that Stafford too has its slums and you will have to live in them. If you stay here you will find life is no country town idyll. For the impoverished shoemaker in Broad Eye or the farm labourer in Brook Street or Clarke's Court the day-to-day grind to survive means conditions can be as hard as those in the big cities. Even so, Stafford offers possibilities that you may be able to exploit.

The family environment of the Stafford area

It is a theme of this book that families from similar backgrounds might follow different trajectories, and this applies equally to Stafford's host population and the immigrant Irish. A distinction can be made between the environment of Stafford town and that in the surrounding countryside. In the countryside 'traditional' family life was still largely maintained. A strictly hierarchical society existed in which the local landowning families and their agents largely set the terms of their tenants' lives and the social norms of the rural population. The dominant families – the Littletons, Ansons, Ryders, Talbots, Chetwynds – were part of the nation's ruling class, and their family links were nationwide as well as local. Below them were many smaller families from the petty aristocracy and the local squirearchy. All these families and their managers employed people from the local population and they also drew on supplies of casual labour such as the Irish. Social or familial links with such people were strictly distant and instrumental. There is, never-theless, circumstantial evidence that Catholic owners like the Staffords, Whitgreaves and Wolseleys were more willing to take on Catholic Irish workers than others. In time some more prosperous families with Protestant Irish backgrounds took up residence in the countryside and undoubtedly became part of local privileged society. The peer group of the poorer Catholic Irish was clearly the local rural working class, how-ever. They were mainly dependent on farm labouring and related occu-pations, but many such people, particularly the young, were moving out of the district in search of jobs in Stafford town itself, the Black Country, Birmingham and the Potteries. People making this move nevertheless retained family connections to people in the area and brought rural workers into contact with the norms and attitudes of industrial society. Even so, most families were likely to be long-settled in the district, and their kinship relations were complex and close. Most were at least nom-inally Anglican, although a minority deviated towards Non-Conformity and there was, as we have seen, a sprinkling of Catholics. Superficially the latter might have offered an entry route into local society for Irish Catholics, but the local Catholics' identity was profoundly moulded by the faith and attitudes of upper-class recusants. The Irish might be seen as threatening interlopers as much as fellow co-religionists. The family environment of the rural district was, therefore, generally one of trad-ition, conservatism and stability. It was not one that offered much of an opening to Irish incomers, particularly single migrant workers.

Stafford town was rather different. It was at heart a class-stratified society just like the countryside, but the boundaries were more fluid. We have seen that perhaps 150 elite families dominated the political and eco-nomic affairs of the town. Even so, the growth of the shoe trade along with Stafford's increasing significance as a market, transport and admin-istrative centre offered opportunities for both native and incoming entre-preneurs and manual workers. Many people living in Stafford were native Staffordians or had family ties with the surrounding countryside, so even here local kinship networks and obligations were strong. The family envir-onment was, nevertheless, more open. The growing economy meant an increasing number of in-migrant workers and their families. Shoemakers were particularly mobile, going 'on-tramp' around shoe towns like Stafford to find work. The implications of this are discussed in Chapter 8. A per-ennial shortage of housing meant that many family households included lodgers. Although initially instrumental in motivation – lodgers need-ing accommodation, occupiers needing an income to pay rent and liv-ing expenses – such households could develop quasi-family relationships around work, social life, sexual intimacy, bonding and marriage. 'Home' was often the workplace. Life was insecure. The town's small size meant that social networks overlapped – everybody knew everybody else, by repute if not in actuality. The social control exerted by the elite through social and religious institutions, as well as directly through the criminal justice system, served to put limits on workers' independence. It could be risky to step out of line. Even so, Stafford's freeman vote and electoral corruption served to bolster a robust independence amongst many in the working class. The religious truce operated by the elite meant that one obvious touchstone for intercommunal violence was lacking.

Stafford's nineteenth-century ethos was increasingly moulded by the shoe trade, but its other functions also influenced its family environment. Its central location, market trade, law courts and administrative functions meant its inhabitants were relatively outward-looking rather than parochial. Its position as county town, addled as it was, meant that many Staffordians were aware of the wider context. The *Staffordshire Advertiser* (founded in 1795) put the literate classes in touch with regional, national and international affairs. In class-ridden nineteenth-century society the odds were always stacked against the poor, in Stafford as elsewhere. Nevertheless, it was a place where incomers like the Irish might get on through exploiting openings in the economy and amongst local social networks.

For Irish people and families living in Stafford, and even more for their children growing up there, the nature of the town was bound to be a major factor influencing their lives. Immigrants who aspired to economic and social success were forced to accept publicly the class attitudes and ideologies of the elite groups, whatever their private thoughts. They needed to enter and exploit the network that dominated the town's affairs. Even so, the boundaries separating the lower bourgeoisie, the artisans and the unskilled residuum were porous. Immigrants such as the Irish faced a complex social environment but one that was relatively benign in comparison with the polarised situation to be found in the big cities and the areas of heavy industry and mining. Stafford was no paradise. Living conditions were often bad and poverty was widespread. It offered little to migrants determined to maintain publicly an exclusive Catholic and Irish identity and transmit it to their descendants. Irish individuals and families almost immediately faced challenges to their identity, and they and their descendants had to take decisions on how they would relate to the various elements of the host society. We now go on to document the range of responses that families were to make.

Notes

1 R. J. Scally, *The End of Hidden Ireland: Rebellion, Famine and Emigration* (Oxford: Oxford University Press, 1995), Part 2.

2 A. O'Dowd, *Spalpeens and Tatty Hokers: History and Folklore of the Irish Migratory Agricultural Worker in Ireland and Britain* (Blackrock: Irish

Academic Press, 1991), pp. 58 and 67, and Figures 22, 23 and 25. S. H. Cousens, 'The regional variation in emigration from Ireland between 1821 and 1841', *Transactions of the Institute of British Geographers*, 37 (1965), pp. 15–30. C. Ó Gráda, *Ireland: A New Economic History, 1780–1939* (Oxford: Clarendon Press, 1995), pp. 74–6.

3 *Royal Commission on the Condition of the Poorer Classes in Ireland* (1836) (hereafter *RC Poorer Classes*), Appendix F: 'Baronial examinations relative to conacre etc', Q. 33, 'Are the landed proprietors absentee or resident?'. The baronial evidence rather conflicts with Patrick Melvin's view that the majority of gentry landowners were resident; P. Melvin, 'The landed gentry of Galway, 1820–1880' (Ph.D. thesis, Trinity College Dublin, 1991), pp. 33 and 100.

4 J. Mokyr, *Why Ireland Starved: A Quantitative and Analytical History of the Irish Economy, 1800–1850* (London: George Allen and Unwin, 1985), p. 20.

5 In the 1831 census there were 2,294 "occupiers employing labour" in the study area, the majority of whom would have been commercial farmers.

6 F. H. A. Aalen, K. Whelan and M. Stout, *Atlas of the Irish Rural Landscape* (Cork: Cork University Press, 1998), pp. 79–83 and Figure 31.

7 I. Weld, *Statistical Survey of the County of Roscommon* (Dublin: R. Graisterry, 1832), p. 475; J. Clarke, *Christopher Dillon Bellew and His Galway Estates, 1763–1826*, Maynooth Studies in Local History, 49 (Dublin: Four Courts Press, 2003), p. 22.

8 National Library of Ireland (NLI), Tithe Applotment Book (TAB) 11/40, film 39, Moylough, Co. Galway; TAB 25/15, film 88, Kilkeevin, Co. Roscommon.

9 *RC Poorer Classes*, Appendix D: 'Baronial examinations relative to the earning of labourers, cottier tenants etc.' (HC1836 XXXI.1), Cos. Galway, Mayo and Roscommon baronies, responses to Q. 1, 'How many labourers are there in your parish? How many are in constant and how many in occasional employment?'.

10 *The Times*, 10 October 1845: Times Commissioner's report from Castlerea, Co. Roscommon.

11 Clarke, *Christopher Dillon Bellew*, p. 58.

12 *Royal Commission of Inquiry into the State of the Law and Practice in Respect of the Occupation of Land in Ireland (Devon Commission), Minutes of Evidence, Pts II and III, 1845*, 23 July 1844, Castlerea, Mr Joseph Sandford, Q. 54, p. 362.

13 *RC Poorer Classes*, Appendices D, E: 'Baronial examinations relative to food, cottages and cabins, clothing and furniture etc.', and G: 'Report on the state of the Irish poor in Great Britain'.

14 *Ibid.*, Appendix E, Connaught, County Galway, Barony Ballymoe (half).

15 *Ibid.*, Appendix D, Connaught, Co. Galway, Baronies of Ballymoe, Dunmore, Tuam and Tyaquin; Co. Mayo, Baronies of Burrishoole, Carra, Clanmorris and Costello; Co. Roscommon, Baronies of Athlone, Ballymoe, Ballintobber and Boyle.

16 *Ibid.*, Appendix F, Qq. 30–2.

17 Cousens, 'Regional variation; Miller, *Emigrants and Exiles*, Chapter 6, esp. pp. 193, 196 and 199–201.

18 The number of beggars in Castlerea in 1834 was stated to be double that of ten years previously, partly because of the loss of the flax and linen trade.

Appendix to the First Report of the … Inquiry into the Poorer Classes in Ireland, Parliamentary Papers (PP) 1835, Vol. 32, Part 1, Baronial Examinations, Ballintobber Barony, Kilkeevin Parish, p. 511. In 1832 Isaac Weld wrote that at the Castlerea market 'linen yard formerly sold in considerable quantity but with cessation of demand the supply stopped'; Weld, *Roscommon*, pp. 480 and 682–4.

19 C. Steedman, *Policing the Victorian Community: The Formation of the English Provincial Police Forces, 1856–80* (London: Routledge and Kegan Paul, 1984), p. 78 and Chapter 3; E. Malcolm, '"What would people say if I became a policeman?": The Irish policeman abroad' in O. Walsh (ed.), *Ireland Abroad: Politics and Professions in the Nineteenth Century* (Dublin: Four Courts Press, 2003), p. 99.

20 E. M. Spiers, 'Army organisation and society in the nineteenth century' in T. Bartlett and K. Jeffery (eds), *A Military History of Ireland* (Cambridge: Cambridge University Press, 1996), Table 15.1, p. 337; P. Karsten, 'Irish soldiers in the British army, 1792–1922': Suborned or subordinate?', *Journal of Social History*, 17 (Autumn 1983), pp. 31–64 (p. 36–7); D. Fitzpatrick, 'Ireland and the Empire' in A. Porter (ed.), *The Oxford History of the British Empire*, Vol. 3: *The Nineteenth Century* (Oxford: Oxford University Press, 1999), pp. 510–12; K. Kenny, 'The Irish in the Empire' in K. Kenny (ed.), *Ireland and the British Empire* (Oxford: Oxford University Press, 2004), pp. 104–5.

21 J. H. Johnson, 'Harvest migration from nineteenth-century Ireland', *Transactions of the Institute of British Geographers*, 41 (June 1967), pp. 97–103, esp. Figure 2; O'Dowd, *Spalpeens and Tatty Hokers*, Chapters 1 and 3.

22 *Appendix to the First Report … Poorer Classes* answers to questions relating to the relief of destitute classes: Q. 5, 'What number of labourers are in the habit of leaving their dwellings periodically to obtain employment, and what proportion of them go to England?'. Evidence of The Revd Thomas Feeny, P.P., Kiltullagh, p. 36 of the Supplement to Appendix (a).

23 M. J. Huggins, 'Agrarian conflict in pre-famine County Roscommon' (D.Phil. thesis, University of Liverpool, 2000), pp. 308–14.

24 Report of magistrate Matthew Browne to Dublin Castle, 17 September 1845, National Archives of Ireland (NAI), Outrage Reports, 1845, Co. Roscommon, 25/19637.

25 Report of magistrate D. Duff to Dublin Castle, 19 September 1845, NAI, Outrage Reports, Roscommon, 25/19819.

26 M. Young and P. Willmott, *The Symmetrical Family: A Study of Work and Leisure in the London Region* (Harmondsworth: Penguin, 1975), pp. 23–30.

27 J. Nolan, *Ourselves Alone: Women's Emigration from Ireland, 1885–1920* (Lexington: University Press of Kentucky, 1989), pp. 27–32.

28 P. Radosh, 'Colonial oppression, gender and women in the Irish diaspora', *Journal of Historical Sociology*, 22:2 (June 2009), pp. 269–89 (p. 272).

29 Nolan, *Ourselves Alone*, p. 29.

30 E. Larkin, 'The devotional revolution in Ireland, 1850–75', *American Historical Review*, 77:3 (June 1972), pp. 625–52.

31 Various attempts were made to estimate the number of deaths and emigrants in the Castlerea district. The fact that the study area overlaps three counties complicated this process, but the main difficulty was the bewildering variety

of possible estimates of the death rate coupled to problematic assumptions about the impact of the Famine on the birth rate. The estimates of deaths in the Castlerea district ranged from 51,795 down to 21,929, but the majority lay between the low 30,000s and the upper 40,000s. The resultant emigration figures mostly ranged from the low to the high 20,000s, hence the figures given in the text. S.H. Cousens, 'The regional pattern of emigration during the Great Irish Famine, 1846–51', *Transactions of the Institute of British Geographers*, Second Series, 28 (1960), pp. 119–34; W. E. Vaughan and A. J. Fitzpatrick, *Irish Historical Statistics: Population 1821–1971* (Dublin: Royal Irish Academy, 1978), Table 42; Mokyr, *Why Ireland Starved*, esp. pp. 266–7.

32 L. Swords, *In Their Own Words: The Famine in North Connacht, 1845–9* (Dublin: The Columba Press, 1999), p. 18.

33 See, for example, C. Kinealy, *This Great Calamity: The Irish Famine, 1845–52* (Dublin: Gill and Macmillan, 1994), Chapter 2.

34 Letter from William French to Fitzstephen French, MP (forwarded to Dublin Castle), 8 October 1846, NAI, Famine Relief Commission Papers, 1844–47, RLFC3/2/25/38; letter from Patrick O'Connor, Chairman, Drumatemple Relief Committee to Dublin Castle, 3 November 1846, NAI, RLFC3/2/25/25; letter from Michael Daniel O'Connor, Secretary, Ballintobber Relief Committee to Dublin Castle, 14 January 1847, NAI RLFC3/2/25/24; letter from Mrs Henry Blake to Dublin Castle, 6 February 1847, NAI, RLFC3/2/11/104; letter from Charles Strickland, 21 February 1847, NAI, RLFC3/2/25/44; letter from Denis O'Connor, Chairman of the Kilcorkey and Baslick Famine Relief Committee, 2 February 1847, NAI, RLFC3/2/25/36.

35 *Tuam Herald*, 10 April 1847 and 3 April 1847.

36 Letter from John N. Gerrard and article, 'Landlordism in Ireland: The Gerrard tenantry', *Freeman's Journal*, 2 April 1846.

37 *Roscommon Journal*, 14 March 1846. The population of the townland was decimated by the eviction, falling from 363 in 1841 to just 4 in 1851.

38 *Tuam Herald*, 4 April 1846. The same list was published with the first *Freeman's Journal* article on 27 March 1846, but with probable typographic errors.

39 J. S. Donnelly, Jr, *The Great Irish Potato Famine* (Stroud: Sutton, 2001), pp. 110–16.

40 Papers relating to aid to distressed unions, letter from Mr Auchmuty to the Commissioners, 29 March 1848 and 4 May 1849, PP 1849.

41 J. Herson, 'Irish immigrant families in the English West Midlands: A long-term view, 1830–1914' in J. Belchem and K. Tenfelde (eds), *Irish and Polish Migration in Comparative Perspective* (Essen: Klartext, 2003), pp. 93–108 (Table 1, p. 106).

42 Ó Gráda, *Ireland*, pp. 74–5.

43 F. Geary, 'Deindustrialisation in Ireland to 1851: Some evidence from the census', *Economic History Review*, 51:3 (August 1998), pp. 512–41.

44 H. Skrine, *Three Successive Tours in the North of England … and Scotland* (1795), cited in R. Butters and N. Thomas, *Stafford: A History and Celebration* (Salisbury: Francis Frith Collection, 2005), p. 49.

45 C. Dickens, 'A plated article', *Household Words*, 24 April 1852.

46 Daniel Defoe, quoted in M. W. Greenslade, D. A. Johnson and C. R. J. Currie, *A History of Stafford* (extract from Greenslade, Johnson and Currie, *The Victoria History of the County of Stafford* (*VCH Stafford*), Vol. 6 (Stafford: Staffordshire County Library, 1982), p. 201).

47 In the mid-1820s associations for the apprehending and prosecuting of felons were established in many of the local parishes. In every case the signatories were clearly the leading local citizens, and the list for Stafford in 1825 consists of 144 names; *SA*, 3 September 1825. Assuming 5 members per family, this represents 10.4% of the town's population of around 7,200 in the mid-1820s.

48 *VCH Stafford*, pp. 225–6.

49 J. Kemp, *The Freemen of Stafford Borough, 1100 to 1997* (Stafford: J. Kemp, 1998), pp. 1–3, 9–15 and 23–35.

50 *VCH Stafford*, p. 238.

51 Kemp, *Freemen*, p. 27.

52 A description from a by-election in 1826 when the London *Globe* reported that 'upwards of one hundred bare-breeched burgesses appeared in rags to poll'; *SA*, 23 December 1826. E. J. Hobsbawm and J. W. Scott, 'Political shoemakers' in Hobsbawm (ed.), *Worlds of Labour* (London: Weidenfeld and Nicolson, 1984), pp. 103–30.

53 M. W. Greenslade, *Catholic Staffordshire* (Leominster: Gracewing, 2006), Chapters 4 and 5; *St Austin's, Stafford, 1791–1991* (Birmingham: Archdiocese of Birmingham Historical Commission, 1991), pp. 9–11; J. D. Herson, 'The English, the Irish and the Catholic Church in Stafford, 1791–1923', *Midland Catholic History*, 14 (2007), pp. 23–46 (p. 23 and table, p. 46).

54 M. J. Fisher and A. Baker, *Stafford's Hidden Gem: St Chad's Church, Greengate Street. A History and Guide* (Stafford: St Chad's Church, 2000), p. 10.

55 The numbers on Figure 2.4 are based on a standard area definition of Stafford town for this study that approximates to the borough boundary of 1917. They therefore differ from the published census populations for Stafford Borough.

56 L. Schwartz, 'On the margins of industrialisation: Lichfield' in J. Stobart and N. Raven, *Towns, Regions and Industries: Urban and Industrial Change in the Midlands, c. 1700–1840* (Manchester: Manchester University Press, 2005), pp. 177–90.

57 An alternative was from Chester to Whitchurch and Newport – the modern A41 – and from thence across to Stafford. Migrants working to the west of the town may well have taken this route.

58 This perambulation has been derived from the author's personal know-ledge and the following sources: John Wood's 'Plan of Stafford from Actual Survey, 1835' in Staffordshire County Council Education Department, *Stafford Maps*, Local History Source Book L3 (Stafford: Staffordshire County Council Education Department, 1969); *VCH Stafford*, pp. 185–96; R. Lewis, *Stafford Past: An Illustrated History* (Chichester: Phillimore, 1997); Butters and Thomas: *Celebration*; R. Lewis and J. Anslow, *Stafford as It Was* (Nelson: Hendon, 1980); J. Anslow and T. Randall, *Around Stafford in Old Photographs* (Stroud: Alan Sutton, 1991); R. Lewis and J. Anslow, *Stafford in Old Picture Postcards* (Zaltbommel: European Library, 1984); R. Lewis, *Around Stafford* (Stroud: Tempus, 1999); R. Lewis, *Stafford and District* (Wilmslow: Sigma Press, 1998); J. Anslow and T. Randall, *Stafford in Old Photographs* (Stroud:

Alan Sutton, 1994); P. Butters, *Yesterday's Town: Stafford* (Buckingham: Barracuda Books, 1984).

59 *VCH Stafford*, p. 191.

60 *Ibid.*, p. 232; Lewis, *Stafford Past*, p. 57.

61 Dickens, 'A plated article'.

62 A reminiscence of the author's childhood in Butters, *Yesterday's Town*, p. 103.

63 *Parliamentary Papers, 1842 (007): Commission on the Sanitary Condition of the Labouring Population of Great Britain. Local Reports on England*, No. 15: E. Knight, 'On the Sanitary State of the Town of Stafford', pp. 225–6.

64 The comment was by Sir Giles Gilbert Scott who restored St Mary's in 1842–4. Quoted in M. J. Fisher, *Staffordshire and the Gothic Revival* (Ashbourne: Landmark Publishing, 2006), p. 50.

3

Stafford's Irish families: the overall picture

Passing through and settling down

Between the 1820s and 1901 members of 206 distinct Irish families were
resident in Stafford for at least ten years.[1] They were the families who, in
the terminology of this book, 'settled' in the town. This chapter outlines
the overall character of this diverse body of immigrants.

We first have to consider the types of family that appeared in the town,
and Table 3.1 sets out the five ways in which they originated. Just over
one-third were Type 1: migrant Irish families. These people moved to
Stafford, often as complex families in a chain migration, and were composed of established partnerships or widowed people with children who
had been born in Ireland, even if more children were later born in Britain.
By contrast, more than one-quarter of the families were Type 2: migrant
Irish adults. This type consisted of people who were doubtless members
of pre-existing kinship networks in Ireland but who arrived in Stafford as
single (or widowed) individuals and established partnerships with other
Irish-born people after arrival in the town. Their children were all born
in Britain. Type 1 and 2 families are the classic 'Irish immigrants' who
are studied, though seldom as families, by most historians of the migrant
experience. Here they will be described as 'full-Irish' families. Historians
have been less interested in Types 3 and 4 – the families with mixed
ethnicity. Over one-third of Stafford's settled families had core partnerships established between an Irish-born person and a non-Irish partner.
Approaching one-quarter were 'male-mixed', an Irish-born man with a
non-Irish woman. This group, Type 3, was twice as large as the opposite
situation, an Irish-born woman with a non-Irish man (Type 4). This substantial body of mixed families poses immediate questions on the extent
and nature of Irish identity. There were, finally, a few of Type 5: British
transient in Ireland. These were families of British people who had lived

Table 3.1 Types of Irish family in Stafford

Type of family	Number	%
1. Migrant Irish family (Migration of pre-existing core unit including children born in Ireland)	73	35.4
2. Migrant Irish adults (Core unit established in Britain; children born after arrival in Britain)	55	26.7
3. Male-mixed family (Core unit established with Irish-born male and non-Irish partner)	48	23.3
4. Female-mixed family (Core unit established with Irish-born female and non-Irish partner)	24	11.7
5. British transient in Ireland (British-born parents with child(-ren) born in Ireland	6	2.9
Total	**206**	**100.0**

Table 3.2 Irish-born individuals in settled and non-settled families, Stafford, 1841–1901

	1841	1851	1861	1871	1881	1891	1901	Total
From settled families	37 (25.5%)	300 (50.7%)	366 (58.2%)	294 (66.4%)	247 (66.8%)	177 (67.3%)	112 (61.9%)	**1533** **(58.4%)**
From non-settled families	108 (74.5%)	292 (49.3%)	263 (41.8%)	149 (33.6%)	123 (33.2%)	86 (32.7%)	69 (38.1%)	**1090** **(41.6%)**
Total	**145**	**592**	**629**	**443**	**370**	**263**	**181**	**2623**

Excludes Irish-born individuals in Stafford Gaol and the lunatic asylums.

in Ireland and had children born there. Obvious questions of identity arise with these people also.

To say 206 Irish families settled long-term in Stafford raises the question of how many people and families came to the town but did not settle – they stayed less than ten years. Answering this question is not easy. Table 3.2 compares the numbers of Irish-born *people* at each census who were in 'settled' families with the numbers of people who were lone individuals or families not recorded in the following census – the 'non-settled'. It shows that the great majority of the 145 Irish-born people in Stafford in 1841 left the town during the 1840s. The Famine immigrants split down the middle – half moved on, but half stayed. After 1851 the proportion of Irish-born who departed fell so that by the last three decades of the century transients formed about one-third of the resident Irish in Stafford at any one time. These figures suggest that the common image of extreme Irish mobility must be modified, particularly since the test of 'settlement' here is very high – people who stayed at least ten years. There is plenty of evidence that many Irish people and families stayed a number of years in Stafford but ultimately 'failed' the ten-year test.

Even so, we need to put some numbers to these more transient people. The total number of non-settled Irish-born people enumerated in the census returns is 1,090 (Table 3.2). In other words, between 1841 and 1901 at least 1,000 Irish-born people came to the town but were only recorded once – they left within ten years. They are, however, merely the ones who happened to be there at the time of the ten-yearly census counts. Others came and went in the intervening years. It is possible to make some estimate of the total number passing through using the burial records of St Austin's Catholic Church. Between 1841 and 1880 there were 185 funerals for adult Irish people (aged over fifteen), only 74 of whom were people recorded in the census returns. They represent 40 per cent of the total Irish funerals. It might be thought that burial records underestimate the proportion of young, mobile adults in the population, but in fact 49 per cent of the adult burials were of people aged forty-five or under. This is striking evidence of how many Irish emigrants died young. Even so, if we allow for some bias against the young in the burial records, it seems reasonable to suggest that only about 35 per cent of the people who passed through Stafford were recorded by the census. This means that if 1,090 non-settled Irish-born were enumerated, then a total of 3,114 must have passed through. In broad terms, over 3,000 Irish probably lived for a time in Stafford between 1841 and 1901 but left (or died) within ten years.[2]

This evidence suggests a complex picture of mobility and settlement. The settled full-Irish and mixed families always lived alongside many transient people, but the proportion of transients declined over time. There was no rigid distinction between the settlers and the transients since most were members of interacting groups. The detailed family histories will show significant cross-over of individuals from transients to settlers and vice versa. Lone individuals or people from transient families could join settled family units whilst members of settled families forged relationships with transients and abandoned Stafford. Despite this, the overall picture shows substantial and increasing *family stability* even though individuals and other families came and went.

Table 3.3 Arrival of settled Irish families, Stafford, 1820s–1901

Arrived	No.	%	Cumulative %
Before 1842	23	11.2	11.2
1842–51	63	30.6	41.7
1852–61	56	27.2	68.9
1862–71	30	14.6	83.5
1872–81	22	10.7	94.2
1882–91	10	4.9	99.0
1892–1901	2	1.0	100.0
Total	**206**	**100.0**	

When they came

The impact of Irish immigration was drawn out over a number of decades and was not just a phenomenon of the immediate Famine catastrophe. Table 3.3 shows how a significant minority of settled families had
already arrived in the 1820s and 1830s. Approaching one-third came in
the 1840s, most, of course, during the Famine from 1846 to 1851. They
were followed by a roughly equal number during the 1850s. These later
arrivals were families whose response to the Famine and its aftermath
was delayed. Many continued to subsist through seasonal work but later
gave up and emigrated. Others were motivated to leave Ireland by the
general lack of prospects and security in post-Famine Ireland and this
group included those who did service in the forces. Some had already
lived elsewhere in England or been in the military forces before arriving in Stafford. Approaching one-third of Stafford's settled Irish families came after 1861. This continued inflow during the 1860s and 1870s
reflected the town's dynamic growth in that period. Only after 1881 did
settlers diminish because Stafford's labour market tightened in response
to problems in the shoe trade, agricultural depression and the general
late Victorian economic downturn. Alternative destinations overseas
were now more attractive.

Province and religion

Historians face the problem that the census returns give no information
on religion and usually little on the precise geographical origin of immigrants from Ireland. Studying the long-term trajectory of families often

Table 3.4 Religious and provincial background of settled Irish families in Stafford, 1820s–1901

(a) All families

	Connacht	Leinster	Munster	Ulster	Province unknown	Total
Catholic	83	14	8	5	45	155 (75.2%)
Protestant	1	13	5	9	12	40 (19.4%)
Unknown	—	2	2	2	5	11 (5.3%)
Total	84	29	15	16	62	206 (100.0%)

(b) Full-Irish families

	Connacht	Leinster	Munster	Ulster	Province unknown	Total
Catholic	72	6	4	5	30	117 (91.4%)
Protestant	—	2	—	5	4	11 (8.6%)
Unknown	—	—	—	—	—	— (0.0%)
Total	72	8	4	10	34	128 (100.0%)

(c) 'Mixed' families and families of British transient in Ireland

	Connacht	Leinster	Munster	Ulster	Province unknown	Total
Catholic	11	8	4	—	15	38 (48.7%)
Protestant	1	11	5	4	8	29 (37.2%)
Unknown	—	2	2	2	5	11 (14.1%)
Total	12	21	11	6	28	78 (100.0%)

means, however, that fragments of information on their geographical origin do emerge. Sometimes a census enumerator recorded the actual place or county of birth of Irish individuals. Evidence of religion can be garnered from church records, newspapers and other sources. Even so, in Stafford there is still a tantalising minority of settled families for whom no definitive answer can be given about their place of origin, their religion or both. Table 3.4 shows what has been achieved.[3]

At least three-quarters of all families were actively or nominally Catholic and one-fifth were Protestant. The residual 5 per cent proved impossible to assign to either religion (Table 3.4a). There was, however, a clear distinction between full-Irish and mixed families. The full-Irish families were dominated by those from Connacht (Table 3.4b). They formed over three-quarters of the full-Irish families whose provincial origin is known, and a substantial number of those whose province is 'unknown' probably came from the same region. The majority of Connacht families came from the Castlerea area examined in Chapter 2. There was a significant minority of Catholics from other parts of Ireland, and some Protestant all-Irish families. The origin of the mixed families was much more varied (Table 3.4c). Their religious split was more evenly balanced with just under half Catholic and more than one-third Protestant; the residue could not be assigned. Less than one-fifth of the Irish-born members of mixed families definitely came from Connacht. Nearly twice as many came from Leinster and there was a significant minority from the other two provinces. The reasons for these differences will be examined in the case-study chapters.

Family structures

What was the structure of the Irish families who settled in Stafford? Table 3.5 shows the range. In assessing this evidence, it is important to stress that *it reflects the revealed character of families over a significant period of time* – by definition, over a minimum of ten years and usually longer. Conventional studies of family structure, for example those by Anderson and Dupree, mostly provide a picture of family structure as revealed by a census snapshot of households at a particular date.[4] This will tend to inflate the apparent importance of nuclear and smaller family units, important as they were. In Stafford just over one-third of the full-Irish families were nuclear (Table 3.5a) but there was significant variation among the different groups. The Connacht Catholics emerge overwhelmingly as complex families of Types O, X and Z. The conventional impression of Catholic immigrants from the poor west of Ireland settling in large and mutually supportive family groups is clearly demonstrated in Stafford. There were, on the other hand, a number of lone individuals. These people were inherently likely to form quasi-familial relationships of various types. The same also applied to a number of childless couples.

All-Irish families from the other provinces, both Catholic and Protestant, with generally higher levels of skill and closer affinity with English culture, were more likely to settle as self-sustaining nuclear families. These characteristics were even more marked with the mixed families, three-quarters of which were nuclear (Table 3.5b). Birthplace evidence suggests that over 40 per cent of these mixed units originated outside Stafford or Staffordshire. It is to be expected that such mobile mixed families would be nuclear.

Table 3.5 Family structure of settled Irish families in Stafford, 1820s–1901

(a) Full-Irish families

	I	K	N	O	X	Z	Total
Connacht Catholic	2 (2.8%)	4 (5.6%)	12 (16.7%)	23 (31.9%)	14 (19.4%)	17 (23.6%)	72
Other Catholic/ uncertain	5 (11.1%)	1 (2.2%)	25 (55.6%)	9 (20.0%)	4 (8.9%)	1 (2.2%)	45
Protestant	1 (9.1%)	0 (0.0%)	8 (72.7%)	0 (0.0%)	2 (18.2%)	0 (0.0%)	11
Total	**8 (6.3%)**	**5 (3.9%)**	**45 (35.2%)**	**32 (25.0%)**	**20 (15.6%)**	**18 (14.1%)**	**128**

(b) Mixed families

	I	K	N	O	X	Z	Total
Connacht Catholic	0 (0.0%)	1 (9.1%)	5 (45.5%)	1 (9.1%)	3 (27.3%)	1 (9.1%)	11
Other Catholic/ uncertain	0 (0.0%)	1 (2.6%)	30 (79.9%)	4 (10.5%)	3 (7.9%)	0 (0.0%)	38
Protestant	0 (0.0%)	2 (6.9%)	23 (79.3%)	1 (3.4%)	3 (10.3%)	0 (0.0%)	29
Total	**0 (0.0%)**	**4 (5.1%)**	**58 (74.4%)**	**6 (7.7%)**	**9 (11.5%)**	**1 (1.3%)**	**78**

Key
I Lone individual
K Couple, no children
N Nuclear family: couple and children
O Joint family: same generation sibling or cousin families (horizontal extension)
X Extended family: three or more generations (vertical extension)
Z Joint/extended (complex) family

The jobs they did

The way people earned their living was an important determinant of life chances. It is necessary, therefore, to consider the range and status of occupations present amongst the Irish families at or before the time they settled in Stafford. Their broad job types can be classified as follows:

• boot and shoe trade occupations;
• labouring and agricultural labour;

- military service;
- other craft, clerical and service work;
- professional and entrepreneurial occupations.

Table 3.6 shows the close relationships between occupational characteristics and family background. The broad picture is what would be
expected. Full-Irish Connacht Catholic families were overwhelmingly
dependent on labouring or farm labouring with the remainder rely-
ing on miscellaneous manual skills or marginal entrepreneurial roles
such as lodging-house keepers and hawkers. The labouring Connacht
Catholics formed the biggest single block of Irish families and their significance was greater than the apparent number suggests because they
tended to be larger and more complex units. In other words, there were
a lot of people with such a background in Stafford, just as there were
elsewhere.

Even so, Table 3.6 emphasises the breadth of occupational background
to be found amongst the Stafford Irish. Boot and shoe families were
mostly mixed- rather than full-Irish, and evenly split between Catholics
and Protestants. The religions were balanced in families with a military
background. Protestants monopolised those in professional, clerical and
entrepreneurial occupations, as would be expected. The Ascendancy's
control of the economy in Ireland was reflected amongst the higher-status Irish who emigrated. The reasons for these variations in background
amongst the different occupational groups will be discussed in the relevant chapters below, and in each case the characteristics of the specific
occupational group will be compared with those of the 'archetypal' Irish
labouring families.

Settlers and transients: a comparison

Were the families who settled in Stafford a cross-section of the Irish
migrants or was there something distinctive about them that predisposed
them to come to the town and stay there? In other words, how 'typical' of
the mass were Stafford's Irish settlers? To answer this question we need
to know more about the families who did *not* settle. There were two types
of short-term transients – firstly, family units with male or female household heads and, secondly, single individuals lodging in other people's
households or in lodging houses. A sample of each type was drawn from
the census returns that reflected the proportion of non-settled families
in Stafford at each census date. This means the sample was weighted
towards the greater numbers of non-settlers in 1841, 1851 and, to some
extent, 1861. The resultant samples were of forty-five family units and
forty-nine individual lodgers. The evidence to assign counties of origin

Table 3.6 Occupational types, settled Irish families, Stafford, 1820s–1901

(a) All families

	B&S	Lab.	Mil.	CC&S	EP	Total
Connacht Catholic	0 (0.0%)	70 (84.3%)	0 (0.0%)	13 (15.7%)	0 (0.0%)	83
Other Catholic/ uncertain	9 (11.1%)	34 (42.0%)	8 (9.9%)	30 (37.0%)	0 (0.0%)	81
Protestant	11 (26.2%)	2 (4.8%)	8 (19.0%)	13 (31.0%)	8 (19.0%)	42
Total	**20 (9.7%)**	**106 (51.5%)**	**16 (7.8%)**	**56 (27.2%)**	**8 (3.9%)**	**206**

(b) Full-Irish families

	B&S	Lab.	Mil.	CC&S	EP	Total
Connacht Catholic	—	65 (90.3%)	—	7 (9.7%)	—	72
Other Catholic/ uncertain	1 (2.2%)	27 (60.0%)	6 (13.3%)	11 (24.4%)	—	45
Protestant	1 (9.1%)	1 (9.1%)	1 (9.1%)	4 (36.4%)	4 (36.4%)	11
Total	**2 (1.6%)**	**93 (72.7%)**	**7 (5.5%)**	**22 (17.2%)**	**4 (3.1%)**	**128**

(c) Mixed families and British transient in Ireland

	B&S	Lab.	Mil.	CC&S	EP	Total
Connacht Catholic	—	5 (45.5%)	—	6 (54.5%)	—	11
Other Catholic/ uncertain	8 (22.2%)	7 (18.4%)	2 (5.6%)	19 (52.8%)	0 (0.0%)	36
Protestant	10 (32.3%)	1 (3.2%)	7 (22.6%)	9 (29.0%)	4 (12.9%)	29
Total	**18 (23.1%)**	**13 (16.7%)**	**9 (11.5%)**	**34 (43.6%)**	**4 (5.1%)**	**78**

Key
B&S Boot and shoe trade
Lab. Labouring: general, farm or building
Mil. Military: active service, pensioner or previous military service
CC&S Other craft, clerical and service occupations
EP Entrepreneurial and professional occupations

Table 3.7 Comparison of the occupations of settled families and transients, Stafford, 1841–1901 (%)

	B&S	Lab.	Mil.	CC&S	EP
Settled families (*n* = 206)	9.7	51.5	7.8	27.2	3.9
All transients (sample = 94)	11.7	42.6	7.4	29.8	8.5
Transient families (sample = 45)	17.8	31.1	15.6	24.4	11.1
Transient lodgers (sample = 49)	6.1	53.1	0.0	34.7	6.1

and religion to the transient families was inevitably scantier because of their shorter stay. Comparing those that are known with the definitely assigned settled families, the data indicate that families and individuals who moved on were more likely to be Protestant – nearly 30 per cent as compared with the 20 per cent of definite Protestants amongst the settled families. Connacht families formed only half the non-settlers, with a striking proportion claiming to come from Leinster. This result contradicts the popular image of the mobile Celtic Irish labourer. It suggests that Protestants and those from the more anglicised east of Ireland were more likely to keep moving than the Catholics from the west. Put the other way round, Stafford's settled families conformed *more* strongly to the classic picture of Catholic emigrants from the west of Ireland than did the transients.

The occupations of the settlers and transients were broadly similar (Table 3.7). It will be seen that all the sampled transients – families and individual lodgers combined – had a rather lower proportion of labourers and military than the settled families, whereas those in the other occupations were somewhat more significant. In other words, the transients tended overall to be *more skilled* than the settlers. This reflects the greater mobility of those with more to sell in the labour market. There were, however, clear contrasts between the transient families and the transient individual lodgers. The former were more evenly scattered across the occupations whereas the latter were much more likely to be labourers and people in other manual occupations. It is, however, significant that the profile of the individual lodgers was *more* akin to that of the settled families than was that of the transient families. It reflects the fact that many of the settled families were themselves established in Stafford by people who were initially lodgers.

The overall evidence suggests, however, that this study of Stafford's settled Irish families is broadly representative of the more general emigrant population in England. They were not an idiosyncratic group who settled in Stafford for local reasons.

Where the Irish lived

The lives of Stafford's Irish families were conditioned by the jobs they had. This determined what sort of houses they lived in and where they were. In Victorian times, even more than today, the poor had to live in the slums. The better off could afford higher rents and better houses, but if they fell on hard times they too had to find somewhere cheaper and meaner. Stafford had, as we have seen, plenty of slums awaiting the Irish. The supply of housing in this rapidly growing town always failed to keep up with the demand for accommodation. Builders and landlords only put property on the market if it was clearly profitable, and this produced high rents and a chronic shortage of housing. Conditions for the poor were therefore overcrowded, insanitary and miserable. Stafford's first council houses were not built until 1901, and the council's housing record before the Great War remained very poor. The town's Irish families depended totally on the workings of the private housing market.

There was no 'Irishtown' or Irish 'ghetto' in Stafford – these terms have no relevance here. Figure 3.1 shows that in 1861 the Irish were scattered all over the town. That was the year when the Irish were, in fact, most segregated from the host population. Even so, the map shows that whilst there were dense pockets of Irish in the worst slum courts and streets, others were to be found elsewhere. Even in the poorest courts and streets the Irish were not rigidly segregated from those in the host population who were equally poor. English families and households were always to be found close by.

It is important to make some assessment of the degree to which Irish families and households were segregated from the host population since that would have a substantial influence on their experiences and on how their identities might be shaped. Individuals and families who lived in solidly Irish households with other Irish households next door or nearby might rely more on this accessible kin and neighbour support. Most of their lives would be lived in an Irish cultural, religious and ethnic environment. Their children's home life would be relatively closed off from the host society, though they would get more English cultural influences from school – if they attended – or from work. Conversely, all-Irish or mixed households isolated from other Irish households would experience a social milieu dominated by relationships with Staffordians. The pattern of relative segregation would change over time as some of the initial immigrants got better houses and as their children became adults and set up new households.

The degree of segregation experienced by the Irish in British towns was determined partly by their absolute numbers and partly by how diverse they were. If, on the one hand, there were large numbers of Irish in a place, their sheer volume could be sufficient to sustain 'Irish-only' institutions

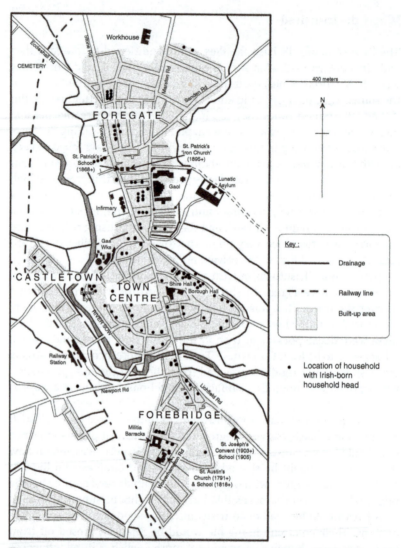

Figure 3.1 Residential distribution of Irish households, Stafford, 1861
(P. Cubbin, Liverpool John Moores University, with author additions)

like churches and pubs. If most of the Irish worked at the same jobs, and
for the same employers, they would have immediate social networks sustained by similar experiences and identities. If those jobs were of low status, poorly paid and insecure, even stronger forces would be at work to
segregate the Irish from the host society. If, on the other hand, the number of Irish was too low to sustain significant 'Irish-only' institutions, if
they had a diverse range of skills and worked for many different employers

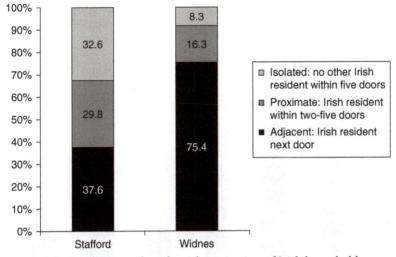

Figure 3.2 Comparison of residential segregation of Irish households, Stafford and Widnes, 1861

alongside local workers, then the forces for segregation would be weaker. Stafford typified the latter situation, and its effects on residential segregation can be seen in Figure 3.2. Here the relative segregation of Stafford's Irish households in 1861 is contrasted with a town at the other end of the spectrum – Widnes.[5] Relative segregation is measured on a three-stage scale. Households were 'adjacent' if they lived next door to another Irish household. This would indicate residential segregation from the host society. They were 'proximate' if there was another Irish household within five doors, suggesting a more ethnically mixed pattern of housing. They were 'isolated' if the nearest Irish neighbour was more than five doors away. This amounted to residential integration with the host population. Widnes and Stafford contrasted greatly. In Widnes there were many more Irish than in Stafford and they mostly worked as labourers in the chemical industry. They were at the bottom of the occupational heap in the town, and that meant they got the worst housing. The result was extreme segregation. Over 90 per cent of the Irish households in Widnes were 'adjacent' or 'proximate'. In Stafford the proportion was less – around two-thirds – and a larger proportion of these were 'proximate' rather than 'adjacent'. In Widnes three-quarters of the Irish actually lived next door to other Irish people – the degree of extreme segregation was very high. In Stafford, on the other hand, over 30 per cent of the Irish lived amongst English people – they were 'isolated' – whereas under 10 per cent were so in Widnes. The residential circumstances of the Irish in Stafford were, therefore, radically different from those in Widnes. The latter town typifies

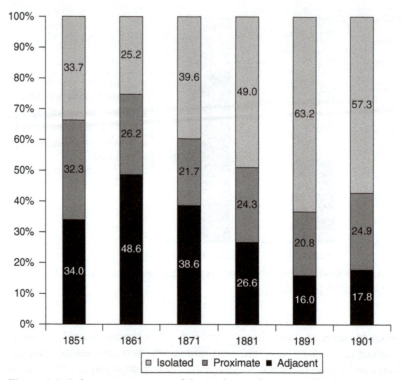

Figure 3.3 Relative segregation of the Irish population, Stafford, 1851–1901

the common image of the Irish living in dense concentrations, whereas Stafford presents a more nuanced pattern determined by their lesser numbers, their social diversity and local factors that will become clearer when we examine the fortunes of specific families.

The degree of relative segregation amongst Stafford's Irish changed over time, as shown on Figure 3.3. In contrast to Figure 3.2, which deals with the numbers of *households*, Figure 3.3 depicts the relative segregation of *Irish-born individuals and their children*. This ensures that people in large households and lodging houses are given due weight. It shows that in the immediate aftermath of the Famine in 1851 the majority of the Irish were close together, split roughly evenly between those living literally next door to other Irish and those with Irish close by but with some English households in between. Only a third were 'isolated'. This relative segregation had increased by 1861 as farm labourers packed into Stafford's Irish lodging houses and other Irish households. After that the proportion of 'isolated' households rose as the Irish and their descendants, together with newer, more secure immigrants, fanned out into relatively better housing. By 1891 over 60 per cent were residentially integrated into the host population. That meant, nevertheless, that a large minority of the Irish and their descendants still lived in the traditional places, and the proportion slightly increased around the turn of the twentieth century, perhaps on account of the out-migration of better off 'isolated' Irish.

This evidence suggests some continuing polarisation of the Irish population and their descendants. On the one hand a residuum of the poorest remained close together in the worst areas because of poverty but also to benefit from continuing links to an Irish social network that was only slowly being transmuted into a Stafford working-class Catholic one. On the other hand, those living more 'isolated' lives – perhaps the more skilled, the more aspirant, the mixed families and the Protestants – avoided the traditional locations and got better housing in more respectable areas.

The histories of Stafford's Irish families took place, therefore, in a specific geographic context. Where they lived, the conditions in which they lived and how these changed clearly affected the opportunities open to them, but the housing in which they lived also reflected the life choices they made and were able to make. It was a complex relationship, but it serves to emphasise that the Irish experience was profoundly affected by the environment in which families lived out their lives and handed on to following generations.

Classifying the families

We can now bring together the information about Stafford's Irish families and use it to choose the case studies in the succeeding chapters. The evidence is summarised in Figure 3.4. The family histories have to represent the character and relative weight of the distinct groups of Irish so that those with similar origins can be compared. The range of characteristics shown on Figure 3.4 could, in theory, produce any number of permutations for such a classification. It seems clear, however, that occupation was a prime determinant of basic circumstances. Other things being equal, the fortunes of agricultural labourers and their families were likely to be different from those of boot and shoe operatives, old soldiers, entrepreneurs or professionals. There was, of course, considerable correlation amongst occupation, religion and geographical background, and these three factors largely determine the classification adopted. The 206 families are therefore classified as follows:

- Catholic labouring families, mostly from Connacht. Total: 106.
- Mostly Catholic craft, clerical and service families from Connacht and other parts of Ireland. Total: 56.

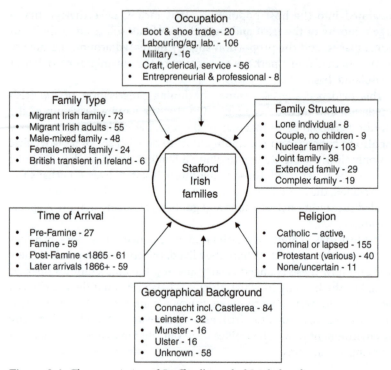

Figure 3.4 Characteristics of Stafford's settled Irish families

- Military and ex-military families, both Catholic and Protestant. Total: 16.
- Boot and shoe families, both Catholic and Protestant. Total: 20.
- Professional, clerical and entrepreneurial families, all Protestant. Total: 8.

The chapters that follow are structured around this classification but within each chapter the case studies are selected to represent the spread of families in terms of the period in which they arrived in Britain, the type of family they were, their religion and their family structure during their time in Stafford – lone individual, nuclear family or complex family. The choice also reflects the final element that needs to be considered – the ultimate fate of families.

Divergent paths: the fate of the Irish families, 1820–1920

The 206 families who settled long-term in Stafford during the nineteenth century were a cross-section of those who left Ireland in that troubled period. What happened to them in the decades after they settled in

Table 3.8 The long-term trajectories of Stafford's Irish families

Trajectory	Number	%
Long-term transient families (Settled at least ten years but ultimately left)	72	35.0
Terminal families (No roots, little out-migration; just faded away)	39	18.9
Integrating families (Intermarried with host society and put down deep roots)	95	46.1
Total	**206**	**100.0**

Stafford? Despite the uniqueness of every family's history, their paths went broadly in one of three directions. These are summarised in Table 3.8. It shows that rather more than one-third of Stafford's Irish families proved to be *long-term transient*. In other words, they settled for a time in the town – at least ten years – but ultimately the initial settlers and/or their descendants left. The long-term transients shaded into a second group, *terminal families*. These families settled long-term in Stafford but put down no permanent roots. Ultimately they just faded away and literally became extinct. Just under one-fifth of the families proved to be of this type, and they form an interesting group whose presence amongst the Irish could not have been identified without the use of family reconstruction techniques. Had things have gone more favourably, some terminal families might have survived to become members of the third category, *integrating families*. Approaching half – 46 per cent – of the 206 families ultimately did put down deep roots in Stafford. They intermarried with local people and produced significant numbers of children. Their descendants are still to be found in the town today, although family members also migrated to other places in the Midlands as well as to the Diaspora in the wider world.

The sheer complexity of family history means that, at the margins, some families demonstrated elements of more than one long-term trajectory. Despite this, the three-way distinction between long-term transient, terminal and integrating families is robust, and it is fundamental to describing the history of Stafford's Irish families. The challenge is to explain *why* particular families followed one of the three paths. The historical data shows no significant correlation between family fate and family type, religion or region of origin. Initial jobs are weakly linked to fate in that families from the military and the shoe trade were rather more likely to integrate whilst a somewhat higher proportion of the terminal families were labourers. The two characteristics that are more significant are date of arrival and family structure. Table 3.9 shows that the

Table 3.9 Family fate by date of arrival (%)

Date of arrival	Integrating	Long-term transient	Terminal	**Total families**
Up to 1845	28.6	57.1	14.3	**28**
1846–51	43.9	43.9	12.3	**57**
1852–65	33.3	34.9	31.8	**63**
1866–1901	70.7	15.5	13.8	**58**
Overall %	**46.1**	**35.0**	**18.9**	**206**

Table 3.10 Family structure and family fate (%)

Family structure	Integrating	Long-term transient	Terminal
I: lone individual	0.0	2.8	15.4
K: couple, no children	0.0	4.2	15.4
N: nuclear family	48.4	51.4	48.7
O: joint (horizontal extension)	13.7	29.2	12.8
X: extended (vertical extension)	25.3	5.6	2.6
Z: complex (joint/extended)	12.6	6.9	5.1
Total no. of families	**95**	**72**	**39**

proportion of families who proved to be terminal was relatively constant except for the cohort that settled in the immediate post-Famine decade. They ultimately died out in Stafford at more than twice the rate of settlers in other periods and the reasons for this are discussed in Chapter Six. Otherwise we can see that the proportion of families who proved to be long-term transients became smaller and, conversely, the proportion who integrated generally grew larger the later they settled. At a general level the increasing tendency to integrate reflected, on the one hand, support from the growing reservoir of existing settlers to help newcomers settle successfully and, on the other hand, the strong likelihood of absorption of settlers and their descendants into the host community because of the relatively small number and proportion of Irish in the local population.[6]

Table 3.10 examines the relationship between family structure and ultimate fate. It shows that nuclear families were equally likely to follow any of the three trajectories. The differences lie at the family extremes.

Over half the integrating families were various forms of complex family whereas only one-fifth of the terminal families were of this type. Conversely, over 30 per cent of terminal families were lone individuals or childless couples whose family units disappeared when they died. These differences might be expected, but the table also shows how the pattern of long-term transient families was closer to that of the integrators than to the terminal families except that joint (sibling) units and a residue of individuals and childless couples were more likely to leave.

It is clear, then, that the fate of families was linked partly to their structure. The causal relationship is, however, not straightforward since the evolving structure of families was in part a reflection of their trajectory rather than a cause of it. Lone individuals demonstrably failed to develop new and family-sustaining relationships whereas extended and complex families emerged precisely because their members intermarried with the host population and became committed to lives in Stafford. The trajectories of Stafford's Irish families and therefore their structure reflected complex and dynamic circumstances. The succeeding chapters analyse a cross-section of family histories to discover why they followed the trajectories they did.

Notes

1 All data discussed in this chapter are derived from the database of Stafford's Irish immigrants and their households described in Chapter 1 and in the Bibliography.
2 Birmingham Archdiocesan Archives (BAA), P255/2/1, Stafford St Austin's, Register of Confirmation, Marriages and Burials, 1828–57; P255/4/1, Stafford St Austin's, Register of Burials, 1858–74; P255/4/2, Stafford St Austin's, Register of Burials, 1875–93.
3 Religious allegiance was gleaned from the records of St Austin's Catholic Church at BAA; Church of England marriage registers at the Staffordshire Record Office (SRO), microfiches for St Mary's, St Chad's, St Thomas's and Christ Church; and SRO D4800/1(Presbyterian Church Records, Stafford), and D4800/2 (Congregational Church Records, Stafford).
4 Anderson, *Family Structure*, p. 44; Dupree, *Family Structure*, Table 2.2.
5 The census enumeration data for the Irish in Widnes were collected by Joanne Hicks, Liverpool John Moores University, to whom acknowledgement is made for the use of her database.
6 P. Collier, *Exodus: Immigration and Multiculturalism in the 21st Century* (London: Allen Lane, 2013), pp. 41–3.

4

Pathfinders: labouring families before the Famine

Typically Irish? Stafford's Irish labouring families

The common image of the immigrant Irish is that of poverty-stricken labourers and their families trapped in the reeking slums of Victorian cities. There they struggled to survive by doing any sort of hard menial work they could find. In Stafford over half the Irish families began their lives in the town depending on this type of job. The overwhelming majority were Catholic. They mostly lived in the town's slum courts and back streets. Drink and drunken disputes sometimes punctuated their lives as they sought escape from their dismal bug-infested surroundings. Even so, differences emerge. The stereotypes can be misleading.

Although a small number of labouring families settled in Stafford before the Famine, the majority came during and after it (Table 4.1). Nearly 40 per cent settled during the immediate Famine years, but well over half came later and a fifth arrived after 1861. This demonstrates the chronic nature of emigration from mid-nineteenth-century Ireland.

The vast majority of Stafford's labouring families came from Connacht, particularly the Castlerea area, and this predominance was especially marked during the Famine immigration (Table 4.2). Only nine labouring families from the other three provinces settled in Stafford. Nearly half the families came from Ireland already formed, and during the Famine an even greater proportion came as Type 1, 'migrant Irish families'. Even so, a large minority of families was established in Stafford by 'migrant Irish adults' (Table 4.3). Only a small minority of labouring families was ethnically mixed.

The classic picture of family kinship amongst the Irish is demonstrated in that nearly 60 per cent of the units overall were various types of extended and complex family (Table 4.4). The proportion amongst Famine settlers was over 70 per cent but it fell to just under half amongst those settling after 1851. Nuclear family units formed a significant

Table 4.1 Date of arrival of labouring families

Date of arrival	No.	%
Before 1845	8	7.6
1846–51	42	39.6
1852–61	35	33.0
After 1861	21	19.8
Total	**106**	**100.0**

Table 4.2 Known provincial origins of labouring families (%)

Province of origin	Before 1845	1846–51	After 1852	Overall %
Connacht	50.0	97.1	85.0	87.5
Leinster	33.3	2.9	5.0	6.3
Munster	—	—	5.0	2.5
Ulster	16.7	—	5.0	3.7
Total no. of families	**6**	**34**	**40**	**80**

Note: the provincial origin of 26 families is unknown.

minority, particularly amongst those arriving after the Famine, and there were also some isolated individuals and couples without children. These nuclear units may well have had relations elsewhere in Britain, but in Stafford they lived independent of blood relatives.

The long-term trajectories of the labouring families are summarized on Table 4.5. Around one-third proved to be long-term transients. They superficially conformed to the image of mobile Irish migrants, but it must be remembered that even these people settled for at least ten years in Stafford and they often invested significant personal capital in their lives in the town. The proportion of long-term transient families was significantly smaller amongst those who settled after 1851. This suggests the later families came deliberately to Stafford and were more committed to the town. Just over one-fifth of the families proved to be terminal, a phenomenon more likely to happen to those settling after 1852. At the other extreme, there were forty-six labouring families who survived long-term and integrated into local society. They formed the biggest group amongst those arriving after the Famine.

Because labouring families were the biggest single group amongst the Irish it is statistically appropriate to devote substantial space to them.

Table 4.3 Types of labouring families (%)

Type of family	Before 1845	1846–51	After 1852	Overall %
1. Migrant Irish family (migration of pre-existing core unit with children born in Ireland)	87.5	54.8	39.3	49.1
2. Migrant Irish adults (core unit established in Britain; children born after arrival in Britain)	—	40.5	42.8	38.7
3. Male-mixed family (core unit with Irish-born male with non-Irish partner)	—	4.8	8.9	6.6
4. Female-mixed family (core unit with Irish-born female with non-Irish partner)	12.5	—	8.9	5.7
5. British transient in Ireland (British-born parent with child(-ren) born in Ireland)	—	—	—	—
Total no. of families	**8**	**42**	**56**	**106**

Table 4.4 Structure of labouring families

Family structure	%
I: lone individual	3.8
K: couple, no children	3.8
N: muclear family in Stafford: couple and children	33.0
O: joint family: same-generation sibling or cousin families (horizontal extension)	26.4
X: Extended family: three or more generations (vertical extension)	17.9
Z: Joint/extended (complex) family	15.1
Total no. of families	**106**

Table 4.5 Long-term trajectories of labouring families (%)

Trajectory	Before 1845	1846–51	After 1852	Overall %
Long-term transient families	62.5	45.3	21.4	34.0
Terminal families	0.0	11.9	33.9	22.6
Integrating families	37.5	42.8	44.7	43.4
Total no. of families	**8**	**42**	**56**	**106**

Their arrival was spread over a considerable period of time, and circumstances for individuals and families arriving in the 1870s were different from those in the 1830s or during the Famine and its aftermath. We shall, therefore, look at a sample of families arriving in each of the following time periods:

- pre-Famine, 1820s–1844;
- the Famine, 1846–51;
- the post-Famine period, after 1852.

The following two chapters look at the Famine and post-Famine periods. Here we look at those who settled before the Famine.

Settlers before the Famine

We have seen how, from the 1820s onwards, the Stafford district was visited each year by hundreds of Irish harvesters, particularly from the Castlerea area. They came to earn money to relieve their poverty back home, and initially there was little incentive to settle permanently. As a result, only six labouring families settled in Stafford before the Famine, and even then, in one case the word 'settled' has to be qualified. In 1841 a Patrick Goodman was lodging in Salter Street, presumably as a migrant worker, although no occupation was stated. He was related to an extensive Goodman family who settled in Stafford during the Famine. In that sense, Patrick was a 'pathfinder', but he was never seen in the town again.

The five other families were a varied group who spanned the range from long-term transients through terminal families to those that ultimately integrated. Michael Byrne was an unmarried farm labourer, a seasonal worker, who in 1841 was found in the loft of a stable at Baswich. In 1851 he was still in Stafford but lodging with his sister and her husband who had also been seasonal migrants in 1841. They all left in the 1850s. There was one pre-Famine female-mixed couple, Thomas Ward and Mary Daly. The Irish element in their heritage was lost rapidly and Mary's Catholic adherence weakened. She failed to transmit it to her children and when she died in 1881 as a pauper inmate of the workhouse her funeral was conducted by an Anglican priest. The family's children, meanwhile, merged seamlessly into Stafford's working class. Three all-Irish families – the McMahons, Carneys and Kearnses – proved to be long-term transients, however, and were the most typical of these early labouring families. The Kearns family has been selected from this group to examine the problems and responses of these pre-Famine settlers.

The Kearns family: poverty and transience

The Kearns family lived in Stafford for over eighty years yet they never integrated into local society. They remained on the economic and social margins, living poverty-stricken lives in miserable slums. Their story superficially conforms to many of the conventional stereotypes of the Irish experience in Britain. Even so, their ultimate identities were a complex mix brought about by changing external circumstances and problematic internal relationships within the family.

Family origins

Farrell and Mary Kearns arrived in Stafford some time around 1826, since they claimed their first known child, Francis, was born in the town around that year. They were certainly there by 1831 and were members of the first Irish family that we know settled long-term in Stafford (Figure 4.1).[1] Although Farrell Kearns said he had been born around 1796 in Dublin, his wife Mary Grenham said she was from Kilbride in Co. Roscommon. The Kearns family came from the same area.[2] Some of them may have been forced off the land and have migrated to Dublin but in the post-Napoleonic War depression Farrell's part of the family may have decided to return to their roots in Roscommon and get money from seasonal work in England. Farrell's upbringing was one of great poverty and insecurity in a family of landless labourers or conacre-holders at the bottom of the social hierarchy. They belonged to a group whose community and social structures were being shattered and whose spiritual links with the Catholic Church were often tenuous.

Family links and obligations were a remaining support in such circumstances, and they seem to have had some significance for the migrant Kearns family in the early days. Farrell and Mary were not the only

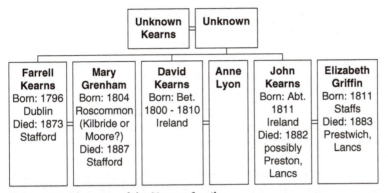

Figure 4.1 The stem of the Kearns family

members of the Kearns clan in Stafford in the 1830s. Two male relatives, David and John Kearns, were there. David Kearns, Farrell's brother or cousin, had married an Anne Lyon and they had at least one child, Mary Ann, in Stafford. They had disappeared by 1841, however.[3] The other, John Kearns, was a hawker and also probably a brother or cousin to Farrell. He came to Staffordshire as a single man and, in the course of his travels, married a local woman, Elizabeth – also known as Eliza – Griffin, at a Catholic church near Lichfield in 1835.[4] They were in Stafford by 1837 and in 1841 were running a lodging house in Eastgate Street. By then they had had three children. Five other hawkers, four of them Irish, were in the house along with two of their spouses. It was an unstable and poverty-stricken household.

Although family links probably explain the presence of the three Kearns families in Stafford in the 1830s, they were not sufficiently close to remain together. As the first in-migrants, Farrell and Mary Kearns offered some basic support to the others, but in the end David and John Kearns had to make their own way and no joint Kearns family emerged in Stafford. Nothing is known of the subsequent whereabouts of David Kearns's family. The path of John's is rather clearer. His work as a hawker meant he spent little time in the family household. Certainly, he was not there in 1841. By 1851 the family had moved ten miles away to Rugeley, but Eliza was still having to bring up the children on her own as a 'hawker's wife'. By then they had four children. They were in poor circumstances, but she was apparently determined to do her best for the family. As a Staffordshire Catholic she could tap into support from the priest or richer Catholics in the local church. How else do we explain the fact that in 1851 her son John, born in Stafford in 1839, was a boarder at St Mary's College, a Catholic school in Upper Woolhampton near Newbury in Berkshire?[5] He grew up to become a railway guard in Shrewsbury, a respectable working-class occupation, and there are numerous descendants from this line of the family. His sister Mary also came under the wing of the Church and ultimately became a member of the Sisters of Charity.[6] In 1861 her younger sister, Anne, was still living at home but working as a schoolmistress. By then she and her mother – and John when he was at home – were in Doncaster, a major move from Staffordshire. Eliza was described as 'formerly an assistant in a shop'. Later they moved to Lancashire, and Eliza Kearns died in Prestwich in 1883.[7]

John and Eliza Kearns depended on occupations at the margins of the economy, but Eliza had aspirations and the family managed to achieve a modest respectability with their children showing clear evidence of upward social mobility. The evidence suggests they grew up in an English Catholic environment in which their often-absent father's Irish identity had little significance. Descendants of the family consistently married non-Irish people and the family's Irish heritage was rapidly diluted. Their trajectory contrasts markedly with that of Farrell and Mary Kearns in Stafford.

The lives of Farrell and Mary Kearns in Stafford

In the 1830s Farrell and Mary ran a lodging house in the small cottage in Brook Street that was the final destination of James O'Connor's imaginary walk round Stafford in 1841 (Chapter 2). By 1844 the Kearns family had had at least eight children, although two died in infancy (Figure 4.2). The house was pretty squalid and it was a rough existence punctuated by drink, conflict and petty crime. In 1836 John Maines, from an Irish family living nearby, was summonsed for throwing 'a large stone' at Mary Kearns. He had quarrelled with Farrell and challenged him to a fight, which the latter had rejected. Mary, who 'admitted she was neither drunk nor sober', then reportedly called Maines 'a cuckold', a jibe at the adultery of his wife, perhaps with Farrell Kearns himself.[8] There was a great deal of bad language, which ended with Mary shouting 'Murder!' It was a pathetic drunken argument, and the case was dismissed.[9] This evidence proves, however, that by the 1830s the Kearns family had lost their Irish language, so there was no linguistic barrier to relationships with local Staffordians. Six years later, in 1842, Mary Kearns was given six months with hard labour for passing counterfeit coin – two base shillings.[10]

These two incidents were symptomatic of the circumstances in which the Kearns family continued to live for the next sixty years. Indeed, their housing got worse. By 1851 they had moved to New Street, a mean street further into town, and by 1861 they had ended up in the slum of Snow's Yard. The family was to remain there for three generations and into the twentieth century, a decline in residential fortunes unusual even amongst the poor Irish.

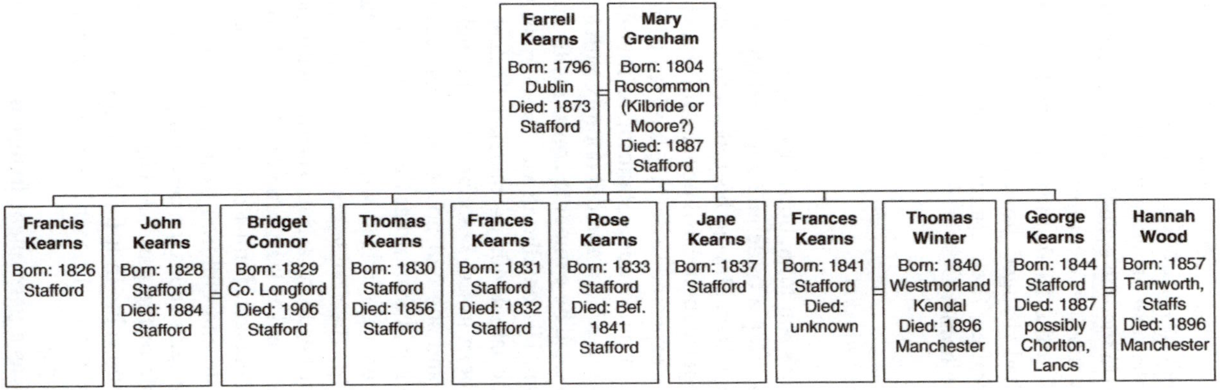

Figure 4.2 The children of Farrell and Mary Kearns

In the 1830s, when their children were young and Farrell Kearns was a casual farm labourer, lodgers were a vital supplement to their income, but when they moved to 51 New Street in the 1840s they stopped taking lodgers. Farrell had, by this time, left the land and was working as a brick-layer's labourer, although in 1851 Mary Kearns was an 'outdoor servant'. Two of the children were also bringing in money, and so it seems they had less need of the extra income even though the Famine Irish arriving in Stafford desperately needed accommodation. Even when the family moved to Snow's Yard in the 1850s they initially lived on their own at no. 5. By 1871 things had changed, however, and the family was forced to take in lodgers thereafter. Their cramped households must have had precious little feeling of 'home'.

John Kearns and his descendants

Farrell and Mary Kearns's son John, born in 1828, became a shoemaker, so he entered Stafford's staple trade and superficially achieved modest upward status over his father. Having been born in Stafford and grow-ing up there when the permanent Irish population was very small, John Kearns might have been expected to develop a mixed Irish-English iden-tity, or even to become a pure young Staffordian. That did not happen, however. He never went to school and did not mix with local children in the school yard. Neither did he come into contact with English Catholic norms in the classroom. His childhood was lived in an Irish environ-ment. Sometime in the late 1840s he married Bridget Connor.[11] She claimed to have been born in Co. Longford, an unusual place of origin for the Stafford Irish, and she had no obvious connection with other people of that name living in Stafford at the time. Perhaps she had been a lone Famine immigrant who lodged with the Kearns family. It was a problematic relationship. The couple continued to live with Farrell and Mary Kearns. Children began to arrive, starting with George in 1850 (Figure 4.3). In total they had at least nine children, although three died in infancy. Being a shoemaker, John Kearns went 'on tramp' in search of work, leaving his wife and children to fend for themselves. He was prosecuted twice in the early 1860s for deserting his wife and family and leaving them chargeable to the parish.[12] Having missed out on educa-tion himself, he saw little value in it for his children. After compulsory primary education began in 1871 he was fined at least once for failing to send his children to school.[13]

The Kearns family was a permanent fixture in Snow's Yard for over fifty years. In such squalid surroundings, and with the Red Cow pub at the yard's entrance, the misery of poverty frequently erupted into drink-fuelled disputes and violence. Things seem to have been particularly

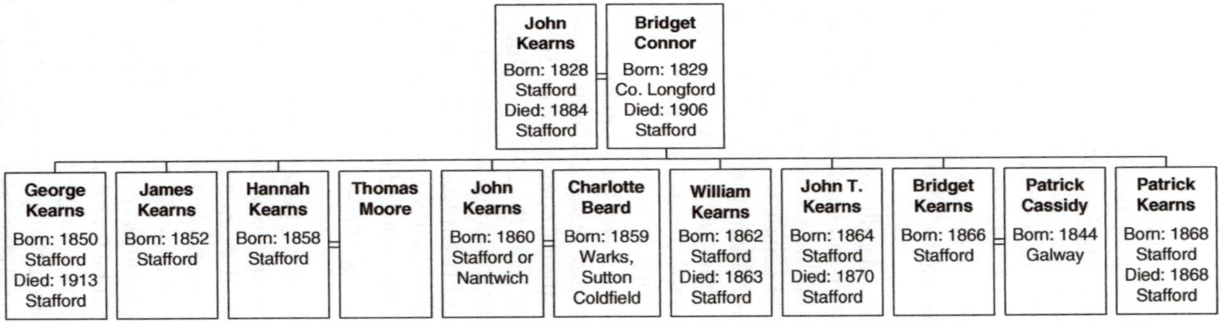

Figure 4.3 The children of John and Bridget Kearns

boisterous for the Kearns family in the years from 1875 to 1881 when they were in a number of 'Irish Rows'. On 30 August 1875, for example, Bridget Kearns and four other people were involved in 'continual disturbances ... kept up among the Irish inhabitants of Red Cow Yard'.[14] In 1877 Catherine Jones, 'a young woman with a disfigured countenance', assaulted 'an old woman' in the yard. The 'old woman' was Bridget Kearns. She was then aged about forty-eight, so we can see the awful toll that poverty, stress and drink had already taken on her. 'A disgraceful row had erupted from a drinking bout.' One of the witnesses said 'the proceedings reminded him of a prize fight'. Bridget Kearns had 'pulled sufficient hair from the defendant's head to make a doormat'. The case was dismissed and the magistrate told the police to 'keep an eye on both women as one was as bad as the other'.[15]

In 1879 John Kearns was found guilty of keeping an unlicensed lodging house – the rooms at no. 7 were too small for the house to be licensed.[16] His parents had passed the business on to their son some time in the late 1860s, and in 1871 the old couple were living on their own at no. 5. This did not last. Farrell Kearns finally died in 1873 at the age of seventy-seven, and Mary had to move back to her son's family at no. 7.

She lived there until her own death in 1887, aged around eighty-three. The couple had remarkably long lives given the stresses under which they had lived, and in their later years they had to offer support to their neglected grandchildren. John and Bridget's children seem to have grown up in a household with little parental commitment. Their first three sons, George, James (b. 1852) and John (b. 1860) became shoemakers and they all left Stafford in the 1870s. George and James probably emigrated, since neither can be found in Britain from 1881 to 1901. No record has been found of what happened to James, but George, who never married, returned to Stafford in the 1900s. He had lost his work in the shoe trade and in 1911 was reduced to being a cattle drover. He died alone at no. 14 Snow's Yard in 1913.

We now need to look at what happened to the rest of the family. For convenience it is best to begin with John and Bridget Kearns's other children. Their third surviving child, Hannah, a servant, married a Thomas Moore in 1875, although with such a common name it has not been possible to identify definitively who he was.[17] It was not a Catholic marriage, an indication that the Kearns family's adherence to the Church was weak by this time. The couple cannot be found in the 1881 Census, so presumably, like Hannah's brothers, they emigrated in the early years of their marriage. In 1882 Hannah's sister Bridget (b. 1866) did marry in the local Catholic church. Her husband was Patrick Cassidy, a bricklayer's labourer from Galway who was living in Mannion's lodging house at no. 11 Snow's Yard. The couple subsequently left Stafford and also emigrated. John Kearns (b. 1860) was the final child of John and Bridget to get married.

When he was an adult, John claimed he was born in Nantwich, Cheshire, and the evidence supports this. It demonstrates that John and Bridget Kearns did have periods away from Stafford when he was 'on tramp'.[18] In 1884 John (Jr) married a woman called Charlotte Beard, also in the Catholic Church. Born in 1859 in Sutton Coldfield, Warwickshire, in 1881 Charlotte was working as a servant in Rugby. She had an illegitimate son, Frederick, who had been born a cripple. Shortly after their marriage John and Charlotte moved to Wolverhampton and they brought up a family of seven children there.

It seems clear that John and Bridget Kearns's children had little commitment to Stafford. There are two obvious explanations for this. The first is that Stafford's economy, and particularly the shoe trade, went into depression after 1874. The three Kearns boys had all gone into the trade at the wrong time. Coming from an impoverished Irish background – and from the notorious Snow's Yard – they were stigmatised and found it hard to get work. This did not apply to all Irish families from such a background, however. Although structural conditions made things difficult, the Kearns offspring also suffered a second problem – their own family circumstances. The evidence shows a lifetime of poverty and neglect in which relationships with their parents, grandparents and siblings were blighted by disorder, drink and the threat of violence.

We have two specific bits of evidence for this relating to John and Bridget's supposed final son, Thomas. He was born in Snow's Yard on 14 April 1871.[19] It took five weeks for Bridget Kearns to register the birth and there must be some doubt about Bridget's claim to be Thomas's mother. The reason is that when he was eleven, in April 1882, he was not living at home in no. 7 Snow's Yard. He was in Stafford Workhouse. He was there for at least six months and was described in the register as an 'orphan'.[20] The workhouse overseers presumably knew a lot about the Kearns family and Thomas was probably given this designation because they knew he was not John and Bridget's real son. One possibility is that he was actually the illegitimate child of Bridget's daughter, Hannah (or Anne) Kearns, conceived when she was working as a servant girl. She was then thirteen and such was the fate of many young girls forced into service. The possibility of an incestuous pregnancy by her father cannot be ruled out either. When Hannah married Thomas Moore in 1875 the latter refused to take young Thomas as part of the deal. He was left to be brought up by his disgruntled and neglectful grandparents, hence his sojourns as an 'orphan' in the workhouse.

There is a second conundrum about Thomas which exemplifies the disordered circumstances of the Kearns family. In 1900 a 'Thomas Kearns' was given three months in gaol for assaulting Bridget, whom the *Staffordshire Advertiser* described as his 'grandmother'. She was then living at no. 14 Snow's Yard and running a lodging house she had taken over from the Mannion family. The 'real' Thomas Kearns was, however, not in Stafford at all but in South Africa serving with the army Medical Corps. In 1891 he had taken the classic route out of his miserable surroundings by signing up. His army papers confirm that his next-of-kin was his 'mother', Bridget Kerns (*sic*), of Red Cow Yard, Stafford, so we know we are dealing with the right person.[21] It seems someone stole Thomas's identity as soon as he joined the army. It was presumably the same 'Thomas Kearns' who was admitted to the workhouse ten times between 1891 and 1896.[22] Bridget must have known of the deception and acquiesced in it for reasons now impossible to fathom. It did her little good. In August 1900 the bogus 'Thomas' crushed her against a door and threatened her with a poker. Bridget managed to escape out of the upstairs window and slid down the drainpipe, a feat of some agility for a seventy-one-year-old woman.[23] Meanwhile, in the army the 'real' Thomas broke free from his family's disordered circumstances. He served for over twenty-two years and had an 'exemplary' record, 'honest, sober and industrious', latterly as a sergeant and with qualifications as a first-aid instructor and medical dispenser. He married in 1907 and the family ultimately settled in Southampton where he died in 1931.[24]

When 'Thomas Kearns' attacked Bridget she had already been a widow for sixteen years. The shoe trade had gone into decline in the late 1870s and her husband John had found it difficult to get work. In 1881 he had managed to get a labouring job at Venables' timber yard on the Doxey Road. It was dangerous work and in August 1884 a pile of logs fell down and crushed him. He received severe head injuries from which he died a few days later.[25] Bridget herself died in 1906.[26]

Family dispersal

John Kearns was the only child of Farrell and Mary Kearns to remain in Stafford for the rest of his life. We need now to examine what became of their other children. Their first known child, Francis (b. 1826), seems to have left Stafford in the 1840s and nothing more is known of him. He probably emigrated. After John, previously discussed, the following three – Thomas (b. 1830), Frances (b. 1831) and Rose (b. 1833) – all died young, though Thomas survived until 1856. The next child, Jane (b. 1837) was working as a servant in 1861. She had left the family household and was living in a lodging house in Mill Street. She presumably married, but her subsequent history has proved impossible to trace. The following child, Frances (the second child with this name, b. 1841) left Stafford in the 1850s and went to Manchester. She must have benefited from distant kinship links or other contacts in the city. Once there she made a decisive break from her Irish background, and in 1864 she married Thomas Winter, a cabinet turner originally from Kendal in Westmorland. It was a Church of England wedding. The couple had a number of children and there are numerous descendants from this branch of the family.[27]

Farrell and Mary's final child, George (b. 1844) began as an agricultural labourer but by 1864 he had left farmwork and entered the twilight world of the socially marginal by keeping a lodging house in Foregate Street. There he lived in a common-law relationship with Sarah Dix, a Staffordshire woman ten years older than him. She already an illegitimate child, Ellen, but during the 1860s she bore two more children to George: Joseph Thomas and George. Both died in infancy. Baby George had been dumped on his father's sister Frances and he died at her house in Manchester in 1868.[28] George Kearns and Sarah Dix subsequently ended their partnership and during the 1870s George moved to Stoke-on-Trent and married Hannah Wood, a Staffordshire woman from Tamworth. Although in 1881 they were living with their two children in Plant's Square, Stafford, their later whereabouts proved difficult to trace but they ultimately moved to the western outskirts of Manchester. Their children had numerous descendants in that area.

The Kearns family environment

When John and Bridget Kearns's son George died alone in Snow's Yard in 1913 he was the only member of the Kearns family left in Stafford. Although they had been there for nearly ninety years, the family put down no real roots in the town. Their origins in impoverished Roscommon, and the fact that they had to seek work in Britain, were important elements in their consciousness. Their status as landless labourers or conacre-holders at the bottom of the social hierarchy probably inculcated attitudes of fatalism mixed with a desire to stay within the familiar and defensible walls of Irish communities. They were doubtless resentful of and hostile to the landlords, middlemen and the forces of State control in Ireland. They may have been involved in, or come into contact with, Ribbonite rural unrest in the 1820s before they came to Britain. To the extent that Ribbonism represented an embryonic physical-force Irish nationalism, the Kearns family may also have had a basic nationalist outlook, but there is no evidence that such ideas played any role in their lives in Stafford. They merely shifted their hostile attitudes to house landlords, the council, the police and the English once they settled in Stafford.

This was particularly the case with Farrell Kearns and Mary Grenham and, from what little we know of them, David Kearns and Anne Lyon. They used their heritage to face the strange and potentially hostile environment of Stafford together. Their view of the new world in which they lived was at root suspicious and combative. Though they used the Church for key life events like baptism and some marriages, there is little to suggest that religion influenced their *mores* or provided spiritual and emotional support. Neither did it open up social contacts. The Kearnses, both male and female, were only nominal Catholics and the women played no role as 'cultural carriers' of the Church's message. The case of Farrell's brother or cousin John Kearns was rather different. He had come to England as a single man, and his involvement in an ethnically mixed marriage both resulted from, and contributed to, an apparently more engaged role in the English environment. He had closer ties with the English Catholic Church and this brought the reward of its tangible support. The history of the two main branches of the Kearns family – those of Farrell and John – therefore diverged significantly.

In Stafford, Farrell and Mary Kearns's surviving children were divided between an early group, Francis, John, Thomas and Jane, born between 1826 and 1837, and the two later arrivals, Frances and George, born in the 1840s. Of the early group, John always stayed at home. His behaviour suggests he was socialised into the outlooks of his parents' Irish mental enclave, although his move into shoemaking shows at least some engagement with the economic and social realities of Stafford. The fact that the two later children left the town and 'married out' into English society suggests they rejected their parents' environment and had the ability and ambition to escape the limited world in which they lived.

We need to consider the kinship, home and household characteristics of the Stafford Kearns family. It has already been suggested that blood ties were significant in their early period of settlement in England. It was a passing phase, however. After 1850 the dominant relationship was between Farrell and Mary Kearns, their remaining children at home, and the next-generation family of John Kearns and Bridget Connor. The bonds between the older couple and Bridget, their daughter-in-law, were strong. John Kearns was a mobile and neglectful father, and it seems likely that Mary Grenham-Kearns and Bridget sustained the main family obligations to their offspring. Even so, the fact that all but one of the children from both generations left the family home and the town of Stafford suggests they had little loyalty or continuing commitment to close family ties. Their parents and grandparents offered them little in terms of affection or the practical benefits of contacts, jobs or better housing.

The Kearns family became stranded in Snow's Yard. The only surviving evidence we have of social life in the yard is from the agencies of social control and from the local newspapers. They present a litany of drunkenness, 'Irish Rows', assaults and other infringements that give the superficial impression of a totally brutalised, shifting and anomic society.

That would be misleading, however. Lodgers and some of the families did come and go quickly, but one of the remarkable features of Snow's Yard was how long some families lived there. For many years the Kearns family lived alongside the Hagans, Mannions, Shiels, MacMahons and others. It was a remarkably stable society – even a community – in which long-term and broadly constructive relationships must have existed among neighbours. Drink-fuelled and angry as some days and nights obviously were, for most of the time the English and Irish families in the yard had to get along. They doubtless helped each other in ways that have left no historical record, and in particular this applied to the women. The men who were doing paid work left during the day and their social circuit in the town was wider. The women's lives were, in contrast, focused on the yard and the Red Cow. Much of the time they were looking after the children and possibly making some attempt to manage the grimy and infested hovels in which they lived. At other times they were drinking in and around the pub. In 1881 Bridget Kearns and two other Irish women were witnesses in a case where Ann Mannion was accused of hitting Ellen Shiel with a mop and throwing water over her. We shall meet Ellen Shiel again in Chapter 6. Their evidence helped convict both women, the one for assault, the other for drunkenness – petty convictions they would have treated with contempt. Overall the evidence from such cases indicates the strong, if sometimes brittle, female social network that existed in Snow's Yard.

The environment of poverty and casual drunken violence inevitably influenced the children growing up in the yard. Down the years a number of its younger inhabitants had brushes with the law, although the Kearns children largely kept clear – or weren't caught. Nevertheless, John and Bridget's son John Kearns (b. 1860) was involved in one case of some interest. In January 1877 he and three other 'mischievous apprentices' were convicted of criminal damage. The others were Peter Daniels, James Concar and William Follows. The first named was an English youth, whilst Concar was from an Irish family. Follows was the son of Henry Follows from a local working-class Catholic family – and the landlord of the Red Cow. We have an indication here of the social network to which John Kearns belonged – mixed English/Irish and local Catholic. The four were apprentices at Elley's shoe factory. They had sneaked off work and damaged the fence and garden of C. H. Dudley, one of the firm's owners. There was possibly more to the case than met the eye. Elley's backed on to Snow's Yard, and only a few months earlier the firm had been publicly rebuked at the Borough Health Committee for creating 'a standing menace to public health' in Snow's Yard. There were no closets at the factory, and it seems the workers merely relieved themselves in and around the yard. The residents must have hated the firm and the children picked up the message.[29]

Identity and dispersal

The Kearns's domestic lives remained within a strongly Irish milieu and this was transmitted to their immediate children. Their identity seems to have been ethnically Irish and it largely remained so for many years. It would have been, however, an unconscious identity defined and sustained by the work and home circumstances of the Irish migrants with whom they lived. Although the second- and third-generation children grew up in this strongly Irish environment, the evidence suggests that even in this family an autonomous Irish identity could not be sustained amongst the descendants. What took its place is less easy to distinguish. The fact that all the surviving children ultimately left Stafford shows they had little commitment to the town and its society, but leaving might equally be interpreted as a rejection of the Kearns family heritage. It is noteworthy that of the six children who married, three, or possibly four, chose ethnically English partners from outside Stafford. They could have found partners amongst the town's Irish families or migrant workers, but only one did so. The second- and third-generation Kearns descendants were faced with the tension between their parents' degraded Irish heritage and the need to reach a workable accommodation with the world in which they grew up. This involved leaving both the stem family and Stafford, and in some cases leaving Britain as well. The descendants of the Stafford Kearns family became geographically dispersed and part of the scattered Irish diaspora.

Pre-Famine families: the overall picture

Although only a small number of labouring families settled in Stafford before the Famine, we can begin the process of seeing how the family histories throw light on the issues concerning the Irish migrant experience outlined in Chapter 1. Most of these early labouring families conformed to the common image of Irish migrants with their Celtic Catholic ethnicity. It might be expected that such all-Irish families would have been forced to integrate, since there were so few Irish in Stafford when they settled there. This proved not to be the case, however. Ethnic forces remained strong. The early families found it difficult to break out of an isolated and alienated lifestyle, even when the next generation of children grew up in Stafford. They had been forced to abandon unsustainable lives in Ireland but their poverty and apparent alienation caused them problems in Stafford. When other labouring families arrived during and after the Famine, these pathfinding families seem to have depended on the social and kinship links provided by the newcomers. Even so, members of these early families were forced to respond to the local social and economic environment, and a limited number of their descendants entered the shoe trade. To that extent, the second and third generations showed signs of being opportunists although their parents' response to emigration bears hallmarks of the classic 'exile' perspective. The descendants' work environment provided opportunities for intermarriage, but many second-generation people who opted for the local industry did so at a time when it had passed its peak and was running into problems. This provided the stimulus to leave. The apparently limited integration demonstrated by members of these families owed as much to changing economic circumstances as to on-going ethnic loyalties.

Though many of these early immigrants tended to stay close to the Irish environment, this was at the level of informal social networks. There were no Irish clubs or associations in the town and no Irish community leaders who operated clientalist networks of influence and identity reinforcement. The early labouring families experienced a long-term shift to ambiguous identities, neither consciously Irish nor demonstrably Staffordian. This ambiguity partly reflected the apparent absence of key individuals able and willing to promote family strategies of social advancement. The women played a significant but limited role in keeping family life going but often at a disordered and basic level.

The Irish who settled in Stafford during the Famine might be expected to have all the problems exhibited by the pre-Famine families and more. The next chapter tests the validity of this assumption.

Notes

1 BAA P255/1/2, Stafford, St Austin's, Register of Baptisms, 1831–58 (9 January 1831).

2 SRO, Census Enumeration Returns, Stafford, 1861 and 1871.

3 We only know of David Kearns and his wife Anne Lyon because their daughter Mary Ann was christened at St Austin's Catholic Church in Stafford on 4 November 1832; BAA P255/1/2. John Kearns and his Staffordshire-born wife Elizabeth Griffin were living in the town at least between 1837 and 1845.

4 Marriage, 5 October 1835, Pipehill/Hopwas, RC Chapel, Lichfield Street: Michael John Kearns and Eliza Griffin. Information from Chrissy Westgarth, a descendant, 2004.

5 Later Douai Abbey School: douaiabbey.org.uk/stmary1.htm#stmary7.gif (accessed 18 July 2013).

6 Information from Chrissy Westgarth, 2005.

7 A John Kearns died in Preston in 1882, probably Eliza's husband. Preston Registration District (RD), Deaths, July–September 1882, 8e/410; Prestwich RD, Deaths, April–June 1883, 8d/250: Eliza Kearns.

8 A. Poulton-Smith, *Bloody British History: Stafford* (Stroud, The History Press, 2013), pp. 57–9.

9 *SA*, 25 June 1836.

10 *SA*, 3 September 1842.

11 The marriage probably took place in Ireland; there is no obvious record of it in England.

12 *SA*, 25 May 1861 and 5 December 1863. His was given three months with hard labour on each occasion.

13 *SA*, 17 April 1875.

14 *SA*, 11 September 1875.

15 *SA*, 5 May 1877.

16 *SA*, 6 December 1879.

17 Stafford RD, Marriages, July–September 1875, 6b/23: Thomas Moore and Hannah Kearns.

18 Nantwich RD, Births, October–December 1859, 8a/289: John Kearns.

19 Stafford RD, Birth Certificate, 6b/8, no. 75, 22 May 1871: Thomas Kearns.

20 SRO D659/1/4/52, Stafford Poor Law Union Indoor Relief List, 1882/83.

21 British Army Service Records, National Archives (NA), WO97 Chelsea: Royal Army Medical Corps, no. 10714: Sgt T. J. Kearns; *Find My Past*, www.findmypast.co.uk (accessed 20 July 2013).

22 *Staffordshire Name Indexes*, www.staffsnameindexes.org.uk, D659/1/4/10, Stafford Poor Law Union, Workhouse Admission Book, 1836–1900.

23 *SA*, 25 August 1900.

24 NA, WO97, RAMC, 10714: Sgt T. J. Kearns; *FindMyPast* (accessed 15 July 2013). Southampton RD, Deaths, October–December 1931, 2c/36: Thomas J. Kearns, born 1871.

25 *SA*, 23 August 1884.

26 Stafford Borough Council (SBC), Burial Register, 09/4658, 15 December 1906.

27 Information from Marilyn Oakfield, 2006.

28 Stafford RD, Birth Certificate, 6b/3, no. 494: George Kearns, 23 July 1867; Chorlton RD, Deaths, April–June 1868, 8c/434: George Kearns, born c. 1867.

29 *SA*, 11 March 1876 and 13 January 1877.

5

Refugees from the Famine

'The fever wards were full'[1]

The Irish population of the Stafford district quadrupled between 1841 and 1851.[2] The Irish Famine had an immediate impact on districts like Stafford as well as on the better-known cities like Liverpool. The flood of emigrants began to hit Liverpool and other western ports in December 1846, and by the beginning of 1847 the refugees had reached Staffordshire. A correspondent to the *Staffordshire Advertiser* wrote that 'It is painful to see these poor fellows in their wanderings through the country. Their suppliant and unoffending manner, and the patience with which they appear to endure the weather and the cravings of hunger, appeal powerfully to every humane mind.'[3] Stafford began to see Famine refugees in February 1847, and they had become a flood by April. The Poor Law authorities struggled to cope but they did fulfil their basic responsibilities to the Irish poor and their performance conformed to the national picture painted by Frank Neal.[4] Between April and June the Stafford Poor Law Guardians gave relief to no fewer than 3,557 paupers; in normal times the total would have been around 800.[5] Times were hard in the local economy, but about two-thirds of those relieved were Irish paupers.[6] The absolutely destitute were forced into the workhouse vagrant wards. Many were suffering from typhus or relapsing fever – then collectively diagnosed as 'Irish fever' – and if they did not have it already, they were likely to pick it up in the appalling conditions of the workhouse. The physician at Staffordshire General Infirmary complained 'of the filthy state in which fever patients were sent from the Union workhouse to the infirmary, and the long period patients suffering from fever were kept in the vagrant wards before their admission into the Infirmary'.[7] A 'temporary detached building' was built to separate the Irish from other workhouse inmates. By July the fever wards were full and in the chaos the destitute Irish were all crammed in together – the sick, the dying, the apparently well, those relapsing into fever and the convalescent. The workhouse only took in those who were ill or had nowhere else to go. The mass of Irish immigrants sought shelter in lodging houses and hovels in the town's back streets and yards. We unfortunately have no contemporary description of their conditions – the articulate local elite showed concern about the distress in Ireland but they failed to probe the horrors on their own doorstep. The result was, however, substantial mortality. At the end of 1847 Stafford's death rate during the year had been 1 in 33 (33 per 1,000), well above the English average and not much below that in Liverpool (1 in 29, or 34.5 per 1,000).[8] Along with better-known destinations, Stafford was a direct witness of the Famine's misery.

Panic in-migration to the Stafford area continued throughout 1847 but dwindled during 1848. It was succeeded by a second wave of refugees who had clung on in Ireland for a time but were then forced out by continuing evictions and utter lack of hope for the future. They arrived in circumstances that were marginally more positive and orderly.[9] Individuals and families, particularly from the Castlerea area, came to Stafford because they knew it and had contacts for work. Many only stayed a short time before moving on to other parts of the west Midlands and elsewhere. Others stayed a number of years but ultimately did not settle long-term. Nevertheless, forty-two distinct labouring families emerged as long-term settlers in Stafford who were refugees from the Famine.

Stafford's Famine labouring families were 'classic' Irish immigrants. They almost all came from Connacht; they were all Catholic; and thirty out of the forty-two were joint, extended or complex families (Table 4.4). Most of the remainder were nuclear families, with just one lone individual and one childless couple. The Famine was itself a factor in family formation. Twenty-one families arrived in Stafford already formed – i.e. they fled Ireland as family groups – but an almost equal number, nineteen, were established in Stafford itself. It is striking how the Famine was followed by a wave of marriages amongst Irish immigrants. There were second marriages by those widowed during the Famine, delayed marriages of existing associates and conventional marriages by single people who met in the town.[10] These latter were often supporting relatives back home in Ireland but they were likely to meet similar people in the lodgings of Stafford and many liaisons developed from these contacts. People whose partners had died during the Famine emigrated, sometimes with their semi-orphaned children, and then formed new partnerships in Stafford. The processes of migration and family formation were complex.

The long-term trajectories of labouring families who settled in Stafford during the Famine proved to be varied, even though their origins were superficially very similar (Table 4.5). Seventeen families (40.5 per cent) were ultimately long-term transients. This proportion was distinctly greater than the overall average for labouring families (34 per cent) and it therefore gives some support to the view that Famine emigrants were particularly mobile after they were forced to leave Ireland. Even so, another seven families were 'terminal' and faded away to extinction. Eighteen Famine families (42.9 per cent) were 'integrators' who put down deep roots in Stafford. Their descendants became part of the local community. Families who cover all three trajectories will now be examined to explore the factors that caused their divergent paths. These families are:

- Coleman: a family strategy of respectability and integration;
- Kelly: troubled, troublesome and transient;
- Jordan: a terminal Famine family that withered away.

The Colemans: a family strategy of respectability and integration

The Colemans overcame an unpromising beginning in Stafford, sought respectability and adopted a clear policy of integrating into the local society. They generally made a success of it. They were a complex family amongst whom kinship links were very strong and active. The various Coleman households tended to cluster in one particular part of town but this did not mean they sought out, or remained trapped in, a purely Irish support network. On the contrary, members of this family engaged rapidly with native Staffordians, and descendants intermarried with people from the host society. It seems clear that for most in the Coleman family Irish identity was fairly rapidly transmuted into a respectable English Catholic one. As one descendant said in an interview, 'the first immigrants looked to home, the second generation looked both ways and the third generation said "forget it".[11]

Difficult early years in Stafford

Like that of many Irish families, the Colemans' arrival was a drawn out process. At the height of the Famine, on 18 October 1847, William Coleman (b. 1805) was stricken with fever and taken into Stafford Workhouse (Figure 5.1).[12] He was there for five weeks. This is the first record we have of the family in Stafford. William Coleman and his family farmed a small patch of land that family legend believes was in Knock, Co. Mayo.[13] The surname Coleman is common in southern Mayo and the family certainly came from that county, though it has not proved possible to confirm the precise locality. Like many stricken by the Famine, William had probably come to Stafford in a desperate attempt to earn money to save his family from the loss of their land. He may already have known the place from earlier seasonal work or from contacts who did. We have no evidence that his wife and children were with him at this

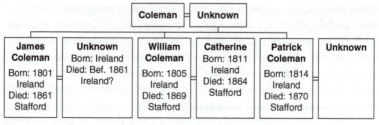

Figure 5.1 The stem of the Coleman family in Stafford

time. They had arrived by 1851, however. Catherine Coleman and four of her children were living in Margaret Morris's lodging house at no. 9 Sash Street, although William was not present and nor were three of his children. They do not seem to have been in England at all, so perhaps they were still clinging to the land back in Mayo. William Coleman had been the family's pathfinder. Early in the 1850s James and Patrick Coleman followed him to Stafford with their surviving children. James (b. 1801) was William's brother, and descendants of these two lines of the family continued to have significant kinship links. Patrick's (b. 1814) relationship to William is unclear, but his small branch does not seem to have been part of the active family network. There were no children and it became extinct in 1870 with Patrick's death.

The early experience of the Colemans in Stafford was hard, with unskilled labour, occasional homelessness and some minor offending. William and Catherine Coleman began in a lodging house. William worked as a labourer. It was a tough and insecure life, and by the 1860s his strength was giving out. In 1864 William was described as a 'rag collector', which suggests life on the absolute margins, although when he died in 1869 his occupation was again given as 'labourer'.[14] In 1856 their son Thomas John (b. 1841) was one of a gang of 'disorderly youths' brought before the Mayor to be admonished (Figure 5.2).[15] It is significant that Thomas's mates were all local Staffordians, not other Irish youths. In 1862 his brother William (b. 1846) was fined 10s along with another Irish lad for assaulting John Griffin, an Irishman, though what prompted the attack is unknown. Things were worse for William's brother James Coleman and his son John (b. 1835). In 1862/63 both were imprisoned for 'wandering abroad without visible means of subsistence'.[16] John Coleman had been living in outhouses and it was James's third offence. In 1861 they had been lodging in Snow Hill, a mean street off Gaol Road, but perhaps they had been thrown out for disorder or not paying their rent. It certainly seems that William and Catherine Coleman did not offer them lodgings, although Catherine died in 1864 and may have been ill when James and John needed somewhere to stay. Family support was not unconditional. In 1865 John got into trouble again. He was caught stealing timber from a

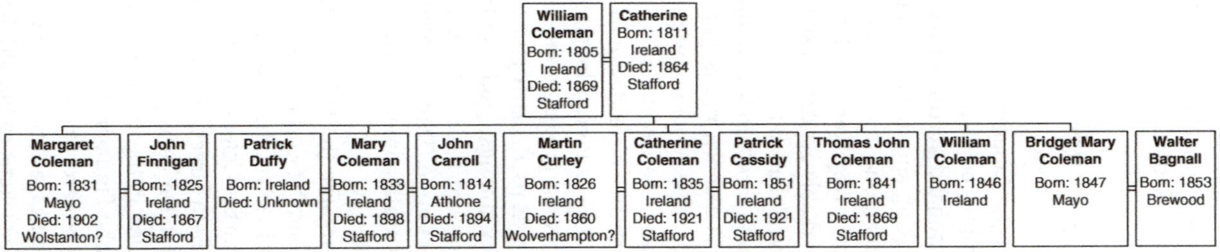

Figure 5.2 William and Catherine Coleman's children

builder's yard and received fourteen days in gaol.[17] Meanwhile, the other relative, Patrick Coleman, had arrived during the 1850s with his son Martin (b. 1835), who later left Stafford. In 1861 they were lodging in an even worse place, Middle Row, also off Gaol Road. All these men worked on local farms along with other settled and migrant Irish.

Descendants who left Stafford

There is little to distinguish the Colemans' early years in Stafford from those of countless Irish immigrants from a similar background. Life was poor and insecure in squalid surroundings. The one thing missing is evidence of hard drinking and its attendant problems, so relative abstemiousness may have been one of the factors that enabled the family to emerge from the depths of poverty and deprivation. The core of the family also showed remarkable residential stability. Some time in the 1850s William and Catherine Coleman moved into no. 5 Bath Street, and branches of the extended family were to live in this property for the next thirty years. Bath Street was a short, rather narrow and gloomy place just west of the town centre. The residents were generally modest but respectable working class and the Colemans were the only Irish family ever to live there. It suggests a clear desire to leave the Irish milieu. Even so, previous time spent in Stafford's lodging houses and amongst the other Famine immigrants did provide opportunities to meet potential marriage partners. This was particularly true for daughters, since eligible women were a minority amongst Stafford's Irish immigrants in the 1850s. In 1861 single or widowed Irish men aged over sixteen outnumbered women by over three to one. Three of William Coleman's daughters married Irish Catholics at this time, and each partnership produced significant branches of the family.

Their first daughter, Margaret (b. 1831) married a labourer, John Finnigan, in 1851. He was almost certainly known to the family from back home, and in 1851 was living in the Middle Row lodging house later occupied by Patrick and Martin Coleman. The couple set up house in Tenterbanks, quite close to Bath Street, and went on to have six children. Their lives in Stafford must have been poor and fairly miserable given that four of their children died in the 1860s and were probably chronically ill before their deaths. John Finnigan died in 1867. He was only forty-two years old. His widow Margaret fell on hard times and in 1871 was living in no. 3 Turner's Buildings, a cottage in the stinking shadow of the gas works. Family connections came to her aid, however. Once her children grew up and started to earn money in the 1870s she was able to able to pay a bit more rent, and when other Colemans moved out of no. 5 Bath Street she took over the tenancy. That is where she was living in 1881.

Her daughter Margaret had become a teacher, and in 1886 married James Mulrooney, a police constable who hailed from Co. Roscommon. They subsequently moved to Tettenhall near Wolverhampton, but in the 1890s decided to emigrate. They may have followed Margaret herself. She seems to have emigrated in the 1880s with her only surviving son, William, so this branch of the Coleman family was extinguished in Stafford.

Another branch also left Stafford in the 1880s but got no farther than Liverpool. William and Catherine Coleman's youngest daughter Bridget (b. 1847) married a Catholic Englishman, Walter Bagnall, in 1876. He was a bricklayer, and things must have been tight for them in the early years. The family connections worked again, however, and the couple moved into no. 5 Bath Street with Bridget's sister Margaret. Stafford's economy was faltering, and jobs for a brickie were short. Around 1881 Walter got work in Liverpool where he boarded with a Scottish family in Kirkdale. Things went well, and during the 1880s the whole family settled in the port city. Their son William – 'Bill' (b. 1878) – became a Poor Law relieving officer, whilst their daughter Mary – or 'May' (b. 1882) – was a teacher. Family links with Stafford remained strong, however, and family legend has it that Bill Bagnall 'put Margaret and William Finnigan on the [emigrant] boat'. The Finnigans probably stayed with the Bagnall family before departure, a significant event for young Bill. Other members of the family continued to visit the Bagnalls in Liverpool in the twentieth century.[18]

A false start but successful marriages: the Coleman–Curley family

So far we have looked at those descendants of the Colemans who ultimately left Stafford. Many remained, however, and it is to these that we now turn. In 1852 William and Catherine Coleman's third daughter, Catherine (b. 1835), married Martin Curley (b. 1826) at St Austin's Church (Figure 5.3). Curley has proved to be an elusive character. He was not in Stafford in 1851, but in 1852 he and his wife were recorded on their marriage certificate as living at 39 Kitling's Lane – another name for part of Tenterbanks.[19] He was a labourer, and family legend believes also a sometime horse dealer. He almost certainly came from the same area as the Coleman family and was known to them. If so, they made an unfortunate choice of son-in-law. Between 1854 and 1859 the couple had four children who survived, but there was some sort of crisis on 27 October 1860 when the whole family was both admitted and then discharged from the workhouse on the same day.[20] By 1861 Martin Curley had disappeared. He did not die in Stafford, although in 1860 someone of that name did die in Wolverhampton.[21] Certainly, Catherine Curley née Coleman was left in the lurch with young children.[22] The only answer was

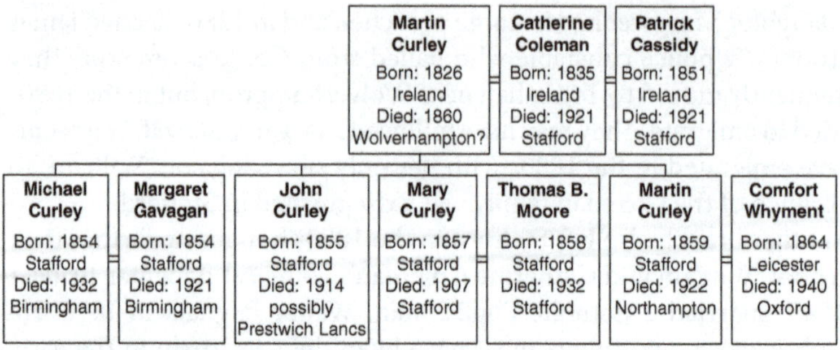

Martin Curley	Catherine Coleman	Patrick Cassidy
Born: 1826 Ireland Died: 1860 Wolverhampton?	Born: 1835 Ireland Died: 1921 Stafford	Born: 1851 Ireland Died: 1921 Stafford

Michael Curley	Margaret Gavagan	John Curley	Mary Curley	Thomas B. Moore	Martin Curley	Comfort Whyment
Born: 1854 Stafford Died: 1932 Birmingham	Born: 1854 Stafford Died: 1921 Birmingham	Born: 1855 Stafford Died: 1914 possibly Prestwich Lancs	Born: 1857 Stafford Died: 1907 Stafford	Born: 1858 Stafford Died: 1932 Stafford	Born: 1859 Stafford Died: 1922 Northampton	Born: 1864 Leicester Died: 1940 Oxford

Figure 5.3 Catherine Coleman/Curley's children

Figure 5.4 Michael Curley (1854–1932), son of Catherine Coleman and the elusive Martin Curley (image courtesy of the late Peter Godwin and the Godwin family)

to move into no. 5 Bath Street with her parents, and that is where she was living in 1861.

Catherine Curley was a determined woman and her children did well. The first was Michael (b. 1854). He became a painter and decorator. Growing up in the west part of the town centre, he would have known many children of Irish settlers, one of whom was Margaret Gavagan (b. 1854). In the early 1870s he decided there was more work to be had in Birmingham. He moved there and in 1877 married his childhood sweetheart, Margaret, in that city.[23] The couple went on to have eight children. A photograph from the 1880s shows a handsome man who was a dapper dresser, exuding success (Figure 5.4). This branch of the family became Brummies, but links with the Stafford Colemans remained strong into the twentieth century.[24]

Figure 5.5 Mary Curley (1857–1907) married local Protestant, Thomas Boydell Moore (image courtesy of Kathleen Boult)

Catherine Curley's only daughter was Mary (b. 1857)(Figure 5.5). She benefited from the increasing mechanization of the shoe trade and became a machinist at W. H. Peach's shoe factory. There she met her future husband, Thomas Boydell Moore, a Protestant Staffordian who worked as a 'clicker' – a skilled leather cutter. The couple married at the Anglican Castle Church on the Newport Road in 1878.[25] Neither Moore nor Mary Curley lived permanently in Castle Church parish and their marriage at this out-of-the-way church was probably a religious compromise. Moore's father, Frederick, was a prominent member of Stafford's main Anglican church, St Mary's. There was undoubtedly a strand of anti-Catholicism running through the Moore family and it was probably too embarrassing for Fred Moore's son to marry an Irish Catholic at either St Mary's or, heaven forbid, St Austin's.[26] Even so, the Moore family did not prevent the marriage. Mary Curley and the Colemans also made a big compromise in not having a Catholic wedding, but as an aspiring and respectable family seeking integration, they must have felt it was in their interests to go along with it. Both Mary and her daughters nevertheless remained practising Catholics even though her son, Thomas, was brought up an Anglican. This gender division of religion amongst the children of mixed parents has been reported in other families in Stafford. It sustains the view that whilst anti-Catholic attitudes were undoubtedly present in the town, the sectarian frontiers were permeable and a religious accommodation generally operated.

Mary Curley and Thomas Moore went on to have six surviving children (another died young). They lived initially in Grey Friars and later in New Street, and they had other Irish-descended and mixed families amongst their neighbours. The family 'had to work at it', but they were never poor.[27] Mary Curley died of diabetes in 1907 at the relatively young age of 50.[28] Although Mary's illness and death must have cast a pall over the household, the children did well and three of them married ethnically English partners in the early decades of the twentieth century. The girls all carried on the family's Catholic faith and were active in social events at St Patrick's Church.[29] Their Irish heritage was, however, rapidly diluted amongst the numerous descendants, and it has formed no active part of the family's identity since the 1920s.

Catherine Curley had two other sons, John (b. 1855) and Martin (b. 1859). Both went into the shoe trade and left Stafford to work in London, although John subsequently worked as a joiner and ended up in the Bury district of Lancashire. Martin settled in Leicester, married a local woman and reputedly became active in shoe-industry trade unionism.

We saw earlier that Catherine Curley probably lost her husband sometime around 1860. She brought up her children with the help of her parents, but once they could support themselves she married for a second time. Her partner was Patrick – or 'Pat' – Cassidy, a bricklayer's labourer about fifteen years her junior. He seems to have arrived in Stafford some time in the early 1870s, and, again, he may already have been known to the family from their home in Co. Mayo. Catherine was lucky with Pat Cassidy, unlike her first husband. A 'full-blown Irishman with an arm as black as a blue brick', he was respected as a good worker.[30] The rest of the family thought a lot of him and the couple had many happy years together. In the 1900s Catherine – or 'Granny Cassidy' (Figure 5.6) as she was known in the family – kept a beer shop, the Curriers Arms, in Sash Street.[31] They both died in 1921.[32]

Bigamy: Mary Coleman's family

William and Catherine Coleman's daughter Mary (b. 1833) also married twice (Figure 5.7). The evidence for her story is complex but intriguing. It shows the problems facing families in the chaotic aftermath of the Famine and the ruses they developed to tackle them. In October 1850 Mary Coleman married a Patrick Duffy at St Austin's.[33] Mary feared she was already pregnant, and Patrick was probably forced to marry her. Having gone through the formalities he ran away. He was not in Stafford at the time of the 1851 Census and was nowhere else in Britain. No death is recorded. He either went back to Ireland or, more likely, got the boat to America. The deserted Mary had to go back to her parents in the lodging house in Sash Street, and in the census she had already reverted to being 'Mary Coleman' and 'unmarried'. Even so, when her baby, Margaret,

Figure 5.6 Catherine Cassidy née Coleman with her granddaughter, Catherine Moore, c. 1900 (image courtesy of Kathleen Boult)

was born in the summer of 1851, the child was christened as 'Margaret Duffy' because the priest knew of Mary's marriage the previous autumn. Nevertheless, Margaret in practice was known as Margaret Coleman.[34] The child was initially brought up in the Coleman household and was probably told her father had died.

In 1857 Mary Coleman met John Carroll. He had been in the army and his earlier career is described in Chapter 8. He was about nineteen years older than Mary, but they nevertheless got married. The marriage was, however, bigamous. As we have seen, Mary was already married. Although Patrick Duffy had left her seven years before, desertion at that time was not grounds for divorce. Even if it had been, petitioning for divorce would have been far too expensive for the impoverished Colemans.[35] Legally she could not marry again, and certainly not at the Catholic church. The family had a stroke of luck, however. Edward Huddleston, the priest who had married Mary to Patrick Duffy in 1850, retired in 1856 and left Stafford.

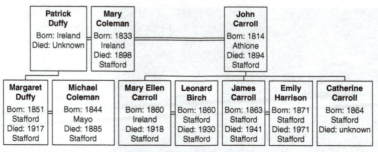

Figure 5.7 Mary Coleman/Duffy/Carroll's children

He was not around to contest proceedings when 'Mary Coleman', a 'spin-ster', turned up at the register office to marry John Carroll. This time her sister Catherine was one of the witnesses.[36] The evidence suggests that the Coleman family, John Carroll and their associates in the Irish net-work colluded to pass Mary off as a single woman.[37] They made no claim that her previous husband had died, and she used her maiden name. The fact that they married at the register office, almost unheard-of amongst the Catholic Irish, is itself suspicious. Mary had found a way of getting her life off to a new and hopefully more stable start. The family now had things to hide, however. That could explain their subsequent search for respectability and their descendants' desire to obscure their Irish origins by being more English than the English.

John Carroll accepted the six-year-old Margaret Duffy as part of the marriage deal. In the 1861 Census she appears as 'Margaret Carroll'. We shall meet her again shortly. The age difference with his wife did not dull John's ardour, and the couple went on to have three children. They all initially entered the shoe trade, and although the subsequent fate of Catherine has not been traced, their first, Mary Ellen, married a local man, Leonard Birch, who was an attendant at the Lunatic Asylum. Birch was a Catholic when he married Mary Ellen Carroll, but he may have con-verted. The Birches were an extensive local family and some at least were Primitive Methodists. There are numerous descendants from this part-nership. James married Emily Harrison, a Stafford-born boot machinist, and they also have descendants.[38]

James Coleman's family: cousin marriage, aspiration and social integration

Although the Coleman children initially found marriage partners amongst other Catholic Irish immigrants, the next generation generally intermar-ried with Staffordians. They and their children assumed a Staffordian

Catholic identity, not a relict Irish one. This trait especially characterised the only branch of the family to retain the Coleman name. We saw that William Coleman was followed to Stafford by his brother James (Figure 5.8). His wife had probably died during the Famine, and he was accompanied by three of his sons, John (b. 1835), Patrick (b. 1838) and Michael (b. 1844). John never married. He worked as an agricultural labourer in the Stafford area, but when farmwork declined became an attendant at the Lunatic Asylum. He died in 1882.[39] Patrick became a baker and married a local Protestant woman, Winifred Dugmore, in 1868.[40] They had their first child, James, in 1869 and a second, Winifred, early in 1871, but mother and daughter both died in May that year. Five weeks later James was dead. Patrick's life must have been shattered by these events, and he died in 1878.[41]

Only James Coleman's third son, Michael, survived to found this part of the family line in Stafford. He became a baker like his brother. His move into a trade was one key to the Coleman family's success. They had the ambition and the ability to lead a focused and relatively sober life, and the strength of family links helped support individuals in their upward mobility. Michael Coleman benefited from all these qualities. By 1861 he had a job with John Myatt, a grocer and baker with a shop in the town centre, and he was living in his employer's household. By 1871 he was lodging with his brother Patrick at their house in Back Walls North. There is a point of some significance here. In the census return both Patrick and Michael are shown as being born in Stafford. This may, of course, be an error on the part of the enumerator, but it is equally likely that the Coleman brothers wanted to obscure their Irish origins. They had, after all, come to Stafford as youngsters and doubtless had local, not Irish, accents. The subsequent history of Michael's family suggests the plausibility of this view.

Nevertheless, connections to the rest of the Coleman family remained important. For Michael they rose to the fore in 1872 when he married Margaret Duffy, daughter of the errant Patrick Duffy and Mary Coleman whom we met earlier. Margaret was, therefore, his second cousin. She knew there were skeletons in her immediate family's cupboard and was anxious for respectability. The couple went on to have eight children, of whom six survived to adulthood. Michael's reputation in the family is of a 'very hard-working baker, working all day and night'.[42] In 1881 he and Margaret were running a grocer's shop and bakery in Cross Street in the north end. It was hard work and wore Michael out. He died in 1885, and Margaret was left a widow with seven young children.[43] She could not keep the shop going, and by 1891 the family had been forced into a cheaper house in Pilgrim Street, a dank and mean street next to the River Sow in Forebridge. Margaret had to make money by taking in washing.

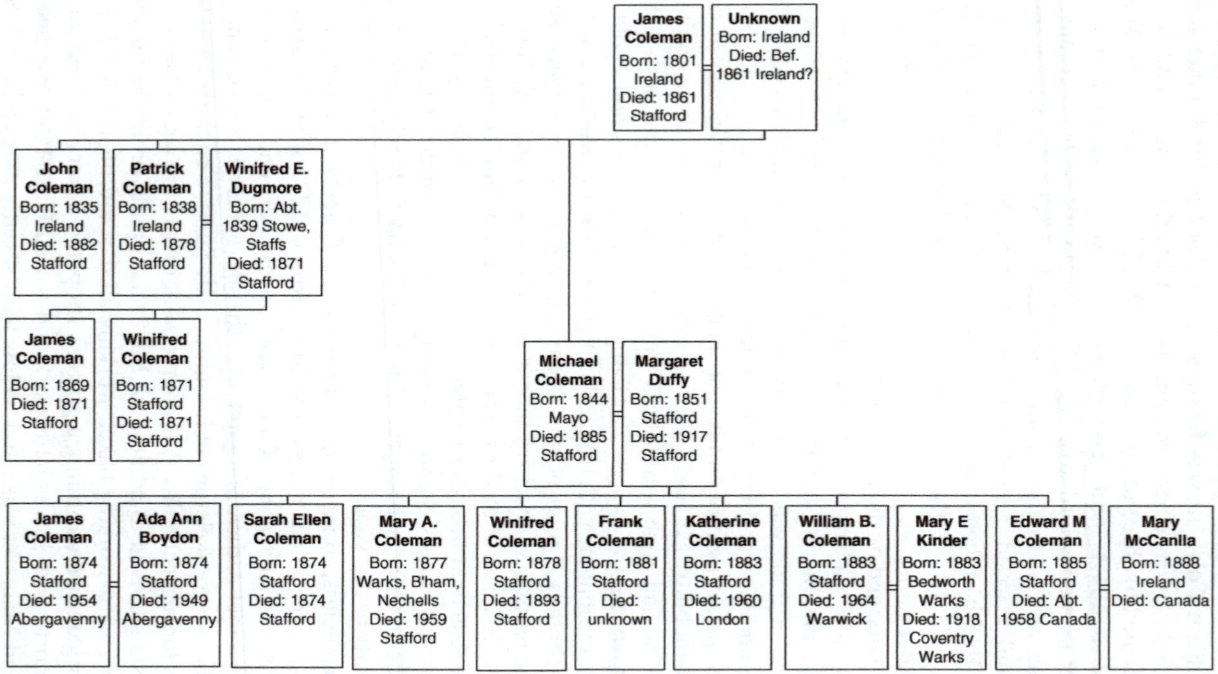

Figure 5.8 James Coleman's children and grandchildren

Family tree of James Coleman's children and grandchildren:

- **James Coleman** — Born: 1801 Ireland; Died: 1861 Stafford
- **Unknown** — Born: Ireland; Died: Bef. 1861 Ireland?

Children:

- **John Coleman** — Born: 1835 Ireland; Died: 1882 Stafford
- **Patrick Coleman** — Born: 1838 Ireland; Died: 1878 Stafford
- **Winifred E. Dugmore** — Born: Abt. 1839 Stowe, Staffs; Died: 1871 Stafford
- **Michael Coleman** — Born: 1844 Mayo; Died: 1885 Stafford
- **Margaret Duffy** — Born: 1851 Stafford; Died: 1917 Stafford

Children of Patrick Coleman and Winifred E. Dugmore:

- **James Coleman** — Born: 1869 Stafford; Died: 1871 Stafford
- **Winifred Coleman** — Born: 1871 Stafford; Died: 1871 Stafford

Children of Michael Coleman and Margaret Duffy:

- **James Coleman** — Born: 1874 Stafford; Died: 1954 Abergavenny
- **Ada Ann Boydon** — Born: 1874 Stafford; Died: 1949 Abergavenny
- **Sarah Ellen Coleman** — Born: 1874 Stafford; Died: 1874 Stafford
- **Mary A. Coleman** — Born: 1877 Warks, B'ham, Nechells; Died: 1959 Stafford
- **Winifred Coleman** — Born: 1878 Stafford; Died: 1893 Stafford
- **Frank Coleman** — Born: 1881 Stafford; Died: unknown
- **Katherine Coleman** — Born: 1883 Stafford; Died: 1960 London
- **William B. Coleman** — Born: 1883 Stafford; Died: 1964 Warwick
- **Mary E Kinder** — Born: 1883 Bedworth Warks; Died: 1918 Coventry Warks
- **Edward M Coleman** — Born: 1885 Stafford; Died: Abt. 1958 Canada
- **Mary McCanlla** — Born: 1888 Ireland; Died: Canada

Family life in that crowded, steamy cottage must have been stressful, and with no father figure around the boys could go astray. That certainly happened with Frank Coleman (b. 1881).[44] He had been four when his father died, and the loss may have traumatised him. He certainly became a disturbed youth, and neither his mother nor his elder brother James could control him. His rebelliousness threatened the family's respectability, particularly in the Catholic community. In desperation his mother sought help from the priest at St Austin's, Canon Acton. His answer was an industrial school, and in 1894 the magistrates ordered Frank to St Joseph's Industrial School in Manchester. He stayed there until he was sixteen and the experience, or shock, seems to have reformed him. He came back to Stafford and got a job on the railway as a telegraph clerk. In September 1898, after a brief spell in the Militia, he joined the army and enlisted in the North Staffordshire Regiment. He saw service in South Africa and the East Indies and served out his full twelve-year term.[45] He used to visit the family in the 1930s, and was remembered as 'a very elegant gentleman with good suits who had clearly arrived'.[46] The family's kinship links were important to him. They were even of significance to the one child who definitely emigrated. Edward Coleman (b. 1885) became an engineer and went to Canada in the 1920s, but he remained in contact with the family in Stafford. He reportedly had a hard time in Canada, but never returned to Britain.

The Coleman traits of hard work and aspiration were demonstrated by Margaret's other children. Once they started work they fought to get the family out of Pilgrim Street and into a respectable lifestyle. By 1901 they had moved into a solid terraced house at no. 28 Shrewsbury Road in Forebridge. The first-born, James, started work as a telegraph messenger on the railway and by 1901 he had been promoted to clerk. He joined the Railway Clerks' Association, and by 1909 was the union's organiser and Vice-Chairman in Stafford.[47] Although railway trade unionism strengthened in the 1900s, it still needed bravery to become an activist in the face of company hostility. This says much about James Coleman's confidence, dynamism and concern to play a socially supportive role. In 1899 he married Ada Ann Boydon, the daughter of a local butcher. She was a Catholic.[48] The couple had five children in the 1900s, but in the midst of this they also played an active role in social events, particularly those connected with St Patrick's Church. In 1913 Stafford celebrated the millennium of its foundation with a pageant and other events. The prime organiser was Martin Mitchell, the child of Irish immigrants and a remarkable man whom we shall meet later. James Coleman was involved as well as at least two other members of the extended Coleman family.[49] This is clear evidence of how the Colemans, as respectable Catholics, consciously tried to identify with the town of Stafford, its social life and its history.

The Colemans actively endeavoured to obscure their poor Irish origins. This was particularly true of Michael and Margaret Coleman's daughter Mary Agnes (b. 1877). She began work in the shoe trade, but later was a clerk at the Stafford Laundry and ultimately became its manageress. That sounds an unglamorous occupation, but in her job Mary Coleman had dealings with members of Stafford's middle and upper class. It reportedly rubbed off on her and she became somewhat snobbish. This branch of the Coleman family became 'English through and through; they might have had an Irish name but they tended to be like English gentlemen.' That did not go down well elsewhere in the family. Billy Bagnall thought they were 'a bit up-tight' and took the rise out of them because they liked to show they had gone up in the world.[50] Perhaps he knew something about the suspicious circumstances of Margaret's mother's marriage.

Conclusion: the leading role of the Coleman women

Three things are clear about the history of the extended Coleman family. Firstly, their initial decade in the town was as deprived as that of most Famine refugees. Secondly, however, they appear to have had a pervasive family strategy to take Stafford as they found it, to exploit it and to succeed by integrating into its social networks. Who determined that strategy? The evidence suggests it was the family's women who largely took up the role. We have seen that a number of the male partners either died young or otherwise disappeared. Catherine Curley/Cassidy, Mary Duffy/Carroll, Margaret Finnigan and Margaret Duffy/Coleman all played pivotal roles in bringing up succeeding generations of the family. These women dominated the household environment and they largely inculcated the family's spiritual and aspirational values. The family's subgroups were initially forced to lodge amongst their fellow refugees from the Famine, and key marriage partners came from these people. The results were mixed. Nevertheless, the Colemans tried as soon as possible to distance themselves from the 'rough' end of the Irish working class. The house in Bath Street symbolised that distancing. They largely kept out of trouble, and certainly avoided the drink-fuelled violence that was endemic to Snow's Yard and similar places. The Stafford-born children who formed the third and fourth generation of Colemans in the town almost all got higher-status jobs than their parents – they made it into skilled manual, clerical and similar jobs. In doing so they socialised with people from the breadth of the local community, and all but two married ethnically English partners. Some were Protestants. Even so, the Catholic Church remained important to the family, again because of the women's dominant role. Its spiritual message was transmitted down the generations. But it also provided opportunities for widening social contacts and gaining marriage partners. The Church was therefore vital for the family's integration into local society. The Colemans became Staffordian Catholics. When Catherine Coleman and Pat Cassidy died in 1921, the final direct link with the family's Irish origins was broken. Memories of these individuals were passed down, but not with any significant attachment to, or even knowledge of, the background from which they came and the traumas they might have experienced.

The third feature of the extended Coleman family was the importance of active family linkages and support. We have seen the conspiracy over Mary Coleman's marriage in 1857. We have found numerous instances of people offering lodgings to other family members and evidence of how the tenancy of no. 5 Bath Street was passed between family sub-units. There are other cases of people living close to each other and being able to offer practical support. Most potently, oral history and legends relating to the period from the 1880s to the 1930s have stressed the extent to which people from all parts of the far-flung family visited each other and offered support when necessary. Family obligations were strong in the Coleman family, and the evidence suggests they were mostly honoured willingly.

The history of the Coleman family illustrates a further feature of the Irish migrant experience. In general terms they 'settled' in Stafford, and descendants remain part of local society today. Yet even here we find numerous instances of sub-elements of the family dying out and others, as individuals and nuclear groups, moving elsewhere in Britain and also emigrating. This complexity underscores again the importance of examining detailed experiences and avoiding simple ethnic generalisations.

The Kellys: troubled, troublesome and transient

Famine refugees who outwitted the Poor Law authorities

The Kellys were trouble. Their history in Stafford was classically that of a 'problem family' and their sojourn of over thirty years demonstrated major symptoms of social stress and deprivation. The Kellys were, however, similar to the Coleman family in one major respect – the dominant role played by the women. They bound the generations together and provided a base from which descendants could ultimately achieve modest upward mobility and integration. That process was largely to take place elsewhere, however. Stafford proved to be an interim phase in the Kelly family's establishment in England.

The definition of the Kellys as a 'problem family' identifies the symptoms of their behaviour but not its causes. Their troubled history raises the question of whether one or more individuals in the family were

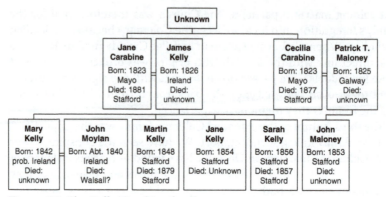

Figure 5.9 The Kelly/Carabine family

suffering PTSD. We shall see evidence of drunkenness and violence; hostility to neighbours; internal family tension; and extreme, if narrow, loyalty to immediate kin. Such behaviour was undoubtedly widespread amongst the impoverished masses of England, but the possibility that in the Kellys' case they were manifestations of deeper psychological problems cannot be discounted. The family was immediately and uniquely identified as troublesome by the Poor Law authorities. This suggests there were deeper issues whose symptoms are now lost to us, and their history should be read with this possibility in mind.

The Kellys and their relatives were victims of the Famine who, like the Colemans, came from Mayo. Jane Kelly's maiden name was Carabine, a rare surname localised in four parishes along Mayo's border with Cos Roscommon and Sligo (Figure 5.9).[51] It was an area close to the Castlerea district but is not the known source of any of Stafford's other Irish immigrants. The Kellys were therefore outsiders to the dominant group, and although they stayed in Stafford for many years, they remained on the margins of local society. Why did they go a different route from the Coleman family?

James and Jane Kelly's arrival during the Famine is documented in some detail. This was because, uniquely in Stafford, the Poor Law authorities tried to deport them back to Ireland. Our first definite record of the family dates from 10 July 1847 when the Relieving Officer, Edward Brannington, applied for 2s 1d to relieve Jane Kelley (*sic*), 'an Irish pauper'. A 'Thomas Kelly' had already been admitted to the workhouse on 29 June, however. He came in because of illness. He was so ill that he was removed to the infirmary on 1 July. 'Thomas' Kelly's recorded age tallies with that of James, and it seems likely they were one and the same. Jane and her five-year old-daughter Mary were destitute because of James's illness, and this would explain why she got outdoor relief. A week later she had received £2 3s 2d, and on 7 August she got another £1 1s 2d, with a further 2s 5d on 21 August.[52] The Poor Law authorities were struggling to cope with the Famine Irish in Stafford. Scores of destitute and fevered Irish paupers were passing through the workhouse vagrant wards. Some died there. Many of their dependants, including Jane and Mary Kelly, were stranded in the town on outdoor relief.

The Guardians started to panic at the cost of coping with the Famine Irish, and on the same day that Jane Kelly got her final payment the Guardians resolved 'that the Act to amend laws relating to the removal of poor persons from England (10 & 11 Vic. Cap. 33) be put into force under the direction of the Overseers of the several parishes of the Union.' The destitute Irish were to be deported back to Ireland.[53] In practice the authorities in Stafford proved reluctant to implement the procedure, but the Kellys became a test case.

On 24 September 1847 James Kelly was again admitted to the workhouse because of illness. The authorities refused to give Jane any more outdoor relief, and she and her daughter were forced inside as well. In effect they were imprisoned there before the next move. The family were discharged on 17 October and an order made for their removal from the parish – and England.[54] A month later came the reckoning. On 13 November Brannington presented his bill of £4 4s 9d 'for conveying three Irish paupers – James Kelley, Jane his wife and one child – to Liverpool and the amount of their fair by steam packett [*sic*] to Dublin.'[55] At this point the Guardians refused to pay up. They thought the relieving officer had exceeded his powers and that the expenditure was too high. They passed the bill to the parish overseers of Stafford with the excuse that the Kellys were chargeable to that parish. The overseers refused to pay and passed the buck back to the Union. Two weeks later Brannington presented his bill again together with the Order of Removal. This time the Guardians questioned the legality of the Order but cravenly decided to seek guidance from the Poor Law Commissioners in London. The Commissioners' ruling does not survive, but the matter surfaced again on 22 January 1848 when Brannington was cross-examined over his actions in the Kelly case. The Chairman supported the relieving officer, arguing that 'Birmingham and other places were removing great quantities of Irish ... and Stafford must do the same.' The other Guardians were not convinced and they did nothing. There is no evidence that the Stafford Poor Law authorities removed any more Famine Irish from the town. It was too much trouble. The Kelly family had, in the short term, been the unlucky victims of a failed experiment. They had the last laugh, however. Although Brannington claimed for their boat fare to Dublin, the family either slipped the net in Liverpool or got the first boat back from Ireland. They returned to Stafford. We know they were back in the town by 1848 because their son Martin was baptised at St Austin's in October of that year.[56]

Violent lives on the social margins

Although the Kellys were treated as unwelcome vagrants in 1847, they did not wash up in Stafford randomly as helpless flotsam of the Famine. It seems pretty clear they already knew the town and, despite the attempt to deport them, it was still worth their while to come back to this unwelcoming place. Jane Kelly's sister Cecilia (or 'Scilley') Carabine also settled in Stafford, and in 1850 she married Thomas Patrick Maloney, a Galway man, at St Austin's.[57] He had arrived around 1849 and got bits of casual farmwork on the Ingestre estate.[58] The lives of the two sisters and their families were to be interwoven for the next twenty years. Other relatives were in Stafford at times, and the social interactions of the Kelly family were more complicated than appears at first sight.

In 1851 James and Jane Kelly were running a lodging house at 52 New Street and were in a situation common to many poor Irish immigrants. Though James worked as a farm labourer and Jane took in washing, the couple's main income came from the lodging houses they ran at various addresses. They are known to have occupied premises in New Street (1851), Bell Yard (1861), Cherry Street (1863–66), Mill Street (1866) and Malt Mill Lane (1868). This was life at the margins of society. From the start the Kellys seem to have been fundamentally alienated both from the host society and from other Irish immigrants, especially those with any pretensions to respectability. They existed in a nether world of petty criminality, violence and disorder. Although there is no evidence of their doings for the ten years after 1848, after 1858 the Kellys' lives become clearer. In December 1858 Scilley's husband Patrick Maloney was given a week in gaol for assaulting James Kelly. We do not know what prompted the fracas, but it shows how intra-family violence stalked their households. Three years later, and contrary to modern gender expectations, Jane Kelly was the perpetrator of domestic violence rather than its victim. In May 1861 she was found guilty of violent assaults and threats against her husband. This was presumably not the first incident, since the magistrates imposed two sureties of £5 on her to keep the peace, failing which she would go to prison for three months.[59]

Jane Kelly was a violent and thoroughly unpleasant character. Two years later she assaulted Anne Goodman, a young woman from a poor Irish family in Cherry Street.[60] Anne worked as a shoe binder, a fairly menial job done by girls, but she aspired to respectability. She began to achieve it that year by marrying Bartholomew Corcoran, and we shall meet them again in Chapter 7. Jane Kelly would have hated such lace-curtain pretensions, and she bullied and intimidated people like Anne. The Kellys were at the rough end. Their squalid lodging houses housed the floating poor – tramps, hawkers, itinerant workers and new immigrants from Ireland. They were summoned twice for breaking lodging-house by-laws, and on occasions lodgers were the victims of petty thefts carried out by other inmates.[61] In 1868 one lodger, William Hodgkiss, a 'besom-maker', assaulted the Kelly's fourteen-year-old daughter, Jane, when he was drunk.[62] The nature of the assault was not stated but was probably sexual. It emphasises the problems faced by children growing up in such conditions.

James Kelly was a cowed and perhaps isolated man. In April 1866 he was given seven days for begging from women in Forebridge, a pathetic crime that suggests Jane kept him short of money from her nefarious activities.[63] She chucked him out around this time – or he perhaps deserted to escape the horror – because in 1871 we find him living on his own in a lodging house in Gnosall, six miles from Stafford. He was working as a farm labourer. It is unclear whether he ever lived with Jane again, although in 1875 he was back in Stafford and was fined 5s for using profane language in Back Walls North at two o'clock in the morning.[64] After that the trail goes cold. In 1881 Jane described herself as a 'widow', but if James had died by then, he did not die in Stafford. With such a common name it is impossible to definitively identify his death elsewhere.

The year 1868 was the low point in Jane Kelly's criminally disruptive activities. She was running a lodging house in Malt Mill Lane that was the base for a gang of juvenile thieves under her control. It came to light when some of its members stole £24 from a butcher's shop in Castletown. They spent the money so freely, and drank so heavily, that the trail rapidly led back to Kelly. It was said in court that 'she led the lads into mischief by harbouring them at her house and supplying them with drink'. One of the culprits was Scilley's son John Maloney (b. 1853). The eight other youths came from a variety of origins – Irish, Catholic Staffordian and non-Catholic – but all from the most deprived backgrounds. When the case came to court the thieves fell out and implicated each other, but all alleged that Jane Kelly had received a cut of the proceeds. They were remanded to prison, 'and on their being placed in the prison van ... a great crowd assembled who hissed the woman Kelly but cheered the other prisoners who, in return, also cheered'.[65] This curious mixture of responses shows Jane Kelly's unpopularity. She was seen as the ring leader and as a malign influence on young lads. She was sentenced to a year in prison, a punishment that clearly identified her central role but also victimised her as an alien and unpopular individual.

The Kelly children: Stafford, Walsall and Longton

In the midst of their disordered lives James and Jane Kelly had three surviving children (Figure 5.9). Their first, Mary, was born in Ireland around 1842 and was with them when they arrived in Stafford. They perhaps had other children during the mid-1840s who died. In 1848 Martin was born in Stafford. He had his mother's violent temper and 'was well-known as a disorderly character' in the 1870s. In 1875 he was accused of an unprovoked attack on John McTighe, an Irishman, in Back Walls North. McTighe gave the Kellys as good as he got and Jane Kelly, 'an elderly woman', appeared in court 'with a conspicuous white bandage round her head'.[66] The evidence strongly suggests Kelly and her family were heartily disliked and publicly abused by other Irish people in the street. Martin worked at labouring jobs and never married. He died in Stafford 1879.[67] The Kellys' daughter Jane was born in 1854. She was accused of receiving in the young thieves case but was acquitted. She was living with her mother in 1871, but her subsequent fate is unknown. She may have settled in the Potteries, but perhaps she emigrated. Sarah, a final child, was born in 1856 but lived for only fifteen months.

Only Mary, the first child, definitely survived to extend the Kelly line. In 1859 she married an Irishman, John Moylan, at St Austin's.[68] Nothing is known about Moylan's origins, but he was presumably already known to the family from Co. Mayo. After the wedding the couple lived with Mary's Aunt Scilley in their lodging house in Cherry Street. This is a demonstration of the kinship bonds in the immediate Kelly family. Their first son, Thomas, was born in Stafford in 1860, but the family soon moved to Walsall where Moylan worked as a furnace labourer. Nothing is known about the Moylans' lives in the Black Country, but the family were undoubtedly poor and stressed. Symptomatic of this is the fact that at various times some of their children lived with Jane Kelly. After her year in Stafford Gaol, Kelly moved to Longton in the Potteries. In 1871 we find her living with her daughter Jane, but her grandson 'Thomas Miller' was also present. This was in fact the Moylans' first child Thomas. Patrick and Scilley Maloney were also 'boarding' there with their son John, aged eighteen, so it seems both branches of the family had decamped from Stafford. Perhaps they had made themselves too unpopular amongst the Irish poor. The immediate family bonds continued to be strong despite, or perhaps because of, Jane Kelly's domineering nature.

The Moylans had at least eleven children in Walsall. Links with Jane Kelly continued. By 1875 she had moved back to Stafford and in 1881 was living in a court off St Chad's Place in the town centre. In the house were two grandchildren, Edward Moylan (b. 1862) and Cornelius Moylan (b. 1875). Edward was working as a farm labourer. Curiously, however, there were three other people listed as 'visitors' with the surname 'Melvin'. One was 'Mary Melvin', thirty-one years of age, married and a hawker. She had two children with her, Frances (b. 1874 in Walsall) and John (b. 1880). The similarity of the surname to Moylan and the coincidence of the age of 'Mary Melvin' to that of Mary Moylan née Kelly suggests strongly that they were one and the same. The Moylans were probably illiterate and the spelling of their name in the records varies wildly, a fact that caused major problems in reconstructing the family's genealogy. Mary Moylan may have moved backwards and forwards between her mother and her husband, although she could also have been in Stafford in 1881 looking after her mother. Jane Kelly was already ill and she died, aged only fifty-six, in September that year. She had a Catholic funeral.[69] With her death the centre of the Kelly–Moylan family moved to Walsall, and there are probably many descendants around there and elsewhere.[70]

The extended family: Patrick Maloney and Patrick Kelly

Discussion so far has centred on James and Jane Kelly's nuclear family, but we have already seen that links remained close, if tempestuous, between the Kellys and Jane's sister's family, the Maloneys. The Maloneys were a similarly disordered household and in 1861 they were running a lodging house in Mill Street, probably unlicensed. Patrick Maloney seems to have been more addicted to drink than James or Jane Kelly and in 1868 he was given fourteen days for disturbing the peace. He was described at that time as 'an old offender'.[71] Scilley Maloney died in Stafford in March 1877.[72] Her death meant Patrick finally went to pieces. Less than two months later his drunken life was publicly exposed by the shocking death in his house of Mary Devlin. Devlin's daughter Elizabeth testified that:

> she went to the house occupied by Patrick Maloney on Mill Bank where she expected to find [her mother]. On entering she saw a woman named Jones drunk in the corner of the room and her daughter in a similar condition lying in the middle of the floor. Maloney was sitting in a child's cradle drunk too, also the witness's sister Mrs Dolan and a woman named White. She saw her mother lying on a heap of bags in the corner and tried to wake her up. Her mouth was swollen as big as a tea cup and foam was oozing from it. The witness pulled her up, she fell down again, and she saw she was dead.[73]

It is noteworthy that five of the seven people in the drunken stupor were women, and the post-mortem showed that Mary Devlin was starving. She had finally succumbed to years of alcoholism. Patrick and his son John left Stafford shortly afterwards. Scilley's branch of the family finally had proved to be long-term transients.

Members of James Kelly's extended family also lived in Stafford for a time. The family connection was not immediately apparent, but the evidence is strong and concerns the brother and sister Patrick and Catherine Kelly. Patrick Kelly was a labourer from Co. Mayo who was born around 1833. He came to Stafford some time before or during 1858 because the first we know of him is when he was fined £1 plus costs for assaulting a police constable.[74] The key thing is that in 1859 he was one of the witnesses at Mary Kelly's marriage to John Moylan, which suggests he was related to her. In the same year he was also a witness at Catherine's marriage to Patrick Mannion. Mannion belonged to an extensive Irish family who put down deep roots in Stafford. In 1861 they were all living in Edward Kelly's lodging house at 10 Snow's Yard and Patrick Kelly was listed as Edward's brother, despite the latter claiming to have been born in Co. Galway, not Mayo. They probably came from the cross-border area separating Galway, Mayo and Roscommon that was home to many of Stafford's immigrants. Edward proved to be transient in Stafford. His wife and only child died in the 1860s and he then left the town.[75]

What was the relationship amongst Patrick, Edward and James Kelly? They could all have been brothers or perhaps James was a cousin to the other two. In 1863 Patrick Kelly married a Margaret Duffey (background unknown) and the couple had at least nine children. They remained in Stafford for a number of years, and Patrick was amongst those charged with riot and assault after the election disturbances of 1868.[76] They left the town shortly afterwards and family links were significant in the move. In 1871 we find Patrick Kelly and his family living in a courtyard behind Short Acre Street in Walsall. Just over the wall in the next court lived John and Mary Moylan! Both men were working as labourers, and the Moylans had clearly helped the Kellys get the house in Walsall and possibly a job. Patrick Kelly's family became settled in Walsall, although one of his sons, also named Patrick, ran away to America and found his way to an aunt and uncle in Scranton, New Jersey. Family legend says that his mother Margaret sailed to America to bring him back 'by the ear'. He subsequently joined the army and served in India and South Africa, but ultimately returned to Walsall.[77] Links between the Moylans and Patrick Kelly's family therefore seem to have been significant. They were mutually trying to survive and bring up large families in the Black Country. There is, however, no surviving evidence that either Patrick or Edward Kelly had active links with James and Jane Kelly whilst in Stafford, or afterwards in Walsall. They probably saw them as rough and unpopular relatives to be avoided.

Explaining the Kelly family's history: alienation, kinship – and trauma?

Jane Kelly's sojourn in Stafford lasted from 1847 to 1881 – thirty-four years – although there was a gap around 1871 when she and her immediate relatives moved to the Potteries. It is clear that their lives in Stafford were deprived, and they lived on the social margins. This was not just in terms of alienation from Staffordian society. Jane Kelly and her son were disliked by the poor Irish amongst whom they lived. What factors explain their experiences in Stafford, their marginal position in local society and their apparent lack of commitment to it?

The evidence points to the women's prime role in the family trajectory, and particularly that of Jane Kelly. She was the dominant personality who determined the family's character. She, James and daughter Mary were a pre-existing family who had experienced the worst of the Famine's effects. Their arrival in Stafford, fevered and destitute, was after eviction from their minimal holding in Co. Mayo. They were an embittered family from the start. Although contacts from back home may explain why they came to Stafford, the attempt to deport them back to Ireland set them apart from all the other Famine immigrants in Stafford. They were immediately marked out as 'troublemakers' amongst the generally suppliant Irish.

The Kellys' experience reinforced a mindset that they would have to fight their corner to survive in a hostile environment. In this situation they relied on the tight kinship links of immediate family rather than support from other Irish people. Jane Kelly and her sister formed a tight bond that involved putting family members up in their respective houses at different times. The two spouses, James Kelly and Patrick Maloney, were peripheral, and weaker, individuals, with James ultimately pushed out and Patrick probably descending into a drunken half-life. We have to ask why. One possibility is that these men were suffering some degree of post-traumatic stress. We know that James Kelly was 'ill' in the infirmary and workhouse in 1847, and that the Poor Law authorities tried to get rid of him and his family as soon as possible. This suggests deviant or even abnormal behaviour seen as disruptive by the overseers and guardians. The family's subsequent relationships also suggest stresses that could have resulted from dealing with James and/or Patrick's traumatised behaviour. It is significant that neither Jane nor Scilley was ever accused of drunkenness, despite the fact that Jane plied her young thieves with drink. This is hardly conclusive evidence, but it suggests the sisters had a single-minded coping strategy to avoid drink's worst excesses whilst battening on the weaknesses of others. The female bonds continued into the next generation with the close domestic links between Mary Moylan, her children, her mother and her aunt. Jane's ruthless pursuit of her interests was probably transmitted to Mary and her descendants, and ultimately they seem to have built modest but relatively successful lives in Walsall and elsewhere.

In Stafford, however, the Kellys and Maloneys were archetypal 'rough' Irish families. In Jane and Scilley's lodging houses home comforts were minimal in the squalid and disordered environment. They were dens dominated by the women with a shifting cast of the deprived and the petty criminal. Kelly, in particular, was isolated from, and hostile to, her neighbours and the feelings were mutual. They had little commitment to either their Irish compatriots or the local host community. The immigrant generation retained a strongly Irish character but there is no evidence that they had any sort of conscious Irish identity. It is noteworthy that Jane was happy to have both English and Irish amongst her nest of thieves. The Kellys were nominally Catholic, but they were distant from the Church except when they commemorated the life-cycle events of birth, marriage and death. They played no visible role in parish life, and faith can have played little or no role in defining either their behaviour or identity. Even so, loyalty and commitment to close kin were transmitted to the next generation and ultimately this helped them integrate into the host society from a position of security and confidence. The Kellys were a troubled, troublesome and transient family in Stafford but their descendants were able to emerge elsewhere as an extensive and apparently more stable family. Their lengthy connection with Stafford was an essential element in that process.

The Jordans: a Famine family that withered away

Lives in respectable poverty

The boundary between families whose members ultimately moved away and those families who died out *in situ* is inevitably blurred, a fact demonstrated by the Jordan family. Although one child married and moved elsewhere, the rest died in Stafford, and the family's presence ceased in 1922. Even so, the picture is not one of simple static existence in Stafford before that date. At least three children worked elsewhere, almost certainly overseas, before returning to the town. Patterns of Irish settlement and mobility were complex, and the Jordans illustrate this well.

Like the Colemans and Kellys, Bartholomew and Margaret Jordan were Famine immigrants to Stafford from Connacht (Figure 5.10). Bartholomew Jordan said his place of birth was Galway or Mayo at different times. Margaret, whose maiden name was Brady, was much more specific. In 1871 she said she had been born in Kilcolman, and in 1891 at Claremorris, which is in the same Co. Mayo parish. The couple came, therefore, from the Claremorris area, having been born there in the 1810s. They married some time before 1837 when their first surviving child, Mary, was born. This part of Mayo suffered greatly in the Famine. In early December 1846 it was said there were 450 poor suffering families in the area, 'the great majority of whom are starving', and by the end of the month 'the people in this parish and surrounding districts [were] starving in multitudes'.[78]

We do not know precisely when the Jordans were evicted or fled from Co. Mayo. Unlike the Kellys, they were not forced into the workhouse vagrant wards in 1847. They slipped quietly into town, and were first recorded in September 1848 when their daughter Margaret was christened at St Austin's Church.[79] Their previous child, Bridget, had been born in Ireland in 1846. Bartholomew Jordan generally worked as a farm

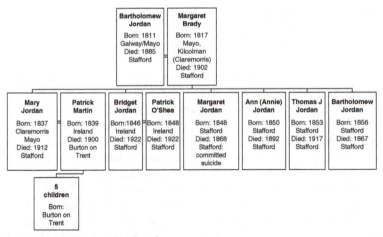

Figure 5.10 The Jordan family

labourer, and he may have come with other Mayo men to Stafford for seasonal work before the Famine. The couple probably had contacts in the
town and settled quickly. In 1851 they were living in Earl's Court, but by
1861 they had moved to Dottell Street, an even meaner place next to the
gas works. Later they moved into Wilson's Court behind Dottell Street,
and remained there for at least thirty years. Life was clearly hard in these
miserable slum cottages, and the Jordans were sometimes forced to take
in other Irish lodgers.

Bartholomew Jordan and his wife were therefore dependent on casual
farmwork and lodgers to survive. Even so, getting stuck in Wilson's Court
shows they remained extremely poor. In such circumstances they might
have been expected to be part of the rough, drunken element of Stafford's
Irish like the Kearns family or the Kellys. In fact they seem to have lived
modest, quiet and generally respectable lives. Bartholomew received the
vote in 1867, and voted Liberal in the 1868 general election and again in
the by-election of 1869.[80] In doing this he was following the lead of many
Irish immigrants and of the Catholic priest who publicly supported the
Liberal candidates. Even so, it shows some identification with the local
and national affairs of their adopted home.[81] Otherwise the couple left little public record of their lives in Stafford. This negative evidence suggests
a poor but relatively steady life making the best of the circumstances.

The sad lives of the Jordan children

In 1860 the Jordans' eldest daughter, Mary, married Patrick Martin at St
Austin's Church.[82] Martin was an Irish bricklayer's labourer but there is

no record of him in Stafford before the couple's marriage. Although they began their married life lodging with an English family at no. 2 Dottell Street, next door to their parents, this was temporary. Some time before 1864 Patrick and Mary moved to Burton-on-Trent. Patrick continued working as a bricklayer's labourer and the family settled in that town. They had at least five children, and there are significant numbers of descendants from this branch of the family today.[83]

Bartholomew and Mary Jordan may have had other children in the late 1830s and early 1840s, but their next surviving child, Bridget, was born in Ireland in 1846 or 1847. She grew up in Stafford and by 1861 was working as a servant in the household of Richard Marklew, a warder at Stafford Gaol. Marklew was transferred to Manchester Prison some time after 1863 and Bridget went with them. That explains why, in 1871, she was working as a cook for Robert Brookhouse, a dental surgeon on Oxford Road, Manchester. By this time, however, she was calling herself 'Elizabeth', not 'Bridget', and she continued to do so for the rest of her life. This suggests she wanted to obscure her Irish origin. Her trail then goes cold for a number of years, but in 1882 she came back to Stafford and married Patrick O'Shea at St Austin's church.[84]

O'Shea had been born in Ireland around 1848, the son of John and Bridget O'Shea from Co. Galway. They had arrived in Stafford in the 1850s. Patrick was working as a farm labourer in 1861. He left the town in the 1860s and nothing more is known of him until his marriage to Elizabeth/Bridget in 1882. Neither he nor she was recorded in Stafford in 1881. They have not been traced elsewhere in Britain either, so they were possibly back in Ireland or had emigrated overseas. By 1891 the couple was living in Colwich, about seven miles south-east of Stafford, but their marriage proved sadly barren of children. By 1901 they had returned to live in town and were living in Back Walls North, the poor area where the O'Sheas had always lived since their arrival in Stafford. Elizabeth and Patrick lived on to a good age. They died within three months of each other in 1922 when they were living at 52 Marston Road, a modestly respectable address in the north end of town.[85]

If Bridget/Elizabeth Jordan lived on to old age, the fate of her sister Margaret was otherwise, and the tale is a sad one. Around Christmas 1867 at the age of nineteen she began work as a servant for Charles Yardley, a farmer in Seighford about four miles outside Stafford. 'She behaved well in service' until April 1868, but at that point she suddenly 'became very unmanageable'. Mrs Yardley then discovered that a sovereign and half-sovereign had gone missing from a chest of drawers, and suspicion fell on Margaret and the other servant in the house, Elizabeth Williams. The two girls accused each other of inciting the crime, but Mrs Yardley said she would forgive them as long as they told their parents what had happened and behaved themselves in future. Margaret Jordan gave the money back to Mrs Yardley and the incident seemed to be over. It was not. An hour later Mrs Yardley heard a scream from the back kitchen and ran down to find Margaret Jordan lying on the floor. She had poisoned herself with sheep dip and died the following day.[86] It looks as though poor Margaret Jordan was led astray by the other girl (who continued to blame her at the inquest) and was totally devastated by the affair.

For Bartholomew and Mary Jordan 1868 was a bad year. Two months before Margaret's suicide her brother Thomas (b. 1853) had appeared in court accused of being one of Jane Kelly's gang of young thieves and receivers.[87] Most received one-month sentences, but Thomas Jordan was acquitted.[88] He had clearly got caught in bad company and was lucky to have escaped gaol, even if only through guilt by association. It is possible that someone, perhaps a priest at St Austin's, put in a good word about the respectability of the Jordan household. Certainly, Thomas Jordan did not get into trouble with the law again, unlike some of his associates in the case. Life was not easy for him, however. In 1871 he was unemployed, and he left Stafford in the 1870s. Like his sister Bridget/Elizabeth and Patrick O'Shea he may have gone abroad.[89] Wherever he went, it did not turn out well and he came back to Stafford in the 1910s clearly a poor man. He died in the workhouse in 1917.[90]

The other two Jordan children also seem to have led sad lives. Ann, or Annie, Jordan was born in 1850, and by 1871 was described as a 'servant', though she was still living with her parents in Wilson's Court. She left home in the 1870s, and, like the others, may have emigrated for a time, perhaps with her brother Thomas. Annie returned to Stafford much sooner than her brother, however, and came back to die. Her burial took place in Stafford on 23 November 1892.[91] Annie's younger brother Bartholomew had an even shorter life. Born as the last child in 1856, he died at the age of eleven in 1867.[92]

Bartholomew Jordan died in 1885, aged around seventy-four.[93] His widow Margaret continued to live in Wilson's Court during the 1890s, but poverty, old age and infirmity finally drove her into the workhouse. There she died a pauper in 1902.[94] The O'Sheas had not taken her in despite the fact that they had no children and appear, later in life, to have had the money to move to a better house. The Martins in Burton-on-Trent similarly seem to have abandoned her. The bonds and commitments in the Jordan family were demonstrably weak in comparison with the Colemans and, paradoxically, the Kellys.

The penalties of isolation

What do we conclude about the Jordan family? Like the other families in this chapter, the Jordans experienced the trauma of the Famine and emigration. Their response was to seek new lives as an independent family unit. They tried to be self-reliant and to make the best of things without much support from their fellow Irish immigrants. It meant they largely avoided trouble and achieved very modest respectability. The fact that Margaret Jordan killed herself rather than tell her parents she had been caught stealing could be interpreted in various ways. She may have feared her father's anger but she may also have felt she had let her family down, particularly after her brother's appearance in court two months earlier. She and her parents showed none of the brazen contempt exhibited by Jane Kelly. But the Jordans' apparent insularity also meant they did not benefit from contacts, and Bartholomew Jordan remained stuck in farmwork to the end of his life. This trapped the family in poverty and miserable living conditions in a rotten part of town.

The Jordan children were caught between two worlds – neither Irish nor English. Bridget's change of name to Elizabeth was symbolic. Their parents showed little sign of positively wanting to stay in an Irish environment, but their poverty isolated them from effective entry into the host society. This left the children with little commitment to either an Irish or a Staffordian environment. They also showed little sign of wishing to stay with or near their parents. Tensions between the generations and the lack of opportunity must have been a strong incentive to leave. They all went away even if, in poor Margaret's case, it was no farther than Seighford. The Martins in Burton-on-Trent made a go of it, but all the rest came back to Stafford, even after a long time away. They do not seem to have had the ruthlessness or adaptability to survive in more challenging places. The two children who married chose Irish partners, but in both cases they were from similarly isolated families rather than from the core group of Stafford's Irish labouring families. The other children stayed single.

The Jordans were Catholics and all their life events were commemorated in the Church. We do not know the strength of their day-to-day commitment, but there is no evidence that it decisively structured their identity or behaviour. They must have been affected – even traumatised – by Margaret's suicide and by Thomas's involvement in the Kelly case. The family household cannot have been a joyous place after these events. The history of the family in Stafford is generally a sad one culminating in 1922 when the Jordans finally died out. Terminal families such as this were perhaps the greatest long-term victims of the Famine.

The Famine labouring families: an overview

We have studied the histories of three representative Irish labouring families who arrived in Stafford during the Famine years. All the adults from these families came from the same part of Ireland. All experienced the agonies of the Famine at first hand. They had grown up in communities struggling to survive on small-holdings and conacre plots. All were Catholics and of Celtic Irish ethnicity. Their knowledge of Stafford had come from earlier harvest work or from contact with people who had been before. When the Famine struck they were forced out and arrived in Stafford more or less destitute. They were compelled to live in lodging houses or the worst slums in town. These people's initial experiences were therefore very similar.

The conventional view would expect to see these families as outcasts from the society into which they had been forced and that they and their descendants then survived by seeking sanctuary within a geographical and mental enclave of Irishness. That would have formed the base from which later generations transmuted their outlook into a more ambiguous Catholic-Irish identity that might, or might not, precede integration into the host society. Stafford's labouring families who arrived during the Famine present a more complex picture. Certain individuals may have suffered clinical symptoms of PTSD, but we have no idea how widespread such problems were.[95] There is no direct testament about how these people responded to their life-changing experiences, since in Stafford no family legends have been reported about the Famine. The absence of such legends suggests that the Famine emigrants tried to blank out the memories – and the trauma? – of those years rather than transmit them to succeeding generations.[96] They had to move on both geographically and mentally. Their trajectories differed, however. One family became well established in Stafford and ultimately 'integrated', whilst the other two showed less commitment and ultimately disappeared from the town. The explanation for this must be sought in factors within the respective families and in their interaction with the local environment.

At the simplest level it seems that in some families there was a desire to make the best of things whereas others exhibited a more hostile or less effective response. These differences can be encapsulated by the tension between the 'exile' and 'opportunist' perspectives. Patterns of family support were always liable to disruption through desertion, incapacity and death. Succeeding generations were also affected by the marriage choices made by the immigrants and their children. We have seen how the desertion and premature death of fathers threw burdens on the mothers. In these circumstances the effectiveness of the women was determined partly by whether they could call on the support of kin. The nature of home and household played a major role in family experiences, though the messages are mixed. These people initially had to live in any available accommodation, including lodging houses, but subsequently two of the families stayed for years in the same houses, showing remarkable residential stability for Victorian Britain. Poor as they were, it was possible to build some notion of a home base.

Evidence of the identities present in these Famine families has to be largely circumstantial, but is telling nonetheless. In each case we are looking at a long period of time – from the late 1840s to 1920 and beyond. By the end of this period people were alive from at least four generations of the family, and in one case (the Colemans) from five. The identities present amongst family members at any point in time would have reflected their place in this generational hierarchy and the influences at work on them. Many writers have discussed the issue of competing and multiple identities in individuals, but it must be remembered that these individuals all had a place in the generational hierarchy of the family. In the case of these Famine families, the immigrants themselves initially had a clearly Irish *character*, but there is no surviving evidence that they had a conscious Irish *identity* that they wished to pass on to their children in order to counter the influence of the English society in which they were growing up. Even so, tensions amongst generations in the Jordan family may have reflected the ambiguous position of second-generation children growing up in Stafford. The ultimately unsuccessful emigration of some of the Jordan children was stimulated partly by economic factors – getting out of poverty – but also by possible alienation both from their parents' Irish character and their isolated position in Stafford.

The evidence suggests, however, that the third and fourth generations in these families retained little Irish identity. As the Famine immigrant generation died off active links with the past died with them. Not all the descendants remained in Stafford, but, wherever they were, they all seem to have become part of the local working-class community. The question of Catholic identity is more complex. The active and secure Church in Stafford clearly sustained the Colemans' Catholic identity down the generations – although it became an English Catholic identity. Catholicism played little obvious role in the root identity of the other two families, however.

The overall picture is, then, of diversity. The paths families followed varied because of the differing reactions made by family members to the challenges of the new environment in which they lived. This theme is repeated when we look at the labouring families who settled in Stafford after the Famine.

Notes

1 SRO, D659/8a/4–5, Stafford Poor Law Union, Board of Guardians Minute Book, 25 May 1844–3 February 1848 (7 July 1847).

2 The number of Irish-born in the Stafford district defined for this study rose from 145 in 1841 to 585 in 1851. The quotation in the opening heading is from

SRO D659/8a/4–5, Stafford Poor Law Union, Board of Guardians Minute Book, 25 May 1844–3 February 1848 (7 July 1847).

3 *SA*, 20 February 1847.

4 Neal, *Black '47*, Chapters 5 and 6, and p. 281.

5 SRO D659/8a/4–5. The average relief was scarcely generous – 2.66d per person.

6 Figure quoted in *SA*, 18 May 1847, from a meeting of the Board of Guardians.

7 SRO D659/8a/4–5, 29 May 1847.

8 *SA*, 20 November 1847.

9 J. D. Herson, 'Irish migration and settlement in Britain: A small town perspective' in R. Swift and S. Gilley (eds), *The Irish in Britain, 1815–1939* (London: Pinter Press, 1989), pp. 84–103 (88–90). This essay discusses at more length the reasons for settlement in Stafford.

10 Herson, 'Migration, "community" or integration?', pp. 172–3. The crude marriage rate amongst the Irish-born and their children between 1845 and 1854 was 13.2 per 1,000. It fell back to between 5.3 and 8.0 per cent in the succeeding decades.

11 The late Peter Godwin, interviewed in 2002.

12 Stafford Workhouse Admission and Discharge Book, 24 September 1847–30 March 1850, in SRO D659/1/4/7–8, Stafford Poor Law Union: Workhouse Admissions, 1847–48.

13 Information from descendants: the late Peter Godwin, 2002, and Kathleen Boult, 2003. In 1852 William Coleman was described as a 'husbandman' on his daughter Catherine's marriage certificate.

14 Catherine Coleman died in 1864, and the Borough burial record described her as the 'wife of William Coleman, rag collector'; SBC Burial Record 2/119.

15 *SA*, 2 February 1856.

16 *SA*, 2 February 1856.

17 *SA*, 9 August 1862, 31 January 1863 and 11 November 1865.

18 Information from Peter Godwin, 2002.

19 Stafford RD, Marriage Certificate, 6b/39, no. 82: Martin Curley and Catherine Coleman, 12 September 1852.

20 SRO D659/1/4/10, Stafford Poor Law Union, Workhouse Admission Book, available online at *Staffordshire Name Indexes* (accessed 23 October 2013).

21 Wolverhampton RD, Deaths, July–September 1860, 6b/228: Martin Curley.

22 Catherine said she was a widow in the 1861 census return.

23 Birmingham RD, Marriages, July–September 1877, 6d/318: Michael Curley and Margaret Gavagan.

24 Information from Peter Godwin, 2002.

25 Stafford RD, Marriages, October–December 1878, 6b/7: Thomas Boydell Moore and Mary Curley.

26 Family knowledge. Frederick Moore (1824–1912) was in the choir at St Mary's for seventy-seven years, supposedly a national record for length of service in the nineteenth century. He was the author's great-great-grandfather through another branch of the family.

27 Comment by Peter Godwin, 2002.

28 Information from Kathleen Boult, 2003.

29 E.g. *SA*, 28 November 1903 and 28 November 1908.

30 Comment by Peter Godwin, 2002.

31 Information from Peter Godwin. Although he was born the year Pat Cassidy died, he spoke of him almost as if he had known him, knowledge that had clearly been passed down the family.

32 SBC Burial Records 11/9824 and 11/9967.

33 Stafford RD, Marriage Certificate, 17/203, no. 24: Patrick Duffy and Mary Coleman, 7 October 1850.

34 Stafford RD, Births, July–September 1851, 17/203: Margaret Duffey (*sic*).

35 Divorce on such grounds became available after January 1858 through the Matrimonial Causes Act of 1857, but that would have been of no benefit to Mary Coleman. L. Stone, *Road to Divorce: England, 1530–1987* (Oxford: Oxford University Press, 1990), Chapter 12.

36 Stafford RD, Marriage Certificate, 6b/52, no. 17: John Carroll and Mary Coleman, 17 November 1857.

37 This case documents further the widespread nature of bigamous marriages in nineteenth-century England explored in G. Frost, *Living in Sin: Husbands and Wives in Nineteenth Century England* (Manchester: Manchester University Press, 2008).

38 BAA P255/3/1, Stafford, St Austin's, Register of Marriages, 1848–80: Leonard Birch and Mary Ellen Carroll, 6 May 1884. SBC Burial Records 11/9044 and 10/9528: Rebecca and Leonard Birch (a relative), 1919/20. Stafford RD, Marriages, April–June 1895, 6b/21: James Carroll and Emily Harrison.

39 SBC Burial Record 4/7605.

40 Stafford RD, Marriages, July–September 1868, 6b/29: Patrick Coleman and Winifred Dugmore, 21 September 1868.

41 SBC Burial Records 2/3882, 2/3883, 2/3914 (1871) and 4/6513 (1878).

42 Information from Peter Godwin, 2002. Mr Godwin's mother was Ellen Mary Moore, and Mary Curley was his grandmother. Born in 1921, in 2002 he was able to speak vividly about members of the family whom he had met as a child, and also about family memories handed down about Michael Coleman, Pat Cassidy and Catherine Coleman. It is, however, significant that he knew of no legends about the Famine trauma and why the Colemans came to Stafford, except that that they were supposed to have come from Knock, Co. Mayo.

43 SBC Burial Record 5/8994.

44 Christened Michael Francis, he was known as Frank in his adult life.

45 NA, WO96, Militia Service Record of Michael Francis Coleman, North Staffordshire Regiment, No. 4286, August/September 1898; WO97, Service Record, North Staffordshire Regiment, No. 5728, 23 September 1898–22 September 1910; *FindMyPast* (accessed 23 October 2013).

46 *SA*, 17 and 24 November 1894; information from Peter Godwin, 2002.

47 *SA*, 21 November 1908, 23 and 30 January 1909.

48 St Austin's Church, Stafford, Register of Marriages: James William Coleman and Ada Ann Boydon, 20 August 1899.

49 *SA*, 2 August 1913 and *passim*; Butters and Thomas, *Celebration*, pp. 11–14.

50 Information from Peter Godwin, 2002.

51 BAA P255/1/2: Martin Kelly, 4 October 1848. Thirteen of the eighteen instances of the name in the Griffith's valuation for Mayo were in the four border parishes of Killasser, Kilconduff, Kilbeagh and Kilgarvan.

52 SRO D659/8a/4–5, 17 April 1845–3 February 1849.

53 *Ibid.*

54 SRO D659/1/4/7–8.

55 SRO D659/8a/4–5, 17 April 1845–3 February 1849 (13 November 1847).

56 BAA P255/1/2, Stafford, St Austin's, Register of Baptisms: Martin Kelly, 4 October 1848.

57 BAA, P255/2/1: Patrick Maloney and Cecilia Carabine, 24 August 1850.

58 SRO D240/E/F/4/7, Ingestre General Estate Wages Book, 1848–55. Maloney worked there from 1 to 13 October 1849 and 29 April to 11 May 1850, for which he was paid 10d a day.

59 *SA*, 11 May 1861.

60 *Ibid.*, 13 June 1863.

61 *Ibid.*, 30 July 1859 and 30 June 1866.

62 *Ibid.*, 25 January 1868.

63 *Ibid.*, 21 April 1866.

64 *Ibid.*, 9 October 1875.

65 *Ibid.*, 1, 8 and 29 February 1868.

66 *Ibid.*, 17 July 1875.

67 SBC Burial Record 4/6855.

68 BAA P255/3/1: John Moylan and Mary Kelly, 3 May 1859.

69 SBC Burial Record 4/7502.

70 Information from a descendant, Stanley Lloyd, in Australia, 2003.

71 *SA*, 25 January 1868.

72 SBC Burial Record 3/5807.

73 *SA*, 5 May 1877.

74 *Ibid.*, 11 December 1858.

75 SBC Burial Records 1/1784: Michael Kelly, 27 December 1863; 2/2902: Hannah Kelly, 28 April 1868.

76 *SA*, 9 January 1869.

77 Information from Margaret Porwal née Kelly, Patrick Jr's granddaughter, 2009.

78 Swords, *In their Own Words*, pp. 99 and 106.

79 BAA, P255/1/2: Margaret Jordan, 3 September 1848.

80 SRO D5008/2/7/11/1, Borough of Stafford Poll Book, Elections of 1868 and 1869.

81 *SA*, 15 August 1868.

82 BAA P255/3/1: Patrick Martin and Mary Jordan, 17 May 1860.

83 Information from Russell Trebilcock, December 2004.

84 St Austin's, Stafford, Register of Marriages: Patrick Shea and Elizabeth Jordan, 18 February 1882.

85 *SA*, 1 April 1922; and Stafford RD, Deaths, June 1922, 6b/13: Patrick O'Shea.

86 Report of the inquest, *SA*, 23 May 1868. A verdict of 'suicide whilst in a state of temporary insanity' was recorded.

87 *SA*, 1 February 1868, report of magistrate's court proceedings.

88 *Ibid.*, 29 February 1868, report of Staffordshire Quarter Sessions.
89 There is no obvious record of him in the UK census between 1881 and 1911.
90 SBC Burial Record 11/8497.
91 SBC Burial Record 6/11502.
92 SBC Burial Record 2/2708.
93 SBC Burial Record 5/8974.
94 SBC Burial Record 8/2947.
95 Turnbull, *Trauma*, pp. 56–7, 289–96. M. S. Wylie, 'The long shadow of trauma', *Psychotherapy Networker*, 13 April 2010, www.psychotherapynetworker.org/magazine/recentissues/2010-marapr/item/810-the-long-shadow-of-trauma (accessed 28 October 2011).
96 Herson, 'Family history and memory', pp. 219–20 and 230.

6

Labouring families in the Famine's aftermath, 1852 onwards

The post-Famine families: an overview

The common perception is that most poor Catholic Irish people came to Britain during the Famine, but the pattern of in-migration to Stafford shows the limitations of this view. More labouring families settled in Stafford in the years after 1852 than during the crisis years (Table 4.1). Although the acute phase of the Famine ended around 1851, the forces unleashed by it continued to force people out of the Castlerea area – and Ireland more generally – during the 1850s and for decades afterwards.

The later emigrants had to decide where to go. Those who came to Stafford had therefore decided it was more attractive than elsewhere, at least in the short term. There had to be jobs available, and for the labouring Irish that meant jobs on the farms and building sites. In Chapter 2 we saw that Stafford's economy at this time was prosperous. The farmers were cashing in on the demand for produce from the surrounding industrial areas, but at the same time they were suffering a labour shortage due to English workers leaving for better paid work in the towns. The Irish filled the gap and Stafford's Irish-born population reached its peak around 1861 because a large number of farm labourers arrived during the 1850s. This process continued until the mid-1860s, at which time increasing mechanisation began to reduce the number of farm jobs.[1] Some adapted to the decline in farmwork by shifting their occupation. The booming shoe trade and the service economy meant more jobs in construction and general labouring. Continued Irish settlement in Stafford during the 1850s and early 1860s therefore reflected both the aftermath of the Famine as a 'push' factor and the relative attractiveness of the town as a 'pull' destination.

Fifty-six labouring families settled long-term in Stafford after 1852. Their ultimate fate shows the variation we have already traced in earlier families. Twenty-five of them became integrated into Stafford's working class and another nineteen families were in the middle group that ultimately proved terminal. At the other extreme, twelve families were long-term transients. These figures show interesting trends when compared with the pre-Famine and Famine immigrants. The proportion of families who integrated rose modestly to nearly 45 per cent. By contrast, the proportion of long-term transient families declined from 45 per cent amongst the Famine immigrants to around a fifth amongst those arriving after 1852, and this was offset by a rise in the number of 'terminal' families (Table 4.5). This suggests that the post-Famine arrivals were more committed to settling long-term in Stafford even though a significant minority ultimately died out. The possible reasons for this will be discussed later after we have looked at the history of a representative selection of families who arrived in the post-Famine period. They are:

- the McDermott family;
- Jane Duffy and her labouring families;
- the Walshes;
- the complex McMahon, Mitchell and Shiel family.

The McDermotts: farmwork, drink and survival

A middle-aged couple and their son

The McDermotts nearly faded out but ultimately the family survived to produce a significant number of descendants. Martin and Elizabeth McDermott had been born in the 1810s, and were already middle-aged when they arrived in Stafford in the 1850s. We have no firm evidence about their place of origin, but they lived for many years in Clarke's Court with other families from the Castlerea area. McDermott is a common surname in Co. Roscommon and to a lesser extent Co. Galway, so we can assume the family came from the heartland of Stafford's in-migrants. They were probably forced out during the continuing evictions of the 1850s, and they then had a difficult choice to make. As middle-aged people they were perhaps fearful of setting out into unknown lands overseas, so a better option was to go where they stood a chance of getting familiar work. Stafford fitted the bill. There were three other McDermott families in Stafford around this time whose breadwinners also worked on the farms, and Martin McDermott was probably related to them. Even so, no definite connection has been proved and this family never lived close to their namesakes.

The McDermotts settled with their son Michael who had been born in Ireland in 1852. He was their last surviving child, since Elizabeth was approaching her forties when he was born. They presumably had other children who had either died or were old enough to go their own way before the couple moved to Stafford. They were clearly poor, and they and their descendants remained rooted in the Clarke's Court and Back Walls area until 1920. Even so, Martin's income from farmwork and Elizabeth's work as a washerwoman meant they earned enough to avoid taking in lodgers. They led quiet and modestly respectable lives, and were never in any reported trouble, unlike many of their neighbours in this area. Martin McDermott was involved enough in local affairs to be a registered voter, and rather idiosyncratically he voted Liberal in the 1868 general election but Tory in the 1869 by-election. He may have been impersonated at the poll but, if genuine, his change of vote was probably due to better bribery by the Tories in the second election.

Some time in the early 1870s Martin McDermott had to give up farm-work. The jobs were disappearing and he was now an old man for whom both the walk to the farms and the heavy manual work involved were too onerous. His new job typified how immigrants, then as now, often end up with the dirty work people in the host society will not do. He was taken on at the Borough Surveyor's depot at Coton Field. Stafford still had no effective sewerage system and Coton Field was where the Council's night soil carts offloaded their noisome contents. Martin McDermott's job was to clean the stinking tubs before their next journey into town. For this he was paid 2s 3d a day, the lowest wage of any of the workers in the cleansing department.[2] It must have been miserable and heavy work, and he did not survive long. He died in February 1877. Elizabeth lived on for another twelve years. Both had Catholic funerals.[3]

Second-generation integration and a problematic marriage

Martin's son Michael avoided labouring, becoming a house painter, and his workmates were native Staffordians rather than Irish. At the time of the 1871 Census he was on a job in Crewe with Stafford men. He seems to have worked hard – even to the point of exhaustion. This is shown by an incident at the King's Head pub on Gaolgate Street in 1876. It was a Saturday afternoon and he was there on his own after finishing work. He had a pint or two, but then dropped off to sleep. When he woke up he discovered his hat had been taken from his head and stolen. A tatty old one had replaced it. Luckily the incident had been witnessed by John Whitney, a shoemaker, and the culprit was speedily found. It was James Kearns, one of the notorious denizens of Red Cow Yard whose family we met in Chapter 4. Kearns got twenty-one days for his opportunist crime.[4]

Michael McDermott lived in Clarke's Court with his parents, and latterly with his mother, until 1882. In that year he got married. Despite growing up in a court surrounded by other Irish families Michael's integration was well advanced when he married a Stafford woman, Margaret Ellen Booth. It was a Catholic marriage, though the Booths are not a known Stafford Catholic family. She was one of six children of William Booth, an agricultural labourer from Littleworth just east of Stafford. Like many girls from such a background, Margaret went into service. In 1871 she was working in Stafford for Samson Ecclestone's family in Union Buildings, a dreary locality. By 1881 she had moved to Birmingham and was servant to seventy-three-year-old Peter Bishop, a 'master bridle cutter'. He lived in a mean street behind the meat market. All the signs are that Margaret got poor jobs in very modest households.

Marriage to Michael McDermott was a route out of such work, but it was not a successful union. Margaret proved to be a drinker, and Michael was prone to violence when provoked. This was exposed to public gaze in July 1887 when he was in court for assaulting his wife. It was said he had already given her eight black eyes, and this time he had trampled her and struck her with his fist. The trigger for this mael-strom was that Margaret – or Ellen as she seems to have been known – had secretly pawned Michael's suit and other articles. It turned out she had nineteen tickets for items at Mottram's shop, one of which was for her wedding ring. She admitted 'it was through drink', and the magistrates dismissed the case, leaving Michael the problem of reclaiming the pawned items.[5]

Ellen McDermott fitted well into the drunken and deprived environ-ment of Back Walls North. She was in court in 1889 for being drunk and disorderly on a Saturday night.[6] In 1897 she was in another fracas, although in this case another woman, Emma Burton, was convicted of assaulting her.[7] These scattered incidents show the McDermott house-hold was stressed. The couple had just one child, Elizabeth, who was born in 1884. She grew up in difficult circumstances, and it may have been a blessing when her mother died in October 1897. She was just forty years old. Elizabeth continued to live with, and look after, her father for another twenty years, and it looked as if she was headed for lonely spin-sterhood. She confounded expectations in 1918, however, by marrying John Hardy, a local shoemaker. The couple had six children in quick suc-cession between 1918 and 1924, and there are doubtless descendants. Michael McDermott lived long enough to see his daughter married but died at the beginning of 1919.

The McDermotts: determination and integration

The McDermott family in Stafford survived two generations of single chil-dren to expand again in the twentieth century, although the McDermott name itself died with Michael in 1919. What were the factors that deter-mined the history of this family? Martin and Elizabeth McDermott were middle-aged emigrants who were superficially similar to many other Irish families forced out during the Famine, yet they hung on into the 1850s and finally came to Stafford as a rump of a family with just their son Michael. Their lives in Stafford suggest Martin and Elizabeth McDermott had some grit and determination.

They did the poorest jobs and lived in one of the poorest areas in a strongly Irish environment. Their poverty meant they could never leave the locality yet they insulated themselves from it to a substan-tial degree. Their cottage in Clarke's Court may have been small and crummy, but it was a *home* to them alone, undisturbed by a turnover of lodgers. Michael could grow up in a relatively secure environment, and he emerged as an independent person who aspired to escape the limited horizon of his father. Although house painting was a modest job, it carried a degree of skill and brought Michael into contact with native Staffordians.

It was ironic that Michael's marriage to an Englishwomen brought the next generation to the brink of disaster. Although Michael did not stop his wife's love for the bottle, he did nevertheless protect himself and their daughter from its worst effects. The fact that Elizabeth stayed at home until her marriage in 1918 can, of course, be interpreted in two ways. On the one hand, she could have been tied there as a ser-vant to her domineering father. On the other hand, she possibly stayed out of loyalty and mutual support developed during the difficult years before Ellen died. The fact that, in the end, Elizabeth did leave to get married suggests she had independent spirit when the right situation arose.

The McDermotts were Catholics but we have no evidence of how religion influenced their lives and identity. There are no reports of any involvement in the Church's social activities, but for a poor family this was not unusual. Elizabeth McDermott attended St Patrick's School and felt the force of the Church's attempts to stop leakage amongst working-class Catholics. The family's descendants merged seamlessly into the partly Catholic working class of Stafford. Although Martin and Elizabeth McDermott must have remained clearly Irish after their arrival in Stafford, their son had no particular attachment to his Irish heritage. The limited evidence suggests he grew up and lived his life as a working-class Staffordian and that this outlook was passed on to his daughter and the succeeding generations. We have seen in other families that it was the women who primarily determined the values and norms passed on to the next generation. In the small McDermott family the male played the more important role.

Jane Duffy and her labouring families

Irish women and English men

Irish settlement in Stafford was always biased towards men because there were more unskilled jobs in the local economy for immigrant men than for women. Lone Irish women seeking work, particularly in domestic service, would find better prospects in the bigger cities and in more fashionable towns. This imbalance was reflected in the town's settled Irish families in that there were only twenty-four where an Irish woman partnered an English man, around 12 per cent of the total. Only nine of those families were created in Stafford itself. The other fifteen 'female-mixed' families were partnerships established elsewhere in England or, in two cases, in Ireland.

Without exhaustive searches and considerable luck it can be difficult to trace the origins of single Irish women forming partnerships with English men. In only five of the nine Stafford-born partnerships is it possible to identify unambiguous marriage evidence. The most interesting case is that of Mary O'Brien (or Bryan). Born in Waterford around 1801, she came to Stafford around 1830. On 27 September 1835 she married Charles Ilsley, a shoemaker, who came from an English Catholic family. His uncles were a schoolmaster and a priest, so he had influential contacts to help his children. Even so, the Ilsleys lived in poor circumstances in Appleyard Court off Tipping Street. There they brought up five children, one of whom was Edward (b. 1838). He became a priest and progressed up the Catholic hierarchy to become Bishop of Birmingham in 1888 and the first Archbishop of the diocese in 1911.[8] This family's history was exceptional but it emphasises the diversity of the female-mixed families. Seven were labouring families, but approximately equal numbers of the rest were in the shoe trade or in other craft, clerical or service occupations. Only two of the women are known to have come from Connacht, about half were Protestant and only one arrived during the Famine. In these ways they deviated from the mass of labouring families from the west who formed the bedrock of Stafford's Irish immigrant population. Over half the female-mixed families survived to integrate into the host society, a higher proportion than the average, but one-third were, nevertheless, long-term transients.

There were, of course, many instances in Stafford where Irish-born daughters from settled families formed partnerships with both Irish and English men. These women could continue to draw on the support and obligations of their kin, and numerous cases are described in this book. Lone Irish women forming such partnerships were, however, more isolated and vulnerable. As outsiders, their lives were shaped by the nature of the relationship with their partner and how they were accepted by his wider family if it was present. The case of Jane Duffy demonstrates some of the problems such women could face.

A baby's death

On 22 September 1853 Jane Duffy married George Moore at St Austin's Church.[9] It is unclear how she arrived in Stafford because there was no family with that name in the town in 1851. In 1861 she claimed she had been born in 1832 in Co. Longford, an unusual place of origin for Stafford's Irish; in 1881 she was vaguer and said 'Leinster'. This gives us some evidence to go on and in 1851 we find a servant named Jane Duffy at New Ferry on the Wirral. Her age tallies and her place of birth is given as Dublin, also in Leinster. She was working for John Trumper, his wife and middle-aged son. Trumper, a retired farmer, was then eighty-five years old and he died in the autumn of 1852.[10] Jane probably lost her job at that point, but the Trumpers came from Herefordshire and would have had contacts in the rural Midlands. That may be why, within a year, Jane had appeared in Stafford and, at the time of her marriage, was living at no. 2 Malt Mill Lane. It was a lodging house and George Moore was living at the same address. We can presume the two young people met there.

Moore was a local man. His father James was a farm labourer and his family lived round the corner in Back Walls North, but in 1851 George was working on a farm at Doxey on the western outskirts of Stafford. Jane Duffy therefore married into a poor local family whose prospects were limited. Some time before 1861 the couple moved to the Broad Eye, much closer to Doxey. There they proceeded to have two sons, William (b. 1855) and John (b. 1858). It seemed as though the family had settled into a modest and largely unrecorded existence in that poor part of town. Things changed, however. In 1864 George died and Jane was left a widow with two young children.[11] She had to find work and she inevitably went back to the only job she knew, domestic service. Who looked after her children when she was at work? The answer is Harriet Moore. She was the second wife of George's father, James, who had married her in 1851 after the death of his first wife.[12] In the 1850s James and Harriet Moore followed his son's family to the Broad Eye, but old James died in 1868.[13] By 1871 the widowed Harriet was living, with just a lodger for company, at no. 47 Broad Eye, four doors down from Jane. The two women were roughly the same age. In her predicament Jane could call on Harriet for kinship support and the latter gave it – after a fashion.

Jane was a poor and vulnerable woman open to exploitation. In 1870 she became pregnant and the following summer she had a baby boy, Charles. His birth was not registered and his father's name went unrecorded, although it was claimed he gave 10s a month for the baby's maintenance.[14] Within three months Charles was dead. The inquest revealed a miserable state of affairs. Jane Moore was now working in Burslem in the Potteries and Harriet was looking after Charles. On 21 September she took him to a surgeon who gave her a ticket for the infirmary. By the time she reached hospital Charles had died. Examination showed he was 'in an exceedingly emaciated condition' and weighed only 5 lb 12 oz, half the normal weight for a three-month old baby. He had starved to death. Who was to blame? Jane Moore claimed the child had been 'a small and weakly one from its birth and it had been troubled with thrush and frequently vomited its food'. Harriet Moore claimed she had fed Charles on 'arrowroot, corn-flour and new milk every day'. The medical men doubted the truth of this but also suggested the baby might have been allergic to cow's milk. It was clear, however, that Charles had really died from neglect. Although the inquest jury found that the baby had died from 'inanition', the coroner followed up by saying Harriet Moore had narrowly escaped being tried for manslaughter.

Charles Moore's death lifts a curtain on the Duffy–Moore families and the deprived community in which they lived. As a servant, Jane was vulnerable to the sexual predations of her employers. The 10s-a-month maintenance may have been the pay-off from such a man. Charles was an unwanted baby, and if he died a troublesome burden would be removed. 'Several witnesses living in the vicinity corroborated the principal portion of [Jane's] evidence' that the child was weakly. Not surprising. It was a street of poor families, a number of whom were Irish. Jane's problem was one they could sympathise with and they stuck together with a consistent story. Jane and Harriet also confused the authorities and the newspaper with inconsistencies over Harriet's name. In the *Staffordshire Advertiser* report of the inquest she was never identified as 'Harriet Moore' but variously as 'Martha Tavenor' and 'Martha Moore', neither of whom existed.[15] After the inquest Harriet covered her tracks. She was not recorded in either the 1881 or 1891 censuses with any likely name or location and disappears from the historical record until she died in Stafford in 1893.[16]

Jane Moore stayed on in the Broad Eye, doubtless as a charwoman or servant. Her two sons left home and the town of Stafford in the early 1870s. They probably emigrated. It is clear they had no lasting commitment to their mother. At this point Jane might have sunk further into lonely and poverty-stricken widowhood, but her life was to have a final twist. In 1876 she remarried. Her new husband was John Trevedon, a labourer at the gas works who was lodging four doors away. He is an elusive character. Born in 1836 near Callington in Cornwall, he began work as a miner but in 1855 joined the Royal Artillery. He was, however, discharged in 1858 as unfit to serve owing to a heart defect. His conduct up to then had been 'very good'.[17] After that he disappears from history until he turns up for his wedding at St Austin's Church on 26 August 1876.[18] There is no obvious reason why this West Countryman settled in Stafford but there are two possible explanations. He may have managed to rejoin the army and been posted to the Militia Barracks, though no further army service record has been found. By contrast, he may have been released after time in Stafford Gaol, though no criminal record has been traced.

The newly-weds continued to live in the Broad Eye and the 1881 Census shows John still working at the gas works. The marriage was not to last, however. Circumstantial evidence suggests John deserted his wife in 1881/82 and emigrated, perhaps to America.[19] On 13 September 1882 the lone Jane 'Tributon' was admitted as a pauper to Stafford Workhouse.[20] It was the end of her life's road from Co. Longford. She died there in March 1884, aged just fifty-two.[21]

The stresses of a female-mixed family

Jane Duffy represents just one of hundreds of thousands of young single women who emigrated from Ireland in the second half of the nineteenth century. She was forced out by both the Famine crisis and the decline of the communal farming economy in rural Ireland. Illiterate girls like her had only their labour power to sell, and Jane, also like many others, went into domestic service. Such work put her into close contact with people from the host society. Her sense of self gained from a Catholic and country family background was immediately challenged by the alien values of urban England. At a simple level she responded flexibly by moving to the Wirral and then to Stafford, but her outlook became potentially anomic with her loss of traditional moral reference points and sudden shift into the bottom reaches of the Stafford working class. Her family economy depended on the low and uncertain earning of her labourer husbands supplemented by work as a charwoman when money was short. She was a victim of the common but capricious forces of Victorian society – early death, desertion and male sexual predation. Her kinship network revolved around her adopted English family and the ethnically mixed population of the Broad Eye. The family's stability in that locality – common to other families too – suggests a mutually supportive community that closed up against unwelcome threats from outside. The behaviour of neighbours over Charles's death demonstrates that. Yet we also see the brutalising effects on family life of poverty and uncertainty in such a community. No public remorse was shown by Jane, Harriet or anybody else over Charles's death. Although Jane was Catholic, the death meant so little that his burial was a perfunctory affair conducted by an Anglican minister.[22]

She probably did not even attend. It is unlikely there were any mourners at Jane's burial either, although she did get a Catholic ceremony.

The family lives of Irish women who married English men have largely passed unrecognised into history but case studies in this book have already demonstrated the importance of women in determining family values and behaviour. That would also have been the case in 'female-mixed' families, and Jane Duffy probably played such a role in her family. Jane Duffy was no Jane Kelly, however. Until Charles Moore's death the family led poor, unpublicised and unremarkable lives. There is no reason to think that Jane and George did not build a nurturing home until the latter's death sundered it. Seven years later Charles's inquest exposed the hard environment of Jane's residual household and its social network. What is clear is that the survival demands imposed on this Irish woman after her arrival in Stafford forced her to assimilate into the English society she had entered. Her heritage was Irish but her identity ceased to be so. It was a strictly instrumental strategy and it built no commitment to Stafford society in her children. The family created by Jane Duffy, George Moore and John Trevedon proved to be a transient unit.

The Walshes: a family who rejected Stafford

Family connections: the Walshes and the Mannions

The Walsh family is unique amongst the Stafford Irish in leaving explicit evidence that it continued to identify with Ireland and Irish national-ist issues. Stafford's social environment was unattractive to such people, and the Walshes ultimately left. Even so, they stayed in Stafford for over twenty years.

John Walsh, a Galway man, married Mary Mannion in Ireland in the late 1850s (Figure 6.1). The newly established Walsh–Mannion partner-ship then became a link in the chain migration of the extensive Mannion family from Co. Galway to Stafford. Most of the Mannions put down roots in the town, and there are many descendants of the family today. The Walshes did not conform to the family pattern, however, and we need to examine why they broke the mould and emigrated.

Patrick Mannion was the family's pathfinder. As we saw in Chapter 2, he and the Walshes may have been victims of the Gerrard evictions in 1846. Patrick was a labourer aged about forty whose wife had died during the Famine. In 1851 he was living in Raftery's lodging house in Allen's Court. That family also came from Co. Galway. Patrick was still a seasonal migrant worker, and during the 1850s his sons Patrick (b. 1836), Martin (b. 1839) and Michael (b. 1841) also came over for seasonal work.[23] In April 1861 Patrick father and son were in Edward Kelly's lodging house

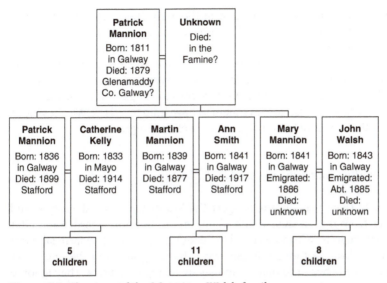

Figure 6.1 The stem of the Mannion–Walsh family

in Snow's Yard. The economy of Stafford was buoyant at this time as farming prospered and the shoe trade expanded. That was the incentive for the Mannions to settle permanently in Stafford. Martin's wife Ann and their young children Michael and Mary arrived some time in 1861.[24] Then Patrick Mannion's daughter Mary came with her husband, John Walsh. They already had a son, Michael, who had been born in Ireland in 1860, but the couple went on to have seven more children in Stafford. In 1859 Patrick junior had married Kitty (Catherine) Kelly, a member of the Kelly family discussed in Chapter 5. Kitty seems to have returned to Ireland after the wedding, but she had settled in Stafford by the end of 1862 because her one-year-old child died in the town. We see, therefore, that the Mannions' process of settlement was drawn out, but from around 1863 there were three branches of the family living in Stafford, all of them initially in Snow's Yard.

The Mannion family remained for many years an integral part of the deprived and sometimes violent Snow's Yard community. Patrick Jr's squalid death in the yard in 1899 was recounted at the start of this book. We now need to see how and why the Walshes broke free from this problematic family embrace, left Snow's Yard and ultimately emigrated. Answering these questions is not easy but a key element must have been the personal characters of John Walsh and Mary Mannion and how they responded to the challenges and opportunities facing them. All we know from the surviving evidence is that John and his family were feisty people who asserted themselves in pursuit of their interests and beliefs. As immigrants to Britain in the early 1860s, they had survived the worst of the Famine and its aftermath, but had seen at first hand the burdens of landlord power, poverty and eviction. They had also been open to the nationalism of Daniel O'Connell, the Young Irelanders, the Tenants' Rights movement and the early Irish Parliamentary Party. The Fenians were also starting their underground organisation at this time. These forces for Irish identity seem to have influenced the Walshes much more than most of Stafford's poor Catholic immigrants.

The Walshes' independence and Irish identity

Initially there was little to suggest the Walsh family's trajectory would differ from that of their rough Mannion kin in Snow's Yard. Soon after his arrival John Walsh was fined for assaulting John Kelly, a farm labourer from Galway. Although Walsh was a building labourer, he and Mary immediately began to making money by taking in lodgers. They ignored the legal regulations and in July 1862 John was fined for keeping an unregistered lodging house. Five years later he was in court again for not whitewashing or cleansing his premises in Snow's Yard.

John Walsh had another life on the building sites. There he stuck up for workers' rights. In 1871 the trade unions' 'nine-hour day' campaign swept through the country like a bush fire, and John Walsh was involved in an incident in Stafford.[25] In August 1871 he and another Irish man, Thomas Carney, were charged with 'molesting' Isaac Rushton, a building foreman. The men were working for Francis Ratcliffe, a builder who employed many Irish workers and was also a slum landlord. Rushton had 'asked' the workers on site to work overtime, but Walsh and Carney tried to get the men to stick to the nine-hour day. When they were present the men went along with them but they later capitulated under pressure from the foreman. Walsh and Carney responded with 'a volley of abuses and threats' against the workers and the foreman. They were charged under the new Criminal Law Amendment Act but avoided prison by agreeing to pay the expenses of the hearing.[26] The case would have confirmed John Walsh's hostility to the power of the British ruling class both in Ireland and against workers in Britain.

John and Mary Walsh clearly wanted to leave the hopeless squalor of Snow's Yard. The final incentive to get out came in 1877 when the family suffered a triple tragedy. Three of their young children, John (b. 1871), Stephen (b. 1872) and Margaret (b. 1875) died within two days of each other. They succumbed to fatal infections that spread easily in that overcrowded and rat-infested slum.[27] The event must have traumatised the family since there is every indication that John and Mary Walsh were conscientious and loving parents. By 1881 three of the surviving children had got jobs in the shoe trade and they showed every sign of upward occupational and social mobility. Their earnings contributed to the family income and bolstered its economic security. John himself must have managed a relatively secure income even in the precarious building trade. All this meant that some time between 1877 and 1881 the family gave up the lodging house and shifted well away from Snow's Yard. They moved into no. 34 Cooperative Street, a house located on the northern edge of town. Although it was next to the workhouse, this was an area of new and solid by-law housing mostly occupied by shoemakers and other artisanal workers. Almost all were English.

It was a massive step up for the family. To help with the costs they still needed to take a lodger and in 1881 they had a young Irish bricklayer's labourer who probably worked with John Walsh. Even so, living in Cooperative Street meant they were able to create a civilised home in the house. Their move was not just geographical, however. It suggests they also wanted to distance themselves socially from their less respectable relatives in Snow's Yard. Members of the Mannion family had numerous brushes with the law during the 1870s and 1880s, but the Walshes were never involved. The kinship bonds were breaking and there is no evidence that the Walshes felt any obligation to help their more deprived relations. The impression is of an independent and increasingly confident family anxious to move on to other things. For most such Irish families in Stafford this meant seeking respectability and acceptance by downplaying their Irish origins. The Walshes did the opposite – they publicly affirmed their Irish identity.

In January 1881 Gladstone's Government introduced the Coercion Bill, which would suspend habeas corpus in Ireland and threatened the mass internment of 'suspects'. It was the Government's response to the campaign of the Irish Land League and the 'agrarian outrages' taking place during the Land War. In February there were fierce debates in Parliament, and Charles Stewart Parnell galvanised the Irish Parliamentary Party into unified and effective opposition. The Speaker's response was to impose the first ever guillotine on debate, something described at the time as a coup d'état.[28] For Irish nationalists it was yet further evidence that the British would always bend the rules to repress Irish nationalism.

These events brought a small flurry of activity amongst the Irish even in Stafford, and John Walsh was at the centre of it. On 12 February 'a numerously attended meeting' was held at the Slipper Inn in the town centre. Walsh presided and proposed two resolutions:

> That we, the Irish electors of Stafford, record our indignant protest against the Coercion Bill introduced by the so-called Liberal Government in order to place a weapon in the hands of the landlord-magistracy of Ireland to crush the just aspirations of a cruelly persecuted people.

That we, the Irish electors of Stafford, tender our grateful thanks to the senior representative of this Borough (Alexander McDonald Esq.) for his noble advocacy and defence of the just claims of the Irish people, and we acknowledge the debt of gratitude due from us to that gentleman who, though suffering from recent illness, generously stood by our countrymen in combating the tyrannical Coercion Bill introduced by the so-called Liberal Government.

The meeting passed the resolutions and agreed to form a branch of the Irish National Land League in Stafford.[29]

This was tepid stuff by the standards of militant Irish nationalism but it was, nevertheless, one of only two documented instances of clearly *Irish nationalist* political activity in nineteenth-century Stafford. The other had occurred in 1876, also at the Slipper Inn, when there was a fight between different factions during an Irish Home Rule Association meeting. The ringleader was James Garra, 'a tall stout-built young Irishman who for a number of years has been employed in and around Stafford'.[30] A farm labourer, he later settled in the Cannock area.[31] His presence reminds us that initially transient and short-term-settled Irish people were always present in Stafford, although in diminishing numbers. Walsh was clearly the instigator of the 1881 Land League meeting. It reveals his continuing identification with Ireland's sufferings and that he was able to motivate others to show at least minimal support for action. The results would have disappointed him. There is no evidence that a functioning branch of the Land League was actually established in Stafford, or that Walsh or anyone else publicly espoused the Irish cause again in the town. Although it was possible to get Irish Catholic workers – mostly the young and migrant – to attend political gatherings in pubs, the Stafford Irish and their descendants were too few and too thin on the ground to nurture committed and effective nationalist activity. The social environment was fundamentally unsupportive. Long-term settlement in Stafford meant rejecting active and overt involvement in the Irish national cause. There was no future in it. People had to move elsewhere if they wanted to retain and transmit such an Irish identity.

That is what John Walsh and his family did. Despite their obvious ability to succeed in Stafford, the family left the town and emigrated to America in 1886.[32] We must beware of imputing purely political reasons for this. They would have read the economic signs. The shoe trade was past its heyday and suffering from foreign competition.[33] West Midland industry generally was depressed in the 1880s, and many people from Staffordshire were emigrating.[34] The local newspapers had frequent advertisements for passages to the Americas and Australasia.[35] Even so, Stafford's social scene was uncongenial to John and Mary Walsh. They had left the Irish environment of Snow's Yard but they also rejected the move to English identity and social conformity shown by other aspirant and respectable Catholics. The Walshes reckoned they could do better elsewhere.

McMahon, Mitchell and Shiel: one family, different outcomes

We now return to Snow's Yard yet again to see what happened to another extended family from Co. Galway who settled in Stafford more than ten years after the Famine. We shall see that one part of the family – the Mitchells – aspired to leave the deprived immigrant environment and find respectability, whilst the other – the Shiels – remained trapped in the slum. In their different ways both sides of the family nevertheless integrated into Stafford society. Kinship bonds were not broken. The branch that did well came to identify strongly with the problems and aspirations of Stafford's people, including the Irish poor and their descendants. The other branch merged into the town's working class.

Three Galway families emerge in Stafford

In 1861 Martin Mitchell was working as a seasonal farm labourer in the Stafford area. He was then about fifty-two years of age. He lodged with the Hart family at no. 4 Allen's Court along with two other migrant farm-workers. The Harts had been Famine immigrants to Stafford from Co. Galway; Martin Mitchell was almost certainly from the same area and knew them directly or through contacts. He was a married man, and we can presume that his wife and family were back in Ireland on a holding they had managed to retain, and perhaps expand, in Famine times. The name Martin Mitchell was not common in the rural west, but the Griffith's Valuation shows a land-holder with that name holding around twelve acres of scattered land in the townlands of Island East and Lettera, Templetogher parish, Co. Galway.[36] In 1871 Martin's son John said he had been born in Dunmore, the parish next to Templetogher. It seems, therefore, that the family came from that locality.

Martin Mitchell was not recorded in Stafford again, though he probably still came for harvest work during the 1860s. His son John (b. 1849) started to come over with him (Figure 6.2). Initially John also worked on the farms but such jobs were disappearing by the late 1860s. He had to do something else, and he became a bricklayer, a distinct jump in skill that epitomised the spirit of initiative that was present in the Mitchell family. John Mitchell was certainly in Stafford by 1869, because in that year he married Bridget McMahon at St Austin's Church. In 1871 the newly married couple was living with Bridget's family at no. 8 Snow's Yard.

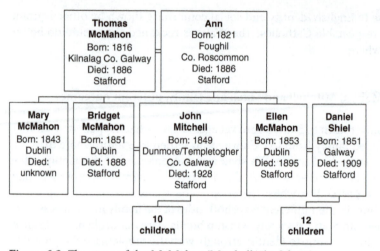

Figure 6.2 The stem of the McMahon/Mitchell/Shiel families

The McMahons originally came from the same area as the Mitchells. Thomas McMahon was born around 1816 in Kilnalag, a townland in Templetogher parish about two miles south of Island East. He married before he came to Britain. His wife was Ann (surname unknown), who was born around 1821, probably in Foughil, a townland in Kiltullagh parish, Co. Roscommon. This was adjacent to the McMahon and Mitchell area of origin.[37] The newly married couple were victims of the land hunger of pre-Famine times, and, like members of the Kearns family discussed in Chapter 4, they moved to Dublin. Dublin was a poor and stagnant city with an overcrowded labour market and most people leaving the impoverished west tended to emigrate either to Britain or overseas. The McMahons bucked the trend, however. They were already living in Dublin by 1843, because their first known child, Mary, was born there in that year. Their two subsequent children, Bridget and Ellen, were also born in Dublin in 1851 and 1853 respectively. Thomas must have managed to find labouring jobs in Dublin for a number of years, but they nevertheless retained their family and social links with Galway. They probably knew the Mitchell family already, and it may have been Martin or John Mitchell who encouraged them to emigrate to Stafford. The move took place some time in the mid-1860s because by 1868 Thomas McMahon was registered to vote in Stafford.[38] Their direct move to the town demonstrates the continuing strength of the connection between Stafford and the Castlerea area.

The McMahon–Mitchell household was superficially similar to others in Snow's Yard. Their one advantage was that the three children were of working age and could contribute to the family income. Mary and

Ellen McMahon both worked as domestic servants, although they seem to have depended on casual 'coming in' work rather than more secure, if exploited, work 'living in' with employers. Mary left Stafford some time in the 1870s, but neither her subsequent address nor any marriage have been traced. Ellen may have fallen victim to an employer's sexual demands, since in 1872 she had an illegitimate child, Thomas. Despite this, in 1874 she married Daniel Shiel, another Galway man, who arrived in Stafford some time between 1871 and 1874.[39] He worked as a bricklayer's labourer and probably lodged in the McMahon household or in one of the others in Snow's Yard. After their marriage Ellen and Daniel set up house next door to the McMahons at no. 9.

The troubled history of the Shiel family

The McMahon–Mitchell and Shiel households were part of the fractious community of Snow's Yard but old Thomas and Ann McMahon tried to avoid the worst of the disorder. They were never prosecuted for involvement in 'Irish Rows', and this suggests they kept themselves to themselves as far as possible. Nevertheless, things got very tight for Thomas and Ann once their children left, and they started running an unlicensed lodging house to make ends meet. In 1878 they were prosecuted after a police raid found four men lodging there. It was not their first offence, and despite Ann's protestations that she would get the house registered, the couple carried on in the murky underworld of unlicensed lodgings.[40] These were the miserable circumstances in which the McMahons lived out their last years. They died within ten days of each other in May 1886 and both had burial services at the Catholic Church.[41]

Ellen and Daniel Shiel continued to inhabit Snow's Yard, and their family did get sucked into the troubled and deprived lifestyle of their neighbours. In 1881 Ann Mannion and Ellen Shiel had a fight:

> The Irish element preponderated in this case and great amusement was caused in court by the effervescence of the parties … It appears the quarrel originated in the Red Cow Inn. Mannion then went to her house, and when Ellen Shiels [*sic*] passed her window she struck her with a mop and threw some water over her, whereupon the latter attempted to force the door and struck Mannion a violent blow with her fist.

Ellen Shiel got off the assault charge but she was fined for being drunk.[42] Such goings-on inevitably influenced the Shiels' children, and their sons got into numerous scrapes. In 1891 Patrick (b. 1879) persistently truanted from St Patrick's School. The case revealed much about the Shiels' circumstances. When his father was brought before the magistrates he pleaded 'he could do nothing with the lad'. The boy had not been at home for at least five days and 'had to be forcibly brought home'. Clearly, Patrick was desperate to get away, but his efforts merely resulted in his being sent to a 'truant school' in Liverpool. His father was ordered to pay 6d a week for his upkeep, a considerable burden since Daniel claimed to be earning only 20s a week at the time. In other words, the family was in grinding poverty.[43] When Patrick reached the age of thirteen he was discharged from the school and came back to Stafford where, in September 1891, he was immediately up before the magistrates for stealing apples.[44] More seriously, in May 1892 Patrick and an English boy were charged with stealing a watch and chain at the public baths. Patrick then pawned the watch for 3s and sold the chain to a militiaman. His parents elected to have the case dealt with summarily since Patrick 'had been in an industrial school recently because his parents could not control him'. He was sent to a reformatory for five years.[45] Patrick Shiel's behaviour was recognisably that of a wild youth growing up in deprived and amoral circumstances.

Daniel and Ellen Shiel clearly had problems coping with their growing family. Ellen bore twelve children between 1872 and 1894, five of whom died in infancy. For her, life was a grinding succession of pregnancies surrounded by squalling children in an overcrowded slum. The Red Cow would have been a welcome diversion, despite alcohol's impact on the next child to be born. Then, in 1895, Ellen died. She was only in her early forties and was worn out by work, pregnancies and drink. Daniel was left to struggle on with his unruly offspring, the youngest of whom was only a toddler. There were bound to be more problems, but he managed to see his surviving children into adulthood before he died, aged fifty-eight, in 1909. Both Ellen and Daniel were buried with Catholic rites. To that extent they had retained an adherence to the Church and passed it on to their children. There is, however, little evidence that the Church's teachings, spiritual support or social activities played any significant role in their day-to-day lives. The Shiels were the type of working-class family in Stafford's north end in danger of 'leaking' from the Church. The only antidote was Catholic education, and the Shiel children went to St Patrick's School. We have, however, seen that, in Patrick's case at least, going to school was no more attractive than life at home.

Patrick Shiel's brothers Daniel (b. 1880), John (b. 1883) and William (b. 1891) got into trouble for illegal gambling, disturbing the peace and wilful damage. These documented cases were presumably only the tip of an iceberg of disruptive behaviour picked up by neglected children in the general environment of Snow's Yard.[46] A case of illegal gambling in 1909 is revealing because it gives an indication of John Shiel's peer group. Was he trapped in the transmitted deprivation of an Irish enclave? The answer is no. Of the five youths involved, one, John Raftery, was from a Stafford Irish family. The other three, Walter Hawkins, Wilfred Williamson and Alfred Ferneyhough, were from English families. They were poor

Staffordian working class, and that was the class to which Shiel family now belonged. John and Daniel Shiel began their adult lives doing exactly the same job as their father – bricklayer's labourer. It is not known what became of them in later life. Two other children did marry in Stafford. Ellen (b. 1895) married a William Woolley in 1911 and James Shiel (b. 1894) married Helen Edwards in 1918. Although the marriages took place at St Patrick's Church, both partners were Protestant and English. This is more evidence that the Shiel family had moved into the Stafford working class.

The Mitchells struggle out of Snow's Yard

So far, the picture presented of the McMahon/Mitchell/Shiel family shows a deprived existence in a poor slum from which descendants escaped, with some difficulty, into the twentieth-century Staffordian working class. Such a trajectory was not universal, however. The history of the Mitchell branch of the family was to be different.

Bridget and John Mitchell lived for a time with their McMahon in-laws in Snow's Yard, but, as a bricklayer, John had a saleable skill and could hope to make better money than his labouring father and father-in-law. Once children started to arrive the Mitchells were desperate to move, and some time in the 1870s they rented no. 11 Sash Street. This was a mean street on the other side of Foregate Street that had been home to numerous Irish families since the Famine. Even so, it was a step up from Snow's Yard. The Mitchells went on to have ten children, although four died in infancy and their first-born, Mary Ellen, died in her early thirties when she was still living at home (Figure 6.3). Bridget Mitchell's married life therefore echoed her sister Ellen's – a succession of pregnancies and the burden of rearing a brood of sickly children in an overcrowded cottage. When he was in work, John Mitchell would have earned reasonable money, but the building trade was volatile and he doubtless had spells out of work. Things got so bad that they were forced back into Snow's Yard, for they were recorded as living at no. 10 in 1885.[47] They managed to move out again shortly afterwards and levered themselves into a house in New Street. That brought little joy, however, for Bridget Mitchell died in 1888.[48] Like Ellen Shiel, she must have been worn out by a hard life in unhealthy, cramped conditions.

John Mitchell and his family nevertheless had aspirations and an independent spirit. Arguably, they had a family strategy to leave their poor Irish background by making use of Stafford's social networks. A portent of this occurred during the 1885 general election. It was the year the Irish Parliamentary Party under Charles Stewart Parnell endorsed the Tories in the mistaken belief that they might deliver Home Rule. As usual, the

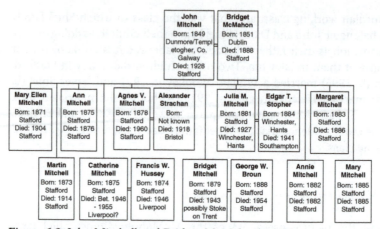

Figure 6.3 John Mitchell and Bridget McMahon's children

election in Stafford was a torrid affair. John Mitchell, a politically aware man, responded to Parnell's tactical shift and voted Tory. This was known to the people in Snow's Yard and on election day, 25 November, he was 'subjected to violent treatment by George Dale, a fish dealer, and other denizens of the yard because he had incurred the displeasure of his neighbours'. Mitchell, in turn, was accused of having 'used offensive expressions with reference to [Dale's] political opinions' and struck him on the ear whilst also bespattering his wife with mud. John's sister-in-law, Ellen Shiel, then 'shielded him as best she could, dragged him into the house, and while dragging him in … received on her left arm a kick … aimed at Mitchell'. Ann Mannion alleged that 'Mitchell would have been a dead man but for the intervention of Mrs Shiel'. Bridget Mitchell was also there. She was wearing a Tory ribbon and Dale assaulted her as well. He received fines totaling 15s for his political anger.[49]

This incident shows three things. The first is that John Mitchell and his wife were politically aware and probably still identified with Irish political issues. More significantly, they were independent-minded. They were prepared to step publicly outside the social culture of Snow's Yard. Nevertheless, and thirdly, kinship bonds and obligations were still important. The Mitchells may have had obvious aspirations to leave the Snow's Yard community, but the support of Ellen Shiel and the favourable evidence of Ann Mannion suggests they were still respected there. The family's later history continued to demonstrate these features.

Martin Mitchell: entrepreneur, activist and politician

There is a direct comparison to be made between Daniel Shiel and John Mitchell. Both their wives died young, and both were left to bring up a

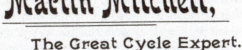

A SHORT BIOGRAPHY
OF A
FAMOUS STAFFORDIAN.

Martin Mitchell,

The Great Cycle Expert.

BEFORE commencing business, had a thorough practical and theoretical engineering training. In 1896, became official cycle expert to the "Exchange & Mart." Writer of special articles on cycling to leading journals. Well-known and deservedly-popular as musician and entertainer. Member of Town Council (6 years), and Board of Guardians. His customers find that they secure reliable quality and absolute fairness.

Figure 6.4 Martin Mitchell: 'The Great Cycle Expert' from an advertisement in *Hibbert's Handbook of Stafford*, 1906

young family on their own. As we have seen, Daniel Shiel's relationship with his children was problematic. He probably tried to control them by brute force, but it was ineffective and they got into trouble. We do not know John Mitchell's parental tactics, but all the evidence points to a desire to build a strong, respectable family. He and his children were regular churchgoers, and the Church's social activities played an important role in their lives. Though John and Bridget Mitchell were themselves handicapped by their impoverished origins – John Mitchell, for example, never learned to write – they saw to it that their children seized the opportunities that were on offer.[50] Their only son, Martin (b. 1873), was to prove the spearhead of the family's advancement.

Martin Mitchell went to St Patrick's School. As the son of deserving Catholic parents, he was encouraged by his teachers. He was an extrovert with a talent for singing and entertainment, and in 1888 we find him as one of the principal characters in a play, 'Bluebeard', put on at Christmas by the Catholic Boys' Club. Of the five named principals, three were from Irish families and two from English ones. Though coming from a solidly Irish background, Mitchell was already part of a mixed social network. His sense of self was moulded by his childhood amongst the Irish of Snow's Yard and the poverty they endured, but also by the opportunities open to him through Stafford's social network, especially the Catholic Church. He benefited too from Stafford's economic diversification. Rather than going into the troubled boot-and-shoe trade, he opted for an engineering apprenticeship, almost certainly at Dorman's engineering works on Foregate Street. This gave him a skill to exploit, and some time in the mid-1890s he saw an opening in the cycling craze then sweeping the country. He set up as a cycle engineer and agent, and in 1896 was 'official cycle expert to the *Exchange and Mart*' sales magazine. By 1900 he had a shop in Crabbery Street in the town centre, and he later moved to a prominent site in Greengate Street. In the 1900s he was styling himself as 'The Great Cycle Expert' (Figure 6.4).[51] He had annual cycle exhibitions and was naturally very active in the Stafford Cycle Club.[52] Martin Mitchell became, in other words, an effective entrepreneur with a flair for publicity but also, it seems, with a reputation for good service and fair dealing. They were qualities he could use in other fields.

We have already seen Martin Mitchell entertaining people when he was young and he continued to do this all through his life. His fine bass voice and entertainment routines were to be heard at all sorts of social gatherings. Even so, he was not just an artist out for hire to anybody who would pay him. Rather, he seems to have given his services to organisations and occasions with which he sympathised. He performed down the years at workhouse concerts, trade-union socials, Catholic soirées, the Gladstone Club, the Reform Club and for many sports organisations. During the Boer War he arranged a 'patriotic concert' in aid of the borough war fund. These venues indicate a man concerned for the plight of the poor; supportive of trade unions; supportive of political Liberalism; and, above all, active in self-improvement through sport. His Boer War concert shows him at that time identifying publicly with British patriotism rather than the Boer resistance widely supported by Irish nationalists. Mitchell became a pillar of St Patrick's Church, where he was choirmaster and organist for a time. He was happy to be seen as a prominent Catholic in Stafford, an indication of the relatively secure place enjoyed by the Church in the town. We find, however, no overt statement or activity related to Irish nationalism or Home Rule. This is not to say he wanted to bury his Irish origins – other evidence, to be discussed later, suggests not. Nevertheless, unlike John Walsh, his Irish identity, such as it was, was not expressed in Irish associational or political activity. He decided there was no scope for such things in Stafford – or perhaps he was just not interested. As a second-generation descendant, it was time to move on.

Mitchell went into politics. In 1898 he stood as an independent for the Borough Council but came bottom of the poll.[53] Two years later he succeeded and was elected for the East Ward. He was only twenty-seven and by far the youngest person on the council. He was also elected to the Board of Guardians. These events show his rapid rise to public prominence. He clearly benefited from his business role and patriotic activities during the Boer War. He remained on the council for the rest of his life. As a young whippersnapper he initially took a low profile. He made no intervention when the thorny issue of financial support for voluntary (including Catholic) schools was debated in 1903. There was an argument between Bartholomew Corcoran – an Irish Catholic – and Nonconformist councillors, but Mitchell took no part. He must have been a good ward councilor, however, because in the same year he was re-elected and came top of the poll. He was elected chairman of the Burial Board in 1904, a post earlier held by Corcoran. It was seen as a safe berth for Catholic representatives.[54] During this period he tended to err on the

side of economy in council spending, and harshness in the policies of the
Poor Law Guardians. In 1906, for example, he supported the building of
four stone-breaking cells for tramps in the workhouse, asserting that it
was 'a step in the right direction as the Workhouse had become a home
of health and a paradise of pleasure for tramps'.[55] In 1908 he made a 'vigorous speech' opposing unnecessary expenditure by the County Council
on medical examinations for all children. He argued the money should
be spent on the 8,000 in the county known to be 'medically defective',
though how these were to be identified from the rest he did not say.[56] This
parsimonious perspective found its reward the same year when he was
elected Vice-President of the Stafford Ratepayers' Association.[57]

Unemployment was high in 1908. Martin Mitchell became a member of the town's Distress Committee, but he came under fire for talking
a lot but doing very little. He in turn rounded on the committee saying 'he was disgusted with what was being done. His suggestions had
been ignored. He could do more as a private person', and he forthwith
resigned.[58] This incident demonstrates that Mitchell was by no means
popular with other councillors. It was also symptomatic of his shift to a
more radical position. He joined the Liberal Party, and during the con-
stitutional crisis of 1910 he seconded a motion at the local association's
annual meeting supporting the removal of the House of Lords veto.[59] In
1911 he began his most important political campaign. Stafford's dynamic
growth in the 1900s had led to a severe housing shortage and worsen-
ing conditions in the town's slums. Coming from Snow's Yard and Sash
Street, and still living nearby, Mitchell knew the conditions well, and
he and a minority of other councillors, as well as the Medical Officer of
Health, fought to get the council to build 250 council houses. Its efforts
so far had been minimal because a strong landlord lobby opposed direct
council provision. Mitchell resigned as Vice-Chairman of the Housing
of the Working Classes Committee because he had been 'beaten by the
Aldermen'.[60] He would 'not belong to any property owners' committee'.
Mitchell even enlisted the Church's support, and a letter was received
from Canon Keating at St Austin's in support of better housing for the
poor. The Stafford Guild of Help, with Mitchell as a member, pursued
a high-profile campaign publicising Stafford's slum conditions – 'there
were places in Stafford where people would not keep animals, and yet
men, women and children had been living there in insanitary dwellings
and in a state of overcrowding'.[61]

In September 1912 the Local Government Board held an inquiry into
complaints that the Borough had failed to fulfil its statutory obligations.
Mitchell was called by the complainants and alleged that:

> there was a dearth of houses. The Council had ignored the MoH's
> reports and requests for ten years. Private enterprise ... had done
> nothing ... The 20 houses that were the subject of the inquiry would

> be absolutely useless ... 100 houses were needed to replace slums
> and another 100 for the general public and the welfare of the people.
> [Applause]

In December 1912 the Local Government Board reported that the Borough Council had indeed failed to carry out its duties under the 1890 Housing of the Working Classes Act, and it was finally forced to come up with a building programme, though one considerably smaller than Mitchell wanted. He nevertheless seconded the Committee's resolution to build, saying that 'although a little disappointed, he was quite willing to fall in with the Committee proposals as they were "getting on" with the job'. He felt the number of houses was too few and the proposed rents were too high but he also 'combated the notion that the housing scheme would be a terrible burden on the rates'. By December 1913 he was able to 'express pleasure at the changed attitude of the Council – he was glad they were now recognizing their duty in the housing matter'.[62]

Though scarcely left-wing or socialist in his politics, Martin Mitchell was progressive and became more radical as time went on. His campaign for council housing reflected his experience of, and concern for, the poor of the north end where he grew up and amongst whom he lived until the end of his life. But he was also interested in modern, eye-catching developments. In 1907 he was involved in promoting Stafford's first motor-bus service.[63] In 1912 he organised a 'grand flying exhibition ... by the world's greatest flyer', Gustav Hamel. The airman made several flights from Lammascote Field, and in a well-known photograph Mitchell was pictured leaning nonchalantly against the aircraft (Figure 6.5). He also held the concession for pleasure boats on the River Sow.[64] He was a larger-than-life character whose reputation was still remembered in the town a century later. One of the interviewees for this research spoke in 2002 of the legend of Martin Mitchell as though he had known him personally, even though he was born ten years after Mitchell's death. The same impression was given by other contacts who knew of him.[65]

The Mitchell family's climb to Stafford Catholic respectability

In the spring of 1914 Martin Mitchell became ill. His last public appearance was at the opening of the new General Post Office in early April, and within three months he was dead, aged only forty.[66] His death was a considerable shock to local social and political life, since he was clearly just reaching the height of his powers and influence. His obituary reported that:

> the town has lost an earnest worker for the public good and one
> who was admired and respected by all who knew him ... By birth an

Figure 6.5 Martin Mitchell the showman, 1912, leaning against the plane, third from the right (Staffordshire County Museums Service)

> Irishman, Mr Mitchell had all the enthusiasm of the race for any cause he took up … In politics he was a Liberal, and as a speaker, singer and entertainer he made appearances on numerous platforms in the Midlands. Mr Mitchell was a Roman Catholic and a prominent member of St Patrick's Church.[67]

The fascinating feature of this obituary is the statement that Mitchell was 'By birth an Irishman'. We know he was not – he was born and brought up in Stafford. It suggests that either he publicly professed an Irish identity or his father wanted to attach such an identity to him after his death. The evidence certainly suggests there was pride in the family's Irish origins, but Mitchell's life also demonstrates that he had no interest maintaining a relict Irish identity in the face of the world as he found it in Stafford. His assets at death of £2,702 19s 1d (around £250,000 at 2012 prices) give an indication of his material success.[68]

Mitchell never married. He had no descendants. His immediate family ties remained strong, however. He lived at home with his father and unmarried sister Bridget (b. 1879) until his death. The family was close-knit and, unlike most of the Snow's Yard families, Catholicism and the Church remained important in the Mitchells' lives. Was it as an Irish Catholic Church? The answer is no. On St Patrick's Day 1896, celebrations were held at St Patrick's schoolroom. A lecture was given on 'The Young Ireland Movement' that 'discussed the aims of Young Ireland and showed the applicability of their doctrines to the present day'. It was 'loudly applauded'.[69] Numerous Irish songs and recitations were performed, and

Martin's eighteen-year-old sister Agnes gave a rendering of 'The Roving Pedlar'. Martin Mitchell did not attend, however, which is significant given that there was rarely a week when he was not on stage somewhere in the area. There is no other mention of the Mitchell family amongst those present. This is shaky evidence, but it suggests the Mitchells were not enthusiastic participants in maudlin expressions of Irish identity. When it came to *Stafford* Catholic events the Mitchells were well to the fore. The family participated in the St Patrick's Church soirées held every year in the Borough Hall. These major social gatherings encompassed Stafford's upper- and middle-class Catholics, respectable Irish families like the Mitchells, and also non-Catholics from the business community and the Council.

The Mitchells clearly wanted to break out of their Irish social background into wider, if still markedly Catholic, Stafford society. Their social outreach was reflected in the marriages of John Mitchell's daughters. In 1900 Agnes Mitchell married Alexander Strachan. The name suggests Scottish ancestry, but it has proved impossible to identify his background or occupation. Though they married in 1900, they were not living in Britain at the time of the 1901 Census. They may have emigrated, or perhaps Strachan was working overseas. In 1914 they were living in Bristol, since 'Alec' Strachan (but not Agnes) was one of the mourners at Martin's funeral.[70]

Martin Mitchell's sister Bridget (b. 1879) acted as housekeeper to her father and Martin Mitchell until, in 1922 and rather late in life, she married George William Moray Broun, a shoe-leather clicker whose family originally came from Cheshire. The partners of two other Mitchell sisters both represented the new, diversified economy of Edwardian Stafford. In 1903 Catherine Mitchell (b. 1875) married Francis William Hussey. He had been born in Stafford in 1874, although his father Thomas, a cabinet-maker, originally came from Liverpool. The family was Catholic, and we can assume the couple met through the Church. In 1901 Francis Hussey was an electrical fitter working in Wolverhampton, but he found an opening with Stafford's major new employer, Siemens Brothers, when they moved their factory to the town in the early 1900s. That move was certainly what brought about Julia Mitchell's marriage in 1908. She married Edgar Stopher, who in 1901 was an electrical apprentice in Charlton, London. He moved to Stafford with Siemens shortly thereafter. He had been born in Winchester in1884, the son of an ironmonger and, like Francis, he seems to have come from a Catholic family.[71] None of the Mitchell sisters married people descended from Stafford's Catholic Irish families. Three of the partners were members of the skilled British working class and the third, Alexander Strachan, probably was. The Mitchell family's search for respectability and integration was demonstrated by these marriages.

After Martin's death John Mitchell and his daughters kept the cycle business going for a number of years. It provided them with a useful income over and above what the sons-in-law brought in. In 1916 they became Stafford's first motor-cycle dealer, but the business was finally sold to Davies Brothers of Chester in 1921. There was a boom in motor-cycling after the Great War, and the Mitchells sold at the top of the market.[72] The proceeds provided John Mitchell with an income for his declining years. He died in 1928, aged seventy-nine. Alec Strachan died in 1918 in Bristol, and his widow Agnes came back to Stafford. She lived to a good age and was buried there in 1960. There may be descendants. The Stophers appear to have moved back to Edgar's home town of Winchester, where Julia died in 1927. She was only forty-six. The Husseys moved to Liverpool. He died there in 1946 and Catherine also died around the same time. There may be descendants from both these families too. The Mitchell family effectively died out in Stafford with Agnes's death in 1960. Their very success in exploiting the opportunities provided by the town ultimately resulted in their dispersal to other parts of England.

The Shiel and Mitchell families: different routes to integration

The McMahon/Mitchell/Shiel family arrived in Stafford well after the Famine, but they came from that same Castlerea area that supplied so many of Stafford's Irish immigrants. They benefited from kinship connections that got them accommodation in the troubled Snow's Yard community. During the period of their arrival and settlement Stafford's economy was starting to change. Irish families like the McMahon/Mitchell/Shiels could not depend on the old staple jobs of farmwork for the immigrant generation and shoemaking for the children. They had to respond to an economy demanding new skills but also offering better opportunities.

The structural environment set the context within which the immigrant families operated, but the history of this family shows again the varied responses people made to these challenges. The personal character of the initial immigrants – the McMahons, John Mitchell and Daniel Shiel – had been forged by their experience of life in Ireland before, during and after the Famine. When they ultimately left, their motivations were doubtless a complex mixture of desiring to escape from Ireland's problems and seeking new opportunities in the known world of England and Stafford. Having emigrated, the interconnected family's ties clearly remained significant, but the trajectories of the two main units diverged. The Shiels remained in the Snow's Yard community and their family history shows unmistakable signs of deprivation and stress, particularly for Ellen Shiel. Their life was squalid and occasionally violent, and in such conditions 'home' could not have been any sort of protective sanctuary from the wider world. Instead, their children found companionship with their peers, and they probably belonged to a gang culture largely beyond the control of both their parents and the forces of law and order. That social grouping was, however, multi-ethnic. The membership criterion was not Irishness but a common experience of poverty and deprivation within the Stafford working class. The Shiel children would have had a mixed identity. They grew up with Irish parents and amongst other Irish adults in Snow's Yard, but this older generation offered little stable or coherent in terms of a meaningful Irish identity; we have seen the evidence that Patrick Shiel positively rejected both his family home and his Catholic school. The Church meant little to them. These children moved out into the surrounding streets and fraternised with children from 'rough' English, particularly Catholic, backgrounds. There was no mileage in presenting an aggressively 'Irish' identity to other such kids, and the evidence is that the Shiel children passed rapidly into the Stafford working class and were absorbed by its culture.

Ellen Shiel's sister Bridget did escape. We cannot know the importance of her character and personality relative to that of her husband John in determining this, but it seems clear that the couple had some sort of strategy to lever themselves into a more respectable Stafford Catholic environment. John's job was of relatively higher status, but it was still insecure, and it seems more likely that the Mitchells' fortunes were shaped by a positive engagement with the Catholic Church. In 1884 a curate was appointed with special responsibility for the north end Catholics. Mass began to be said in St Patrick's schoolroom, and a more lively Catholic community developed in the area that culminated in the opening of St Patrick's Church in 1895.[73] The Mitchells were important players in this development.

The Mitchells therefore became respectable Catholics. Home conditions were difficult but when the family lived in Sash Street and New Street we can envisage a house with lace curtains, some Victorian clutter and almost certainly a piano on which Martin and Agnes honed their musical skills. Their home environment was supportive, and it clearly continued to be so even after Bridget's death. Martin responded to this positive environment. He grew up with confidence, social poise and an engaging personality that clearly charmed people from all backgrounds. John Mitchell's pride in his Irish origin was transmitted to his offspring but their Irish identity was a positive aspect of their outgoing personality, not a defensive bulwark against the 'other' English in a hostile environment. The family reached outwards, and we can see from Martin's interests and campaigns as well as his sisters' marriages a positive engagement with the social and economic environment of Stafford around the turn of the century.

By the 1900s the McMahon/Mitchell/Shiel family had, in different ways, come to terms with the circumstances of their migration to England. Whatever their problems, they had become established in British society.

Labouring families after the Famine

Although more labouring families settled in Stafford after the Famine than during it, many of the comments made in the previous chapter apply also to the post-1852 families. There were some contrasts, however. These later in-migrants were more diverse than their predecessors. Although most were 'migrant Irish families' and 'migrant Irish adults' who moved directly from Ireland, some of the later settlers had previously lived elsewhere in England. There were a number of ethnically mixed families, a contrast with the all-Irish units of the Famine influx. These immigrants had clung on in Ireland during the worst of the catastrophe but were forced out in the succeeding decades by continued evictions and lack of prospects. Many of those who worked on Stafford's farms then experienced a second period of stress when new machinery reduced the demand for casual farmworkers.[74] Many single men and seasonal workers abandoned Stafford, but a substantial minority stayed on because if the job market had gone against them in Stafford, it was likely to be worse in districts where they had no contacts. The adaptable, as well as the old and unemployable, had a strong incentive to hang on in the town, but nearly twenty single farm labourers and labouring families were left, like Martin McDermott, stranded in a shadowy world of casual work and poverty. Many died as paupers in the workhouse. They were the ultimate 'terminal' families and were the saddest social wreckage of the Famine.

Like their Famine predecessors the post-1852 families had experienced stresses, maybe traumas, but they had found ways of surviving afterwards and were perhaps more hardened to the fracturing of the society in which they had grown up. The sense of self present in these families provoked three reactions. The first was that of the Walshes – to emerge as militant nationalists, at least by Stafford's minimal standards. They were, however, exceptional. The second reaction was to retreat. Two-thirds of the long-term transient and terminal families of this period were nuclear units whose lives were a battle for survival within a deprived and predominantly inward-looking Irish milieu. Their environment was often shifting and anomic, and their lack of social interaction with the host society expressed, but also ensured, their withdrawal from Stafford either by leaving the town or through death in it. The Kellys, in the previous chapter, showed many of these characteristics. The identities present within these first two groups were inchoate but remained largely Irish. The third reaction was, however, a lengthy process of accommodation with Stafford society and increasing integration within it. The Shiel/ Mitchell family illustrates this process well. Many of these families were similarly complex units whose kinship links paradoxically provided the security to move out into local society.

Labouring families were close to the bottom of Victorian society. Whether English or Irish, their lives were a struggle to survive in a world of insecure earnings, illness and accident. This and the previous two chapters have examined the particular problems faced by Irish labourers and their families, together with some of the reactions they had to their predicament. The picture is of considerable diversity and helps give focus to commonly vague or stereotypical perceptions of the mass of Irish migrants to Britain and overseas. We now turn to Irish families from other backgrounds to expose the challenges they faced and the responses they made.

Notes

1 Herson, 'Irish migration and settlement', pp. 90–2; M. W. Greenslade, D.A. Johnson and C. R. J. Currie, *The Victoria History of the County of Stafford*, Vol. 6 (Oxford: Oxford University Press for the Institute of Historical Research, University of London, 1979), pp. 109 and 114.
2 SRO D1323/C/4/1–2, SBC Public Health Committee Minutes, 9 March 1875–27 January 1880 and 24 February 1880–25 September 1888. On 17 November 1876 the cleansing department employed twenty-one workers, six of whom were Irish. The highest pay was 2s 10d a day for removing the contents of cesspools. There was no 'Irish differential' in pay. They got the going rate for the job.
3 SBC Burial Record 3/5790: Martin McDermott, 16 February 1877; 6/10305: Elizabeth McDermott, 4 April 1889.
4 *SA*, 16 September 1876.
5 *Ibid.*, 23 July 1887.
6 *Ibid.*, 18 March 1889.
7 *Ibid.*, 2 October 1897.
8 M. McInally, *Edward Ilsley: Bishop of Birmingham, 1888–1911; Archbishop,1911–1921* (London: Burns and Oates, 2002), pp. 1–4 and *passim*.
9 Stafford RD, Marriage Certificate, 6b/35, no. 112: George Moore and Jane Duffy, 22 September 1853.
10 Wirral RD, Deaths, October–December 1852, 8a/260: John Trumper.
11 Stafford RD, Deaths, June–August 1864, 6b/10: George Moore.
12 *Ibid.*, Deaths, April–June 1846, 17/106: Rebecca Moore; Stafford RD, Marriages, July–September 1851, 17/164: James Moore and Harriet Jenkinson.
13 Stafford RD, Deaths, January–March 1868, 6b/3: James Moore, born about 1795.

14 *SA*, 30 September 1871.
15 *Ibid.*, 30 September and 7 October 1871. The *Advertiser* story may have had a typical reporter's error but the rest of the story seems clear and consistent.
16 Stafford RD, Deaths, April–June 1893, 6b/11: Harriet Moore.
17 NA, WO97, Service Record of no. 5043, Gnr. John Treverden (*sic*); *FindMyPast* (accessed 3 September 2013). Trevedon was illiterate and his name was spelt with numerous phonetic variations.
18 Stafford RD, Marriage Certificate, 6b/37, no. 65: John Trevedon and Jane Moore, 26 August 1876.
19 On 26 March 1883 a John 'Trevethan, joiner, aged about 40' arrived in New York aboard the 'City of Paris'. New York Passenger Lists, 1820–1957, Serial M237, Roll 462, Line 16, List no. 33, *Ancestry* (accessed 10 September 2013).
20 *Staffordshire Name Indexes* D659/1/4/10.
21 SBC Burial Record 05/847: Jane 'Tributon', pauper, Stafford Union Workhouse 1, 13 March 1884.
22 SBC Burial Record 2/3979, 25 September 1871.
23 Michael was subsequently a migrant farmworker in Staffordshire and Shropshire and never lived with the rest of the family in Stafford.
24 The family was not present in the 1861 Census but Ann's baby Bridget was baptised at St Austin's on 28 December 1861.
25 E. H. Hunt, *British Labour History, 1815–1914* (London: Weidenfeld and Nicolson, 1981), pp. 263–7.
26 *SA*, 12 August 1871.
27 SBC Burial Records 3/6010, 3/6011, 3/6015 (16–18 October 1877).
28 P. Bew, *Ireland: The Politics of Enmity* (Oxford: Oxford University Press, 2007), pp. 323–4.
29 *SA*, 19 February 1881.
30 *Ibid.*, 23 December 1876.
31 In the 1881 Census he was at Teddesley Farm, Teddesley Hay, and in 1901 in Cheslyn Hay. He was not, however, present in 1891.
32 New York Passenger Lists, 1820–1957, Microfiche M237, Roll 498, Line 19, List no. 1111, arrival 13 September 1886: Mary Walsh (40), Bridget Walsh (8), James Walsh (4) and Bernard Walsh (3), from Liverpool aboard SS *Celtic*. John Walsh presumably arrived ahead of his wife and children but has not been traced. *Ancestry* (accessed 16 January 2014).
33 A. M. Harrison, 'The development of boot and shoe manufacturing in Stafford, 1850–1880', *Journal of the Staffordshire Industrial Archaeology Society*, 10 (1981), pp. 1–80; A. Fox, *A History of the National Union of Boot and Shoe Operatives, 1874–1957* (Oxford: Basil Blackwell, 1958), Chapters 9–13; *SA*, *passim*, 1880s.
34 R. Lawton, 'Population migration to and from Warwickshire and Staffordshire, 1841–91' (M.A. thesis, n.d.) (copy of Staffordshire section in William Salt Library, Stafford, TH48), Chapter 12.
35 E.g. *SA*, 30 June 1883, when there were three advertisements for ships to Australia/New Zealand and five for the USA/Canada together with an advertisement by the New South Wales Government for assisted passages.
36 (Griffith's) General Valuation of Ireland, 1848–64, *Ancestry* (accessed 25 October 2013).

37 The census enumerator in 1871 recorded Thomas's birthplace as 'Galway Kinevad', but Kilnalag is the nearest phonetic approximation to such a place to be found in the area. McMahon is not a common name in Galway, although Mahon is. Perhaps he altered it. There is considerable doubt about Thomas's birth date. His quoted age in the census puts it between 1811 and 1816, but his burial records imply a later date, 1825/26. Ann claimed she was born in 'Fakal', Co. Galway, but this almost certainly meant Foughil, which lies less than a mile from the Galway border.

38 In the general election that year he voted for the Liberal Disestablishment candidate.

39 The family name is variously spelt Shiel, Sheil, Shiels, Shield and Shields in the surviving records. Unfortunately, no descendant of the family emerged to say which is the family's preferred version.

40 *SA*, 8 June 1878. SRO D3704, SBC, Register of Common Lodging Houses, Stafford, 1878–1940.

41 SBC Burial Records 5/9281 and 5/9298.

42 *SA*, 4 June 1881.

43 *Ibid.*, 30 May, 6 June, 22 August and 17 September 1891.

44 *Ibid.*, 12 September 1891.

45 *Ibid.*, 21 May 1892.

46 *Ibid.*, 24 June 1899, 31 August 1901, 22 October 1904 and 27 March 1909.

47 *Ibid.*, 5 December 1885.

48 BAA P255/4/2, Stafford, St Austin's, Register of Burials, 1875–93 (25 January 1888).

49 *SA*, 5 December 1885.

50 John Mitchell registered his son's death in 1914, but was unable to sign his name on the death certificate. Stafford RD, Death Certificate, 6b/27, no. 156: Martin Mitchell, 29 June 1914.

51 *SA*, 21 April 1900; 2 May 1903; advertisement in *Hibbert's Handbook of Stafford* (1906).

52 *SA*, e.g. 12 December 1903, 30 April 1904, 22 May 1905.

53 *Ibid.*, 19 November 1898.

54 *Ibid.*, 9 May 1903, 24 October 1903 and 12 November 1904.

55 *Ibid.*, 10 February 1905.

56 *Ibid.*, 8 February 1908.

57 *Ibid.*, 9 May 1908.

58 *Ibid.*, 4 and 21 November, and 5 December 1908.

59 *Ibid.*, 9 April 1910.

60 *Ibid.*, 9 September, 4 November, 23 December 1911 and 13 January 1912.

61 *Ibid.*, 9 March and 18 May 1912.

62 *Ibid.*, 14 September, 7 December, 28 December 1912; 8 March and 3 December 1913.

63 *Ibid.*, 23 November 1907.

64 Lewis, *Around Stafford*, p. 120.

65 The interviewee was the late Peter Godwin.

66 His death certificate says he was thirty-eight; however, his birth was registered in July–September 1873 (Stafford RD, 6b/14). His father, who registered Martin's death, was illiterate and presumably had only a hazy notion of how

old his son was, hence the discrepancy. Martin died from nephritis – kidney inflammation and failure – and a cerebral haemorrhage. Stafford RD, Death Certificate, 6b/27, no. 156, 29 June 1914. I am indebted to Dr Richard Nelson of Chester for a diagnosis and discussion of the nature of his illness.

67 *SA*, 4 July 1914.
68 England and Wales National Probate Calendar (Index of Wills and Administrations), 1856–1966: Martin Mitchell, probate granted Lichfield, 12 October 1914; *Ancestry* (accessed 9 September 2012).
69 *SA*, 21 March 1896.
70 Stafford RD, Marriages, July–September 1900, 6b/37: Agnes Mitchell and Alexander Strachan; *SA*, 4 July 1914.
71 Stafford RD, Marriages, April–June 1922, 6b/45: Bridget Mitchell and George William Moray Broun; October–December 1903, 6b/38: Catherine (Kitty) Mitchell and Francis William Hussey; April–June 1908, 6b/48: Julia Magdalen Mitchell and Edgar Thomas Stopher.
72 Information from the late Roy Mitchell (not related), 2005.
73 Herson, 'The English, the Irish and the Catholic Church in Stafford', pp. 34–5.
74 *VCH Stafford*, Vol. 6, pp. 109 and 114.

7

Lace curtain Irish? The families of craft, clerical and service workers

Non-labouring families and their social roles

The previous chapters have shown that families whose origins were in the Irish labouring class had varied trajectories. Those who integrated mostly moved into the Stafford working class, but over the generations a minority showed distinct upward social mobility. We now begin the study of the families who from the start did not have the archetypal labouring background but depended on a diverse range of other occupations.

Nearly half Stafford's settled Irish families initially depended on occupations other than labouring. They spanned a wide range of jobs. At one extreme they did work of the lowest social status and were essentially similar to the labourers. At the other extreme there were people with privileged occupations. In the middle were those with various sorts of craft, clerical or service jobs. The history of these families was not predictable. A small number climbed into Stafford's economic, religious and political elite. Others were always poor or left for more promising pastures elsewhere.

In studying these families we have to be conscious of the conceptual tension between their ethnicity and their status within the host society. Do we see them primarily as Irish or primarily as respectable working class or middle class? They themselves would have been conscious of the same tension, particularly in the years after coming to Britain. Their evolving class position would have reflected, and been reflected in, distinct traits of identity, attitude and behaviour. Davidoff *et al.* summarise features that characterised nineteenth-century middle-class families and that typified aspiring working-class families too. These include the importance of 'respectability' and status, the strength of the male breadwinner norm, the role of women as home-makers, and the sharper division of gender roles brought about by the separation of home and workplace. The houses of these people would have the well-washed lace curtains of respectability in their windows. Even so, the sharpened boundaries between male and female roles, with the assumption of male dominance and female subservience, could bring stress within families. The bonds of kinship and obligation within extended families might be weakened by assertions of independence and status within the constituent units or in geographically isolated nuclear families.[1] We have to see to what extent this broad swathe of Irish families exhibited these characteristics, the factors that caused them and whether they experienced faster 'ethnic fade' than the unskilled families.

Historians of the Irish have shown increasing interest in the more skilled and middle-class immigrants, particularly amongst the Catholics. In doing this they have taken up the baton from contemporary observers. Hugh Heinrick, writing in 1872 from a nationalist perspective, saw an evil influence at work:

> At the top there is a class – fortunately not large in numbers, but not less baleful in their example and its results – who, having attained comparative prosperity, wish to forget their nativity, and in all things conform to English thought and English habit ... Their defection is greatly facilitated by intermarriage with English families, and the consequent conformity which follows ... The misfortune is that the class which feeds this defection is the class whose means would enable them to be of greatest benefit to their country and their kindred did they not thus fall away from the standard of patriotic duty.[2]

Heinrick specifically identified one of the contextual factors at work when he commented that 'In the town of Stafford, and in the locality known as the Potteries ... are numerous Irish residents, but so scattered as not to constitute a power relatively.'[3] John Denvir, writing twenty years after Heinrick, focused on the fact that 'A number of our fellow-countrymen in Stafford and Stone are engaged in the staple industries of these places – boot and shoemaking. It cannot but be noticed that shoemaking and tailoring are the only trades in which, up to the last few years, you found any considerable number of artisans in this country.'[4] Denvir commented more generally in the 1890s that:

> Although not so numerous among the substantial 'middle-class' traders as one would wish to find them, they [the Irish] are making fair progress, and it is no uncommon thing to find substantial shopkeepers and wholesale dealers who have been costers or the sons of costers; while in every calling and profession you find Irishmen in most responsible positions. In London, as elsewhere throughout Great Britain, you meet with a numerous body who prove that 'with a fair field and no favour' Irishmen are bound to come to the front.[5]

Heinrick and Denvir picked up issues concerning the roles of the skilled and middle-class Irish that are still discussed today. The first concerns their economic roles. John Belchem has emphasised that amongst the vast numbers of Irish in Liverpool some in the Catholic bourgeoisie were important as commercial suppliers to the 'enclave economy' and as economic power brokers, offering jobs and opportunities to their compatriots.[6] However, this was not the whole picture. As 'Micks on the make on the Mersey' they were as likely to seek escape from the 'ghetto' through trade with, and assimilation into, the host society, just as Heinrick had seen in 1872.[7] In this chapter a study of the Corcoran family will explore whether there was any possibility that similar families could make a living servicing the Irish population of Stafford or whether their aspirations inevitably encouraged them to integrate rapidly into the host economy.

Irish families who achieved some wealth and status had opportunities to engage in other identifiable roles. They could carry out two distinct, though complementary, cultural roles. On the one hand they could be cultural leaders amongst the Irish themselves. Writers such as O'Leary, Belchem and William Jenkins (who emphasises the role of women in the process) have identified the importance of the Irish Catholic middle class in defining and reinforcing particular forms of Irish identity amongst the immigrant population.[8] They were active role models promoting acceptable, moderate Irish identity and 'respectability' through the cult of domesticity, associational culture, membership of friendly societies and the temperance movement.[9] The simplest form of such analysis documents the Irish organisations promoted and sustained by such cultural leaders, but Louise Miskell has cautioned against overemphasising this type of activity amongst numerically small immigrant communities, in her case in South Wales. She suggests that we need to look for informal practices and types of association based around support and interaction in the household and family. These processes, hard as they are to expose, played a vital role defining the nature of communal identity. This insight clearly has relevance to Irish families and households in Stafford.[10]

The Irish Catholic middle and skilled working class could also play a role as intermediary 'culture brokers', interpreting and promoting the Irish in the host community. O'Leary particularly emphasises this process, arguing that:

> the views of elites in the host society were challenged by those who claimed to speak on behalf of the Irish, including both the Catholic clergy and the emerging Irish middle class. Derogatory perceptions of the Irish ... were countered by alternative views which stressed the orderliness, religiosity and moral integrity of the immigrant community.[11]

Whilst this may have been a consciously adopted role by some aspirant individuals, we need to remember that many people developed multiple identities through contact with the host population. Being 'Irish' was not necessarily the primary focus of their lives.[12] We also have to remember that the Protestant Irish were likely to have distinctly different identities and roles in relation to both the host society and the mass of Catholic Irish. It is often assumed that their integration with the host society was unproblematic but the investigation of particular families will explore the validity of that assumption.

The aspirant Irish – both Catholic and Protestant – could also play distinct religious roles. It must be remembered that Irish priests and ministers were themselves overwhelmingly middle class by background and by the nature of their calling. They were inherently leaders of their flocks. Irish Catholic priests would clearly aim to promote and reinforce religious practice, but this process could either sustain Irish identity or be a force to negate it. After Emancipation the Catholic Church was desperate to gain a secure and respectable position in English society and pressure from the hierarchy was towards incorporating the Irish into the English Church and society.[13] Individual priests might fail to toe the party line, however, and we need to see whether such forces operated in Stafford. These issues are examined particularly in Chapter 10.

In the religious nineteenth century the aspirant and middle-class Irish were likely to adhere to church and chapel as both a spiritual and a social focus in their lives. It was a further element in the drive for respectability.[14] In this process they could emerge as lay religious and social leaders amongst the Irish population, a role carried out by both men and women. In the case of Liverpool, Belchem argues they promoted Irish Catholic apartness in the city, but in Stafford the strength of the recusant tradition was likely to dictate incorporation into a Church dominated by the English upper-class elite.[15] The Irish middle class could act as religious culture brokers promoting working-class adherence and practice within the evolving Catholic missions. O'Leary has, however, suggested that the extension of the political franchise forced members of the middle class to defend their interests, and paradoxically they could emerge as an alternative source of leadership contesting the Church's authority in secular matters.[16]

The aspirant Irish could potentially emerge as political leaders, but in various forms. They might be leaders of the local Irish in pursuit of the national struggle or the articulation of ethnic demands in local politics, but they could equally be politicians integrated into English power structures. In Stafford we have already seen how Martin Mitchell's success in business and social affairs led him to become an influential local politician. It is clear he was motivated partly by a desire to improve conditions for the people in the north end amongst whom he lived. He was, however, no leader of 'the Irish' in any form of overt nationalism or even in terms of local politics. This contrasts with the situation in Liverpool, where the centrality of the Irish ethnic and religious dimension in local politics has been documented by Belchem, Sam Davies and P. J. Waller.[17]

The Liverpool case was exceptional, however, and the Irish middle classes elsewhere usually sought involvement within the established political parties. Their adherence to Irish political movements – Fenianism, Home Rule, the Land War or Gaelic Nationalism – waxed and waned, but, outside Liverpool, Irish middle-class activists never mobilised the masses on Irish issues to influence local or national electoral politics significantly in Britain.[18] Their leadership roles were increasingly defined by the politics of the Tories and Liberals or by the emergent class politics of the Labour movement.[19]

The craft, clerical and service families

Bearing the previous discussion in mind, we need to examine the traits shown by Stafford's non-labouring families and the factors that seem to have determined them. This will involve exploring the identities and values that they exhibited and the economic, cultural, religious and political roles they performed, or failed to perform, amongst their Irish compatriots and within the wider Stafford society. In Chapters 8 to 10 we shall look at the families with origins in the military and shoemaking, and the small class of professionals and substantial entrepreneurs. These groups had specific reasons for settling in Stafford. A feature of Stafford's Irish settlers was, however, the broad range of other occupational backgrounds to be found amongst them, and in this chapter we focus on the large group of families who had miscellaneous occupations lying outside labouring or the locally specific occupations just mentioned. In broad terms these families had craft, clerical and service (CC&S) occupations or were marginal entrepreneurs. There were fifty-six of these families, and their profile differed significantly from Stafford's Irish labouring families. In the tables that follow the two classes are compared.

Somewhat under one-fifth of the CC&S families had settled before the Famine, a substantially higher proportion than amongst the labouring families (Table 7.1). These early arrivals were a mixed bunch. Four families existed on the margins of society as pedlars, rag dealers, bone collectors and lodging-house keepers. Others conformed to the picture of skilled workers leaving Ireland in the decades after 1800 because of the 'deindustrialisation' of the country after the Act of Union.[20] Of the other six families who had more aspirant occupations, three worked on the railway after the Grand Junction line opened in 1837. A cabinet-maker, a policeman and the Irish wife of the town's miller made up the rest of these early arrivals. The numbers settling as a direct result of the Famine were fewer, but more quit Ireland in the decade following the Famine. They were the longer-term casualties forced to leave because of reduced prospects in the shattered economy. Most notable, however,

Table 7.1 Date of arrival of craft, clerical and service, and labouring families

Date of arrival	CC&S families %	Labouring families %
Before 1845	17.8	6.6
1846–51	12.5	39.6
1852–61	28.6	33.0
After 1861	41.1	19.8
Total no. of families	**56**	**106**

Table 7.2 Provincial origin of craft, clerical and service, and labouring families

Province of origin	CC&S families %	Labouring families %
Connacht	35.0	87.5
Leinster	25.0	6.3
Munster	20.0	2.5
Ulster	20.0	3.8
Total no. of families	**40**	**80**

Note: the provincial origin of 16 CC&S and 26 labouring families is unknown.

is the fact that over 40 per cent of the CC&S families settled in Stafford after 1861. Marginal workers formed only a small proportion of these families. Most were engaged in a broad range of skilled crafts or service activities.

The regional origins of the CC&S families also differed from the labouring families (Table 7.2). They came from all parts of Ireland. Although Connacht immigrants were still the largest group, only just over one-third came from there. The other three provinces were equally represented. This even distribution of origins reflected the fact that those in CC&S jobs were able to weigh the advantages of staying in Ireland with those of leaving. These emigrants might, therefore, come from anywhere in Ireland and might end up anywhere in England. The reasons why some came to Stafford were more diffuse than was the case for the labouring families.

There was a contrast in the types of family who settled in Stafford. A small minority are identified in Table 7.3 as 'British Transient in Ireland'. These families will not be considered further but they emphasise that Irish migration was not all one-way. British individuals and families frequently went to Ireland for craft work or as part of the military or the

Table 7.3 Types of craft, clerical and service, and labouring families

Type of family	CC&S %	Labouring %
1. Migrant Irish family (Migration of pre-existing core unit with children born in Ireland)	28.6	49.1
2. Migrant Irish adults (Core unit established in Britain; children born after arrival in Britain)	10.7	38.7
3. Male-mixed family (Core unit with Irish-born male with non-Irish partner)	41.1	6.6
4. Female-mixed family (Core unit with Irish-born female with non-Irish partner)	16.1	5.7
5. British transient in Ireland (British-born parent with child(-ren) born in Ireland)	3.6	—
Total no. of families	**56**	**106**

British administration. Children born in Ireland to such families technic-ally count as Irish emigrants and may indeed have had some identifica-tion with their birthplace. Some such families turned up in Stafford.

Over half the CC&S families were ethnically mixed units, a contrast with the labouring families who were overwhelmingly 'all-Irish'. This sug-gests that many of the more skilled immigrants came to Britain as single people and that their stronger bidding position in the labour market also opened up more opportunities in the market for wives and husbands from the host society. Even so, around 40 per cent of the CC&S families were wholly Irish, and three-quarters of these had emigrated as complete fam-ily units with children born in Ireland. Only about one in ten had formed families after arrival in England. If they had a choice, the all-Irish CC&S families were unlikely to live amongst their compatriots of the labouring class. Class and status considerations influenced relations amongst Irish immigrants as much as between them and the host population.

Another factor affecting relationships was, of course, religion. We have seen that almost all the labouring families were Catholic. Around two-thirds (63.6 per cent) of the CC&S families were also Catholic, but that leaves thirteen families (23.6 per cent) who were definitely Protestant and another seven (12.7 per cent) whose religion is unknown but were probably nominal Protestants. This significant body of Protestant emi-grants reflects their relatively better education and skill prospects in

Table 7.4 The fate of the craft, clerical and service, and labouring families

Ultimate fate	CC&S families %	Labouring families %
Long-term transient	39.3	34.0
Terminal	17.9	22.6
Integrating	42.9	43.4
Total no. of families	**56**	**106**

Ireland, their willingness to move and their ability to integrate into a generally Protestant society in England. Things were inherently easier for them than for their Catholic counterparts, although that was not always the case as we shall see. Family structure reflected these families' mobility and ability to compete in the labour market. Eighty per cent were individuals, couples or nuclear families, and more complex units were a minority. The bonds of family support and obligation were inherently much weaker than amongst the labouring families, where nearly 60 per cent were complex.

There were, therefore, many contrasts between the CC&S and the labouring families that reflected their origins and the circumstances of their settlement in Stafford. Did the ultimate fate of these families also differ markedly from that of the labouring families? The answer is negative. Table 7.4 shows that the long-term trajectories of the two groups were remarkably similar. The CC&S families were rather more likely to be transient in the long term, probably because they had the incentive to gain promotion or better jobs by moving away. Relatively fewer of these families died out in Stafford. Most notable, however, is that the proportion who integrated into local society was almost identical. This demonstrates yet again that the ultimate fate of Irish immigrant families was not determined simply by their superficial character – their jobs, religion, origin or whatever. These factors were merely the backcloth against which the drama of family relationships was played out.

The case study families reflect the diversity of the craft, trade and service in-migrants to Stafford. The initial occupations of the three familes discussed in this chapter – the Corcorans, the Larkins and the Giltraps – were joinery, the railways and the prison service, all jobs with modest status. Margaret Carr was at the other end of the occupational spectrum. She was a washerwoman. These families were of varied structure. The Corcorans and Giltraps became large and complex families. The Larkins were a nuclear family in Stafford, though they had extensive kin elsewhere, whereas Margaret Carr was a lone widow who lived in quasi-familial households with unrelated but similarly poor people. The Corcoran family integrated into Stafford society, though ultimately with an idiosyncratic twist. Margaret Carr died in Stafford as a lone individual whereas the other two families proved to be long-term transients. The Catholic Larkin family demonstrated arrested integration and evidence of tension over the nature of their identity.

The Corcoran family: aspiration and respectability with a twist

This book began with an extract from Bartholomew Corcoran's obituary in 1908.[21] It described his successful business career and his 'keen interest in public affairs.' Here was a man, and a family, who seem to have created successful lives in Stafford. They exploited various opportunities to gain a secure foothold in local society whilst maintaining limited contact with their Catholic Irish peers. They showed hints of acting as brokers amongst the Catholic Irish, but only within very strict limits. They were cautious and avoided anything that might threaten their integration into respectable Stafford society. Family events did not take a totally predictable course, however. During the 1900s most of the family's descendants abandoned Stafford, but at the same time a new family nucleus emerged to carry on the Corcoran name into the twentieth century.

The Corcorans' arrival in Stafford

The Corcorans came from Tibohine parish, about six miles north of Castlerea in Co. Roscommon. They therefore came from the same area as many of Stafford's Irish. The family were particularly located in the townland of Cloonfad, and they experienced the pressures bearing down on poorer tenants in the west in the first half of the nineteenth century. Their land-holding was in transition. Even after the Famine they were still involved in land co-partnerships, but as early as 1825 four members of the family were already individual tenants of five- or six-acre holdings.[22] Land hunger and poor prospects led some to abandon both co-partnership and individual land-holding in favour of working at a trade in the commercial world. Patrick Corcoran was one of them. His father was probably Bartholomew Corcoran of Cloonfad.[23] Patrick had been born in the 1800s and married a local woman, Catherine Crews, around 1830.[24] He then left the land and became a joiner.[25] The family moved nearer to the town of Castlerea, and in the 1840s they and their growing family were occupying a cabin at Ballindrumlea about a mile outside the town.[26] It was still a miserable existence. Even before the Famine it was reported that, in Castlerea, people in trade were often forced to beg.[27]

Patrick and Catherine's family survived the immediate impact of the Famine, but moved to England in the 1850s. Corcoran's occupation depended on the building trade. The Famine undermined many of the small- to medium-sized farmers as well as those landlords whose estates were effectively bankrupt. They consequently had neither the need nor money to use craft workers, so people like Patrick Corcoran were in turn impoverished. Many had to emigrate. Patrick must have used existing connections to make Stafford his bolt-hole rather than choose the uncertainty of going to America. The family had arrived by 1856 but we only know that because Patrick died that year.[28] Before he died he seems to have found work as a carpenter in the Haywood district to the east of Stafford, though it may have been interspersed with labouring.[29] After his death the family moved into Stafford town. At that point the Corcorans seemed a stereotypically deprived immigrant family. They were fatherless and struggling to survive in one of Stafford's worst slums. Nevertheless, Patrick's shift to independent artisan status in Roscommon demonstrated an ambitious mentality and a determination to free himself and his family from the dying communal land economy. His aspirational approach was passed on to his children in their new environment.

Patrick and Catherine Corcoran had at least five children, of whom four survived to settle in Stafford (Figure 7.1).[30] In 1861 the widowed Catherine was living at no. 5 Plant's Square. Irish families occupied all but one of the houses in the square. The Corcorans were clearly poor, but there was a strong and supportive network amongst them. The Bowen family lived across the yard at no. 7. They were Famine immigrants who also came from Tibohine and they are considered further in Chapter 9. They helped Catherine survive her difficult early years in the town.[31] In 1861 only three of Catherine's children were living with her. Mary Corcoran, who was then twenty-three and the eldest daughter, was not there or elsewhere in Britain. She may have been clinging on in Ireland in some sort of job, or perhaps she was just visiting home. She settled permanently in Stafford in the early 1860s and the surviving Corcoran family was then complete.

Catherine Corcoran's children and their marriages

In the absence of Patrick, Catherine's son Bartholomew (b. 1834) played a major role in defining the Corcoran family's fortunes. In the 1861 Census he claimed to be a plumber, glazier and painter, so he could turn his hand to a range of building trades. These activities were to make him a good living. He began modestly, and in the 1860s presumably worked for other employers. Hard work enabled him to get out of Plant's Square and by 1865 he was living in Friar Street, a solid working-class address.[32] By 1871 he had done well enough to begin working on his own account, operating from substantial premises on Foregate Street just where it became Grey

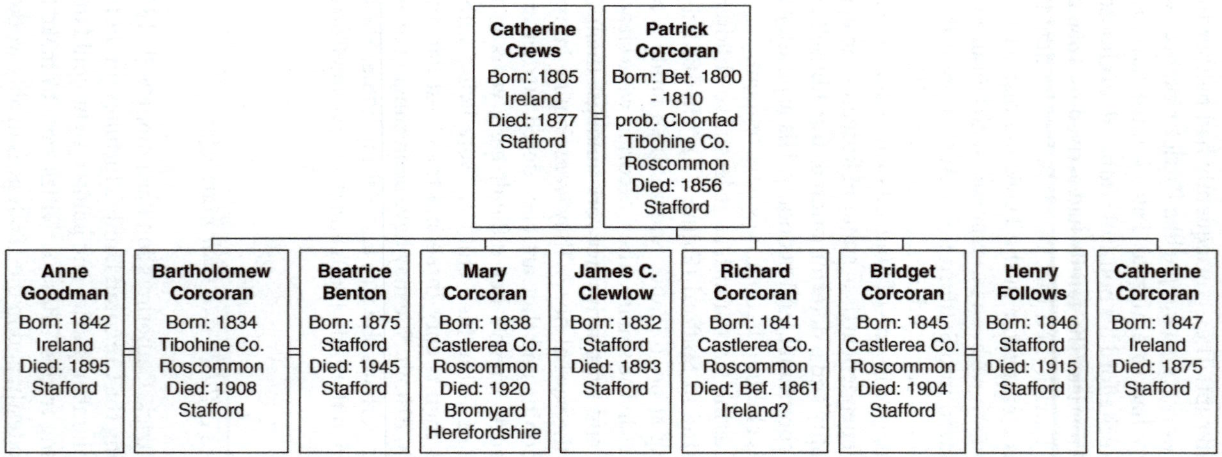

Figure 7.1 The Corcoran stem family in Stafford

Friars.[33] He, his family and his business were to occupy this property for over forty years.

In 1863 Bartholomew married Anne Goodman at St Austin's. She was the woman we saw in Chapter 5, bullied by Jane Kelly. Their marriage was unique in the Stafford Corcoran family in that Anne was also an Irish immigrant from a poor Connacht family because, at that stage, the Corcorans' main contacts were still amongst the working-class Irish from the west. Superficially it did not look a propitious marriage. Like the Corcorans, the Goodmans were a single-parent family, although in their case the father had died in the Famine. They lived in another slum, Cherry Street, and Anne Goodman's two brothers were clearly 'teenage tearaways' with a run of convictions for petty crime. One of them was described by a magistrate in 1862 as 'one of the worst characters in the Borough'.[34] Anne herself was illiterate.[35] Even so, she clearly aspired to break free from this deprived and troublesome background, and in Bartholomew Corcoran she found a kindred spirit. For the next thirty-two years the couple worked hard to achieve a position of respectability.

Bartholomew's three sisters, Mary, Bridget and Catherine, all got jobs in the shoe trade, and this broadened their contacts with the host community. Two married local men quite quickly. In Mary's case the circumstances were suspicious. In 1866 she married James Charles Clewlow, a non-Catholic. He was a shoemaker, and in 1871 was a 'manufacturer employing two men'. He carried on his business at no. 2 Grey Friars Place, premises that backed on to the Corcoran household on Grey Friars/Foregate Street. Mary therefore knew Clewlow as a neighbour. It was James's second marriage. In 1852 he had married a local woman, Mary Ann Moore, and the couple had four children. In the spring of 1866 Mary Ann died and James wasted no time replacing her. His marriage to Mary Corcoran took place at St Austin's on 9 October. The couple needed to be quick, since the liaison had obviously begun before Mary Ann's death. Their first child, Agnes Cora Clewlow, was born in December 1866. We shall examine this family's subsequent history later.[36]

In 1868 Bridget Corcoran also married a Staffordian, Henry Follows.[37] He was a clicker from an extensive Catholic family. In 1871 they were living at no. 45 Friar Street and by the mid-1870s they had moved to no. 48 Rowley Street, an address with distinctly higher social status. The Follows family showed some evidence of accepting kinship obligations, since Bridget's mother, Catherine, and her sister, also named Catherine, were living with them in 1871. The younger Catherine had a short life. She never married and died in 1875. Her mother succumbed two years later to what was diagnosed as 'general decay' after living in Stafford for about twenty years. It was a miserable end. Catherine Corcoran died in the workhouse and it seems only an overseer was there to witness her death.[38]

Bartholomew Corcoran and his family

We now need to trace the history of Bartholomew and Anne Corcoran. The superficial picture is of a hard-working couple who exploited connections in business, the Church and politics to achieve a secure and respectable position in local society. In spite of this – or perhaps because of it – their personalities and character remain rather opaque. Bartholomew Corcoran was no Martin Mitchell. Mitchell was an extrovert character with clear views, strongly articulated. Corcoran's career paralleled Mitchell's in many ways but his aims were more mundane and family-centred. His origins explain this. Martin Mitchell was the Stafford-born son of immigrant parents. Bartholomew Corcoran, by contrast, had grown up in Ireland and witnessed the Famine at first hand. His early years in both Ireland and in Stafford were hard. These experiences led him to seek security by working assiduously, exploiting openings and taking care to avoid conflict with anybody influential. As a result he may have been a somewhat repressed individual for much of his life, but towards the end the old man broke free from his life's traditional restraints.

Bartholomew did well enough in the 1860s to be able to move into the substantial house and yard in Foregate Street. His premises were only two doors from the entrance to Snow's Yard but they were already in a different social world. His neighbours were skilled workers, shopkeepers or minor public servants. They were all English, although a significant minority were in-migrants from elsewhere in England. Bartholomew and his family were always the only Irish people to live on this stretch of the street, and their residential integration into the host community was clear from an early stage.

Bartholomew Corcoran prospered both from the general growth of the building industry in the later nineteenth century and from the higher quality of maintenance, construction and services imposed by new building regulations. His business was consistently listed in directories from 1872 onwards, and it became more substantial during that decade.[39] In 1879 his tender of £40 to paint the outside of Stafford Workhouse was accepted by the Board of Guardians.[40] In 1888 he was admitted to membership of the Worshipful Company of Plumbers, whose object was to promote good workmanship by its members.[41] From 1891 his firm was also listed amongst the more limited group of 'waterworks plumbers – authorised' as well as under the general heading of 'painters, glaziers and plumbers'.[42] This indicates a well-founded business allowed to undertake substantial public work. There is unfortunately no direct evidence as to the ultimate size of Corcoran's firm, but some indication of its relative size can be gleaned from money given by its workmen to the 'Hospital Saturday' collections that took place in the late nineteenth century. In 1888 Corcoran's workpeople collected £2 5s. This was around half the total given by employees of the London and North Western Railway (LNWR) (£5 3s 7d) and of the timber merchants Henry Venables (£4 8s 6d), both substantial employers in the town. It was, however, fifteen times that from the Corporation Gas Works (2s 11½d). In 1891 Thomas Sneath, one of the firm's plumbers, entered a national competition sponsored by the *Plumber and Decorator* and won a certificate of merit for his practical plumbing work.[43] This indicates that Bartholomew was an outward-looking entrepreneur keen to raise the public prestige of his business.

Once the firm was secure and well known, Corcoran branched out into other activities, some of which doubtless put more work his way. Both Bartholomew and Anne became active in the social life of the Catholic Church. By 1884 he was a man of substance amongst the laity. In February of that year he was present at the inauguration of the St Patrick's Young Men's Association, which took place at the Borough Hall. Corcoran was a member of the platform party alongside five Catholic priests and four members of the Catholic elite. It was he who was chosen to propose the vote of thanks to the Chairman, The Revd Canon Michael O'Sullivan, former priest at St Austin's.[44] Thereafter we see the Corcorans consistently present at, and making donations to, the Catholic soirées that were a distinctive feature of Stafford church life from the 1870s onwards. He also became President of the local St Vincent de Paul society.[45]

By 1891 Bartholomew was moving towards his career as a local politician. He was already one of the managers of St Austin's and St Patrick's Catholic schools, and in September that year he seconded a motion to declare the schools free of charges under the new Free Education Act. The proposer was Henry Sandy, a prominent local Catholic who was a surveyor and estate agent. Corcoran's network in the building and property trade is apparent here. A year previously he had indicated his political allegiance by joining the organising committee (with sixty-six other people!) of the 'Grand County Conservative Ball'. The event took place at the Borough Hall in January 1890, and many local business leaders were present, a significant number of whom were Catholics.[46] Twenty years previously Bartholomew Corcoran had been a Liberal.[47] Now he was linked to the Tories. Even so, he was cautious enough to avoid a party allegiance when he finally went on the Council. At the municipal elections in 1894 he stood as an independent for the East Ward and came top of the poll amongst the four councillors elected for this multi-member ward.[48] Of those voting, 56 per cent voted for him.

Did Bartholomew Corcoran get elected through the Irish Catholic vote? The answer is clearly negative. Irish Catholics certainly would have voted for him but there were not enough of them to get him elected. In the 1890s there were about 500 Irish or mixed-Irish Catholics in Stafford of whom perhaps 300 lived in the East Ward.[49] Leaving out children and

most women, as well as men not having the residence or property quali-
fication to vote, there were probably only about seventy Irish Catholic
voters in the ward.[50] By the same token there were probably about ninety-
five Staffordian Catholic voters, so the potential Catholic vote was only
165. Bartholomew Corcoran actually received 634 votes and it is clear
that most of those who voted for him were neither Irish nor Catholic. It
shows again that sectarian forces were feeble. Even so, it must have taken
courage to stand. Corcoran was the first Irish or Irish-descended Catholic
to be elected to Stafford Borough Council. He was the trail-blazer and
he deserves recognition for that fact alone. Perhaps because of this, his
subsequent history as a local politician was stolid rather than inspiring.
Despite his ethnic origin, in most ways Bartholomew conformed to the
common picture of councillors in small-town England. He was a local
businessman with substantial means and a network of profitable contacts in building, commerce and property. Ultimately he owned a block
of twelve houses in Stone Road as well as a parcel of land and four properties in other parts of the north end.[51] He was also not unusual amongst
Stafford councillors in being an outsider. At the turn of the century only
five out of twenty-four members were native Staffordians, and at least
thirteen originated from outside Staffordshire.[52]

Having got on to the Council Corcoran was immediately elected a
Poor Law Guardian.[53] On the Council he was appropriately put on the
Sewerage Committee and on the sub-committee identifying a location
for the town's urgently needed sewage works.[54] By 1899 he had progressed to chairmanship of the Council's Burial Board where, in 1901,
he faced his most embarrassing public incident. In May of that year a fire
at the workhouse killed seven of the pauper inmates. The ensuing burials at the cemetery were bungled because the coffins were 'of a curious
oblong shape' and 'of extraordinary size'. Corcoran claimed the problems
were 'not the fault of the officials of the cemetery'.[55] All of this was parish pump stuff. Unlike Martin Mitchell, Bartholomew Corcoran had no
obvious political vision or dynamic agenda. He was in it for the status,
the contacts and, doubtless, to respond to the day-to-day problems of
people in his ward. He wanted to avoid controversy and conflict, particularly if there was a religious dimension. In 1903 the Council debated
whether to take up powers under the 1902 Education Act. It proposed
to appoint a special committee to consider the issue and membership
was to be determined by religious allegiance. Martin Mitchell, by this
time on the Council, was nominated as the Catholic representative but
said that the Catholics deserved two places. He nominated Bartholomew
Corcoran, but the latter responded by saying 'he was not over-anxious
to serve. He did not want squabble but amiable work.'[56] They were worthy sentiments but demonstrate his avoidance of the contentious areas
of local government. In this case, however, his prudence was justified.

Sectarian arguments exploded between the Nonconformists and the rest, and Corcoran, perhaps through frustration, then made his most vigorous recorded intervention in debate:

> Mr Corcoran observed that the Non-Conformists were very glad in days gone by to avail themselves of the education given in Church of England and Roman Catholic schools, and did not put their hands in their pockets to build schools of their own. Now that some justice was being done to Voluntary Schools, Non-Conformists in a sectarian spirit said they would refuse to pay the rate.[57]

The Council gave up the hopeless task of trying to set up an Education Committee and in July 1903 voted narrowly to cede its education powers to the County Council. Bartholomew Corcoran and Martin Mitchell were amongst those who voted in favour of that solution.[58]

By the autumn of 1903 Bartholomew Corcoran had had enough of being a councillor. He was now an old man, nearly seventy, and he decided not to seek re-election.[59] He also left the Board of Guardians around the same time. The pinnacle of his local government career had been the chairmanship of the Burial Board. He was not, however, quite in his dotage. His affairs had already taken a new twist, and to understand this we need to return to the family home in Foregate Street.

Exodus from Stafford: the history of Bartholomew's children

Bartholomew and Anne Corcoran had five children (Figure 7.2). They were spaced at regular intervals over a thirteen-year period, a fact that suggests both frugality and careful family planning. The household may have been frugal too. Only from 1881 do we know they employed a live-in servant, although they may have had daily women before that. By that time they had taken in Anne's aged mother and she lived with them until her death in 1893. Their hard background made the Corcorans careful. Their objective was a secure environment out of which their children could emerge confidently into respectable Stafford society. The evidence is that they achieved it. The children attended the Catholic schools, and as far as we know got into no serious scrapes. Both Mary and Agnes dutifully embroidered the samplers that respectable young women of the age produced.[60] After leaving school the two girls stayed at home for some years before enrolling together, in 1889, at Our Lady's (Notre Dame) Women's Training College for teachers in Liverpool. They graduated with Elementary School Teachers' Certificates: Mary in 1893 and Agnes in 1894. Both spent some time at schools in Liverpool before returning to Stafford.[61] They were, however, forced to give up teaching when they married.

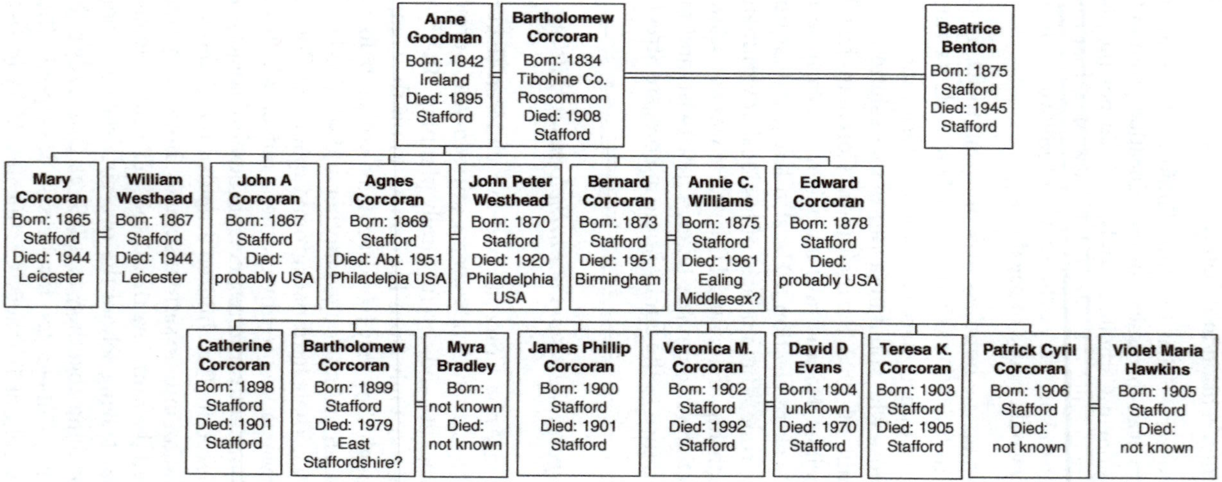

Figure 7.2 Bartholomew Corcoran's children

There were only two Corcoran marriages to ethnically Irish people. All the others were to English partners. This indicates the extent of the family's integration into the host society and suggests it was part of a conscious strategy to do so. Mary and Agnes Corcoran's marriages exemplify this. In 1893 Mary married William Westhead, and seven years later Agnes married his brother John Peter (usually known as Peter). The Westhead family came from Aspull in Lancashire and their aspirant working-class origins were similar to the Corcorans'. Their father, also William Westhead, had started work as a wagoner in a coal mine, but some time in the 1850s he became a fireman on the LNWR.[62] He moved to Stafford around 1861 when it was made a key shed on the line, and he rose to be a driver. William therefore made it into the aristocracy of labour. In 1863 he married Mary Goodall from a Stafford shoemaker's family. William and Mary Westhead's children in turn worked hard to move up the social hierarchy. The eldest, Thomas (b. 1864) became an accountant and a prominent local businessman active in the Tory Party, ultimately becoming Mayor of Stafford in 1910.[63] The younger William (b. 1867) trained as a dispensing chemist whilst his brother Peter (b. 1870) also went into accountancy. Although the Westheads' social aspirations were similar to those of the Corcorans, it was not inevitable that the two families would become linked. There were obvious differences. The Westheads were English, Protestant and also possibly Freemasons.[64] In cities like Liverpool the chances of Mary Corcoran and William Westhead meeting and marrying would have been small, yet in Stafford such a liaison could occur. The Corcorans were members of the Stafford business network and its social connections, and the Westheads were also insinuating themselves into this social circle. Bartholomew probably began to use Thomas's services as an accountant. We know that Bartholomew's son John was already friendly with young William Westhead in 1891 because he was staying at the latter's digs in Birmingham on census night. Thus it came about that Mary Corcoran and William Westhead formed the relationship that led to their marriage in 1893. Whether William's parents totally approved of this mixed-religion marriage is uncertain. Figure 7.3 shows the marriage party assembled in the back yard of the Corcorans' Foregate Street property. Bartholomew is the bearded man in the centre of the picture and Anne sits in front of him. Both stare proudly and confidently at the photographer. The bridegroom, William, stands to the right of Bartholomew, looking satisfied but a trace nervous. The man to the right is his father. Old William Westhead has turned grimly away from both his new in-laws and the camera. His wife Mary, the woman in the dark dress seated below him, stares at the ground. Do these poses betray embarrassment or dislike at the situation? If they do, the Westhead parents must have got over it by the time Peter married Agnes a few years later. The success

Figure 7.3 Respectability and integration: the mixed marriage of Mary Corcoran and William Westhead, 10 August 1893 (image courtesy of Sally Ann Harrison)

of these socially advantageous marriages overcame any sectarian doubts held by the two families.

The two Westhead–Corcoran couples went on to lead successful and respectable lives – but not in Stafford. They left, as did all Bartholomew and Anne's children. Mary and William Westhead stayed on for about ten years after their marriage, and in 1901 they were living at no. 54 Corporation Street, a classic address for aspiring middle-class people. William was still a pharmacist, but to further his career the couple moved to Leicester where he worked at the Provident Dispensary. The family remained in the Leicester area thereafter. Agnes and Peter Westhead took a more radical course of action. After a period in Shrewsbury they emigrated to America in 1908. The couple settled in Philadelphia and did well, and there are numerous descendants living in the United States today.[65]

Bartholomew and Anne's son Bernard (b. 1873) also left Stafford after his marriage. As a young man he worked as a plumber in his father's business. He seemed set to become part of the Stafford business network, and his marriage in 1896 looked part of the same pattern. His bride was Annie Catherine (or Kate) Williams, from a family of local Catholics who were also moving up the social scale from relatively humble beginnings. Kate's grandfather George had opened a butcher's shop, and from the 1860s his business was just a few doors up from the Corcorans. His son Frederick developed the enterprise and became wealthy.[66] From the 1880s he described himself as a 'cattle dealer' and by 1891 the family had moved along the road to Brook House, a substantial dwelling in its own grounds at the edge of the town. It looked as though Bernard Corcoran had made a good catch in Kate Williams and would be set to take over, in partnership, his father's business. That did not happen. Within five years of their marriage Bernard and Kate had decamped to Derby and around 1902 they moved to Birmingham, where he got a job in the cycle industry. His occupation in 1911 was described as 'handle bar builder' at a cycle works.

The exodus from Stafford of the Corcoran children was completed by John Anthony (b. 1867) and Edward (b. 1878). John also began as a plumber in the business, and during the 1890s it looked as though he would also become a member of the middle-class Catholic elite. His name crops up amongst the organisers and stewards of Catholic soirées, dances and similar events.[67] By 1901 he and his brother Edward had taken over the premises in Foregate Street from their father. John then unexpectedly rejected life in Stafford. He spent some time in California in 1900 or 1901, and in December 1905 he emigrated permanently. In New York he told the authorities he was going to Philadelphia, which is plausible, since we have seen his sister Agnes also went there later. The trail then goes cold, however, and John's subsequent history is unknown. His New York entry record does, however, contain a bit of evidence that hints at how John defined his own identity and perhaps his apparent alienation. His nationality was stated as 'Ireland'.[68] This may have been a simple clerk's error, but, if genuine, it suggests identification with his ethnic roots and rejection of his parents' strategy of integration into Stafford society. We do not know whether his brother Edward had the same perspective, but in 1907 he also emigrated to the USA. In 1910 he was living with Agnes and Peter Westhead in Philadelphia.[69]

Anne and Beatrice

So, in the 1900s, Bartholomew and Anne Corcoran's children deserted the family home, the family firm and Stafford. This was a radical shift in the trajectory of this strand of the Corcoran family. They had seemed a classic example of the strategy of integration, yet in the end the fate of the second generation appeared to be one of long-term transients. Why did this happen? The key lies in the death of Anne Corcoran née Goodman on 5 March 1895.[70]

There seems little doubt that Bartholomew and Anne's marriage had been a conventionally dutiful and apparently successful relationship. The couple had sacrificed much in their early years to establish the business and create a nurturing environment for their children. They made their way into Stafford's middle class, especially its Catholic social side. Anne particularly threw herself into Church society, and during the 1880s she consistently turns up amongst the people organising Catholic soirées.[71]

Figure 7.4 Irish and English Catholic families in Stafford: Bernard Corcoran's marriage to Kate Williams, 25 June 1896 (image courtesy of Sally Ann Harrison)

Once they were grown up her children also became involved. The evidence is, therefore, that Anne was at the centre of this tight family. Her relationship with her children was probably stern but loyal and it produced a cohesive family unit. Her death at the early age of fifty-two shattered things. Bartholomew expressed his grief publicly by donating the Stations of the Cross, as a memorial to his wife, to the new St Patrick's Church opened four months after her death.[72]

For a time the remaining family held together. On 25 June 1896 they gathered for Bernard's wedding to Kate Williams, and we see Bartholomew amongst them looking prosperous but solemn in top hat and massive beard (Figure 7.4). Now, of course, he was on his own.[73] But Bartholomew had a shock in store for his family and friends. Seven months after Bernard's wedding, on 28 January 1897, Bartholomew arrived at the Sacred Heart Catholic Church in Blackpool and got married again. His new wife was Beatrice Benton. She was twenty-two years old – forty-one years younger than her husband. The couple had sneaked off to Blackpool to avoid the embarrassment of a ceremony in Stafford, and it all must have created quite a scandal.[74]

The marriage shows Bartholomew breaking free from earlier constraints. He was an old man in a hurry. We do not know precisely how the couple got involved because the apparently respectable public figure had married a young woman from a pretty humble background. Her father, William, had been a blacksmith, railway porter and, in 1900, kept the Brown Horse beer shop on Grey Friars.[75] In 1891 Beatrice was a servant at Lammascote Farm. She may later have served in the Corcoran household because there was a family connection. Beatrice's mother, Mary Ann Follows, was a very distant cousin of Henry Follows who married Bartholomew's sister Bridget. Whatever the age and social disparity between the couple, the marriage put new life into Bartholomew. He was still active in politics and local society but between 1898 and 1906 he also fathered six children with Beatrice, although only three survived infancy (Figure 7.2). Unlike their step brothers and sisters, members of this branch of the Corcoran family were to remain in the Stafford area throughout the twentieth century.

Anne Goodman's children were unable to accept their father's radical change of life and became increasingly estranged from him. The division of his property suggests some of the family politics. Bartholomew owned a row of twelve houses in Stone Road, but some time in the 1900s he gifted them specifically to his son Edward and daughter Agnes (Westhead). Perhaps it was to help them set up in America. When he died all the rest of his property and effects went to his new wife, Beatrice. This included a piece of land nearby that Bartholomew stated was 'not included and was not intended by me to be included' in the deed of gift of the twelve houses in Stone Road. This implies there had been a family dispute over it whilst he was alive. There were various other properties in the north end and the gross value of the estate was £1,033 11s 11d (worth around £102,370 at 2012 prices). Beatrice certainly needed the money since she was now a widow with three young children to bring up. It meant, however, that the other children – Mary, John and Bernard – received nothing.[76]

Bartholomew Corcoran died in June 1908 at the age of seventy-four. He merited an obituary in the *Staffordshire Advertiser*, which said that he came to Stafford about fifty years previously but made no mention of his Irish origin.[77] It paid tribute to his interest in public affairs and as a liberal benefactor to St Patrick's Church and schools, and it suggests a man still respected in the district despite his somewhat surprising final years. What are we to make of Bartholomew Corcoran and his families? Both he and his wife sought security through hard work and a willingness to take the Stafford social environment as they found it. Their faith was important to them, but the Church was valuable for contacts in the host society as much as for spiritual support. That meant, however, largely sublimating their Irish identity and allying themselves with English Catholicism. There is only one public record of Bartholomew showing an interest in Irish affairs. On St Patrick's Day 1896, amidst the celebrations at St Patrick's schoolroom, an outside speaker lectured on 'The Young Ireland Movement'. He was 'loudly applauded' and Councillor B. Corcoran proposed 'a hearty vote of thanks'.[78] This event took place a year after Anne Corcoran's death. Perhaps he was already loosening the shackles after years of caution and conformism. Even so, a brief dose of enthusiasm

amidst the bonhomie of St Patrick's celebrations was but a modest nod
to his Irish origins.

This is not to say that the family's Irish origin was immaterial. Rather,
it is an example of Alan O'Day's concept of 'mutative identity' affected
by the inherent and changing circumstances of the place in which they
settled. The Corcorans' ethnic identity was not maintained as an active
force because in Stafford it could not distribute meaningful benefits.[79]
The fact that Anne Corcoran's children dispersed and John Anthony *may*
have decided to reassert an Irish identity was determined by the accident of Anne's death and the internal family relationships amongst this
group of people. Their general strategy of integration, most notably by
intermarriage with people from the host society, was ultimately still the
dominant force. That is illustrated equally by the history of Bartholomew
Corcoran's sisters.

Mixed marriages: Catherine Corcoran's daughters

As was pointed out earlier, both Mary and Bridget Corcoran speedily
married ethnically English men: one Catholic, the other Protestant. Mary
Corcoran had to take over James Charles Clewlow's young Protestant
children from his first marriage, so she was faced immediately by a household with potentially conflicting identities. Nevertheless, the couple went
on to have six surviving children of their own and they were brought up
as Catholics. Both Mary and her own children (but not James nor his first
wife's children) took an active part in the Catholic social scene alongside
her brother's family. James Clewlow was similar to his brother-in-law in
wanting to run his own business, but the trends in the shoe trade were
against such small operators and he was declared bankrupt in 1873.[80]
He ultimately became a foreman in a shoe factory and died in 1893. It
is noteworthy that the four Clewlow–Corcoran children who married
chose ethnically English partners, and all ultimately left Stafford for other
destinations in the Midlands. After Clewlow's death the widowed Mary
went to live with her daughter Ruth and her husband Arthur Shaw. The
latter was a brickworks manager, and the family ultimately settled in
Bromyard in Herefordshire. Mary Corcoran's son Ernest became a mech-
anic and his brother-in-law gave him a job at the Bromyard brickworks.
Family obligations seem to have been a significant force in the second
Clewlow family.

Bridget Corcoran's marriage to Henry Follows was an all-Catholic
affair. This family was more active on the Catholic social scene but they
were basically English Catholics. Follows worked in the shoe trade and
also wanted to be an entrepreneur. With Austin Dale, from another
Stafford Catholic family, he set up as a dealer in leather and grindery

materials for the shoe trade but the partnership was undercapitalised and Follows's contribution borrowed. In 1884 he was declared bankrupt with a deficit of £192 5s 6d (about £19,200 at 2013 prices), a fate blamed on the bad state of trade and 'death and sickness in his large family'.[81] This could have shattered the family, but Henry bounced back. He got work as a foreman in a shoe factory and the family continued to live at a respectable address in Rowley Street. His brother-in-law Bartholomew may have rescued them by paying Henry's debts, though there is no evidence. The two families seem to have been close and this is just the sort of obligation Bartholomew might have honoured.

Things were not to end happily, however. Around 1900 Bridget slipped into dementia, and by 1901 she was incarcerated as a 'lunatic' in the County Lunatic Asylum. She died there in 1904.[82] By then six of her children had married and left the family home. All but one of the Follows' seven children continued the family pattern of marrying ethnically English partners. Five ultimately left Stafford, two settling in Birmingham and Chelmsford respectively, and three in Southampton. Close sibling ties clearly operated amongst this last group. Only Catherine and Rose Mary Follows stayed in Stafford. Catherine married in 1899 but she died within the year and her husband, an elementary school headmaster, left the town. This tragedy could have been a factor undermining Bridget's mental state. Rose Mary was unique in being the only Corcoran descendant in Stafford to marry an ethnically Irish partner. He was John Gheoghegan, a second-generation Irishman born in 1854 in Bridgnorth, and considerably older than his wife. He was employed in white-collar jobs in engineering, and he and his family became respected members of the St Patrick's congregation. John played an active part in parish affairs until his death in 1927, and there are numerous descendants.

The aspirant Corcorans

The Corcoran family demonstrate a number of features. Firstly, their strategy reflected a clear desire to escape from the stress of their early lives in Ireland and Stafford. Bartholomew implemented it in partnership with Anne Goodman for the next thirty years, and Bridget and Mary did it by marrying out into the local community. The three new branches of the family moved in the same social scene and continued to show a strong sense of kinship. From their homes in Stafford's north end they reached out as respectable families to their peers in the local community and especially into the life of the emerging St Patrick's parish. Secondly, however, there is little evidence that they identified with their poor Irish neighbours and their problems, even those in nearby Snow's Yard. Bartholomew was the patron of worthy organisations – the Young Men's Association and the St Vincent de Paul Society – but there is no evidence that he did direct work with these client groups. It is similarly doubtful whether he went out of his way to employ Irish or Irish-descended workers in his business.[83] His role as a broker amongst the Irish is very indistinct. Thirdly, we see how the fortunes of the branches of this family were affected by the wider economic environment in which they operated. Bartholomew made the right choice. His business benefited from the expansion of the building trade and its greater sophistication in the second half of the nineteenth century. His sisters were less fortunate since both their husbands depended on the shoe trade, which was past its peak.

It is not surprising that the majority of the children in this extended family chose to leave Stafford. Their mobility, including emigration, was common to large numbers of English people in the late nineteenth century. It did not necessarily represent some legacy of inherent mobility amongst the Famine Irish and their descendants. People's behaviour was determined predominantly by their reaction to specific circumstances at the time and their estimate of future prospects in different situations. The *general mobility* of the Corcoran family descendants was influenced by their economic context, but the *specific decisions* they made also reflected family relationships. This leads to the final point. The history of the extended Corcoran family emphasises how the nature of family relationships could provoke either cohesion or atomisation. For most of its history in Stafford the forces of cohesion were the stronger amongst the Corcorans, but the deaths of Anne Goodman and, even, perhaps, Bridget Follows née Corcoran were life-course events that provoked atomisation after the turn of the century.

The shadowy figure of Margaret Carr

The history of the Corcoran family in Stafford is reasonably well documented. That of Margaret Carr is quite otherwise. We only have the most basic sources to trace her presence in the town. She is a classic case of someone whose testimony is lost but who deserves recognition precisely because there were thousands of migrants like her who lived with no obvious blood relatives to provide mutual support.

Margaret Carr was born in Belfast around the year 1801. She was a Catholic but we know nothing about her life before she came to Stafford in the 1850s.[84] By then she was a widow but where and when her husband died is unknown. We have no idea why she ended up in Stafford. The first we know of her was when, on census day in 1861, Edward Dawson, the enumerator, worked his way up Tipping Street in the town centre. He came to no. 14, a decrepit cottage backing on to the pig market. There he found Harriett Riley, an unmarried shoe binder of twenty-nine. This woman was eking out her sketchy earnings by taking in other lone women who had fallen on hard times. All her lodgers came originally from outside Stafford. Annie Heywood and Ann Parker were destitute widows of seventy-seven and eighty respectively, both reduced to being 'paupers on the parish'. They were dead within eighteen months.[85] Matilda Moore was a young shoe binder from Gloucestershire. And there was Margaret Carr. She was by then sixty years old and described herself as a washerwoman. This assorted group of women crammed together in a small cottage exemplifies the countless Victorian households in which people were forced into intimate relationships by poverty and housing shortage. Margaret Carr's associates formed a shifting 'pseudo-family' whose members co-existed, maybe supported each other, but also suffered the tensions of living with strangers.

Margaret may not have lost all her family links, however. Just round the corner stood no. 88 Eastgate Street, a much more elegant dwelling occupied by The Revd Thomas Smith Chalmers, a Nonconformist minister. He was running a 'classical and commercial boarding school'. And the servant there was another Margaret Carr. She was a twenty-six-year-old single woman who had been born in Ireland. Was she old Margaret Carr's daughter? It seems likely. If so, the elderly Margaret may have made some money by taking in washing from the school. It was not to last, however. By 1871 The Revd Chalmers had moved to a much posher house in Rowley Park but his servant Margaret had gone. She left Stafford altogether and she may have emigrated, possibly in 1865.[86] The family kinship bond was broken and the elderly Margaret now depended totally on strangers.

In 1871 we find her lodging at no. 17 Mill Street with the White family. Ellen White, a forty-year-old charwoman, came from Castlerea. She was, at this time, living alone with her three children whilst her husband, a labourer, was working elsewhere. It was a poor household. Ellen would have earned a pittance, her daughter Mary very little more as a shoe binder, whilst her son Thomas was an unemployed labourer. Margaret Carr's rent was therefore a vital supplement to the household income, but her ability to earn money was now feeble. The relationship between the White family and Margaret was instrumental. If she could not pay she would have to go, and for her there was only one destination – the workhouse. She died there, a pauper, in June 1873.

Margaret Carr lived in Stafford for at least twelve years – probably more. Her passage through the town went almost unnoticed and left little in the historical record. She had a life of poverty and shifting personal relationships. The battle to survive ultimately meant that blood relations, ethnic identity or religious bonds counted for little. Margaret died alone amid the corporate anonymity of the workhouse. Her sojourn as a lone individual proved to be an extreme example of a terminal 'family' in Stafford.

The Giltrap family and the benefits of Protestant connections

The history of the Giltrap family allows us to explore the background, kinship patterns and identity of a class of immigrants often neglected by historians of the Irish. They were from an Anglo-Irish background in Leinster and were Protestant, probably Methodist.[87] Although they were Unionist, as immigrants they had no involvement in the obtrusive Orangeism imported by many Irish Protestants into Lancashire, Cumbria or Scotland. Rather, they merged seamlessly into English society. They were transients in the Stafford area but some became established in another Staffordshire town, Burton-upon-Trent.

Migrant brothers: Henry and John William Giltrap

The Giltrap family came from Mullycagh, Co. Wicklow, a townland in Hollywood parish on the road from Dublin to Tullow that skirts the west-ern flank of the Wicklow Mountains. Much of the land was rather poor.[88] Descendants have no definite evidence of how the family came to that area but they were English settlers during either the Cromwellian planta-tions or perhaps in the eighteenth century.[89] In the 1830s and 1840s there were at least five closely related strands of the family living in Mullycagh and they held parcels of land ranging from around thirteen to twenty-nine acres, which means they were small-to-middling tenants.[90] Their landlord was The Revd Lord John Beresford, but that family had been absentees since their property was burnt during the '98 Rebellion.[91] There is a legend that members of the Giltrap family actively fought against the rebels and took part in the bloody retribution that followed.[92] It can be assumed, therefore, that the sense of self of members of the Giltrap fam-ily was conditioned by Protestant and Unionist superiority together with deference to members of the Ascendancy. This background was to be sig-nificant in the jobs the emigrants took in England.

Henry (b. 1827) and John William Giltrap (b. 1826) came to England in 1846/47. Their father, William Giltrap, is believed to have kept a public house.[93] Publicans needed to keep on the right side of the authorities, and William's Protestant contacts were useful to help his sons find jobs. Henry and John initially worked as servants in Wicklow, presumably in local big houses, and this gave them more contacts with the ruling elite, which were valuable when the Famine came.[94] Although Wicklow was not one of the most afflicted areas, the Giltrap brothers decided their prospects would be better in England. They emigrated and immediately joined the Staffordshire police force. How did they get these jobs so easily? Wicklow connections were the answer. The first Chief Constable of Staffordshire, John Hayes Hatton, was a Wicklow man who had joined the Leinster provincial police force in 1822.[95] He rose up the ranks to Lieutenant and would have known all the Protestant land-owning families of the county. In 1840 he left to become first Chief Constable of Suffolk and two years later took up the same role with the new Staffordshire force. When Henry Giltrap decided to go to England a Wicklow clergyman recommended him to Hatton. The Chief Constable was happy to take him on and his police service began on 1 July 1846. Some time later Mr Richard Horne of Tulfarris House, Hollywood parish, similarly recommended John Giltrap to Hatton. He started in the Staffordshire force on 1 July 1847.[96]

These events show how advantageous contacts could benefit Protestant people of modest means when they emigrated. The Giltrap brothers slid easily into jobs in England through patterns of influence largely denied to their Catholic Celtic compatriots. Their settlement in Staffordshire was fortuitous and owed nothing to the attraction of the area itself. We now need to see what use the Giltraps made of their flying start. The family's connections to Stafford proved to be lengthy but both the nature of their work and family factors ultimately meant they were long-term transients whose commitment to the locality proved to be weak.

Henry Giltrap and his family

Henry Giltrap put in a good first year's service with the Staffordshire force and was promoted to a third-class constable.[97] His career appeared to be going well but, out of the blue, things changed. Picture the scene on 26 June 1847. It was the ceremonial opening of the Trent Valley railway from Stafford to Tamworth and Rugby, a key link in the route from London to the north-west. The church bells were ringing, the flags were flying and crowds gathered to see the first train pass. Eighty members of the Staffordshire Constabulary had been dropped off by a special train to keep order along the line. Henry Giltrap was amongst them. At the end of the day the train returned from Tamworth to Stafford, picking up the exhausted policemen on the way. Chief Constable Hatton was on board to supervise the operation. Henry Giltrap got back on at Rugeley, but passing Colwich his hat fell off. In trying to grab it he overbalanced and fell out of the open carriage just as they were passing over a bridge. He managed to cling on to the train but was dragged between the carriage and the bridge parapet. His left arm was smashed. Hatton took charge and when the train got to Stafford twenty minutes later Giltrap was taken to the infirmary where his arm had to be amputated.[98] In the medical conditions of the 1840s Henry was lucky to live, but three months later he had recovered. He was, however, now useless to the police. Many others who suffered such traumas in Victorian England would have ended up penniless rejects eking out an existence on the margins of society. Not Henry Giltrap. Hatton ensured he received a gratuity of £100 from the police superannuation fund (equivalent to about £9,600 today).[99] More importantly, and luckily for him, in the early days of the railways Hatton also appointed the railway police in Staffordshire, although their wages were reimbursed by the railway company.[100] He therefore ensured that on 15 September 1847 Henry was transferred to the LNWR's Police Department at Stafford. There was work for a one-armed man there. It was the day limited services actually began on the Trent Valley line following its ceremonial opening in July.[101] Henry was no ordinary police constable, however. In those early days 'policemen' on the railways also signalled the trains, and Henry was sent to the Shugborough Tunnel three miles east of Stafford (Figure 8.1). He was paid 16s a week, later raised to 18s.[102] He was to work for the LNWR for the next forty-eight years.

Henry found lodgings in Great Haywood, a pleasant walk of three-quarters of a mile through the Earl of Lichfield's estate at Shugborough. As a railway policeman he had modest local status, and he quickly met and married a local butcher's daughter, Ann Corvesor.[103] The couple lived initially in Great Haywood, but by 1861 they had moved to a cottage in Shugborough close to Henry's work. Some time in the 1860s Henry was moved to the signal box at the other end of Shugborough Tunnel, Milford and Brocton, and the family rented a house in the straggly settlement of Milford. They lived there for at least twelve years and became part of the local community. Ann's parents lived half a mile down the road at Walton. Milford and Brocton became a much busier place when the passenger station opened in 1877.[104] The locality was, and remains, a favourite local beauty spot, and hoards of people came on the train from Stafford, Rugeley and elsewhere. Henry's work at Milford signal box was hard, particularly for a man with one arm and now in his middle age. It was shiftwork and this was a very busy stretch of railway. Until an over-bridge was built in 1877 he also had to open and close the level-crossing gates on the local road.[105]

Henry and Ann Giltrap had seven children, two of whom died young. Their son Henry (b. 1850) followed his father into service on the LNWR. He did well. Starting as a humble goods clerk, by the 1870s he was working his way up the promotional ladder in north Wales and became a station master, first at Llanberis and later at Abergele on the coast line to Holyhead. He subsequently left the railway and worked for the Singer Sewing Machine Company in London.[106] Henry and Ann's final child, Thomas Arthur Giltrap (b. 1862) also had a career on the railway. One of Thomas's children, John Maddocks Giltrap (b. 1904) emigrated to New Zealand in 1922 and founded a branch of the family there.[107] Another of Henry and Ann's sons, William (b. 1851), benefited directly from his father's status as a railwayman and from living next to the Earl of

Lichfield's estate. He became a footman at Shugborough Hall. There he met and married a nursery maid, Harriett Cockrill. William later became a butler, and the couple reputedly adopted the upper-class airs typical of deferential people serving the aristocracy. After William's death the couple's connections with England's ruling class saw Harriett become a dresser to Queen Alexandra at Sandringham.[108]

By the early 1880s Henry was getting too old for the heavy work at Milford box. He had been a reliable worker, however, and such men were valued by the railway companies. The LNWR therefore moved him to a new box in a quieter location. On 16 April 1883 the Charnwood Forest Railway was opened to the town of Loughborough in Leicestershire and Henry Giltrap was there to signal the first trains into the station.[109] The new posting meant Henry and Ann finally moved away from the Stafford area. They were only in Loughborough for five years before Ann died.[110] Left on his own, Henry moved into lodgings with Harriett Atkinson, a widowed 'retired dressmaker' of fifty-one. Her son Charles was a railway clerk, so Henry presumably got the room through him. After twelve years in Loughborough, Henry retired with a pension in June 1895 and then went to live with his son Thomas at Ainsdale in Lancashire. He died there in 1902, leaving the modest effects of £52 14s 3d.[111]

John Giltrap and his cousins: police, prison, brewery and domestic service

Although John William Giltrap began work in Staffordshire in a situation identical to that of his brother, his career was to take a different route. He did more varied jobs but ultimately his family showed more residential stability – but not in Stafford. We know that John was taken on by the Staffordshire Constabulary in 1847 but John Hayes Hatton may have considered transferring him to the railway police at the same time as Henry. The LNWR records state that 'Giltrap, J.' was appointed in September 1847 as a signalman but there is a comment in faint pencil that says 'no trace at Stafford'.[112] By 1851 John was certainly in the main force and serving in the brewing town of Burton-upon-Trent.[113] Like his brother, John soon met and married a local woman. She was Sarah Simnett, the daughter of a maltster in the brewing trade. They wed in August 1850 and his marriage to Sarah enfolded him in her family's network in the Burton area.[114] John's career in the police proved to be short, however. He resigned from the force on 1 February 1853 because he had got a job as a warder at Stafford gaol. We do not know why he switched careers at this point. His record in the police had been good and the force's recommendation would have been important to get his new job.[115] Beyond that we cannot say. In 1861 John and Sarah Giltrap were living with their three children in Gaol Road, Stafford. They had modest status and employed a fourteen-year-old servant girl, Rosetta Merricks.

John's sojourn in Stafford and the prison service was limited to between ten and fifteen years. Sarah may never have settled away from her home town or perhaps the job proved too unpleasant and held few prospects, but in the 1860s the family moved back to Burton-upon-Trent and John got a job in the brewing trade. That was not to last long, however, because in 1869 he was killed in an accident at the brewery. Even so, by then he and Sarah had had six children and they established a strong branch of the Giltrap family in the Burton area and beyond with many descendants.[116]

The Giltrap family is a classic case of sequential migration amongst kin. Henry and John Giltrap had established the family in Staffordshire in 1846/47, and it was the base that enabled two of their cousins to follow.[117] By 1851 Margaret Giltrap (b. 1823) had arrived and was a servant in Lichfield. Her employer was Samuel Spofforth, an organist at the Cathedral, and church connections in Wicklow probably helped get her the job. John Giltrap almost certainly helped her get a later position because in 1861 she was living in Stafford at the same time as John and his family were in the town. Margaret's employer was Robert Hand, a wealthy solicitor who lived at Rowley Hall in a posh southern suburb of the town. She did not stay in Stafford, however. When John Giltrap and his family moved back to Burton upon Trent in the 1860s, Margaret followed and she died there in 1876. She never married. Margaret's sister, Martha Giltrap (b. between 1834 and 1836) had also arrived in Staffordshire by 1851 and gone straight to John William's base in Burton-upon-Trent. She was housemaid to Henry Whitehead – a land agent – and his family. It is noteworthy that both these Giltrap sisters found work with middle-class and professional employers, and it suggests a respectable demeanour and the ability to call on good references from their background in Wicklow. Martha stayed in Burton-upon-Trent and in 1856 married a cooper from Co. Sligo, Charles Lyons. They had a large family and there are descendants in the area as well as, through subsequent emigration, in South Africa.[118]

The benefits of a Leinster Protestant background

During their time in the Stafford area the Giltraps were the type of family that causes considerable problems for the historian. They were not prominent enough to earn much local publicity. They did not feature as reported participants in church or social activities, but neither did they indulge in petty crime, drunkenness or any of the other activities that might have brought them to the attention of the courts and local journalists. They lived lives that were hard-working and respectable, and their children showed significant upward social mobility. They are representative of the many Irish families, both Protestant and Catholic, who lived quietly, intermarried and ultimately merged seamlessly into the host society. Even so, we have seen that the Giltraps had the advantage of being able to exploit Protestant networks in Wicklow to smooth the process of emigration and settlement in Staffordshire. With Henry as the pathfinder, members of the Giltrap family helped each other to settle, and a commitment to kinship bonds and obligations amongst them endured. Henry and John William immediately married Staffordshire women. There was little ethnic or cultural distinction between these working-class Anglo-Irish Protestants and the women they married, and the resultant families grew up with an overwhelmingly English identity. They were respectable, modestly aspirant and little different from their neighbours except in terms of their heritage. That was something that had little day-to-day significance in their social relationships.

The Giltraps' relationship with the town of Stafford was, nevertheless, peripheral. Henry and his family lived the whole time a few miles out of town, though they doubtless came in for shopping and also to visit John William and his family when he was at the gaol. The nature of both brothers' jobs inherently meant their social interaction with the local community was limited. Henry existed in the shiftworking community of the railway and John's prison job also orientated him to an inward-looking work culture. In both cases they and their descendants proved to be long-term transients in the Stafford area and the same applied even more forcibly to Margaret Giltrap. Like many other migrants, the Giltraps came, settled, but ultimately moved on because of the interplay of work opportunities and family idiosyncrasies.

Larkin/Mullarkey: contested identity in a Catholic family?

The final family amongst these general workers also proved to be long-term transient, but in this case the process took forty-five years. The history of the Larkin family in Stafford provides rare evidence of possible identity tensions affecting in-migrant families down the generations. Explaining the origin of those tensions is not straightforward, but they expressed key choices made by family members.

Immigrants to Preston: Mullarkey or Larkin?

James Larkin moved to Stafford from Preston in Lancashire in 1862, when he was a young man of twenty-two. Although he was born in Ireland in 1840, his family came to Britain during the Famine and he had already lived the majority of his life in England. He presumably spoke with a hybrid Irish-Lancashire accent. His sense of self was influenced by the tension between an Irish family home and the need to make his way in the wider society, initially in the hard environment of an Industrial Revolution town. His history is illustrative of many Famine immigrants who had been young children in Ireland, had then experienced the searing impact of the Famine and subsequently lived most of their youth in stressful conditions in England. It gives us some idea of the dilemmas he faced and the consequences for his family down the generations.

James Larkin's real name was James Mullarkey. He changed it to Larkin when he moved to Stafford. We therefore need to begin the story with a look at his family's earlier history in Preston. The Mullarkey family came from Connacht, and, although the surname is commonest in Sligo and Mayo, family legend is that these Mullarkeys came from Co. Galway.[119] James Mullarkey's father was also called James, and in 1851 he was working as a cooper, a relatively skilled job but one he may have been doing as a back-street enterprise on his own account. The fact that his son Patrick and daughter Bridget were also coopers suggests they worked as a family unit. James, his wife Mary and their six children were packed into a slum in Back Simpson Street with two other families. It was a grim existence typical of impoverished Famine immigrants. James Sr was already fifty-seven and he died in 1854, but four of the children were adult by this time and able to earn money for the family household.[120] Family cohesion was strong, since five of the six children were still living with their widowed mother in 1861 when they were in their twenties and thirties. In the mid-1850s young James Mullarkey started work and he got jobs in the cotton mills. By 1861 he was a self-acting spinning-mule minder and it looked as though he was destined for a life in the textile industry, but James then made a radical shift of occupation. On 4 July 1862, using the name Larkin, he started work as a railway engine cleaner at Stafford shed.[121] He had moved outside the tight family unit. Why did he change his job and, more importantly, why did he change his name?

Family descendants do not know why James Mullarkey became James Larkin; there is no surviving evidence. We are therefore left to speculate, and there are three possibilities. The first is that he had something to hide and that he changed both his name and job location to escape his past in Preston. The evidence does not support this. During the 1860s James still went back to his home town, and in 1869 he was married there – as James Mularkey (*sic*).[122] His bride was Anne Nesbitt, an Irish cotton worker whose family had settled in Preston in the 1850s. Furthermore, in Stafford the couple's children were baptised at St Austin's under the name 'Mullarkey alias Larkin', so his alternative name was no secret in the local Catholic community.[123] The births were registered under the name Mullarkey. These facts also tend to disprove a second explanation – that

James Larkin wanted to bury his Irish origins because he had experienced hostility and discrimination in Preston and was making a new start with an English identity in Stafford. He may well have experienced anti-Irish hostility in Preston, but the fact that in 1861 he was a self-actor minder, a relatively skilled and well-paid job rare amongst the Irish, suggests he had not suffered crippling discrimination.[124] If he had really wanted to hide his Irish origins he would not have chosen the ethnically ambiguous, but frequently Irish, surname of Larkin. He clearly wanted to keep an element of the Mullarkey name. This all points to a final possibility – that he just did not like the name Mullarkey or was embarrassed by it. Although use of the word 'malarkey' to mean contemptible nonsense did not become current until the 1920s, the surname Mullarkey may well have carried comic 'stage-Irish' connotations before that.[125] James perhaps thought it was a burden he could do without and that he wanted a less obtrusively 'Irish' name whilst not totally rejecting his Irish heritage. He made a quirky individual decision but it was to leave his children with a dilemma.

The Stafford railway family

Why did James Larkin switch to railway work and come to Stafford? The reason was that he lost his job in the mill during the 'Cotton Famine' in Lancashire caused by the American Civil War. By July 1862 more than a quarter of the Preston population was destitute and in December 1862 49 per cent of all operatives in the cotton districts of Lancashire were out of work.[126] James Mullarkey was one of them and his answer was to look for a more secure job on the railways. Although Preston was an important junction on the LNWR line to Scotland, too many men were now looking for railway work there and James had no luck. He was, however, a reliable single man who had had a good job in the mills, and he was told that if he would move there were openings elsewhere. That is how he arrived in Stafford. In 1860 the LNWR directors decided to make Stafford the border station between the company's Southern and Northern divisions. It meant that all trains passing from one division to the other changed engines there, and a sudden and large increase in railway activity took place in Stafford in 1861–62.[127] The company was taking on more men and James Mullarkey – or Larkin – was one of them.

Having started as a cleaner, James moved on to the footplate as a fireman in May 1864. Five years later he was driving trains as a 'passed fireman', although he was still learning his trade. In March 1869 he was fined £1 – nearly a week's wages – for not having his train under control and crashing into a bridge at the end of a loop line.[128] He officially became a driver on 30 March 1871 and worked the routes to

Shrewsbury, Welshpool, Rugby and Birmingham for the rest of his career. He did not become a 'top link' driver, probably because his discip-
linary record continued to be punctuated by incidents of carelessness.
He was, however, fairly typical of most drivers at Stafford shed and it
reflected the nature of the job – shift work with long hours, poor conditions and draconian discipline imposed by a parsimonious company.[129]
Overall, James Larkin's work put him amongst the labour aristocracy of
Victorian England and provided the security to develop a respectable
lifestyle in the town.

James lodged with other railway families in his early years in Stafford.
As we have seen, he married Anne Nesbitt in 1869. Anne probably came
from an army family that had fallen on hard times. There is no record of
her father in Britain, but her mother Mary had been born in Spike Island,
Co. Cork, and two of her daughters were born in the West Indies, all of
which suggest a forces family. By 1861 the widowed Mary was scraping
an existence as a sweeper in Preston. Her daughters worked in the mills,
but Anne had already moved out of the family home and was lodging in
Walton-le-Dale, a southern suburb of the town. This suggests an independent streak. Her marriage to James Larkin brought together a couple
who could aspire to a respectable artisanal lifestyle. In 1871 the couple
were living at 35 Railway Terrace in Castletown, Stafford's railway suburb, and they already had one child, Alfred. Between 1872 and 1884 they
went on to have seven more surviving children. The house in Railway
Terrace proved too small and by 1881 they had moved to New Garden
Street, a respectable street in Forebridge. The family was to remain there
for over twenty-five years.

Although the Larkins had the trappings of a lace curtain lifestyle, the
evidence suggests a family with tensions. In 1882 James was summoned
before the magistrates for failing to send his children to school. The other
miscreant in court that day was the much less respectable John Kearns
from Red Cow Yard. This brush with Stafford's deprived underclass must
have shaken the couple. Anne Larkin would have been ashamed and
made sure it never happened again.[130] Some of the children now settled
down to diligent school careers that led to modest preferment by their
teachers. In 1886, for example, Frances (b. 1872) was one of the cast in
St Austin's School's production of the operetta *Genevieve*.[131] The Larkin
family continued to be practising Catholics, but life in the Larkin household was not all Catholic respectability. In 1886 their son James, who was
twelve at the time, stole a cash box containing papers from St Austin's
Church. He thought there was money in it. His father said in court that
he was 'a bad boy' and Canon Acton put the boot in by describing him
as 'incorrigible', reporting that he had been turned out of school for corrupting others. James was detained for one month and then sent to a
reformatory for five years.[132]

Contested family heritage or practical problems?

James's case opens up the issue of the family surname – Larkin or Mullarkey? After his time in the reformatory he initially returned to Stafford and his father got him a job as an engine cleaner.[133] He did not stick at it and some time before 1898 joined the navy.[134] By 1903 he was a leading first-class petty officer on HMS *Hearty*, but his life was cut short that year. With two others he hired a sailing boat on the River Waveney in Norfolk, but it capsized and James was drowned. Most significantly, his death was recorded as being that of James Mullarkey. He had reverted to the old family name. The funeral took place in Lowestoft and was attended by his father and his brother Joseph, and the newspaper report also referred to his father and brother by the name Mullarkey.[135]

Like James, the other Larkin children all left Stafford as soon as they were old enough to do so, and some, though not all, reverted to the name Mullarkey. It would be easy to see these two developments as triggered purely by conflicts arising from the father's ambivalence about his family heritage and his choice of a new life in Stafford. That would be facile, however. Families may be sundered by apparent ideological conflicts, but other factors always come into play. In this case, one was the job market. Stafford's economy was relatively depressed during the 1880s and 1890s and more people were leaving the town than coming to it. Children growing up in that period would commonly have felt there was more to be gained by leaving Stafford than staying, and the Larkin children saw things that way. There was, however, a more acute factor pointing in the same direction. Anne Larkin née Nesbitt died in the County Lunatic Asylum in 1894 of 'cerebro-spinal disease', or vascular dementia, and late-onset diabetes.[136] She was only fifty-one years old. The deterioration in Anne's condition in the preceding years must have created great stresses in the family. Given that James Larkin was always on shiftwork, Anne was the primary home-maker and the centre of the children's lives. With the onset of her illness the older children had to take over basic household duties and look after their ailing mother. Her illness came at a crucial time when the children were adolescents consciously defining their own senses of self. Anne's vital influence in this process was first impaired and then removed. An already sad and stressful situation was worsened when, just twelve months after Anne's death, James Larkin remarried. His new wife was Myra Furber, the fifty-three-year-old widow of a grocer, John Furber, from Hanford near Stoke-on-Trent. It seemed an unlikely pairing, but the late John Furber had a cousin, Henry, who was an engine driver at Stafford shed, so James presumably met Myra through him.[137]

At the time of Anne's death and James's remarriage up to six of the children were still living at home. By 1901 only the youngest, Annie, was still there. It would have been natural for some, as adults, to leave the family home, but the fact that they all left Stafford as well points to a desire to get away from both the town and the new domestic situation. When they gained their independence each of the children had to choose their preferred family name. At St Austin's School the children had all been known as Larkin and that is how James entered them in the census returns between 1871 and 1901. Half of the children – Frances, Mary, Edward and Annie – decided, at least initially, to retain the surname Larkin as they became adults. In day-to-day life that was probably the easier option, but it was not without difficulty, since they would face problems if they had to present birth certificates showing the name Mullarkey. Even so, the path taken by this group of children suggests a lack of commitment to the family's Mullarkey heritage. The children were leaving home under stress from the events leading to Anne's death and James's remarriage. In some cases their subsequent history proved problematic. That was certainly the case with Mary Larkin. She and her brother Joseph Patrick were twins born in 1875, but their lives took very different paths. Mary retained the name Larkin and in 1898 was working as a 'music teacher, domestic servant etc.' in Cheshire. Her musical skills, hallmark of a respectable background, must have been learned at school or in the family house in New Garden Street. In February of that year she was arrested in Birkenhead and admitted a string of thefts, mostly of money, from houses across Cheshire. The newspaper reported, rather ambiguously, that 'the prisoner associated herself with the Catholic minister at Stockport and is said to have successfully filled the role of adventuress throughout Cheshire'.[138] It would seem that she fell back on her Catholic roots and was given some support by the Church in her predicament. She was sent to the Convent and Home of the Good Shepherd Reformatory in Litherland near Liverpool.[139] What she did after her release is unknown but she may have emigrated.

Mary's elder sister Frances Ellen took a more respectable path as a teacher, and in 1891 was attending, under the Larkin name, the Notre Dame teacher-training college in Liverpool at the same time as the Corcoran sisters. That indicates the Larkins were respectable enough to afford the fees or to tap some charitable source of money. It has not proved possible to discover what happened to her after that but she certainly did not return to Stafford. She also may have emigrated.

We know most about the early adult years of Edward Larkin (b. 1880). His is the only case where we have specific evidence about why, having started out as Larkin, he ultimately changed his name back to Mullarkey. He left home as soon as he could and moved to Birmingham. He initially worked as a machinist in the city's gun trade, but on 28 May 1903 he joined the army – as Edward Larkin.[140] He served in the Sherwood Foresters, the North Staffordshire Regiment Reserve and, during the Great War, the West Yorkshire Regiment. By 1905 he had been sent to the garrison at Ambala in India and in 1910 he was at Peshawar near the North-West Frontier, but in March 1911 he left the army and was transferred to the reserve. He went back to Birmingham.

It was at that point that a practical problem arose over his surname. He got a job as a wagon repairer on the LNWR, but things had changed since his father had been taken on with his assumed name in 1862. In the 1900s the company checked potential employees' birth certificates and they insisted that Edward use his registered name, Mullarkey. We know this because on 20 May 1911 he wrote to the army record office in Lichfield and, although now damaged and indistinct, his respectful letter asks if 'I could be allowed to change my name'. He explains the LNWR's position and concludes that 'I thought it best to adopt my own name'.[141] The key point is that Edward obviously regarded Mullarkey as his genuine family name but made it clear that he was forced to use it now for practical reasons rather than because it was a burning identity issue for him. The change hardly turned out to be worthwhile. He soon quit the railway job and went back to the army. The bridge had been crossed, however, and he was generally known thereafter as Mullarkey, though not always. In August 1912, as Edward Mullarkey, he received a seven-day sentence with hard labour for begging at Fulwood in Preston, presumably outside the army barracks there.[142] It is a sorry tale and it suggests he had no contact with his Mullarkey relatives in Preston. He had already passed the pinnacle of his army career since he had lost his lance corporal's stripe in 1910 for being absent from a roll call at Peshawar. He served during the Great War, though not on the Western Front, and ended his service in the garrison in Malta. He was invalided out of the army in April 1919.[143]

Annie Larkin (b. 1884), the youngest child, remained with James and Myra in the family home. She was only eleven when James remarried so she had little choice but to accept her new step-mother's presence. As she grew up she also showed some commitment to Stafford. Events connected with St Austin's Church seem to have been significant in her life and she attended reunions and soirées, at least once in the company of her step-mother.[144] Even so, she escaped home fairly quickly. In 1905 she married – as Annie Larkin – Samuel Shotton, a native Staffordian from a modest family who worked as a putter-up in the shoe trade.[145] The couple had their first child, Winifred Annie, in Stafford, but at the beginning of October 1908 their relatives went down to the station to see them off on the train to Liverpool. They were emigrating. At Liverpool they boarded the SS *Essex*, bound for Sydney.[146] The Shottons settled in that city, had six more children and created an extensive family in Australia.[147]

This pattern of exodus from Stafford was completed by James and Anne's other sons, and they all adopted the name Mullarkey. Edward and James were not the only sons to join the forces. Alfred John (b. 1871) went into the navy. Joining the military was a way for poorly qualified young men to get a guaranteed job away from where they had grown up. It was, in other words, an easy escape route. The fact that three of the Larkin children took it suggests that they had a strong desire to get out of both Stafford and the family home. In 1898 Alfred John married – with the name Mullarkey – a local girl, Florida Carr, daughter of an innkeeper in Littleworth. She was his only continuing link with Stafford. By 1901 the couple were living in Portsmouth and Alfred was a chief petty officer. In November 1914 he was serving on the battleship HMS *Bulwark* when it blew up at anchor in Sheerness. Only twelve of the crew survived and Alfred Mullarkey was one of 738 men who died.[148]

There is no evidence that Dennis (b. 1877) went into the forces but he did the nearest thing and also got well away from Stafford. He became a seaman – of sorts. In 1901 we find him – as Dennis Larkin – as a ship's fireman living on a hulk, the SS *Lady Jocelyn*, laid up in Victoria Dock, London.[149] In 1907 he married, however, under the name Mullarkey, and by 1911 was a stationary engine driver living, also under the name Mullarkey, in Forest Gate, London, with his wife and two children. So Dennis reverted to the Mullarkey name when he got married. Joseph Patrick, Mary Larkin's twin brother, did much better than his sister and was the only child who successfully aspired to a higher-status occupation. He became an elementary school teacher and in 1901 was lodging in Middlesbrough under the name Mullarkey. We have no direct evidence as to why he reverted to the old family name, but he probably needed to present his birth certificate to gain entry into the teaching profession. He did well and in 1911 had become headmaster of an elementary school in West Ham. There is a family legend that he wrote speeches for Keir Hardie which, even if dubious as to detail, probably stems from his identification with British Labour politics rather than Irish issues.[150] He was still single, and at that time lodging with his brother Dennis and his family in Forest Gate. That is the only example we have of family obligations coming into play amongst the Larkin/Mullarkey children. Otherwise, they scattered to the four winds.

Interpreting the Larkins' history

The Larkin family that developed in Stafford after James's arrival in 1862 proved to be long-term transient. The family broke up. On 4 December 1906 James was compulsorily retired from the railway on the grounds of 'old age and ill-health'.[151] He died just seven months later.[152] Only Myra was then left in the family home in New Garden Street. A combination of factors had produced that outcome. Lack of job prospects during the 1890s was undoubtedly one force pushing the Larkin children out of Stafford. It seems clear, however, that their commitment to the family home and to Stafford weakened following Anne Larkin's death. It was the mother who had acted as the prime focus of this family. James Larkin gives the impression of a somewhat peripheral figure struggling to define his sense of self and his personal identity. The saga of his name change underlines this. He had shown a streak of determination by leaving Preston, but otherwise his behaviour was irresolute. He clearly had a problem with his name but there was some force preventing him going the whole hog and abandoning his previous identity. Perhaps it was pressure, even ridicule, from his family back in Preston. Perhaps it was an unwillingness totally to abandon his family heritage – or even his Irish identity. There is no surviving testimony on why James took his decision, but he left each of his children with a dilemma that they had to resolve when they grew up.

The choices made by the children split on gender lines. The daughters all stuck with the name Larkin, but we should be cautious in drawing much from this since our knowledge of Frances and Mary's adult life is limited, and Annie married when she was twenty-one. The sons all made a clear, though in one case delayed, choice to return to the Mullarkey name. This was partly a matter of bureaucratic convenience, as Edward clearly demonstrated, but we cannot avoid the conclusion that there were deeper factors at work. The decision inherently involved rejecting their father's choice of name and his assumed identity. It must, in part, have been a rejection of him and his role in the family. He had publicly described his son James as 'a bad boy' when he got into trouble for stealing, and that reveals a troubled relationship between father and son. Was this symptomatic of a wider malaise in the relationship between James and all his sons? The fact that they all left Stafford as soon as possible certainly points in that direction. The reasons presumably lay in James's failings as a family home-maker and problems with his personality. The name issue became a weapon in a wider conflict between the sons and their father but it could also have been a conflict over the rejection or retention of an Irish identity. The sons' ultimate choice of 'Mullarkey' clearly shows willing acceptance of a demonstrably 'Irish' surname and the family heritage it embodied, but farther than that we cannot go. Although the children were youngish adults during the struggle for Irish independence, we have no evidence that they identified politically or culturally with their Irish compatriots.

The history of the Larkin/Mullarkey family in Stafford shows how the experience of even a nuclear migrant family could be complex. They had the trappings of an aspiring working-class family – a secure income from a skilled job, a sound house in a respectable street and adherence to organised religion. A more detailed examination of its history illustrates, nevertheless, the stresses that stemmed from the migrant background of its founders. The ultimate expression of those tensions took over forty years to work through but they resulted in the effective demise of the Larkin/Mullarkey presence in Stafford.

Craft, clerical and service families: conclusions

The Corcoran, Giltrap and Larkin families, together with Margaret Carr, demonstrate some of the variety of non-labouring people who left Ireland in the nineteenth century. Any generalisations must be made with caution. For a start, the families spanned a wide range of social status. Margaret Carr was close to the bottom of society, reduced to taking in washing to survive. Her history is set apart from the other three families considered in this chapter. These families also had modest beginnings but after arrival in Staffordshire they got jobs with some skill and status. In the case of James Larkin and the Giltrap brothers it was the specific jobs that brought them to Staffordshire rather than any prior connection with the area, but it was the other way round for the Corcorans. They arrived because of the long-term links between Castlerea and Stafford and they then had to find their way into jobs in the local economy.

The individuals who initially came to Britain and established these families had all experienced the Famine decade in Ireland. The Corcorans and the Mullarkeys had lived through the Famine in the west of Ireland whereas the Giltraps and Margaret Carr came from areas generally less affected. Even so, its overall impact on Ireland's economy and psyche was a factor in bringing them to England too. Once here the Giltraps got on because of their origins, whilst James Mullarkey did so in negation of his. The Corcorans lay in between.

We can make some general conclusions about these CC&S families. All four had kinship ties and obligations, although the disappearance of Margaret Carr's presumed daughter ultimately left her alone. The problems caused by the premature death of wives emphasise the pivotal role played by women in their roles as wives, mothers and home-makers in creating and sustaining – where they chose to do so – a nurturing family ethos. These families showed a clear division of labour, with the men bringing in money from relatively secure work and the women creating the secure home environment. The Corcorans, Larkins and even Henry Giltrap's family lived for years in the same houses. They could afford decent accommodation and use their residential stability to create respectable and homely surroundings for their families. They were, in other words, lace curtain Irish. None, as far as we know, had to take in lodgers.

By the 1900s the three main families were beginning the third generation since their arrival, and we have to consider their mutating identities in the intervening half-century. The Giltraps and their descendants retained little meaningful identification with their specific origins in

Wicklow, though they had had to come to terms with the fact that they were now merely individuals in a mass rather than members of a community indoctrinated with the superiority of the Protestant Ascendancy and its hangers-on in Ireland. The situation for the Corcorans and Larkins was different. These Celtic Catholics from the West had a world view that contrasted with dominant forces in their new host society, but we have seen contrasts in their responses. The Mullarkey/Larkin family were an extreme and public demonstration of multiple identities whereas the Corcoran family were more businesslike. Their strategy was rapid integration into the economic and social life of Stafford. They wanted to survive and get on. This small group of CC&S families was diverse in both its origins and its trajectories, and it cautions against generalising on the Irish experience in Britain on the basis of ethnic, religious or class stereotypes. We have seen here some evidence of the complex mixture of structural, cultural and individual forces that were played out down the generations of migrant families.

Notes

1 Davidoff *et al.*, *Family Story*, pp. 123–7.
2 H. Heinrick, *A Survey of the Irish in England (1872)*, ed. A. O'Day (London: The Hambledon Press, 1990), p. 127.
3 *Ibid.*, p. 59.
4 J. Denvir, *The Irish in Britain from the Earliest Times to the Fall and Death of Parnell* (London: Kegan Paul, Trench, Trübner, 1892), p. 426.
5 *Ibid.*, pp. 398–9.
6 Belchem, *Irish, Catholic and Scouse*, pp. 45–7.
7 The term was coined by Foster in his seminal essay 'Marginal men and Micks on the make: The uses of Irish exile, c. 1840–1922' in R. F. Foster, *Paddy and Mr Punch: Connections in Irish and English History* (Harmondsworth: Penguin, 1995), pp. 281–305. It was taken up by Belchem in *Merseypride*, pp. 129–51.
8 W. Jenkins, 'In search of the lace curtain: Residential mobility, class transformation and everyday practice among Buffalo's Irish, 1880–1910', *Journal of Urban History*, 35:7 (2009), pp. 970–97; P. O'Leary, *Immigration and Integration: The Irish in Wales, 1798–1922* (Cardiff: University of Wales Press, 2000), esp. pp. 187 and 203; J. Belchem, 'Class, creed and country: The Irish middle class in Victorian Liverpool' in R. Swift and S. Gilley (eds), *The Irish in Victorian Britain: The Local Dimension* (Dublin: Four Courts Press, 1999), pp. 190–211.
9 P. O'Leary, 'The cult of respectability and the Irish in mid-nineteenth century Wales' in O'Leary (ed.), *Irish Migrants in Modern Wales* (Liverpool: Liverpool University Press, 2004), pp. 109–40 (pp. 119–38).
10 L. Miskell, 'Informal arrangements: Irish associational culture and the immigrant household in industrial South Wales' in Belchem and Tenfelde, *Irish and Polish Migration*, pp. 111–12.

11 O'Leary, *Immigration and Integration*, p. 131.

12 Akenson, *Irish Diaspora*, p. 15; S. Fielding, *Class and Ethnicity: Irish Catholics in England, 1880–1939* (Buckingham: Open University Press, 1993), Chapter 1.

13 M. J. Hickman, *Religion, Class and Identity: The State, the Catholic Church and the Education of the Irish in Britain* (Aldershot: Ashgate, 1995).

14 Jenkins, 'In search of the lace curtain', p. 973.

15 Belchem, 'Class, creed and country', p. 211; J. Herson, 'The English, the Irish and the Catholic Church in Stafford'.

16 O'Leary, *Immigration and Integration*, p. 299.

17 Belchem, *Irish, Catholic and Scouse*; P. J. Waller, *Democracy and Sectarianism: A Political and Social History of Liverpool, 1868–1939* (Liverpool: Liverpool University Press, 1981); S. Davies, *Liverpool Labour: Social and Political Influences on the Development of the Labour Party in Liverpool, 1900–1939* (Keele: Keele University Press, 1996).

18 A. O'Day, 'The political behaviour of the Irish in Great Britain in the later nineteenth and early twentieth centuries', in Belchem and Tenfelde, *Irish and Polish Migration*, pp. 75–92.

19 Fielding, *Class and Ethnicity*, Chapters 5 and 6; J. Hutchinson and A. O'Day, 'The Gaelic revival in London: 1900–1922. Limits of ethnic identity' in Swift and Gilley, *Irish in Victorian Britain*, pp. 254–76.

20 F. Geary, 'Deindustrialisation in Ireland'.

21 *SA*, 6 June 1908.

22 NLI, Dublin, Tithe Applotment Books, Co. Roscommon, 25/10 Tibohine Parish; Griffith's Valuation, Tibohine Parish taken from Leitrim-Roscommon web-site, Griffith's Valuation data, www.leitrim-roscommon.com/cgi-bin/lrgrifnew, accessed 15 July 2010.

23 Patrick Corcoran's first son was also named Bartholomew, and the Irish practice of naming first-born sons after their paternal grandfathers seems to have applied. The 1825 Tithe Applotment is difficult to decipher, but a number of Corcorans held land in Cloonfad, one of whom is indistinctly written but could be B. Corcoran. He held six acres of third-class land. NLI, TAB 25/10, film 87, Tibohine, Co. Roscommon (1825).

24 The Catholic register for Tibohine parish only dates from 1833 and the precise date of Patrick's marriage is unknown; NLI, Roman Catholic Parish Records (microfilm) P6955, Tibohine, Co. Roscommon, baptisms, 1833–64.

25 Stafford RD, Marriage Certificate, 6b/25, no. 183: Bartholomew Corcoran and Ann Goodman, 12 February 1863.

26 Griffith's Valuation, Roscommon: the rental value of the cabin was 5s, so it was of the meanest class.

27 PP1835, *Royal Commission on the Condition of the Poorer Classes*, p. 512.

28 Stafford RD, Deaths, January–March 1856, 6b/7.

29 When Catherine Corcoran died in 1877 the SBC Burial Record 3/6007 described her as 'the widow of the late Patrick Corcoran, labourer', but the death certificate elevated him to 'carpenter (at Haywood)'; Stafford RD, Death Certificate, 6b/3, no. 335: Catherine Corcoran, 11 October 1877 (made available by Dave O'Meara, a descendant).

30 The third, Richard Corcoran, was christened in Castlerea on 20 February 1841. He may have died during the Famine. NLI microfilm P4619, Kilkeevin, Co. Roscommon, baptisms, 1826–60 (1840–60).

31 For an analysis of the residents of Plant's Square in 1861 and 1871 see Herson, 'Why the Irish went to Stafford', Figure 4.3 and pp. 65–8.

32 Stafford RD, Birth Certificate, 6b/12, no. 425: Mary Corcoran, 15 May 1865.

33 Their address was variably given as Foregate Street and Grey Friars in both census returns and trade directories, but they were clearly in the same premises all the time.

34 *SA*, 30 August 1862. They left Stafford during the 1860s.

35 She was unable to sign her name when she registered Mary Corcoran's birth on 12 June 1865.

36 Stafford RD, Marriage Certificates, 6b/26, no. 153: James Charles Clewlow and Mary Ann Moore, 28 March 1852; 6b/40, no. 160: James Charles Clewlow and Mary Corcoran, 9 October 1866. Stafford RD, Deaths, April–June 1866, 6b/12: Mary Ann Clewlow, aged thirty-six. Agnes Cora Clewlow's birth was not registered but her brother Henry was born in September 1867 which makes Agnes's latest possible birth December 1866. Stafford RD, Births, July–September 1867, 6b/6: Henry Clewlow.

37 Stafford RD, Marriage Certificate, 6b/34, no. 15: Henry Follows and Bridget Corcoran, 18 February 1868. Copy of certificate made available by Dave O'Meara.

38 SBC Burial Record, 3/5275: Catherine Corcoran [Jr], 18 August 1875; 3/6007: Catherine Corcoran [Sr], 15 October 1877; and Stafford RD, Death Certificate, 6b/3, no. 335: Catherine Corcoran, 11 October 1877.

39 His first entry, as 'Bartlett [*sic*] Corcoran, painter and glazier', gives his address as no. 2 Grey Friars *Place*. This was actually the address of James Charles Clewlow and Mary Clewlow née Corcoran. The 1871 Census nevertheless shows Bartholomew and his family living at no. 2 Grey Friars, so the directory got his address wrong as well as his Christian name. *Kelly's Directory of Birmingham, Staffordshire, Worcestershire and Warwickshire*, Part 2: *Staffordshire* (London: Kelly, 1872), p. 726.

40 *SA*, 25 October 1879.

41 *Ibid.*, 21 April 1888.

42 J. Halden, *Stafford and District Directory and Almanack* (Stafford: *Stafford Advertiser*, 1891–1907).

43 *SA*, 11 April 1891.

44 *Ibid.*, 23 February 1884.

45 *Ibid.*, 6 June 1908.

46 *Ibid.*, 30 November 1889 and 11 January 1890.

47 SRO D5008/2/7/11/1.

48 *SA*, 20 October 1894 and 3 November 1894. This poll was significant because the first 'labour' councillor was elected in Stafford: F. Evans, who had been sponsored by the Trades Council.

49 The East Ward covered about half the population of the town overall but included most of the working-class north end, hence the greater proportion of Irish Catholics there. Herson, 'The English, the Irish and the Catholic Church in Stafford', p. 46.

50 Davies, *Liverpool Labour*, p. 119; B. Keith-Lucas, *The English Local Government Franchise: A Short History* (Oxford: Basil Blackwell, 1952), pp. 74–6; H. Jones, *Women in British Public Life, 1914–50: Gender, Power and Social Policy* (Harlow: Pearson, 2000), p. 9.

51 Probate Registry, London, will of Bartholomew Corcoran, died 3 June 1908, probate granted 17 July 1908.

52 SRO D3180/1, Corporation of Stafford Year Book, 1899–1900 and 1901: census returns. The birthplaces of two councillors have not been traced.

53 *SA*, 22 December 1894.

54 *Ibid.*, 17 November 1894 and 26 January 1895. The works at Lammascote Farm were opened in 1897.

55 Halden, *Stafford and District Directory*, 1899; *SA*, 18 May 1895.

56 *SA*, 14 March 1903.

57 *Ibid.*, 9 May 1903.

58 *Ibid.*, 25 July 1903.

59 *Ibid.*, 24 October 1903.

60 Personal information from Sheila Leslie-Miller, a descendant, 2002.

61 Evidence contained in a letter from Sister Jean Bunn, Provincial Archivist, Sisters of Notre Dame, Liverpool to Sheila Leslie-Miller, 27 September 1991.

62 Census returns, 1841 and 1851, Aspull, Lancashire. There were a number of Westhead families in the Aspull area and genealogies produced by descendants of the family disagree on William's antecedents. The evidence suggests they were Thomas Westhead, a labourer, born in Aspull in 1806 and Ann (surname unknown) from the same place and also born in 1806.

63 Obituary, *Express and Star* (Wolverhampton), 6 November 1930.

64 William Westhead's son Thomas was a Freemason, though membership may have begun with him because of the advantage to his business; *ibid.*

65 Information from Barrie Jones, Brian Westhead, Michael Harrison and Sheila Leslie-Miller, descendants. New York Passenger Lists, *Adriatic*, arrived 29 October 1908 from Southampton; *Ancestry* (accessed 20 September 2013).

66 When he died in 1904 his estate was worth £12,863 7s 11d: about £1.3 million at today's prices.

67 *SA*, for example 25 January 1890, 21 January 1893, 28 November 1896, 14 January 1899.

68 New York Passenger Lists, 21 December 1905, *Oceanic*; *Ancestry* (accessed 15 January 2013).

69 US Census Returns, 1910, Philadelphia Ward 40, District 1013. The return gives his year of entry as 1907.

70 Memory card of Anne's death in the possession of Sheila Leslie-Miller, a descendant.

71 *SA*, for example 13 March 1886, 26 February and 1 April 1887, 21 April 1888, 9 March 1889.

72 *Souvenir of the Golden Jubilee of St Patrick's, Stafford, with the History of the Parish* (Stafford: St Patrick's Church, 1945), p. 2.

73 Private photograph.

74 Fylde RD, Marriages, January–March 1897, 8e/938: Bartholomew Corcoran and Beatrice Benton. Information from Nick Griffin, a relative of the Benton family, April 2007.

75 1901 census return and *Kelly's Directory of Staffordshire*, 1900; *Ancestry* (accessed 28 October 2013).

76 Will of Bartholomew Corcoran. His executors were the priest at St Patrick's, Joseph Lillis, and Patrick Donnelly, a rising stalwart of the parish. This suggests Bartholomew's standing in the local Catholic community was still high.

77 *SA*, 6 June 1908.

78 *Ibid.*, 21 March 1896.

79 O'Day, 'Conundrum'.

80 Notice of second dividend on bankruptcy dated 11 October 1873, made available by Dave O'Meara.

81 *SA*, 19 July 1884.

82 Stafford RD, Death Certificate, 6b/2, no. 80: Bridget Follows, 9 April 1904. Certificate made available by Dave O'Meara.

83 In the census returns between 1871 and 1901 there were only seven 'plumbers, glaziers, painters' or combinations of these occupations living in Stafford who were Irish or Irish-descended and who might have been employed in Corcoran's firm. One was Mary Corcoran's son, Frederick Clewlow.

84 SBC, Burial Record 4/3551, 20 June 1873; the priest at the committal was Catholic.

85 Stafford RD, Deaths, October–December 1862, 6b/13: Annie Heywood; July–September 1862, 6b/4: Ann Parker.

86 New York Passenger Lists, arrival 2 November 1865: Margaret Carr, servant, aged about twenty-six, Irish, port of departure Liverpool, ship *Sir Robert Peel*. This might have been the young Margaret from Stafford, though it is impossible to prove. *Ancestry* (accessed 10 March 2013).

87 Information from a descendant, Rachel Taylor, November 2007.

88 S. Lewis, *A Topographical Dictionary of Ireland* (London: S. Lewis, 1839): Hollymount Parish, Co. Wicklow.

89 Correspondence with Eileen Ramsey, April 2008; and Robert Giltrap, September 2003.

90 Tithe Applotment Books, Mullaca, Hollywood, Co. Wicklow, 1833; Ireland, Griffith's Valuation, 1848–64. *Ancestry* (accessed 5 December 2012).

91 Lewis, *Topographical Dictionary*: Hollywood parish.

92 Information from Rachel Taylor, 2007.

93 Information from Robert Giltrap, July 2003.

94 Both gave their previous 'trade or occupation' in the Staffordshire police records as 'servant'. SRO C/PC/1/6/1, Staffordshire Police Force Register, 1842–63, nos 601: Henry Giltrap,723: John Giltrap.

95 J. Reakes (compiler), *Ireland: The Royal Irish Constabulary, 1816–1921*; *Ancestry* (accessed 18 December 2012).

96 SRO C/PC/1/6/1, no. 601: Henry Giltrap. The clergyman's name is unfortunately illegible in the original record, but he was 'The Hon. and Revd Archdeacon' and clearly of elite status; no. 723: John Giltrap.

97 *Ibid.*: promoted to third class, 1 October 1846.

98 *SA*, 26 July 1847 (2nd edn) and 3 July 1847.

99 SRO C/PC/1/6/1, no. 601: Henry Giltrap, Observations; resigned 21 September 1847.

100 *SA*, 23 October 1847. Chief Constable's report to the Staffordshire Quarter Sessions.

101 R. Christiansen, *A Regional History of the Railways of Great Britain*, Vol. 7: *The West Midlands* (Newton Abbot: David and Charles, 1973), pp. 134–8 and 266.

102 NA, RAIL410, Piece 1859, Staff Register, Stafford Station, Police Department (Trent Valley Section); *Ancestry* (accessed 3 December 2012).

103 Stafford RD, Marriages, October–December 1849, 17/195: Henry Giltrap and Ann Corvesor.

104 L. M. Midgley (ed.), *The Victoria History of the County of Stafford*, Vol. 5: *East Cuttlestone Hundred* (1959), at www.british-history.ac.uk/report/aspx?compid=53393&strquery (accessed 23 September 2013).

105 E. Talbot, *Railways in and around Stafford* (Stockport: Foxline, 1994), p. 36.

106 Information from Alison Souster, a descendant, March 2006.

107 Information from Robert Giltrap, July 2003.

108 'A Queen's maid', obituary, *Daily Sketch*, 21 November 1930; and information from Alison Souster, 2006.

109 NA, RAIL410, Piece 1797, LNWR Staff Register, 14 April 1883, Loughborough; *Ancestry* (accessed 12 December 2012): 'Milford and Brocton, signalman, station, 24s'; 13 April 1883: 'to Loughborough'; M. C. Reed, *The London and North Western Railway: A History* (Penryn: Atlantic Transport, 1996), p. 128.

110 Loughborough RD, Deaths, January–March 1888, 7a/88: Ann Giltrap.

111 England and Wales, National Probate Calendar (Index of Wills and Administrations), 1858–1966: Probate Office, Liverpool, Henry Giltrap, probate granted 10 March 1902; *Ancestry* (accessed 23 September 2013).

112 NA, RAIL410, piece 1858, LNWR Register of Permanent Officers and Servants, Trent Valley Stations, Police Department (Northern Division); *Ancestry* (accessed 12 December 2012).

113 *White's Historical Gazetteer and Directory for Staffordshire*, 1851; *Ancestry* (accessed 17 January 2013). 1851 Census Returns, Station Street, Schedule 209, Burton-upon-Trent.

114 Burton upon Trent RD, Marriages, July–September 1850, 17/5: John William Giltrap and Sarah Simnett.

115 SRO C/PC/1/6/1.

116 Information from Eileen Ramsey, a descendant, September/October 2004 and March 2008.

117 It is impossible to tell the relationship from census information, but family knowledge is that she was John's cousin or niece, not his sister. Information from Eileen Ramsey, July 2004 and March 2008.

118 Information from Eileen Ramsey, July 2004.

119 Information from John Macrae, a descendant, derived from Paul Mullarkey and Joseph Patrick Mullarkey, October 2008.

120 Preston RD, Deaths, January–March 1854, 8e/289: James Mullarkey.

121 SRO D1225, LNWR Staff Register, Stafford, 1898–1927. The register includes details of all staff recruited since 1858 who were still working in Stafford in 1898.

122 Preston RD, Marriages, April–June 1869, 8e/739: Ann Nesbitt and James Mularkey. Ann's name was variably spelt Anne and Nesbit.

123 BAA P255/1/4–5, Stafford, St Austin's, Registers of Baptisms, 1870–83, 1883–90; evidence contained in letter from SRO to Mary Nobbs, communicated to the author, August 2003.

124 D. Osgood, 'The Irish in Ashton-under-Lyne in the 1860s', *Transactions of the Historic Society of Lancashire and Cheshire*, 149 (2000), pp. 145–71 (Table 5).

125 C. Soanes and A. Stevenson (eds), *Concise Oxford English Dictionary*, 11th edn (Oxford: Oxford University Press, 2004).

126 J. Watts, *The Facts of the Cotton Famine* (London: Frank Cass, 1968 [1866]), p. 117; J. K. Walton, *Lancashire: A Social History, 1558–1939* (Manchester: Manchester University Press, 1987), p. 241.

127 Talbot, *Railways in and around Stafford*, p. 6.

128 SRO D1225: James Larkin, conduct record, 1 April 1869. He was earning 4s a day at this time.

129 *Ibid*. He was fined or suspended twenty-seven times over a period of thirty-eight years.

130 *SA*, 14 October 1882.

131 *Ibid*., 2 January 1886. Her name is given as 'Florence', presumably a reporter's error.

132 *Ibid*., 17 April 1886.

133 The 1891 census return shows him as a 'railway engine cleaner'; he was living with his parents.

134 He does not appear in the LNWR staff list that records those already working on the railway in 1898.

135 *SA*, 29 August 1903.

136 SBC Burial Record 6/11938, 13 January 1894. Her age is there given as forty-nine, which is slightly younger than that suggested by the census records. Her illnesses were inherited conditions that Annie Larkin passed on to some of her descendants. Information from John Macrae, September and November 2008.

137 Stafford RD, Deaths, October–December 1893, 6b/11: John Furber. St Austin's Marriage Register, 26 January 1895.

138 *SA*, 12/19 February 1898.

139 1901 census enumeration return, Orrell and Ford, Litherland Sub-district, West Derby Registration District.

140 Census enumeration return, 1901, which merely says 'gun trade', and his stated occupation on his short service attestation form, 28 May 1903. NA, WO363, British Army World War I Service Records, 1914–20, 6913: Pte Edward Larkin; *Ancestry* (accessed 23 September 2013).

141 Reply, 23 May 1911, from C. Layton, Infantry Record Office, Lichfield, to Edward Larkin's letter of 20 May 1911; NA, WO363: Pte Edward Larkin; *Ancestry* (accessed 7 January 2013).

142 HM Prison, Preston: Particulars of the conviction of a soldier … Edward Mullarkey, Army [illegible] Office, 24 August 1912; NA, WO363: Pte Edward Larkin; *Ancestry* (accessed 7 January 2013). The offence appeared thereafter in his army records.

143 NA, WO363: Pte Edward Larkin; *Ancestry* (7 January 2013).

144 *SA*, 13 April 1901, 15 February 1902, 28 February 1903.

145 A 'putter-up' was a man who collected the hides or rough leather and distributed it to the skilled 'clickers' who cut it out for the shoes. It was an unskilled and fairly menial task.

146 Third-class-steerage passenger contract ticket dated 23 September 1908, Federal-Houlder-Shire Lines, SS *Essex*, departing Liverpool 10 October

1908: Mr Samuel Shotton, Mrs Annie Shotton and Winifred Annie Shotton. Copy made available by John Macrae.

147 Information from John Macrae, 2008.

148 World War I: Casualty Lists of the Royal Navy and Dominion Navy, 26 November 1914, Loss of Battleship Bulwark from Internal Explosion, Mullarkey, Alfred J., CPO, 139722 (Po); www.naval-history.net (accessed 23 September 2013).

149 The enumeration return gives his place of birth as Liverpool, but that also applies to the man above him in the list and is almost certainly carelessness by the enumerator.

150 Information from Mary Nobbs, July 2005. Hardie was MP for West Ham South, 1892–95, well before Joseph Mullarkey's arrival in London; but the latter may have been active in the West Ham Labour Party.

151 SRO D1225, final entry in the conduct record.

152 SBC, Burial Record 9/4976, 15 July 1907.

8

Old soldiers and their families

The Irish in the British forces

In 1830, when Ireland comprised about one-third of the population of the United Kingdom, over 40 per cent of the British army consisted of Irish recruits. This over-representation of the Irish continued throughout the rest of the nineteenth century.[1] The Irish were essential to the army's strength yet we are still lacking a full-scale study of their role and its paradoxes.[2] Historians of the Irish in Britain have almost totally ignored them. For local but not unique reasons, the case of Stafford shows the value of examining Irish individuals and families who had a military background. Many Irish soldiers passed through the town, and seventeen settled families had their origins in the military.

Irishmen joined the forces, and particularly the army, for a number of reasons. Conditions were bad in the rural areas, and in the big cities and towns they were little better. The strongest areas of recruitment were in fact the counties of Dublin, Cork, Antrim and Galway, which had the major urban centres.[3] The British army depended increasingly on Irish recruits because military wages were low. By 1850 army pay was equivalent to only the lowest farm labourer's wages in Britain. From then on the increasing gap between British civilian and military wages caused a chronic shortage of British recruits, whereas in Ireland army pay was still competitive with the miserable local incomes. The army also offered security and the prospect of adventure and camaraderie, and joining up remained a preferable, even attractive, option for many.[4] This was still the case amongst the labouring Irish who emigrated to Britain, and Fitzpatrick has emphasised that it continued into the second-generation born in Britain.[5] We have seen evidence of this already amongst Stafford's families. Another factor encouraging second-generation recruitment was the establishment of a military tradition within families that led to sons following their fathers into the forces. We shall see this in Stafford too.

A century after the nationalist struggle targeted the alien forces of the British Crown it can appear paradoxical that so many Irishmen continued to join the British army right up until the 1916–18 period. Karsten has argued, however, that in the nineteenth century most Irishmen did not view themselves as joining the 'British army' but rather 'the army'. He suggests that most of the poor Catholics who enlisted were essentially apolitical, and that after seven centuries of British rule they implicitly regarded the United Kingdom and the Crown as a fixed entity.[6] Although there were nationalists and republicans who always refused to enlist, they were a small minority until the War of Independence. Even during the Fenian infiltration of the 1860s, and certainly at other times, most of the recruits were in practice faithful to their oath, generally followed orders and identified with the *esprit de corps* of their regiments. One reason was that until 1847 they had to sign up for a minimum of twenty-one years. Even after 1847 enlistment was for at least ten years.[7] Long service was designed to indoctrinate soldiers into army discipline, divorce them from local connections, and ensure that their loyalty and commitment were to their comrades and the regiment.

The majority of the Irish recruits, unskilled and often ill-educated, were in the infantry. Many served in Irish regiments but they were also essential to the strength of Scots and English regiments where, in some cases, they formed more than half the strength.[8] If they stuck it out, soldiers serving at least seven years received a gratuity and those who lasted twenty-one years got a pension. In 1892 a retired colour sergeant, the highest rank open to ordinary recruits, received a pension of £65 a year.[9] Irish soldiers were almost certain to be drafted to overseas and they can be seen as both the subjects and the agents of British imperialism. Kevin Kenny has argued, however, that this paradox is more apparent than real.[10] The Irish were at the metropolitan core of the Empire, and he suggests that in the nineteenth century it was inevitable they would take advantage of imperial career opportunities. For ordinary soldiers that was service in garrisons throughout the Empire and, at times, fighting Britain's imperial wars. Thousands of those discharged in the second half of the century had also fought in the Crimean War.

After discharge soldiers faced all the challenges and many of the traumas with which we became familiar in the twentieth century. On the one hand their military experience might be welcomed by employers seeking disciplined and deferential workers, for example the railway companies and various public services. They might find avenues open to them that were denied to their deprived labouring cousins. On the other hand, service often left men disabled, debilitated, troubled and with few skills. Some suffered from what would now be diagnosed as PTSD, particularly those who had been on the front line in the Crimean War, the Indian Mutiny and other overseas engagements. Many were unable to compete in the harsh job market. Poverty, drink and petty violence were hazards that lay in wait for those out of luck and unable to cope. We need, therefore, to consider how previous service in the army coupled with an earlier childhood in Ireland impacted on the family lives of Stafford's military families. How did their earlier experiences influence their sense of self and their identity, and were there distinctive patterns of family life and wider relationships amongst these families?

Stafford's military families

The seventeen military families who settled in Stafford arrived at different times and by three different routes.[11] In the 1840s four Chelsea pensioners settled in Stafford with their families. The reasons why Leicester-born William Peach settled in the town with his Irish wife and children are now lost in the mists of history, and the same is true for the families headed by Protestant Irish-born soldiers John Carroll and William Gibbs. Thomas Salt had been born in Stafford and he was merely coming home with his wife and children, some of whom had been born during his posting in Ireland.

By contrast, the largest group of nine military families settled in Stafford for a clear reason. In 1852 the King's Own Staffordshire Militia was re-embodied, having been in abeyance since 1816.[12] It was a volunteer force in which men enlisted, undertook basic training, and then returned for regular weapons training and an annual two-week camp. Militia regiments could also be sent on garrison duty elsewhere. During their service the soldiers received military pay, bad as it was, and also an annual retainer. The main recruits were farm labourers and others in low-paid casual work for whom the money was useful and a dose of army life a change from drudgery and insecurity. In 1856 Stafford became the base for the Second Staffordshire Militia, and new barracks were built in Forebridge. They housed the militia stores and administration, and also a small garrison of regular soldiers. These men were long-service recruits, mostly sergeants in their forties, who were approaching the end of their army careers. Some had already been pensioned off. The barracks acted as married quarters and in 1861 they housed nine families, of which three were headed by Irish-born soldiers. Two of the resident wives were Irish and thirteen of the children in various families had been born during service in Ireland. Six militia staff also lived in the town. By 1871 the number of Irish-born soldiers in the barracks had increased to five. There were then four Irish-born wives but the number of Irish-born children had dropped to four. None now lived in the town. There was a frequent turnover of these regular militia staff and most moved on to postings elsewhere. Not all, however. In the period between 1852 and 1881 nine

Table 8.1 Date of arrival of military and labouring families

Date of arrival	Military families %	Labouring families %
Before 1845	—	6.6
1846–51	23.5	39.6
1852–61	17.6	33.0
After 1861	58.9	19.8
Total no. of families	**17**	**106**

chose to settle in Stafford with their families. This source of settlers was lost in 1881, however, when the town ceased to be a militia base and the barracks were taken over by the police force.

Work in Stafford brought the other four military families who settled. Andrew Higgins, a Catholic from Co. Carlow, had got a job on the railway after leaving the army and was transferred to Stafford around 1861. James McDonald, also Catholic, gravitated to the prison service after the forces and was a warder at Stafford Gaol in the 1870s. He later became full-time manager of the County Conservative Club, a reflection of the ideological influences in his earlier career. Army life had left Edward Tallent with few obvious skills. After twenty-three years in the 54th Regiment he had ended up in 1891 as a labourer in Salford. Nevertheless he aspired to better things somewhat and, perhaps through army connections, he moved to Stafford in the early 1890s and worked as an attendant at the lunatic asylum. The family became respectable working-class Catholics in the town.[13] The special case of John Ryan is dealt with later.

We can compare the characteristics of these seventeen military families with those of the labouring families. They generally arrived later, with three-quarters settling after the Famine and over half after 1861 (Table 8.1).Under one-fifth of the labouring families came at this late stage. Information on provincial origins is limited but sustains the picture of military enrolment described earlier in this chapter. The majority were from Leinster together with a minority from Munster (Table 8.2). Only one family originated in Connacht, which contrasted with the overwhelming proportion of labouring families from the west. Military families also diverged from the norm in having one-quarter who represented the British transient in Ireland (Table 8.3). The children in these families were 'accidentally Irish', and reflect the mobility of army life and the role played by British soldiers in enforcing State power in Ireland. Nearly 30 per cent of the families were of mixed ethnicity, with an Irish soldier marrying a non-Irish woman. Though none settled in Stafford, reverse mixed families – British soldiers marrying Irish women during service

Table 8.2 Provincial origin of military and labouring families

Province of origin	Military families %	Labouring families %
Connacht	9.1	87.5
Leinster	72.7	6.3
Munster	18.2	2.5
Ulster	—	3.8
Total no. of families	**11**	**80**

Provincial origins for six military and twenty-six labouring families not known.

Table 8.3 Types of military and labouring families

Type of family	Military %	Labouring %
1. Migrant Irish family (Migration of pre-existing core unit with children born in Ireland)	29.4	49.1
2. Migrant Irish adults (Core unit established in Britain; children born after arrival in Britain)	17.6	38.7
3. Male-mixed family (Core unit with Irish-born male with non-Irish partner)	29.4	6.6
4. Female-mixed family (Core unit with Irish-born female with non-Irish partner)	—	5.7
5. British transient in Ireland (British-born parent with child(-ren) born in Ireland)	23.5	—
Total no. of families	**17**	**106**

in Ireland – were also stationed in the militia barracks. This pattern contrasts with the overwhelming dominance of migrant Irish families and adults amongst the labouring families. The British transient in Ireland also served to increase rather spuriously the proportion of Protestants amongst the military families. The religious mix was evenly split. If the transients are disregarded, over two-thirds of the service families were Catholic. Although a lower proportion than the labourers, this demonstrates how the army was a refuge for poor Catholics despite the apparent conflict with Catholic nationalist sentiment in Ireland.

Table 8.4 The fate of military and labouring families

Ultimate fate	Military families %	Labouring families %
Long-term transient	23.5	34.0
Terminal	17.6	22.6
Integrating	58.8	43.4
Total no. of families	**17**	**106**

The military families who settled in Stafford showed a stronger propensity to integrate than was the case with the labouring families (Table 8.4). Even so, over 40 per cent of these families proved to be either long-term transient or died out.

Four case studies examine the experience of military families. They are:

- John Carroll and the Coleman family;
- the Disney family and Trench Nugent;
- the Cronin family;
- John Ryan and the Blundon family.

John Carroll and his integration with the Coleman family

The Catholic John Carroll has already appeared in this book because, in Chapter 5, we saw that in 1857 Mary Coleman bigamously married John Carroll, a 'pensioner'. The suspicious nature of their marriage meant their family subsequently had things to hide, and they did so by being ultra-respectable and becoming 'more English than the English'. These family traits also reflected John Carroll's previous history, however, and here we briefly trace his earlier life and how he arrived in Stafford.

Born in Athlone in 1814, Carroll signed up with the 84th Regiment of Infantry in Jersey in 1830. He subsequently served in the East Indies for over fourteen years, and his reckonable service came to the magical twenty-one years that qualified him for a pension when he was discharged in 1857. His left the army because of 'general debility' caused by his long service in the tropics, but his body also bore 'the marks of Corporal Punishment'. They revealed a far from perfect record in his first fifteen years. He had numerous court martial appearances for petty infringements of army discipline, but in the 1850s settled down. 'His character [was] latterly Good and he [was] in possession of One Good Conduct Badge.'[14] John Carroll was now thoroughly inculcated with the attitudes and identity of a common soldier in the imperial British army. After his discharge at Chatham in July 1857, he must have been posted briefly to the new Second Staffordshire Militia, since there is no other obvious explanation of why he ended up in Stafford. He probably met Mary Duffy née Coleman after Mass or through lodging with, or close to, her in Mill Street. The liaison certainly developed rapidly and the couple married at the Register Office on 17 November 1857. Mary had been deserted with a baby daughter six years previously, and for her, marriage to a man twenty years older but with a secure pension must have been deliverance from difficult circumstances. Despite his 'general debility', John went on to sire three children with Mary, and he almost certainly dominated his new family unit. Even so, he was joining a family, the Colemans, with strong kinship links. These provided support, and John and Mary used them as the base for a strategy of merging into respectable working-class Stafford society. It worked. They lived quiet lives together for thirty-seven years and their children stayed with them into adulthood, which suggests a cohesive home environment. The youngest, Catherine (b. 1864), was still living at home when her father died in 1894.

In John Carroll we have an example of an ex-army man who, with modest skills but apparent determination, made a successful transition into civilian life and marriage and put down deep roots in Stafford society. We now turn to a Protestant army family where the path of readjustment proved to be more problematic.

The Disney family and Trench Nugent: Anglo-Irish officers in Stafford

At 6.30 am on Friday 13 December 1867, platelayer William Greatholder came upon a dreadful sight in Shugborough Railway Tunnel near Stafford. The still warm body of a man was lying between the rails with its head and one foot severed. At the ensuing inquest the driver of a luggage train, John Matthews, stated that he had entered the tunnel at 5.30 am and had felt a sudden jerk near the southern end. At Colwich he reported a problem with the track, and Greatholder was dispatched to the tunnel to inspect it. There he made his gruesome find. The remains proved to be those of Captain Lambert Disney, paymaster of the 2nd Staffordshire Militia in Stafford.[15]

The story of the Disney family and their associate Trench Nugent underlines how people play out their lives with a complex interaction between their individuality, their social relationships and the wider societies of which they may be members. These particular people's lives were interwoven closely but their responses to resettlement from Ireland to England differed. They came from a group – the Anglo-Irish Protestant Ascendancy of southern Ireland – who have been effectively ignored in

Figure 8.1 Shugbrough Tunnel near Stafford, where Henry Giltrap was a signalman and Lambert Disney met his death

the literature on Irish migration. Writings on Protestant emigrants concentrate on their most obvious manifestation, the Scots-Irish of Ulster and particularly the Orangeism that many, though not all, brought to Britain. No study has been done of Church of Ireland adherents from the south who came to England in substantial but uncharted numbers. They lack historical visibility and it is generally assumed that, as in the case of the Giltraps, their emigration was opportunistic and that they integrated easily into English life and culture. The Disney family contradicts that assumption. Their emigration came about through family crisis and their settlement in England was reluctant and uncommitted. They are in this chapter because they arrived in Stafford through Disney's role in the military, but the ultimate explanation for their insecurity and his death on the railway line must be sought from before, as well as during, his militia service. By contrast, though closely associated with the Disneys, Trench Nugent did conform more closely to standard assumptions concerning Anglo-Irish Protestant emigrants.

Explaining Disney's death

Lambert Disney was born in Galtrim, Co. Meath, in 1807. His family were middling landowners and, as Church of Ireland adherents, they partially funded the local parochial school.[16] In the 1840s Disney himself continued to hold about 150 acres of land in the parish.[17] The connections amongst members of the Protestant Ascendancy opened up opportunities, as we have seen already at a modest level with the Giltrap family, and, as a landowner, Lambert Disney benefited even more. His social network explains how, by the late 1830s, he had become agent on the Earl of Darnley's estate around the small town of Athboy, Co. Meath. The Earl was at that time a minor, and Disney first comes to historical notice with evidence that he sought to eject Thomas Anniskey, 'a most wretched, squalid-looking old man', from bog-land near Jamestown. That incident demonstrates the easy and arrogant use of power that Ascendancy attitudes inculcated in men such as Disney. The eviction should have been done under the names of the Earl's guardians rather than his own as agent, and the Quarter Sessions held it to be illegal.[18] His behaviour was typical of the agents of absentee landlords, and in that time of agrarian unrest he was a likely target of hatred, even more so because he was also a local magistrate. In 1842 he was the victim of a 'robbery of daring boldness' when his horse and harnesses were stolen from his house, Clifton Lodge, at Athboy.[19]

The picture was not all repressive, however. In 1843 Disney got the Earl's guardians to agree a 25 per cent reduction in estate rents, 'an act of great liberality'.[20] During the Famine he was chairman and treasurer of the Relief Committee in the Barony of Lune, based at Athboy.[21] He undoubtedly worked hard but with mixed objectives. On the one hand he pursued the local public works programme with vigour in order to get at least some money into the hands of local people and keep them on the land. On the other hand he operated the Darnley estate's landlord-assisted emigration policy to get rid of 'surplus' tenants. Some ended up destitute in Quebec when his agent failed to give them the promised start-up money, but 'No blame can fairly be attached to me' was his offhand response when the issue was publicised.[22] It seems clear, however, that the exertions of the Famine period sapped Disney's health and in the end he was the victim of a 'severe and protracted' illness that led him to give up his duties in 1850.[23] Disney represented that class of Anglo-Irish whom Buckland describes as 'prominent in Ireland at a local level' as agents, magistrates and social leaders.[24] His record up to 1850 was of an agent diligently administering his employer's estate but also trying to ameliorate the effects of the Famine within the structural flaws of British Government policy.

There was another facet to Disney's character, however, which was to lead more specifically to the railway track in Shugborough Tunnel. His Anglo-Irish Protestant background put him continually on the defensive against perceived threats to his status and religion. That was common in people of his class, but the hypothesis advanced here – and it can only be a hypothesis – is that Disney so internalised the politics of Irish religion and class that it ultimately gnawed at his whole being. It is also possible that he experienced some trauma, perhaps connected with his experiences during the Famine. The evidence is fragmentary but telling. In the second half of the 1830s, in an attempt to head off the growing Repeal movement, the Irish administration pursued policies that moved Catholics into positions of influence, such as the magistracy, that were previously reserved for Protestants. This 'green' shift was also associated with attempts to undermine the Orange Order. The Protestant landlord class held that the Government was attacking property rights and showing dangerous signs of weakness towards rural crime and popular movements.[25] On 24 January 1837 a 'grand aggregate meeting of the Protestant nobility, gentry, clergy &c of Ireland' was held at the Mansion House, Dublin, and 'Mr Lambert Disney of the County of Meath' was there on the platform amongst scores of others. He publicly gave support to a plethora of speeches and resolutions that repeated the mantras of 'no surrender', 'preserving life and property', 'our Protestant institutions menaced' and so on.[26] His presence suggests he may have been an Orangeman, though we have no confirmation of this.

Disney's attendance at the meeting in Dublin shows he carried the baggage of Protestant ruling-class insecurities in nineteenth-century Ireland. It does not prove he was mentally obsessed by these issues, however. For that we have to turn to other evidence. In 1844 he filed a libel suit against the proprietor of the *Athlone Sentinel* alleging that the latter had published a fake letter 'with reference to the private concerns of Mr Disney and his political and religious tendencies and his conduct in relation to the tenantry of the Ballyleeran estate', of which he was agent.[27] No smoke without fire. It seems that Disney's obsessions were widely known. Other evidence survives from his death. It was reported in the press that 'the deceased was religiously disposed and, on more than one occasion, he has circulated among the inhabitants of the town religious and other publications.'[28] Though we do not know the content of those publications, they suggest he was on a one-man crusade against threats to his religion and his class. That brings us to a second point – the timing of his death on 13 December 1867. It was the height of the Fenian campaign in Britain – indeed, the Clerkenwell Prison bombing took place later the same day.[29] As a Protestant military man Disney would have seen the Fenians as the ultimate threat to his religious and political identity. But the same period also saw the public conversion of Gladstone and the Liberals to Irish reform – notably the disestablishment of the Church of Ireland and around the land question. Gladstone had come out for disestablishment in May 1867 and he was to make his famous Southport speech on Ireland six days after Disney's death.[30] We know Disney was no friend of the Liberals. Stafford was a two-member seat, but, in the general election of 1865 there was only one Conservative candidate although there were two Liberals. Disney voted only for the

Conservative.[31] Fenianism and Gladstone's shift of policy both struck at Disney's whole world view and could have been the factors that tipped this obsessive man towards suicide.

At the inquest the jury returned a verdict of 'accidental death'. That was a polite fiction to save the family from shame. The evidence points to suicide. A key role was played by his militia associate Trench Nugent. He testified that he had been with Disney on the evening before his death and that he 'had not been in his usual spirits. He had, indeed, been suffering much depression – of a religious character – for some time past.' Nugent claimed that Disney had never given him reason to think he might be suicidal, but the evidence of his behaviour that night is bizarre. Having gone to bed but then not sleeping, he got up in the early hours of the morning and left the house. Nugent tried to explain this by saying it was possible he wanted to see his doctor who lived at Colton near Rugeley, and that the railway line was the most direct route. But why go in the middle of the night and along such a dangerous and illegal route? It would have been difficult to walk along the track in the dark and no witness said he was carrying a lantern. When the level-crossing keeper at Queensville asked where he was going he failed to respond but turned quickly on to the road up Radford Bank.[32] He must subsequently have returned to the railway and walked into the pitch-black of Shugborough Tunnel. He was near the far end when the luggage train came up behind him but he must surely have heard it and even perhaps seen its headlamps. He could then have stepped on to the opposite track, squeezed against the wall or laid down between the rails. He did none of these things. Instead, his head was on the rail itself. It might have been a tragic accident, but the weight of evidence points to depression and suicide.

The Disneys and Trench Nugent: career connections

In Stafford the outstanding feature of Disney's life was his unfortunate death. His life in England had come to a miserable end, but before we explore further the reasons why and the significance of this case for the Irish immigrant story we need to look further into his family's history. His sense of self was determined by his position in the commanding Anglo-Irish landed class that equated Ireland's best interests with its own.[33] He does not seem to have been hostile to Catholics at a personal or professional level, or discriminated against them – as long as they knew their place on the estate or in the barracks. In 1845 a Protestant acquaintance wrote to the *Freeman's Journal* pointing out that 'Mr Disney is a Protestant gentleman – the tenants are Roman Catholic almost to a man', yet as agent he gave 'good wages and permanent employment to all the labourers, without distinction, upon the estate (morality and obedience to the laws being the only passports to his favour)'.[34] In 1861, in Stafford, the family employed an Irish servant girl, Jane Walsh, who was almost certainly Catholic.

Disney married a Dublin-born woman, Anna Henrietta, some time in the 1830s, although neither the marriage date nor his wife's identity have been traced. They had at least two children. The first was a daughter born in 1839 who was rather secretively listed in the 1861 Census only with her initials – C. L. The second was a son, Lambert John Robert, born in 1842. These children grew up at the family house, Clifton Lodge, in Athboy. They would have seen their father's work during the Famine and also his serious illness afterwards. When he gave up his job as agent we can assume his employer gave Disney a gratuity, but he had to find alternative employment, and that meant leaving Co. Meath. It was at that point that Trench Nugent came to play a fundamental role in their lives. The Nugents were an extensive landed family from Co. Westmeath. Eyre Trench John Richard Nugent was born in France in 1817 but seems to have come from the Nugents of Ballinlough Castle, Killua, Co. Westmeath. It was only five miles from Disney's home in Athboy.[35] Indeed, Trench Nugent had a small property in Athboy.[36] The two men were associates in the same Ascendancy circle, but Nugent was well connected. In 1848, for example, he was hob-nobbing with the aristocracy at a charity ball for Kells Fever Hospital.[37] Five years later, in May 1853, he was commissioned in England as a captain in the 2nd Regiment, Duke of Lancaster's Own Militia at Preston.[38] That was Disney's chance. Just nine months later, 'Lambert Disney, gent.' was commissioned into the same regiment.[39] Nugent had got him the job despite the fact that he had no obvious military experience. His contacts as well as his experience as an agent handling money and accounts had come to his aid.

Disney was lucky that the British Militia regiments were being revived in the early 1850s since they provided undemanding jobs at various locations throughout the country. In 1856 Nugent was appointed adjutant in the newly embodied 2nd Staffordshire Militia and within a year he had found Disney a job there too as paymaster.[40] The family moved to Stafford.[41] We have here, therefore, an extreme case of how networks amongst the Anglo-Irish Ascendancy could smooth the passage of its members into positions in Britain. In 1861 the Disneys and Nugent were living next door to each other in Garden Street, a narrow but pretty and respectable street off the Wolverhampton Road.[42] Nugent himself moved into the local upper-class network and became committed to life in Staffordshire. On the night of the 1861 census he was socialising as a 'visitor' at Teddesley Hall, the seat of Lord Hatherton five miles outside Stafford. Also there was Hatherton's son, Edward Littleton, the commander of the militia and Nugent's immediate superior. Nugent later became Master of the North Staffordshire Hunt and also a County

Magistrate.[43] He remained single but it is clear that he replaced the elite social network of Co. Westmeath with that of Staffordshire and integrated successfully and lucratively into its social life. He died in 1889, leaving a fortune of £13,327 (worth about £1.46 million at today's prices). One of his executors was from Co. Westmeath, so it seems he had kept his connections and inheritances there too.[44]

Members of the Disney family lived in Stafford for about eighteen years but, in contrast to Nugent, they ultimately proved to be long-term transients. They were never reconciled to leaving Ireland and to the loss of their respected status in the Meath community. They named their house in Garden Street 'Clifton Lodge' after their old home in Athboy, a clear sign of nostalgia for a lost past. There is little evidence that either Disney or his wife engaged with Stafford's social scene or its organised religion. He did attend a 'sumptuous and recherché' mayoral banquet at the Swan Hotel in February 1867 but that is the total of the couple's publicised activities.[45] It contrasts with Disney's numerous recorded attendances at social and professional gatherings in Dublin.

By the time the Disneys arrived in Stafford, Lambert was fifty and Anna Henrietta forty-two. Given Lambert's religious and class obsessions, we can assume that their gender roles were distinct, with Anna performing the duties of diligent but subservient home-maker. We have no specific evidence of their family relationships. The fact that Lambert stole away unseen in the middle of the night for his walk to Shugborough suggests his wife could not help with his depression and that they may not even have shared the same bedroom. Their daughter left home some time after 1861 and she has not been traced subsequently in Britain. It is likely she returned to her family's roots Ireland.

Their son does seem to have had a loyal relationship with his father and, to some extent, followed in his footsteps. Just before the family moved to Stafford, Lambert junior was commissioned as an ensign in his father's Lancashire militia regiment. He transferred at that rank to the Staffordshire militia but then decided to join the regular army. In 1858 he became an ensign in the 12th Regiment of Foot, but by 1861 he had transferred to the 69th Foot and become an instructor in musketry.[46] He subsequently served in India, Canada and Britain, as well as in Ireland. After twelve years' service he bought himself out in 1871 but remained a lieutenant on the regiment's reserve.[47]

Lambert Disney Jr was serving in Britain when his father committed suicide. On the day after his death he was in Stafford to identify the body and support his mother. He was also anxious to preserve his father and family from the shame of suicide. That led him to write a letter the same day to *The Times* emphasising that 'at the inquest the jury, on the most conclusive evidence, found a verdict of "accidental death".[48] He was responding to the paper's first report of a 'Mysterious Death' that clearly hinted at suicide.[49] The letter's tone was short, businesslike and unemotional. There is no specific mention of his father, just 'the unfortunate accident', and it suggests a stiff upper lip and, perhaps, a family in which relationships were stilted, even distant.

Four years later, in 1871, Lambert Disney Jr was appointed Deputy Chief Constable of the Staffordshire Constabulary.[50] Local connections – presumably the Littletons or Nugent – must have helped him get the job. At the time of his appointment Disney was still single, and it is curious that in 1871 he was living in the police barracks alongside ordinary constables and sergeants. Why was he not living with his widowed mother in Clifton Lodge, which was less than five minutes' walk away? It suggests his relationship with his mother was not close, even in her lonely and declining years. She died just two years later aged only fifty-seven.[51] Her son clearly wanted to leave Stafford once his mother had died. Within four months he had applied for the post of Governor of Swansea Gaol but was not appointed. He really wanted to get back to Ireland and he succeeded by becoming Governor of Castlebar Gaol in Co. Mayo. After his years as a single man in the army and police force, Lambert Jr then married a Dublin woman, Mary Isabella Dobbs, in 1881.[52] Tragedy was, however, to strike the family again. In December that year he became Governor of Omagh Gaol in Co. Tyrone, and he moved with his wife and new baby into the Governor's apartment at the gaol. It proved to be his death warrant. The whole place was sitting in its own sewage – sanitary conditions were appalling. Within weeks Disney contracted typhoid and died.[53]

The heritage and identity problems of a Protestant family

The Disney family were never reconciled to their exile from Ireland. Such a conclusion is often made in relation to Catholic Celtic emigrants but rarely in relation to Protestant ones. Yet the evidence clearly suggests it in relation to this family. They failed to settle in Britain for a number of reasons. Firstly, they experienced a drop in social status. They had enjoyed a privileged existence in Ireland as members of the Ascendancy, but from a life networking with people at all levels of the Protestant establishment Lambert Disney descended to working in a back-street barracks and dealing with the burghers of a small English town. Clifton Lodge in the Co. Meath countryside had been swapped for Clifton Lodge in a side street in Stafford. These changes must have been unpalatable to him and his wife.

Loss of status was the common lot of most Irish emigrants when they arrived in overseas destinations, and life was a struggle to rebuild in new and difficult circumstances. Things were usually far worse for the poor, Catholic and Celtic Irish. Protestants usually had an easier route to integration. So why did the Disney family remain apparent outsiders in Britain? The answer to this question must lie in the fundamental outlook of Lambert Disney and other members of his family. He was obsessed by perceived threats to his religion and his class in Ireland and in England. His practice of giving out religious pamphlets would not have endeared him to people in the barracks or the town, and he was probably treated as a crank. In 1866 he applied to be secretary of the Stafford Savings Bank but only received three out of twenty-three trustees' votes and came bottom of their poll. That shows he had built up no significant constituency amongst the Stafford elite even though the Savings Bank had Protestant connections.[54] Finally, Disney may also have been suspicious of 'corrupting' influences in Stafford. That may explain why neither his wife nor daughter was recorded at social events in the town. The family remained aloof. Their son Lambert did make more of a go of life outside Ireland and even, for a time, in Stafford. Nevertheless, he had little commitment to it. After 1867 both Anna and Lambert Disney Jr must have hated everything to do with the town. Anna Disney presumably died a depressed and broken woman, and after his mother had died Lambert Jr was keen to get out and further his career back in Ireland.

The passage of Lambert and Anna Henrietta Disney through Stafford was affected profoundly by their attitudes and identities, and it demonstrates how the influence of Irish origins was always mediated by the specific circumstances of the migrant family itself. The story of the Disneys and Trench Nugent shines a rare light on Ascendancy emigrants from nineteenth-century Ireland.

The Cronin family: respectability, integration and advancement

John Cronin was posted to Stafford Militia Barracks as a staff sergeant around the beginning of 1862. For more than five years he worked alongside Lambert Disney but there the connection between them ends. John Cronin was to make a success of life in Stafford and members of his family were present in the town for over 110 years. We see here a family that retained, and indeed promoted, a strong identification with Catholicism, but whose ethnic Irish identity was rapidly transmuted into an English Catholic one. That process began with John Cronin's career in the army, and was enhanced by his marriage and the family's evolution in Stafford. Their case illustrates how service in the forces could open up opportunities to Irish emigrants, but only if they were prepared to sacrifice any residual commitment to an active Irish identity.

A railwayman's family

The story of the Cronin family in Stafford does not begin with John Cronin but back in the 1830s with a railwayman, Robert Moyers. Moyers was a

porter at Stafford station, having started there when the line opened in
1837 or shortly thereafter. He had been born in Ireland between 1804 and
1811, but we do not know where he came from. The most likely places
are either the Cashel area of Co. Tipperary or Rathfarnham near Dublin
or Strokestown, Co. Roscommon, all home to extensive families with
that rather uncommon name.[55] Moyers was a Catholic and he had not
been long in Stafford before, in 1841, he married a local Catholic woman,
Susannah Follows. She was a servant from a humble family in Bednall,
four miles south of Stafford, and the marriage was one of social equals.
Even so, with his job on the railway, Robert and Susannah could aspire to
modest security. They had four children in the 1840s, and in 1851 were
living in a small house in Mill Bank, five minutes' walk from the station.
Two of Susannah's young relatives, Charles and Susan Follows, were also
living with them, the former listed as a solicitor's writing clerk though he
was only thirteen. It suggests an aspirant household determined to do
well. Unfortunately, Robert died in 1854, aged only forty-eight, and the
family struggled before the children started earning. Even so, their commitment to Catholicism and St Austin's Church provided them with both
spiritual and material sustenance from the clergy and more prosperous
members of the mission. Their eldest child, Susannah, immediately rose
from her humble origins, went into the Church and became a nun.[56] The
Moyers's second child was Elizabeth (b. 1844), and it was she who, in
1867, married John Cronin. We now turn to look at his life beforehand.

John Cronin's career and family

John Cronin was born in 1824 in the parish of Ballymodan, Co. Cork. The
parish includes the town of Bandon and he probably lived there because
his occupation was a tailor when he enlisted in the army on 29 August
1840. The evidence suggests he came from a modest but aspirant artisanal family and had had a reasonable education. Joining up in the city of
Cork, he was attached to the 68th Regiment of Foot and served in Ireland,
Malta, Guinea, the Ionian Islands and the Burmese Wars, and also in
the Crimean War where he received a medal and four clasps recording
service in that squalid conflict. He had worked his way up from private
to sergeant by 1847 and was promoted to colour sergeant, the highest
non-commissioned rank, in 1857. Finally discharged at the garrison town
of Fermoy, Co. Cork, on 26 November 1861, Cronin had served over
twenty-one years in the army. He therefore qualified for a full pension.

John Cronin was a model soldier. His record was described as
'extremely good', he was never tried at a court martial and he received a
gratuity and a number of good-conduct medals during his service.[57] To
achieve such a record he had to embrace publicly the identity and ethos

of the British army in its imperial roles. His subsequent history suggests he internalised those values as well. He made no attempt to return to his home town after discharge but immediately enlisted for militia duty and was sent as staff sergeant to Stafford. He arrived in the town as an eligible man in his late thirties. We know nothing specific of his first few years in Stafford but that silence suggests he carried out his duties as orderly room clerk quietly and diligently. It was vital clerical experience that would bring him benefits. The barracks backed on to St Austin's Church and John Cronin could be at Mass within two minutes. He was a regular communicant and got to know others in the congregation. Amongst the people walking past the barracks on their way to St Austin's were Susannah Moyers and her children. At that time they were living just down the road in Middle Friars and they would have been pointed out as a devout and respectable family. At some point Cronin was introduced to young Elizabeth Moyers, who was then around twenty years of age. She was helping the family income by working as a dressmaker, a job with few prospects. Despite their age difference, the smart and eligible John Cronin was a good catch and they married at St Austin's on 30 November 1867. Ironically it was just two weeks before Cronin's colleague Lambert Disney killed himself.

The Cronins set up home initially at no. 15 Queen Street in the town centre. Elizabeth's widowed mother Susannah was living with them in 1871, a demonstrable commitment to fulfilling kinship obligations, but she died in 1874.[58] Around this time the family moved back to Forebridge and in 1881 they lived at no. 4 Friar's Terrace, a house they were to occupy for more than thirty years. It was a solid terraced property with a garden and a pleasant view across open ground to the playing field of King Edward's School. It was, furthermore, just a minute away from the barracks. Cronin's time in the militia was coming to an end, but his subsequent activities demonstrate how service personnel with contacts, a good record and a respectful demeanour could find new opportunities in civilian life. In 1874 the Stafford Urban Sanitary Authority was being established as a result of the Public Health Act of 1872. A collector of rates was needed and John Cronin applied. He was one of two short-listed applicants and his appointment was seconded by Alderman Hugh Gibson, an Ulster Presbyterian who had already served one term as Stafford's Mayor. It demonstrates the esteem with which Cronin was already held but also the lack of sectarianism amongst Stafford's elite. Cronin received 'flattering testimonials' from his militia sponsors, Lord Hatherton and Trench Nugent, but the Authority members voted for a local man by eight votes to the seven cast for Cronin.[59] The following year he did succeed and was appointed collector of the Watch Rate. He subsequently became collector of the District General Rate when the 1875 Public Health Act was implemented. He held these posts until shortly before his death, at which time it was said, rather ungrammatically, that his 'urbanity of manner and kindliness rendered a difficult post as little unpleasant as possible'. He collected around £100,000 in his time in the job.[60]

From their modest origins the Cronins were now moving into respectable Stafford society, but the focus of their social life remained St Austin's Church. Elizabeth Cronin was involved in the school's amateur dramatics, and as the children grew up they could attend social gatherings such as soirées more frequently.[61] John Cronin was involved in the St Vincent de Paul Society. The ultimate problem for Elizabeth Cronin was, of course, that her husband was twenty years older than her and always likely to die first. He passed away in April 1889 at the age of sixty-five, and his funeral expressed the regard in which the family was then held. His coffin was followed to the grave by old militia comrades, and there were representatives from the Borough Council, the St Vincent de Paul Society; and doubtless, many from St Austin's congregation.[62]

The Cronins' children and the end of the family line

The home created at Friar's Terrace by Elizabeth and John Cronin was a classic of respectable Victoriana. The couple had five surviving children, and their history shows a quasi-Irish family with a service background that integrated smoothly into British life. It also demonstrates, however, how a family may ultimately die out completely and we now turn to see how that happened. The Cronin's first child, Francis, was born in 1868.[63] He did well enough at school and began work as a clerk. He decided, however, to follow in his father's footsteps and on 2 September 1884, when he was sixteen, he enlisted with the Durham Light Infantry. His army career was as exemplary as his father's and by 1896 he had reached the rank of sergeant. At that point he re-engaged as a clerk with the Medical Staff Corps and was ultimately discharged with the rank of sergeant-major in February 1906. He had completed his twenty-one years of pensionable service and had served in Britain, India, Hong Kong and South Africa.[64] He was, however, not to repeat his father's experience following discharge. Within nine months he was dead, killed by consumption of the throat. The illness must have struck rapidly and he died at the family home in Friar's Terrace on 12 November 1906.[65]

The Cronins' second child, Charles John (b. 1871) followed the family tradition pioneered by his Aunt Susannah and went into the Church. Charles went to St Austin's School and did so well that in 1881 he was sent to the prestigious St Wilfred's College, Cotton, in the north Staffordshire moorlands. This Catholic boarding school was famed for educating boys towards the priesthood, and that is the path followed by Charles Cronin.[66] The priest at St Austin's at that time was Canon John Hawksford, who

Figure 8.2 The Rt Revd Monsignor Charles Cronin in the 1900s

had previously been prefect of studies at Cotton College. He was instrumental in getting Charles Cronin a place there and the money to support him. In 1885 Hawksford went back to Cotton as President whilst Charles was still a pupil, so the Stafford connection was strengthened.[67]

Charles proved to be a high-flyer. He was 'at the top of the school ... brilliant at studies, conscientious in performing all the duties assigned to him'.[68] In 1888 he was sent to train for the priesthood at the English College in Rome and was ordained in 1894. He came back to the Birmingham Diocese for four years but in 1898 returned to Rome to become Vice-Rector of the English College. His work there was highly regarded and in recognition he was made a Monsignor and Private Chamberlain to Pope Pius X in 1907 (Figure 8.2). In 1909 he wrote an article on the history of the English College that is still a standard source today.[69] At the outbreak of the Great War Charles finally left Rome and was made Chancellor of the Diocese of Birmingham; he also returned to parish work and did teaching at the Catholic College at Oscott in Birmingham where, in 1924, he became Rector and was appointed Vicar-General.[70] He retired from that post in 1929 and died in 1942. His obituary described him as 'an outstanding figure in the Birmingham Diocese', having spent:

> a conspicuous life in the service of the Church as parish priest, teacher, administrator and as a mentor to prospective priests ... [he] was a conspicuous theologian, perhaps more effective in the lecture room than in the pulpit and more facile with the pen than in speech. To the outer world his appearance of austerity masked a kindly personality ... He was a shy man and, like shy men, very sensitive. He was full of kindness and thoughtfulness, particularly for anyone in any sort of trouble.[71]

Charles Cronin's career benefited from his family's strong adherence to the Church, which ensured the goodwill of teachers and clerics such as Canon Hawksford. The Cronins' Catholicism was sustained by John Cronin and Robert Moyers's Irish tradition but also by the Stafford Catholic tradition of the Follows family. Cronin's whole career was demonstrably that of an English cleric moulded by experience in the international environment of Rome. Even though he reached high office in the Church, Charles Cronin did not sever his ties with either his family or his Stafford Church background. Bonds were strong. He came home when circumstances allowed and was in the town, for example, at the opening of St Patrick's Church in 1895, the annual charity Mass for the St Vincent de Paul Socity in 1908 and the golden jubilee of St Austin's Church in 1912.[72]

The careers of Elizabeth and John Cronin's daughters, Catherine (b. 1873), Winifred (b. 1875) and Margaret (b. 1878), were more prosaic. The social life of all three women centred around the Church, and all are recorded organising and attending soirées and other Church functions. Winifred picked up amateur dramatics from her mother and, in 1915, took part in a 'humorous play' at a concert in aid of Belgian refugees.[73] Catherine and Winifred stayed on at no. 4 Friars Terrace after their mother died in 1904. In 1901 Catherine worked as a dressmaker like her mother before her, but in 1911 had no stated occupation. She died in 1924 and her health may have been poor before that.[74] In the 1900s Winifred was an assistant in a 'fancy shop', but her subsequent career is not known except that she never left Stafford and died there in 1961.[75] Margaret became a school mistress and taught for many years at St Patrick's School.[76] She died in Stafford in 1972.[77]

John and Elizabeth Cronin had five children but not one of them married. The reasons why the two sons remained single are obvious, and for the daughters marriage and domestic drudgery may have been profoundly unattractive options. The Cronin sisters lived respectable, socially fulfilled and generally respected lives in Stafford, though it has to be said that one interviewee for this book remembered Margaret from her schooldays and said she was 'an evil old so-and-so'. What is remarkable is that when Margaret finally died in 1972 an Irish family that had originated in the 1840s with Robert Moyers and been consolidated in the 1860s with John Cronin died out completely. It had lasted over 130 years but encompassed just three generations in that time. The Cronin family demonstrates how there is nothing inevitable about the process of family reproduction down the generations.

John Ryan: the life and death of a Mutiny veteran

On 25 January 1908 the *Staffordshire Advertiser* reported the 'sad death of a military veteran'. He was John Ryan, and his life in Stafford was a great contrast to that of John Cronin and demonstrates how army service was no simple passport to security and advancement. It could presage poverty and a squalid death.

Ryan was born in Co. Galway around 1836. His father probably died in the Famine, but his mother turned up in Stafford in the early 1850s, and in 1855 married John Blundon, a hawker, also from Co. Galway. John must have joined the army before his mother left Ireland, and although his military record has not been traced, we know he was serving in India at the time of the 'Mutiny' in 1857.[78] John had a brother, Michael, who in 1861 was living with his mother and stepfather in Plant's Square. Michael became a shoemaker and in 1864 he married Rose Ward, the Stafford-born daughter of Irish immigrants.[79] The couple subsequently lived in London where Rose worked as a shoe machinist.

John Ryan left the army some time in the 1870s. He had served his full twenty-one years and received a pension, but he had also been wounded and that made him 'feeble on his legs' in later life. Military service had left him unfitted to compete in the labour market and he may have had mental traumas in addition to his physical injury. After discharge he had nowhere to go and so, by 1881, he had settled in Stafford and thereafter lived with the Blundons in their various miserable dwellings. It was a wretched household. John Blundon was a violent drunkard who assaulted his cowed wife; 'she declined to bring charges against him.'[80] In 1878 John Ryan assaulted his stepfather after the latter had again attacked his mother and hit Ryan 'with a formidable stick'.[81] These were poverty-stricken people living in squalid conditions, and John's army service had left him unstable and prone to violence. He got by doing labouring jobs and also selling on the streets with his stepfather, but his army pension was key to his survival. Even so, he must have been semi-destitute. In the end John and Ann Blundon left Stafford and disappeared. They perhaps went back to Ireland – no record has been found of their deaths or residence in other locations in Britain after 1891. John Ryan was left to subsist as best he could.

John's brother Michael died in London in the 1890s, though it has not been possible to trace his death. His widow Rose was presumably left penniless, and by 1901 she had returned to Stafford. There she moved in with her lone brother-in-law and the couple were living as man and wife in another rotten house, no. 9 Snow's Yard. She had a job as a needle fitter in a shoe factory but, even so, their income must have been very poor and by 1907 they were at no. 1 Plant's Square. They had sunk to the bottom of the housing market and, ironically, it was next door to where the Blundons had started over forty years previously. There John Ryan died at the beginning of January 1908. His inquest revealed shocking conditions. His 'widow' Rose reported that he was an army pensioner who had served through the Indian Mutiny, but also that he had had bronchitis for a number of years as well as his enfeebling leg wound. He had fallen down and fractured his arm but refused to go into the workhouse infirmary. He died of 'congestive pneumonia' at home, a house where the 'surroundings were very filthy and the stench was overpowering' according to the doctor who attended him. The inquest jury expressed 'regret that a man who had served his country as the deceased had done should have been allowed to live in such squalid surroundings'.[82] Just two years later Rose Ryan died a pauper in the workhouse.[83] The Ryan army 'family of convenience' had proved to be terminal in Stafford.

John Ryan's sense of self had been formed first in the poverty of Galway during the Famine and then by his army experiences. It is difficult to speculate on the identities that John Ryan and his associates internalised. Life was a miserable struggle to survive an alien environment, but the marriage of convenience between widowed Rose Ryan and her brother-in-law at least meant John achieved some relational stability in his final years. Rose's mention of John's service in the Mutiny and his army pension suggests that those experiences had left an element of residual pride. As with many old soldiers, his service years were the biggest thing that happened in his life. Nevertheless, the squalor of his final days demonstrates that neither he nor Rose was able to impose a basic structure on their lives after years of poverty and disruption. The contrast with the Cronin family could not be greater and is a grim reminder of how service in the military could cripple some migrants' prospects for the rest of their lives.

The military families

This sample of four military families has demonstrated the considerable contrasts that existed in the trajectories of old soldiers and their families. We have seen that three of the families – Carroll, Cronin and Ryan – contained ex-soldiers who had served around the world and stayed long enough to receive an army pension after discharge. These families substantially conformed to the classic pattern of Irish recruits reviewed at the start of this chapter but the individual stories demonstrate the nuanced effects of individual character and circumstances on their subsequent history. What is clear is that army service had thoroughly indoctrinated these men into accepting, consciously or unconsciously, the values and norms of the society into which they settled. Carroll and Cronin clearly identified with the lifestyles of respectable English Catholics and Ryan was trapped in the anomic underworld of Stafford's poor. The Disney family was exceptional in every way but we have seen how its greatest exception was to the stereotype of smooth Anglo-Irish and Protestant integration. Lambert Disney became a military man by accident and his easy militia service was a world away from the hard conditions that the other three regular soldiers had experienced. Yet Disney's life was the ultimate tragedy.

The introduction to this chapter questioned whether there were distinctive patterns of family life and wider relationships amongst service families. The answer is negative. The evidence provided by the case studies suggests that the strength of individual and family characteristics outweighed the general legacy of service in the forces. It might have been expected that these families would exhibit extreme male domination and female subservience but, whilst that may have been the case in the Disney family, the other three do not sustain that view. The key conclusion remains that it is important to understand the interplay of specific individual, family, social and environmental forces in determining people's lives.

Notes

1 E. M. Speirs, 'Army organisation in the nineteenth century' in Bartlett and Jeffery, *A Military History of Ireland*, pp. 335–57 (pp. 335–6 and Table 15.1).

2 I. F. W. Beckett, 'War, identity and memory in Ireland', *Irish Economic and Social History*, 36 (2009), pp. 63–84 (p. 78).

3 T. E. Jordan, 'Queen Victoria's Irish soldiers: Quality of life and social origins of the thin *green* line', *Social Indicators Research*, 57 (2002), pp. 73–88 (pp. 77–8 and Table 1). This reports data on 1,032 recruits.

4 Speirs, 'Army organisation', pp. 39–40; Karsten, 'Irish soldiers in the British army', pp. 38–41; D. M. Rowe, 'Binding Prometheus: How the nineteenth century expansion of trade impeded Britain's ability to raise an army', *International Studies Quarterly*, 46:4 (December 2002), pp. 551–78 (pp. 562–3).

5 D. Fitzpatrick, 'A curious middle place: The Irish in Britain, 1871–1921' in Swift and Gilley, *The Irish in Britain*, pp. 10–59 (p. 23).

6 Karsten, 'Irish soldiers in the British army', pp. 41–7.

7 W. McElwee, *The Art of War: Waterloo to Mons* (London: Purnell, 1974), p. 81.

8 Speirs, 'Army organisation', p. 339.

9 Karsten, 'Irish soldiers', p. 52.

10 K. Kenny, 'The Irish in the Empire' in Kenny, *Ireland and the British Empire*, pp. 92–5.

11 John Ryan is included here as a 'military family' but was also amongst the labouring families with his mother's family in Stafford. No classification can be watertight.

12 D. Cooper, *The Staffordshire Regiments: Imperial, Regular and Volunteer Regiments, 1705–1919* (Leek: Churnet Valley Books, 2003), pp. 12–13.

13 Obituary of Edward Tallent, *SA*, 26 April 1919.

14 NA, WO97, military papers of no. 629: Pte John Carroll, 84th Regiment of Infantry; *FindMyPast* (accessed 1 February 2013).

15 *Birmingham Post*, 16 December 1867.

16 Lewis, *Topographical Dictionary*, p. 639: Galtrim, Co. Meath.

17 Griffith's Valuation, Co. Meath, Ballynamona Townland, Galtrim Parish: c. 150 acres leased by the Representatives of Lambert Disney to Margaret Gallagher and Denis Sweeney; *Ancestry* (accessed 10 February 2013).

18 *Freeman's Journal and Daily Commercial Advertiser*, 2 February 1839.

19 *Freeman's Journal*, 27 September 1842.

20 *Ibid.*, 29 September 1843.

21 Famine Relief Commission Papers, 1844–47, RLFC3/1: 4338 (15 July 1846); 2809 (6 March 1846); 2943 (6 June 1846). *Ancestry* (accessed 5 February 2013).

22 *Daily News*, 13 January 1848.

23 *Freeman's Journal*, 4 March 1850.

24 P. Buckland, *Irish Unionism I: The Anglo-Irish and the New Ireland, 1885–1922* (Dublin: Gill and Macmillan, 1972), p. xv.

25 Bew, *Ireland: the Politics of Enmity*, pp. 144–9.

26 Extracts from the speeches of the Marquis of Downshire and Earl of Donoughmore, *The Times*, 27 January 1837.

27 *Freeman's Journal*, 13 November 1844. The judge granted an order against Daly.

28 *The Times*, 17 December 1867.

29 P. Quinlivan and P. Rose, *The Fenians in England, 1865–72: A Sense of Insecurity* (London: John Calder Press, 1982), p. 87.

30 J. Morley, *The Life of William Ewart Gladstone*, Vol. 2 (London: Macmillan, 1903), pp. 241–3; R. Jenkins, *Gladstone* (London: Pan Macmillan, 2002), pp. 280–4; D. G. Boyce, 'Gladstone and Ireland' in P. J. Jagger (ed.), *Gladstone* (London: The Hambledon Press, 1998), pp. 105–22 (p.107).

31 London Metropolitan Archive and Guildhall Library, UK Poll Books and Electoral Registers, 1865, July 12, Borough of Stafford; *Ancestry* (accessed 4 February 2013).

32 *Birmingham Daily Post*, 16 December 1867.

33 Buckland, *Irish Unionism I*, p. xx.

34 'A good agent', *Freeman's Journal*, 5 July 1845.

35 Lewis, *Topographical Dictionary*, p. 386: Ballinlough Castle, seat of Sir G. Nugent, Bart.

36 Griffith's Valuation, Co. Meath, Trench Nugent, Townparks (Athboy): 'offices' worth £10, sublet to James Walker; *Ancestry* (accessed 10 February 2013).

37 *Freeman's Journal*, 21 November 1848.

38 *The Times*, 18 May 1853.

39 *Ibid.*, 15 February 1854; *Preston Guardian*, 18 February 1854.

40 Obituary of Colonel Nugent, *Birmingham Daily Post*, 7 May 1889.

41 *Preston Guardian*, 20 March 1858.

42 In the 1861 Census the house next door to Disney's was listed as 'uninhabited' because Nugent was at Teddesley Hall on census night. He was in residence for the 1871 Census (schedules 158–9).

43 Obituary of Colonel Nugent, *Birmingham Daily Post*, 7 May 1889.

44 England and Wales, National Probate Calendar (Index of Wills and Administrations), 1858–1966, Probate Office, Lichfield: Eyre Trench John Richard Nugent, probate granted 28 June 1889. *Ancestry* (accessed 24 September 2013).

45 *SA*, 2 February 1867.

46 *Morning Chronicle*, 16 September 1857; *Daily News*, 27 October 1858; *Caledonian Mercury*, 20 May 1861.

47 Death notice of Lambert Disney Jr, *SA*, 18 February 1882.

48 *The Times*, 17 December 1867.

49 *Ibid.*, 14 December 1867.

50 SRO C/PC/1/6/2, Staffordshire Police Personnel Register, 1863–94, no. 1182: Disney, Lambert John Robert, appointed 1 February 1871.

51 SBC Burial Record 3/4505: Anna Henrietta Disney, 17 April 1873.

52 Dublin South RD, 1881, 2/613: Lambert Disney and Mary Isabella Dobbs.

53 *SA*, 18 February 1882.

54 *Ibid.*, 20 September 1866. The chairman of the appointment panel was The Revd Thomas Harrison, the anti-Catholic vicar of Christchurch in Foregate Street.

55 Griffith's Valuation, Cos Tipperary, Dublin and Roscommon.

56 She has not been found in Britain in 1861 and 1871, and it is likely she was sent abroad. In 1881 and 1891 she was a nun at St Scholastica's Abbey in Teignmouth, Devon, and died there in 1896.

57 NA, WO97/1584/129, no. 1733: Colour Sergeant John Cronin; *FindMyPast* (accessed 25 January 2013).

58 Stafford RD, Deaths, October–December 1874, 6b/15: Susannah Moyers.

59 *SA*, 8 August 1874.

60 Obituary of John Cronin, *ibid.*, 6 April 1889.

61 E.g. *ibid.*, 29 December 1877, 26 February and 1 April 1887, 21 April 1888, 9 March 1889.

62 Obituary of John Cronin, *ibid.*, 6 April 1889.

63 Stafford RD, Births, October–December 1868, 6b/14: Francis Cronin.

64 NA, WO97/4611/172, no. 7810: Francis Cronin, Service Record; *FindMyPast* (accessed 30 January 2013).

65 Stafford RD, Death Certificate, 6b/7, No. 138: Francis Cronin.

66 M. W. Greenslade, 'Cotton College, formerly Sedgley Park School', in *VCH Stafford*, Vol. 6, pp. 156–8; F. Roberts and N. Henshaw, *A History of Sedgley Park and Cotton College* (Preston: T. Snape, 1985).

67 Greenslade, *St Austin's, Stafford*, p. 28; www.freewebs.com/cottoncollege/ (accessed 4 March 2013).

68 Obituary of Charles Cronin, *Catholic Herald*, 9 January 1942.

69 C. Cronin, 'The English College, in Rome', in *The Catholic Encyclopedia* (New York: Robert Appleton, 1909), http://paperspast.natlib.govt.nz/cgi/papers (accessed 20 January 2013).

70 M.E. Williams, *Oscott College in the Twentieth Century* (Leominster: Gracewing, 2001), pp. 48–9.

71 *Catholic Herald*, 9 January 1942.

72 *SA*, 27 July 1895, 17 October 1908, 27 July 1912.

73 *Ibid.*, 6 March 1915.

74 Stafford RD, Deaths, October–December 1924, 6b/22: Catherine M. Cronin.

75 Stafford RD, Deaths, July–September 1961, 9b/342: Winifred M. Cronin.

76 Information from the late Roy Mitchell, a pupil at the school in the 1930s.

77 Stafford RD, Deaths, April–June 1972, 9b/1070: Margaret M. Cronin.

78 Report of inquest into John Ryan's death, *SA*, 25 January 1908. The name John or J. Ryan was so common amongst army recruits that it is impossible to make a definitive identification of his service record.

79 Stafford RD, Marriages, October–December 1864, 6b/29: Michael Ryan and Rose Ward.

80 *SA*, 2 June 1877.

81 *Ibid.*, 17 August 1878.

82 *Ibid.*, 25 January 1908.

83 SBC Burial Record 9/5901, 23 May 1910: Rose Ryan.

9

The Irish in the shoe trade

Irish decline and Stafford's growth

In October 1855 over 500 shoemakers, both men and women, attended a mass meeting in Stafford's Market Square. They were protesting against the trial of a sewing machine by Edwin Bostock, one of the town's leading shoe manufacturers. The meeting passed a number of resolutions, and 'The fourth resolution proposed by Mr A. Brew and seconded by Mr A. Prosser condemned machinery as injurious to the interests of the working classes, and solicited the higher and middle classes of Stafford to assist them with their sympathy and support.'[1] The proposer, Andrew Brew, was Irish, and until his death in 1866 he was in the forefront of the fight by Stafford's shoemakers to prevent the introduction of machinery into the industry. Born in Downpatrick, Co. Down, in 1806, one of eight children from a poor Protestant family, he grew up in a town whose industries, based on the linen trade, were in decline by the 1830s. He became a shoemaker and in the late 1820s or early 1830s emigrated to Manchester where he married an Irish woman, Ann Turpin.[2] In 1841 they were living close to Angel Meadow, a notorious slum that was home to many Irish Catholic families, but in the 1840s the Brews decided their prospects were better in the specialist shoe town of Stafford than in the squalor of east Manchester.

Andrew Brew was one of many Irish shoemakers who came to Stafford during the nineteenth century. Between 1841 and 1901 almost one in ten of the town's adult Irish workforce was in the footwear industry, and many of the children of Irish families entered the trade when they grew up. This body of workers was a classic example of how emigration and settlement were fuelled by the shift in economic power between Irish and British capitalism. Ireland suffered 'deindustrialisation' in the nineteenth century, and Stafford's shoe trade illustrates how industrialisation and deindustrialisation were combined forces.[3] Traditionally shoes were bespoke products made by cobblers selling directly to their customers, but in Britain the growth of London and the industrial cities created a profitable market for mass-produced 'ready-mades'. This was exploited most profitably when entrepreneurs used economies of scale, division of labour, and cheaper road and rail transport. The trade increasingly concentrated in specialised shoe towns and villages, and Stafford emerged as one of them.[4] There the development was mainly due to William Horton (1750–1832), the first 'manufacturer' to orchestrate production on a large scale, although most of the work was still done in workers' houses. Shoemaking was a sweated domestic trade until the second half of the nineteenth century. The shoe manufacturers marketed their products both at home and abroad, and Stafford's growing dependence on the overseas and ladies' fashion markets produced sharp booms and slumps in the trade.[5] This volatility meant workers often had to go 'on-tramp' in search of work elsewhere. They had an easily transferable skill that used simple tools and had an organised system to provide support during the search for work. By the 1820s Dublin trades had tramping links with England, and in the shoe trade there was a broadly open labour market between Britain and Ireland.[6]

Shoemaking declined drastically in nineteenth-century Ireland. In 1841, 50,334 'boot and shoemakers' were recorded in the census. The number had dropped to 45,421 by 1861 and decline after 1861 was precipitous.[7] Employment fell to 25,650 in 1881 and 13,627 in 1911. By the 1900s the majority were not makers of shoes but shoe-shop assistants or cobblers repairing footwear imported from British factories.[8] We have seen that in Stafford Andrew Brew fought the introduction of sewing machines, but he and his comrades lost the battle. The employers imposed them rapidly in the 1860s and followed up with other machines that de-skilled the work and reduced the unit costs of production. The industry was moved into purpose-built factories and workshops. These more efficient methods, as well as vicious competition by British shoe firms, eliminated artisan producers in Ireland and more or less strangled the growth of factory production there.[9] The 1907 Census of Production recorded a mere 2,026 factory shoemakers in Ireland.[10] British firms particularly targeted the Irish market because overseas sales were hit by tariff barriers and American competition.[11] Mass-produced footwear from Britain flooded an Irish economy that was becoming more commercialised in the decades after the Famine. Cormac Ó Gráda's comment that 'the dealers, shops and mail traders who displayed and encouraged the purchase of imported wares played their part in the decline of native Irish industries' is an apt description of the relationship between Stafford's shoe trade and the Irish industry.[12] Louis Cullen specifically identified how imported ladies' shoes, Stafford's speciality, dominated the Irish market.[13] In these conditions it is no wonder that Irish shoemakers turned up in Stafford.

Table 9.1 Types of shoemaking and labouring families

Type of family	Shoemaking %	Labouring %
1. Migrant Irish family (Migration of pre-existing core unit with children born in Ireland)	5.0	49.1
2. Migrant Irish adults (Core unit established in Britain; children born after arrival in Britain)	5.0	38.7
3. Male-mixed family (Core unit with Irish-born male with non-Irish partner)	55.0	6.6
4. Female-mixed family (Core unit with Irish-born female with non-Irish partner)	35.0	5.7
5. British transient in Ireland (British-born parent with child(-ren) born in Ireland)	—	—
Total no. of families	**20**	**106**

Stafford's Irish shoemaking families

In Stafford the number of male workers in the shoe trade rose from 899 in 1841 to 1,607 in 1871, an increase of 79 per cent.[14] By then footwear workers formed 19 per cent of the *total* population of the town. Census returns recorded 175 Irish-born shoemakers in Stafford between 1841 and 1901; the real number who passed through was probably three times that. They formed only a small minority of the shoemakers who left Ireland in the nineteenth century, but those who settled were a microcosm of the mass.

Twenty Irish shoemaking families settled long-term in Stafford and they were a quite distinctive group in comparison with the labouring families. Table 9.1 shows that they were overwhelmingly of mixed ethnicity. Furthermore, although Irish male-mixed families were over half the total, female-mixed units formed over a third. These characteristics reflect the peripatetic nature of the shoe trade. Single workers emigrated and then moved around the shoe towns meeting partners either elsewhere or in Stafford itself. In only two cases did already-established migrant Irish families or adults settle in Stafford.

It follows that nuclear families were predominant amongst the shoemakers, with fourteen out of twenty being nuclear. All but one of the remainder were complex units enfolded within Stafford's native

Table 9.2 Date of arrival of shoemaking and labouring families

Date of arrival	Shoemaking families %	Labouring families %
Before 1845	30.0	6.6
1846–51	15.0	39.6
1852–61	10.0	33.0
After 1861	45.0	19.8
Total no. of families	**20**	**106**

shoemaking families. Shoe-trade families emerged throughout the study period (Table 9.2) but particularly in the years before the Famine and then after 1861. Those establishing before the Famine were formed by workers who came to Stafford 'on-tramp' or with a planned decision to go there to better themselves through local contacts. That was certainly the case with Hugh Woods Gibson, who later became an owner of a substantial shoe firm. His case will be examined in the next chapter. Although five families emerged during the Famine and immediate post-Famine period, at least three, of whom the Brew family were one, had lived elsewhere in England before settling in Stafford and were not, therefore, 'real' Famine emigrants from Ireland. The biggest group of nine families settled after 1861, and although some had lived elsewhere in England before they came to Stafford, they typified the emigration of shoemakers brought about by the rapid decline of the Irish shoe trade from the 1860s. They were attracted to Stafford by the rapid growth of the trade there during the same period.

Stafford's shoe-trade families contrasted greatly with the provincial origins of the labouring families. None of those whose origin is known came from Connacht (Table 9.3). They were evenly spread amongst the other three provinces, a distribution that reflected the concentration of craft shoemakers in Ireland's more prosperous and urbanised areas. Protestant families slightly outnumbered Catholic ones, again a big contrast with the labourers, but although the higher proportion of Protestants reflected their favoured status in Ireland, the substantial body of Catholics is an indication of how an artisanal trade like shoemaking offered a route to Catholic advancement.

Having settled in Stafford, nearly two-thirds of the shoemaking families integrated into the local community (Table 9.4). That was a substantially higher proportion than amongst the labouring families. Only one settled family died out, much lower than amongst the labourers, but the residual proportion who ultimately left was similar. We see, then, a polarisation between the majority who integrated and a distinct minority who

Table 9.3 Provincial origin of shoemaking and labouring families

Province of origin	Shoemaking families %	Labouring families %
Connacht	—	87.5
Leinster	36.4	6.3
Munster	36.4	2.5
Ulster	27.3	3.8
Total no. of families	**11**	**80**

Provincial origins for nine shoemaking and twenty-six labouring families not known.

Table 9.4 The fate of shoemaking and labouring families

Ultimate fate	Shoemaking families %	Labouring families %
Long-term transient	30.0	34.0
Terminal	5.0	22.6
Integrating	65.0	43.4
Total no. of families	**20**	**106**

apparently did not. This latter group had some interesting features, how-ever. Five out of six were Protestant and two of the families – Gibson and Livingstone – became substantial employers. Both in fact integrated into Stafford's social life but the Gibsons retired to Birmingham after they had made their fortune, whereas the Livingstones left when their firm went bankrupt in 1887. The other transients were typically mobile footwear operatives who ultimately moved to other shoe towns. Catholic families slightly outnumbered the Protestants amongst the integrating families.

Until the 1880s Stafford's shoe trade attracted many in-migrant work-ers and their families, not just the Irish. In 1871 almost one-third of the town's shoe operatives had been born elsewhere, nearly one-fifth outside Staffordshire.[15] That meant that outsiders were common, and although perhaps not positively welcomed there was acceptance of the shoe-maker's right to come and go in search of work. A perennial shortage of housing meant that many households included lodgers and were over-crowded. Although initially instrumental in motivation such households could develop quasi-family relationships around work, social life, sexual intimacy, bonding and marriage. Because shoemaking was still largely domestic until the 1870s, 'home' was usually the workplace. Booms and slumps meant work was frequently difficult to get and incomes varied from week to week. Times were often hard. The nature of the trade meant the shoemaker's household and family environment could be inherently stressful. Gender roles were complex, with women both home-making and earning money in lower-grade jobs like shoe binding. Their children were exploited with long hours, hard work and insanitary conditions.[16] Even when the work was moved into workshops children were still exploited so that it was said around 1880 that boy labour was paid 'at wages only just a remove from the pauper's dole'.[17]

At home men were likely to dominate the household, particularly if they did 'superior' work like clicking and hand-sewing. The male shoemaker's sense of self was moulded by the worth of his skill, a willingness to go anywhere and solidarity in the face of hard employers and uncertain work. Male domination could, however, be undermined when the men were forced into low-grade work or were unemployed. Domestic routines were frequently disrupted, particularly by the shoemakers' fabled addiction to weekend and 'St Monday' drinking.[18] Even so, 'St Monday' was as much a symptom of the shoemakers' independence as of their intemperance. Running through their lives was a sense of craft pride under threat, and that encouraged solidarity and determination to control as far as possible the terms of their work. The national Riveters' Union was founded in Stafford in 1874 but the battle to control pay and conditions was long and hard. Most workers remained outside the union and many endured a life of drudgery, uncertainty and crippling work done in unhealthy conditions.[19]

Two Irish shoemaking families, the Hamiltons and the Mulrooneys, have been selected as case studies that encapsulate some of the key features of this distinctive group.

The Hamiltons: a poor Protestant family

The history of the Hamilton family again cautions us against making simple assumptions about the ability of Protestant Irish immigrants to merge seamlessly with the host society. They came from Carrickfergus in Co. Antrim, a town 'never … distinguished for the extent of its manufactures' and that in 1841 had just eighty-seven shoemakers.[20] The surname suggests they were originally a Scottish planter family. The first we know about the Hamiltons in England is when, on 5 June 1860, Edward Hamilton, a nineteen-year-old boot and shoemaker, married Harriet Adelina Lockley, a shoe binder. The marriage did not take place in Stafford, however, but at St Andrew's Church, Ancoats, in Manchester.[21] This was where Andrew Brew had lived, and Edward Hamilton took the same route from Ulster to Stafford. In his case one reason was that his wife was a Staffordshire woman from the Stone area. The newly-weds presumably decided that Stafford offered more than the Ancoats slums and within a year they had moved to the town. In 1861 they were living in a mean house in Clark Street in the town centre. They were not alone, however. Edward's sixty-year-old widowed father, also a shoemaker, was there and the census return identifies him as the head of the household, so we can conclude father and son had come to England together. Things were clearly tight because a middle-aged butcher and his wife lodged with them.

Three members of the Hamilton family in fact came to Stafford, because in 1861 a William Hamilton, 'cordwainer' (the traditional name for a shoemaker), was lodging with the Harris family at 37 Gaol Road in the north end. He was a year older than Edward Hamilton and they were probably brothers. William left Stafford in the 1860s and disappears from history.[22] The same applies to his father. He vanished and no death or alternative residence has been traced. Perhaps father and son moved off together and emigrated. In the end only Edward and Harriet Hamilton settled long-term in Stafford and even they took time to become committed to the town. Although their first child, Albert James, was born there in 1861, they had moved to Newcastle-under-Lyme by the time their daughter Mary arrived in 1864. That was a brief sojourn because they were back in Stafford the next year for Arthur's birth. The couple went on to have eight children, but three died as infants and there was a considerable gap in the surviving family between Edward, born in 1868, and Ada, the final arrival, ten years later.

Poor lives in Stafford

The Hamiltons remained a poor shoemaking family. Unlike the Giltraps and the Disneys, there is no evidence that they benefited from Protestant Irish connections to help them on their way. They had no natural supporters in the local community. As adherents, nominally at least, of the Church of Ireland, they were part of the neglected group of Ulster emigrants identified by Ian Meredith who were neither Catholic nor Presbyterian but Episcopalian.[23] In Stafford they had no tight faith community to support them. If they were Orangemen, as many Church of Ireland people in Ulster were, Stafford was barren territory. Harriet's Staffordshire origins were of no help since her family were humble labourers from fifteen miles away. Even worse, the Hamiltons settled in Stafford just when the shoe trade was starting its shift to machine production in workshops and factories. In 1871 Edward described himself as a 'journeyman', which implies he had served his apprenticeship as a craft shoemaker. Times were moving against him, however, since the new production methods brought division of labour and de-skilling. We have no evidence of whom Edward Hamilton worked for but by 1881 he had

sunk to being a 'shoemaker finisher', a relatively low-grade occupation at
the end of the production process. Much of it was still outwork, though
even this was being brought into the factories.[24] In the same year Harriet
was a dressmaker, also a marginal and sweated occupation, and in 1891
she was selling second-hand clothes, something she still did in 1911.The
Hamiltons therefore subsisted on low-grade, ill-paid and uncertain work
on the margins of the economy, and their lives reflected that. In 1878
Edward was fined for not sending his children to school. It suggests one
or more of the children were working to supplement the family income.[25]
The family earned a modest living but little more.

Their housing remained mean. They lived in at least nine different
houses between 1861 and 1915 but showed no evidence of upward social
mobility. They shifted from the dreary town-centre locality of Clark
Street to Mill Street – little better – in the second half of the 1860s, but
had an intervening period in Newcastle-under-Lyme. They then had a
rather better address on Sandon Road in the north end around 1876.[26]
From 1878 until the 1900s they lived in three different houses in dingy
Browning Street, and in their declining years they ended up round the
corner in Grey Friars.[27] These repeated house moves undermined the
Hamiltons' ability to create a stable and nurturing home environment,
although their aspiration to a basic respectability is indicated by membership of the Stafford Humane Burial Society in the 1870s. The family needed to make use of the Society's insurance payments because,
between 1871 and 1875, Harriet had three successive babies who died
within months of their birth. Those years must have been particularly
miserable and stressful for the family.

Despite glimmers of respectability, Edward Hamilton's behaviour also
undermined family life. He was a drinker and could be violent. In 1868
he was arrested for being drunk and, when in the cells, assaulted a policeman who tried to stop him kicking the door and making a racket. The
fight allegedly went on for some minutes.[28] Nineteen years later he was
out with his son Arthur at the Crown Inn, Hyde Lea, and joined in kicking a police inspector who had already been attacked by the violently
drunk Arthur.[29] These incidents were probably only the tip of an iceberg
of anger and violence that existed within the Hamilton household and of
which Harriet and the children were probably the chief victims.

Edward Hamilton came from Carrickfergus, a strongly Protestant
town, and we must speculate to what extent he, his brother and his father
carried their Ulster Protestant identity with them to Stafford. Edward
was, of course, a young man when he arrived in Stafford, and his marriage to a local woman when he was still a teenager immediately invested
his family with a mixed identity. Even so, in the 1868 election he voted
Tory, so he was probably swayed by hostility to the proposed disestablishment of the Church of Ireland and concessions to Catholics.[30] It

seems that for many years Edward in fact wanted to obscure his Irish origin. Although in the 1871 Census he specifically said he had been born in Carrickfergus, in the three succeeding census returns he changed his story and said he had been born in Scotland. If that had happened once it might have been an enumerator's error, but three times suggests a conscious decision to deny his Irish origin. There is also one known incident that suggests a strand of anti-Irishness, and perhaps anti-Catholicism, in the family. In April 1888 Edward Hamilton's son Arthur was fined 10s for an assault at the Working Men's Club in Stafford. The key witness was Thomas Maloney, an Irish Catholic who was an official at the club. In a dispute over membership rules Arthur Hamilton called Maloney 'an Irish something (Laughter)', assaulted him and then ran away.[31] Trivial as the incident was, it clearly indicates that at least one of Edward Hamilton's children had no inherited Irish identity and some apparent antipathy to the Irish. The attitude was probably general in the family and it suggests that although they were near the bottom of the social hierarchy they strove to differentiate themselves from those they regarded as inferiors, the Catholic Irish.

The Hamilton children depart

Harriet and Edward Hamilton's children showed little commitment either to their family or to Stafford when they grew up. Born between 1861 and 1877, they entered the labour force when the shoe trade was often depressed and jobs were beginning to disappear. Their parents had barely managed to scrape a living from the trade, so it held little attraction for the children. Neither Edward nor Harriet was well enough connected to get their children secure jobs in footwear or anywhere else in the local economy. Although Stafford's economic base was beginning to diversify into engineering and administration, before 1900 the switch had not yet created many new jobs and more people were leaving the town than coming to it. With their stressed home life and interrupted schooling, the Hamilton children emerged with poor skills and prospects. Their subsequent lives generally reflected this.

Albert James, the first-born, initially started work with his father as a finisher in the shoe trade but rapidly decided there was no future in it. He took the easy route out of Stafford and in 1881 joined the army. He was with the 12th Lancers, a cavalry regiment, on active service until 1891 and with another five years in the reserve, but his record was mediocre. He never rose above private and had a number of infractions resulting in imprisonment. Despite serving for four years in India he received no medals or good conduct awards and his ultimate pension entitlement was only seven years.[32] It was a record that could have portended problems like those of John Ryan (Chapter 8), but in fact Albert made good in his adult life. He got a job in Rugby and immediately married a local woman, although they failed to have children. By 1911 he was assembling motors in the electrical engineering industry.[33]

The two other Hamilton boys also joined the army. Arthur started work as a butcher's boy. He seems to have been a Jekyll-and-Hyde character, since in the census of 1881, when he was boarding with his employer, he got himself listed as *Richard* Hamilton, whereas, a month later, he gave his name in the magistrate's court as *Edward* Hamilton, his younger brother's name.[34] He was fined for disobeying the market inspector. Nevertheless, he stuck at being a butcher until 1889 when he joined the Royal Artillery – as Arthur Hamilton. He served for just over three years, including one spell in India but also one in prison. In 1892 he was discharged as medically unfit because he had received a compound fracture of his leg whilst on duty. The army just threw him on the scrap heap with a pension of only 12d a week for one year.[35] He returned to Stafford but then moved to Cannock, where he married in 1894. He died, however, in 1897, aged only thirty-two.[36] Edward Hamilton (b. 1868) also died relatively young. In Stafford he worked as a labourer before also joining the Royal Artillery in 1886. He served not a day longer than his pensionable twelve years and managed to avoid any overseas posting. His medical record shows two cases of gonorrhoea, and in 1892 he was diagnosed with primary syphilis. He received no awards or medals and his record was described as 'indifferent'.[37] Even so, when he left the army in 1898 his service background helped him get a job as an ostler at the Crewe Arms Hotel next to the railway station in Crewe. Six years later he had sunk, however, to being a general labourer. In 1898 he had married a widow, Hannah Bebbington, who already had four children. Edward and Hannah went on to have two children themselves, but Edward died of 'hemiplegia' in 1907, aged only thirty-eight. This was almost certainly tertiary syphilis, so his army past had caught up with him.[38]

The Hamiltons' second child, Mary, also had a problematic life. She was still at home in 1881 working as a dressmaker, but in 1884 she had an illegitimate child, Adelina (named after her grandmother). Although born in Stafford, Adelina died in Wolverhampton a year later.[39] Then in the mid-1880s Mary had a liaison with a man called Evans and the result was Emily, born in 1887. It has proved impossible to identify either him or any marriage, and the relationship was clearly short. By 1891 Mary and Emily 'Evans' were living in the Hamilton house in Browning Street, with Mary claiming to be a widow. She went on to have another illegitimate child, Edward, in 1894 or 1895. It was said he was born in Brighton, not Stafford, but no matching birth has been positively identified there. Mary's elusive but clearly promiscuous behaviour suggests she may have made money from casual prostitution. In 1901 Emily (or 'Emmie') and

Edward, both now surnamed Hamilton, were still living with their grand-parents, but Mary was not there and it has proved impossible to trace her. She could have changed her name and identity and gone off to ply her trade elsewhere. Emily also disappears after 1901 so an alternative view is that both she and her mother emigrated in the 1900s. Young Edward was still living with his grandparents in 1911, by which time he was working as a house painter. In 1916 he married Lizzie Sturland, the daughter of a blacksmith's striker.[40] Their subsequent history is unknown, but Edward died in Stafford in 1953.[41]

Harriet and Edward Hamilton's final child was Ada (b. 1877), and she also left Stafford. She was the only child to work long-term in the shoe trade and became a paste fitter, a menial female job. In 1901 she married Charles Conlin, a railway fireman from Crewe whom she probably met through her brother Edward, who, as we have seen, was then living in the railway town.[42] They have not been traced again in Britain and it can only be assumed that they left amidst the tide of emigrants in the 1900s.

The elusive Hamiltons

Edward Hamilton, Mary's son, was the only survivor of the Hamilton family in Stafford after 1915. His presence means the family were tech-nically 'integrators', but we have seen that all the other children left. Even old Edward seems to have died elsewhere after he was widowed in 1915, though his death has not been traced. In essence the family proved to be mainly long-term transients. They were a poor family with internal stresses who struggled to survive in an economic climate that was against them. The children's strategy was to get out of Stafford, but with limited success. This pattern must have stemmed, at least in part, from their fam-ily and social environment in Stafford.

The Hamiltons entered a society alien to the secure reference points of Ulster Protestant life. The sense of self they derived from their back-ground was always going to be challenged by life in Britain, and Edward Jr only became committed to life in England because of his marriage to Harriet. We have no direct evidence of her sense of self or character, and the picture that emerges of the couple's relationship is mixed. On the one hand they fulfilled, in later life, their obligations by taking in their way-ward daughter and bringing up her illegitimate children in the house-hold. That suggests some closeness, commitment and perhaps even contentment in their later life. On the other hand we see in incidents of Edward and Arthur's drunkenness, violence and indifference to school-ing evidence of a disordered household and weak family ties. They were a deprived family that continually moved house and found it difficult to provide a nurturing home.

Evidence is elusive of how the Hamilton family related to their neighbours and the wider working-class community. They needed contact with other shoemakers and employers to get the outwork on which they depended, but their failure to get better houses suggests those contacts were fickle. Harriet's switch to selling second-hand clothes indicates a family relating to Stafford's poorest rather than to the artisans who could still make a respectable living in the shoe trade. Their frequent switches of address imply they never built close relations with their neighbours, whilst Arthur's fracas at the Working Men's Club suggests ineffectual, perhaps even abrasive, relations with working-class peers. It seems clear that Edward wanted to negate his Irish background, but in claiming to be Scottish he was still admitting a different identity from native Staffordians, and we are left with the picture of a mixed-ethnicity family aloof from its social context.

All in all, the Hamiltons' experience of life in Stafford was difficult and their circumstances as poor as, or poorer than, those of many Catholic Irish families. This picture emphasises the need to investigate seriously the economic and social experiences of working-class Irish Protestants rather than just their sectarian proclivities.[43]

The Bowen–Mulrooney family in the shoe trade and beyond

On 15 October 1870 John Mulrooney married Mary Bowen at St Austin's Church.[44] John was a shoemaker who had been born in Limerick in 1851 and Mary had been born in Stafford of Irish parents in 1854. The history of the conjoined Bowen–Mulrooney family contrasts greatly with that of the forlorn Hamiltons. From difficult origins they became a complex and well-established family in the shoe trade of Stafford and elsewhere, but they also showed an ability to diversify into the new industries of the town. In doing so they integrated deeply into the community but also fanned out more widely into British society. There is no space here to cover all the ramifications of this extended family, and this study highlights the spine established by John Mulrooney's marriage to Mary Bowen.

The Bowen family in Plant's Square

The story starts with John Bowen, a 'classic' Famine immigrant. Born in Co. Roscommon in 1831, he probably came to Stafford before the Famine as a seasonal worker on the farms. His formative years were therefore spent in the same land-hungry and poverty-stricken environment that moulded many of Stafford's Irish immigrants. His life in Stafford suggests John emerged from it as a dogged and self-reliant individual with a strong commitment to nurturing family relationships. We shall see indirect evidence that he retained pride in his Irish origins, but his reaction to enforced emigration was to make the best of it and accept – or even encourage – his children to embrace the society into which they were born.

When the Famine struck John Bowen fled, and in September 1847 he staggered into Stafford ill and destitute. He was dumped in the temporary huts erected at the workhouse for the vagrant Irish and was for there for eleven days, but by 4 October he had recovered enough to leave and find somewhere to live in town.[45] His Roscommon connections directed him to no. 9, Plant's Square, a lodging 'house' in a two-room hovel run by Margaret Paton, a sixty-year-old widow from the same county. She had also come to Stafford during the Famine with at least three of her children, one of whom was Ellen (b. 1831). The cramped surroundings of this tiny dwelling thrust John Bowen and Ellen together. The couple married at St Austin's on 7 May 1849. The Bowen–Paton dynasty was now established (Fig. 9.1).

John and Ellen Bowen quickly left her mother's lodging house at no. 9 Plant's Square and moved into the equally small no. 5 at the other end of the yard. There, in 1851, they lived with the Hazle family and two other Irish lodgers. By 1861 no. 5 had been taken over by the Corcoran family (Chapter 7), and John and Ellen had moved across the court to no. 7. There they at least managed to set up house on their own and remarkably, unlike the ever-moving Hamiltons, they stayed in that tiny cottage for over twenty years. Superficially this suggests an Irish family 'trapped' in a miserable slum by endless poverty and lack of prospects, yet the actual picture is more complex. John Bowen certainly had poor jobs and an insecure income. He was an agricultural labourer until farm-work started to decline in the mid-1860s. Redundancy on the land left him with no saleable skills and he ended up a hawker selling goods on the street. Ellen could do little to supplement the household income since she had a growing family to look after in terrible surroundings. Her first child, Sarah, died within a year, but between 1854 and 1873 Ellen had another nine children, all but one of whom survived to adulthood.

Despite these difficulties, three factors helped the Bowen family to survive and ultimately emerge with some long-term success. One was the nature of the Plant's Square community. The houses there were even smaller and more squalid than those in Snow's Yard, with just one polluted water pump and a row of reeking privies. Even so, a community of Roscommon people, frequently related, dominated the Square from Famine times until the 1880s, and a culture of mutual support existed for struggling families like the Bowens. This cohesiveness meant that, in contrast to the drunkenness and fights of Snow's Yard, Plant's Square was quieter. It had no recorded incidents of violence.

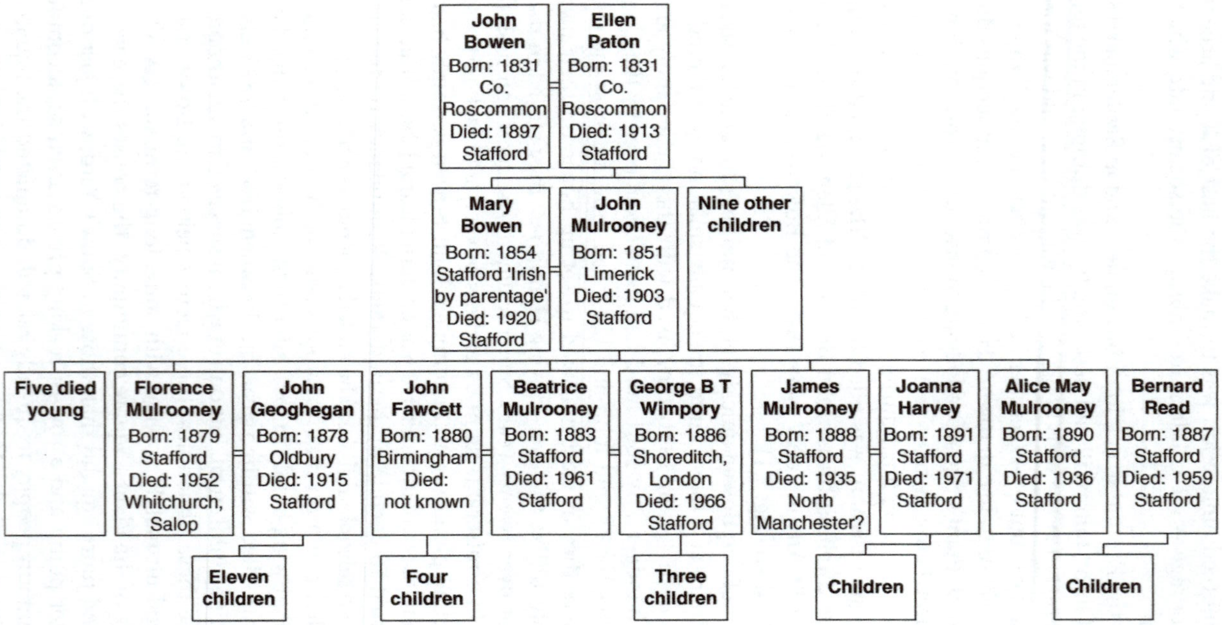

Figure 9.1 Outline of the Bowen–Mulrooney family

The second factor lay with John and Ellen Bowen themselves. They were a steadfast couple who stuck to the business of making a living and bringing up their children. Apart from the census returns, John's only surviving public record is that he (or someone using his name) voted Liberal in the elections of 1868–69. If true, this was political involvement impressive for someone living in such circumstances.[46] If he liked a drink, it was never to such excess that he ended up in court. The family lived, therefore, modestly respectable lives and created a nurturing home out of the two rooms they could afford. That bore fruit in the third factor improving the family's prospects, the lives of the Bowen offspring. The eight surviving children all grew up when the shoe trade was booming and manufacturers were mechanising the industry. Six of them seized this opportunity and got jobs in footwear. Two subsequently saw better prospects in the shoe towns of Leicestershire and left Stafford, whilst one emigrated in the 1880s. Two other children did not go into the shoe trade, of whom one emigrated in the 1870s. The other became a hairdresser but died young in 1901.The key point is that jobs in the workshops gave the Bowen children ample opportunities for social interaction beyond the community of Plant's Square. Four of them met and married ethnically English partners in the shoe trade, and at least two were Protestants. The Irish ethnicity of the Bowen family was diluted rapidly.

The Bowen–Mulrooney family is formed

Mary was the only child of John and Ellen Bowen to marry an Irish partner, and it is their line that forms the rest of this case study. As we have seen, John Mulrooney was born in Limerick around the year 1851. His father Peter had been a gardener, but when John entered the labour market in the 1860s he must have aspired to something slightly better in becoming a shoemaker.[47] Even so, conditions in Limerick were only starting to improve from those Thackeray described in pre-Famine times:

> After you get out of the Main Street the handsome part of the town is at an end, and you suddenly find yourself in such a labyrinth of busy swarming poverty and squalid commerce as never was seen ... Here every house was almost a half ruin, and swarming with people ... Above [the cellars] was a tinsman or a shoemaker, or other craftsman, his battered ensign at the door, and his small wares peering through the cracked panes of his shop.[48]

These were the circumstances in which John Mulrooney entered the shoe trade in his native city, and things were only going to get worse as machine-made British footwear invaded the Irish market. He decided that he would do better in Britain, and he ended up in Stafford either because it was the easiest shoe town to reach from Liverpool or because he was directed there through tramping connections. He certainly moved rapidly into the shoemaking community of the north end, and at the time of his marriage was lodging with the family of a Staffordian cordwainer, Henry Bunn, at no. 5 Back Browning Street. He could have met Mary Bowen either through his work or social connections in the dense shoemaking community of the area. It is significant that both the witnesses at their wedding were English, not Catholic Irish. The new Mulrooney family was to continue its integration into the Stafford working class. Bonds nevertheless remained strong with the Bowens. After their marriage John and Mary initially lodged at no. 31 Grey Friars, the home of another local shoemaker, Henry Draper. It was just a temporary expedient, however, because the couple speedily returned to the Bowen family base in Plant's Square. They lived at no. 8, next door to Mary's family, during most of the 1870s.[49]

Despite the close Bowen family embrace, the early years of John and Mary's married life were pretty miserable. Plant's Square was a death trap for weakly children and Mary Mulrooney's offspring proved the point. She had three babies between 1872 and 1877 but all died within six months. Mary was almost certainly working as a machinist at this time – she certainly was in 1881 – so the babies were left with their grandmother whilst Mary was at work. Despite her own success as a mother, Ellen Bowen now conspicuously failed to get her daughter's babies through their lethal first year in Plant's Square. The family needed to get somewhere better, and by 1881 they had managed to rent a house close by on Grey Friars. That proved to be a turning point because there they had another six children, four of whom did survive to adulthood. Even so, infant death always lurked over the Mulrooney household.

The Mulrooneys became part of the working-class community of Grey Friars and the nearby streets. Like the Hamiltons, they tended to move from house to house as their income and prospects varied so that between 1881 and 1920 the family lived in at least seven different houses in the area. Unlike the Hamiltons, however, they aimed at respectability. The developing mission at St Patrick's School and Church sought to prevent leakage from the church amongst the poor of the north end, and it succeeded with the aspirant Mulrooney family. Mary and her children were actively involved in soirées, sales of work and similar events. Three of the children – Florence (b. 1879), James (b. 1888) and Alice May (b. 1890) – are recorded singing and performing at these functions.[50] On St Patrick's Day 1896, Florence Mulrooney was to be found amongst the Mitchells and Corcorans taking part in a concert of Irish music. Her contribution was the song 'Killarney'.[51] We have here limited but revealing evidence of continued identification with the family's Irish roots, but, as we saw with the Corcorans and Mitchells, such sentimentalism did not extend into any active role in nationalist or Home Rule politics. The influential Irish in Stafford neither promoted nor supported such involvements and the Mulrooneys followed suit.

John and Mary had a last child, Bernard, in 1893 but he died within two years. The couple's middle age was therefore tinged with sadness and things worsened when John Mulrooney himself died in 1903 at the relatively early age of fifty-two. At this time three teenage children were still living at home and presumably contributing to the household income. The pull of Bowen family obligations was, however, still power-ful for Mary Mulrooney. In 1883 her parents Ellen and John Bowen had finally left Plant's Square and moved to no. 54 Grey Friars. There they opened a lodging house that was registered as catering for ten occu-pants in three rooms.[52] Running lodging houses had, of course, always been a means by which needy Irish immigrants made money from their desperate compatriots, but John and Ellen's lodging house catered for a somewhat higher-status clientele.[53] Their late move into the business represented a distinct shift in their life course, since John had switched the insecure life of a hawker to that of a fixed entrepreneur, lowly as the occupation was. He used his new security to also become a coal dealer, something he was still doing when he died in 1897.[54] Surprisingly, his death did not mean the end of the coal business because Ellen Bowen kept it going and Mary Mulrooney helped her. Although in the 1901 Census she was still described as a machinist in the shoe trade, the fam-ily legend is that Mary Mulrooney 'had a coal wharf' and could be seen about town 'with a sack on her shoulders'.[55] Both Ellen and her daugh-ter Mary needed the money after their respective husbands had died, but their hard work brought results. It is said that Mary Mulrooney ended up owning property, some of which she donated to St Patrick's Church.[56]

The Mulrooney children and the Geoghegan family: loss of Irish identity

John and Mary Mulrooney's four surviving children continued the pro-cess of integration into the host society and the changing economy. Beatrice (b. 1883) also became a machinist in a shoe factory, but in the early 1900s she left home and moved to Birmingham. There she married John Fawcett, a Brummy who worked in a bicycle factory. The couple had four children before 1910 (though two died), but around that year Fawcett seems to have abandoned his family and fled abroad. Certainly, no record of his death has been found and in the 1911 Census Beatrice was liv-ing alone, although still describing herself as married. Three years later she married again, also in Birmingham. Her new husband was George Wimpory, a Londoner.[57] In the 1920s the couple returned to Stafford and established a new branch of the family in the town.

James Mulrooney (b. 1888) moved into the growing engineering industry. In 1910 he also followed the general family trait of going outside his Irish ethnic origins by marrying Jenny (Joanna) Harvey from a local Protestant family. In 1911 the couple were living apart because James was in Coventry working as a fitter in the engineering industry. There he boarded with Jenny's brother and his family who had also moved to Coventry. The couple were subsequently reunited in Stafford and there are extensive descendants from this line of the Mulrooney family.[58] Alice May Mulrooney (b. 1890) followed in her mother's footsteps and became a shoe-trade machinist. In 1913 she married Bernard Read, a clerk in a shoe factory from a Stafford family who lived nearby in Grey Friars. There are also descendants from this branch of the family.

The Mulrooney family therefore fanned out into English society and its Irish heritage became increasingly diluted. This also became true of John and Mary's other surviving child, Florence (b. 1879), even though she did marry a person with some Irish roots. On 16 July 1898 the wedding took place, at St Patrick's, of Florence Mulrooney and John Geoghegan. He had been born in 1878 in Oldbury in the Black Country, the son of John and Annie Geoghegan. John Geoghegan Sr had been born in Bridgnorth, Shropshire, in 1854, and was almost certainly the child of Famine immigrants, although the family's origins have not been traced.[59] His wife, Annie Lewis, was an English woman also born in Oldbury.[60] John (Sr) became an engineer's clerk, a clearly aspirant job, and the family moved to Stafford in the 1870s. He probably worked at Dorman's engineering works in the Foregate.[61] The whole Geoghegan family flourished in Stafford and there are numerous descendants. Even so, John Geoghegan (Jr) was ethnically only half-Irish so the dilution of the family's Irish identity and heritage was already at work when he married Florence Mulrooney. The trend was to continue. The couple went on to have seven surviving children and all subsequently married ethnically English partners, a number of whom were Protestant.[62]

Despite a surname name that was demonstrably Irish, the family's Irish consciousness and heritage were largely wiped out after the Great War so that a descendant could say in 2003 that, when growing up in the 1930s and 1940s, they 'had no perception of Irishness'. This loss of identity was further strengthened amongst the Geoghegans because Florence and John's children largely lapsed from active Catholicism.[63] Nevertheless, many of their offspring were sent to Stafford's Catholic schools and this reclaimed some for the Church. They were, however, subjected to a vigorously English Catholic education that demonstrates the partial validity of Mary Hickman's argument that the English Catholic Church's role was to 'denationalise' the Irish.[64] The history of the Geoghegan family shows that the process could be generated actively within the family itself.

The Geoghegan family's shift in identity also resulted from the ability of its members to seize opportunities in the new economy. John Geoghegan followed his father into the engineering industry as a turner. He was fortunate with his timing. In 1900 news broke that Siemens Brothers were buying land in Forebridge to build a big electrical engineering works.[65] Siemens's main factory was at Woolwich in south-east London, and John Geoghegan must have decided he would get work at Siemens, ultimately in Stafford, by first going to the Woolwich factory. The family therefore moved to Erith in Kent in the winter of 1900–01 and they stayed there until around 1907.[66] John then got his anticipated job at the Stafford works and the family returned to their base in Grey Friars, despite its being the other end of town from Siemens. They now had a good income from John's skilled job and their children ultimately fanned out into a wide range of occupations both in Stafford and elsewhere. The Bowen/Mulrooney/Geoghegan family had, over four generations, demonstrated striking upward occupational mobility from farm labour and hawking through shoemaking to skilled engineering.

Adaptation, integration and identity in the Bowen/Mulrooney/Geoghegan family

Mary Mulrooney née Bowen's schooling in the 1850s was sketchy or non-existent. She just about learned to write, but her literacy was probably poor.[67] When faced with the 1911 census form she asked Alice's boyfriend Bernard Read to fill it in. When he asked her where she was born she replied 'Stafford', but she then added a telling point. She said she was 'Irish by parentage'.

This comment *appears* to show that Mary was proud of her parents and their Irish origin. It clearly suggests she 'inherited' a conscious identity that was at least partly Irish. By this standard she was one of the 'effectively Irish' identified by J. H. Clapham, a concept that carries the implication that Irish identity was transmitted almost *in toto* to children like Mary who were born in Britain.[68] Whilst it may have some validity when applied to concentrations of second-generation Irish in some big cities, its relevance to Stafford is negligible. Mary had pride in her heritage but her life demonstrates the family's process of integration into local society. She was now approaching old age – she was to die in 1920 – and she was looking back over her family's life lived for the most part in poverty and miserable surroundings. She could see that the Bowen family had made the best of a poor hand. They had created an apparently nurturing home amidst the hubbub of Plant's Square and laid the foundations of a complex family that adapted to the changing opportunities offered in Stafford and the wider Midland area. They had become part of the Catholic community of the north end, and their offspring with the Mulrooneys and Geoghegans had begun to appear amongst the respectable social circle of St Patrick's parish.

The evidence so far has suggested that the Bowen–Mulrooney family was cohesive and had a strong sense of mutual obligation amongst its members. It aspired to a respectable lifestyle even though John Bowen's occupations were mostly at the bottom end of the labour market. The Bowens kept out of trouble and their children mostly moved into Stafford's growth industry, the shoe trade. Adaptability brought social interaction with the host community and a consistent pattern of intermarriage. That process meant dilution of the family's Irish heritage and brought the complete elimination of its Irish identity by the interwar period. We see here clear evidence of the wastage of memory and reorientation of identity that takes places over four or more generations of a family. There is a small conundrum, however. In 1911 Mary Mulrooney expressed a superficially strong Irish identity based on apparent loyalty to – perhaps even love of – her parents and their origin. Her mother Ellen was then still alive but a widow of eighty. In these circumstances, and in those days, we might expect to find Mary had taken in her mother and was looking after her. Not here. Mary Mulrooney was living with her daughter Alice in a four-room house in Grey Friars but Ellen was not with them. She was lodging with a young English family in Browning Street and living, she said, on 'private means'. The relationship with her landlord was so tenuous that he knew neither her Christian name nor where she was born. This suggests that family obligations had either broken down for some reason or that old Ellen Bowen wanted to preserve a sturdy independence in her old age. Some time in the next two years Mary Mulrooney moved to a small house round the corner at no. 69 New Street and she did finally take in her mother. Ellen was by now an enfeebled old woman and she died there on 4 February 1913.[69] Her death severed the direct link with the knowledge, attitudes and identity of the family's Famine generation.

The significance of shoemaking

The shoe trade peaked as Stafford's major industry in the generation following the Famine and it played a significant role in the history of Irish families in the town. Capitalism's uneven development meant that Stafford's gain was Ireland's loss. In Stafford the trade was valuable because it was the route by which many second-generation Irish found a footing in the core of the local economy. The increasing subdivision and de-skilling of the labour process provided openings for young people from an unskilled labouring background, like many of the Irish. Furthermore, the trade was open to both women and men and, although jobs remained markedly gendered, women in many shoe-trade households played a major role in income generation as well as in home-making. Shoemaking therefore offered a modest but attainable step in upward social mobility. It was the route taken by most of the Bowen children, but in the short term it was no automatic passport out of places like Plant's Square. The incomes of shoe-trade workers remained low and fickle, and most still lived cheek-by-jowl with Stafford's unskilled working class in the town centre and north end. Nevertheless, the diversity of jobs and the increasing concentration of work in factories and workshops offered advancement possibilities to ambitious people. For those trapped in the old domestic trade, like the Hamiltons, shoemaking was a dead end and the position worsened for all as the industry passed its peak and started to decline. Even so, the industry and the clustering of its workers provided multiple possibilities for social interaction that were seized by families like the Bowens and Mulrooneys. The two case studies have illustrated differences in family creation, circumstances, behaviour and trajectory amongst shoe-trade workers. The long-term history of these immigrant families was determined by how individuals in evolving family relationships responded to the specific opportunities and associational networks open to them.

Notes

1   *SA*, 20 October 1855.
2   Information from Rachel Clayton, a descendant, May 2006.
3   For reviews of the issues, with differing perspectives, see C. Ó Gráda, 'Did Ireland "under"-industrialise?', *Irish Economic and Social History*, 37 (2010), pp. 117–23; A. Bielenberg, *Ireland and the Industrial Revolution: The Impact of the Industrial Revolution on Irish Industry, 1801–1922* (London: Routledge, 2009); C. Ó Gráda, *Ireland: A New Economic History, 1780–1939* (Oxford: Oxford University Press, 1994), esp. Chapter 13; Geary, 'Deindustrialisation in Ireland'; Mokyr, *Why Ireland Starved*, esp. Chapters 6 and 7.
4   Harrison, 'The development of boot and shoe manufacturing', p. 1.
5   *VCH Stafford*, Vol. 6, p. 217; A. Middlefell, *The Ancient Town of Stafford from the Eighth to the Twentieth Century* (Stafford: A. Middlefell, 2000), pp. 50–4.
6   E. J. Hobsbawm, 'The tramping artisan' in Hobsbawm, *Labouring Men, Studies in the History of Labour* (London: Weidenfeld and Nicolson, 1968), p. 36.
7   *Census of Ireland, 1841: General Summary and County Tables. Table VI, Table of Occupations; Census of Ireland, 1861*, Part 4, Vol. 2: *Occupations*.
8   J. Press, *The Footwear Industry in Ireland, 1922–1973* (Dublin: Irish Academic Press, 1989), p. 20.
9   *Ibid.*, pp. 18–20; J. Press, 'Protectionism and the Irish footwear industry', *Irish Economic and Social History*, 13 (1986), pp. 74–89 (p. 75); A. Fox, *A History of the National Union of Boot and Shoe Operatives, 1874–1957* (Oxford: Basil Blackwell, 1958), Chapter 2.
10 *Census of Ireland, 1881: Occupations, Tables 18/19; Census of Ireland, 1911: Occupations, Table 20, Occupations of Males and Females by Ages, Religious*

Persuasion and Education; A. Bielenberg, 'What happened to Irish industry after the British industrial revolution? Some evidence from the first UK Census of Production, 1907', *Economic History Review*, 61:4 (November 2008), pp. 820–41 (Appendix, Table 3).

11 Press, *Footwear Industry*, p. 18.

12 Ó Gráda, *Ireland*, p. 268.

13 L. M. Cullen, *An Economic History of Ireland since 1660* (London: B. T. Batsford, 1972), p. 163.

14 The 1841 figure for women, 94, is clearly defective. *Census, 1841: County of Stafford. Occupations, Stafford Borough*; *Census, 1871: Occupations of Males and Females in Principal Towns. Stafford Borough*.

15 Derived from Harrison, 'The development of boot and shoe manufacturing', Figure 16.

16 *Parliamentary Papers, 1865, XX: Children's Employment Commission, 1862, 4th Report; Report on Bootmakers, Tailors, Hatters, Glovers etc.*: 'Bootmakers', pp. 123–6.

17 British Library of Political Science, London School of Economics, Webb Trade Union Collection, Vol. 24, leather trades and National Union of Boot and Shoe Operatives, p. 142.

18 D. A. Reid, 'The decline of St Monday, 1766–1876', *Past & Present*, 71 (1976), pp. 76–101.

19 Webb Trade Union Collection, Vol. 24, pp. 96–9, 112, 160, 201.

20 Lewis, *Topographical Dictionary of Ireland*, p. 271; *Census of Ireland, 1841, Table VI*.

21 Parish Registers, St Andrew's Church, Ancoats, Manchester; *Ancestry* (accessed 3 April 2013).

22 No death or other place of residence in Britain has been traced.

23 I. Meredith, 'Irish migrants in the Scottish Episcopal Church' in M. J. Mitchell (ed.), *New Perspectives on the Irish in Scotland* (Edinburgh: John Donald, 2008), pp. 46–8; Church of England clergy officiated at the family's four recorded burials in the cemetery. SBC Burial Records 2/3970, 3/5362 and 3/4460, 10/7651. The Hamilton boys gave their religion as 'Church of England' when they were attested into the army.

24 Harrison, 'Boot and shoe manufacturing', p. 37.

25 *SA*, 14 September 1878.

26 In 1871 they were at 4 Mill Street but by 1875 they had moved next door to no. 5. William Salt Library, Jones Collection, C. H. Gillard, auctioneers, sale catalogues, property in slum areas, 1860–89: sale catalogue, 1875, 'valuable freehold house properties ... 2 houses, gardens & premises at 5/6 Mill Street in the occupation of Edward Hamilton & Nicholas Maddocks'. By 1877 they were living at Victoria Terrace, Sandon Road. SRO D4338/E/1/5, Stafford and District Humane Burial Society Register, 1876–1930s. In 1881 they were living at 31 Browning Street but by 1891 they had moved to 18 Browning Street, a small four-roomed cottage; in 1901 they were next door at no. 17.

27 They lived at 7 Grey Friars in 1911 and Harriet died at no. 9 Grey Friars in 1915.

28 *SA*, 2 May 1868.

29 *Ibid.*, 13 August 1887.

30 SRO D5008/2/7/11/1.

31 *SA*, 21 April 1888.

32 NA, WO97, no. 2296: Pte Albert James Hamilton, service record; *FindMyPast* (accessed 27 February 2013).

33 Rugby RD, Marriages, April–June 1896, 6d/1011: Albert James Hamilton and Mary Hetty Howlett; 1911 census return.

34 *SA*, 7 May 1881.

35 NA, WO97, no. 72126: Pte Arthur Hamilton, service record; *FindMyPast* (accessed 27 February 2013).

36 Cannock RD, Marriages, July–September 1894, 6b/753: Arthur Hamilton and Mary Merrick; Deaths, January–March 1897, 6b/328: Arthur Hamilton.

37 NA, WO97, no. 52897: Pte Edward Hamilton, service record; *FindMyPast* (accessed 27 February 2013).

38 Nantwich RD, Marriages, October–December 1898, 8a/629: Edward Hamilton and Hannah Bebbington; Nantwich RD, Death Certificate, 8a/210, No. 475: Edward Hamilton, 16 May 1907; R. Banister, *Brain's Clinical Neurology*, 5th edn (Oxford: Oxford University Press, 1978), pp. 428–39; opinion of Dr Richard Nelson, Chester, April 2013.

39 Stafford RD, Births, April–June 1884, 6b/10: Adelina Hamilton; Wolverhampton RD, Deaths, April–June 1885, 6b/326: Adelina Elkin Hamilton.

40 Stafford RD, Marriages, April–June 1916, 6b/46: Edward Hamilton and Lizzie Sturland.

41 Stafford RD, Deaths, April–June 1953, 9b/356: Edward Hamilton, age '56'. (This is the 'official' (but probably inaccurate) age reported by someone to the registrar when the death was registered. Given the mysterious circumstances of his birth, described above (p. 250), it is highly unlikely that the person reporting his death knew his real birth date, or even if there was a birth certificate. There is therefore no guarantee that this was actually his correct age and the discussion above gives my best estimate of Edward's actual likely date of birth: 1894/95.)

42 Stafford RD, Marriage Certificate, 6b/25, no. 149: Ada Hamilton and Charles Henry Conlin, 16 May 1907.

43 See D. M. MacRaild, *Culture, Conflict and Migration: The Irish in Victorian Cumbria* (Liverpool: Liverpool University Press, 1998), esp. Chapters 4, 5 and 6, for an analysis emphasising the sectarian perspective.

44 Stafford RD, Marriage Certificate, 6b/44, no. 158: John 'Muroney' (*sic*) and Mary Bowen. There are many possible spellings of the name Mulrooney, which made it doubly difficult to track this family's history.

45 SRO D659/1/4/8, 24 September 1847–30 March 1850.

46 SRO D5008/2/7/11/1.

47 Stafford RD, Marriage Certificate, 6b/44, no. 158: John Murony and Mary Bowen.

48 W. M. Thackeray, *The Irish Sketch Book* in *Works*, Vol. 17 (London 1888), p. 142; quoted in Ó Gráda, *Ireland*, p. 265.

49 SBC Burial Records 3/4067, 17 January 1872; 3/5028, 12 January 1875; 4/6133, 1 January 1878. All give Plant's Square as the place of residence, the last record specifying no. 8.

50 E.g. *SA*, 26 February 1887, 4 January 1896, 30 December 1899, 24 November 1906.

51 *Ibid.*, 21 March 1896.

52 SRO D3704.

53 In 1891 it held the ten permitted occupants. None was Irish, there were three married couples and one of the other occupants claimed to be a clerk.

54 SBC Burial Records 7/1184: John Bowen, 21 August 1897.

55 Information from Sheila Bayliffe, Mary Mulrooney's great-granddaughter, July 2003.

56 Interview with Sheila Bayliffe, Stafford, July 2003.

57 Information partly obtained from Cathy Witkay, a descendant of the Fawcett family, September 2009.

58 Information partly from Fiona Mulrooney, great-granddaughter of James and Jenny Mulrooney, May 2003.

59 In 1881 a John and Julia 'Gahagan' were living in a court off Ward Street in Wolverhampton. They were of the right age to have been John Geoghegan's parents. John Gahagan had been born in Strokestown, Co. Roscommon, in 1825 and Julia had been born in the same county four years earlier. They came, therefore, from an area where many of the Irish immigrants in Stafford and the Midlands originated. John Gahagan was a bricklayer, a peripatetic occupation that could easily explain why their son had been born in Bridgnorth.

60 No marriage record has been found, but Annie gave her maiden name as Lewis to the parish priest at St Austin's when their son Albert was christened on 13 September 1879; BAA P255/1/4.

61 W. H. Dorman and Co. was established in 1869 and initially made machinery for the shoe trade. The firm diversified rapidly into other fields and became a major employer. Staffordshire Industrial Archaeology Society, *100 Years of Business in Stafford, 1900–2000* (Stafford, SIAS, 2000), pp. 20–4.

62 Information from Sheila Bayliffe, 2003.

63 She did, however, recall that some mothers in Grey Friars stopped their children playing with them because they were Catholic, interesting evidence of twentieth-century anti-Catholicism. Sheila Bayliffe, 2003.

64 Hickman, *Religion, Class and Identity*, Chapter 3.

65 *SA*, 29 September 1900 and 30 March 1901.

66 Their baby Florence Clare was registered in Stafford in 1900 and her death similarly that year, but by the time of the 1901 Census they were living at 43 Ripley Road, Erith.

67 Her 'signature' in the register of marriages does not have the customary 'X' to indicate inability to sign her name.

68 J. H. Clapham, 'Irish immigration into Great Britain in the nineteenth century', *Bulletin of the International Committee of Historical Sciences*, 20 (July 1933), pp. 596–605 (p. 603).

69 Stafford RD, Death Certificate, 6b/11, no. 363, 4 February 1913. The cause of death was 'bronchitis and pneumonia' and Mary Mulrooney was present at the death.

10

The forgotten Irish: entrepreneurs and professionals

Irish entrepreneurs and professionals in Stafford

Although we know most of the emigrants from Ireland were manual workers, actual figures on the occupational status of emigrants are sketchy. In the nineteenth century the authorities collected no data on the occupations of Irish people entering Britain, and the British census failed to publish statistics on people's jobs related to their places of birth. The only way to link the two is through local studies like this, and the general picture for Stafford between 1841 and 1901 is shown in Table 10.1. This shows that Stafford conformed to the expected picture in that almost 70 per cent of the Irish were semi-skilled or unskilled workers, whilst around one-quarter reported skilled or clerical occupations. Nevertheless, around 5 per cent of men and a somewhat lower proportion of women were engaged in professional, entrepreneurial or managerial occupations. Was Stafford typical?

Evidence about Irish emigrants leaving for the Americas, South Africa and Australasia does indeed show a similar picture. Between 1877 and 1880, 5.7 per cent of males going overseas were in occupations covering commerce; finance; insurance; the professions; and, rather quirkily, students.[1] That figure is remarkably close to Stafford's proportion of professional, entrepreneurial and managerial immigrants. It might be argued, however, that higher-status emigrants disproportionately went to overseas destinations and that Britain mainly received those too poor and unskilled to go anywhere else. The only way to assess this is by collating evidence from local studies, and Figure 10.1 attempts to do this.[2] Although we must be cautious in making comparisons because of differences in classifying occupations and allocating people to them, the evidence suggests Stafford's proportion of professional and entrepreneurial Irish was relatively high but not out of line. Northallerton had nearly 10 per cent of Irish in this class. Contrary to what many might expect,

Table 10.1 Occupational status of Irish-born males and females aged 15 upwards, Stafford, 1841–1901

Occupational Status	Males %	Females %
I–II: Professional, entrepreneurial and managerial	5.2	3.1
III: Skilled manual and clerical	25.7	28.7
IV–V: Semi-skilled and unskilled	69.1	68.2
Total no. of individuals	**918**	**296**

Source: census enumeration returns; those reporting specific occupations.

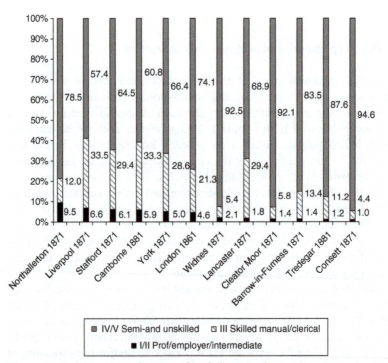

Figure 10.1 Occupational status of Irish-born males, various towns, 1861–81 (for sources see n. 2)

Liverpool had the second-highest proportion, somewhat above that in Stafford. Although our image of the Liverpool Irish is dominated by the labourers and carters of the docks, a significant proportion also worked in the skilled trades and higher-status jobs that clustered in the commercial city. Places as diverse as Camborne, York, London and Widnes all had professional and entrepreneurial proportions in the same range as Stafford. These places contrast with one-industry settlements like Cleator Moor or Consett, in which there was little to attract higher-status immigrants. It is clear, however, that Stafford's cohort of professional and entrepreneurial Irish was, in simple numerical terms, pretty typical of a wide range of places in England and Wales.

A Protestant elite

This chapter now examines the families from this small group who settled in Stafford. Although nearly sixty Irish-born professional, entrepreneurial or managerial individuals are recorded in Stafford between 1841 and 1901, only nine such families settled in the town for more than ten years. They formed 4.4 per cent of the 206 settled Irish families. All were Protestant, which demonstrates how access to higher-status occupations in Ireland was still largely restricted to members of the Anglo-Irish Ascendancy and Ulster Protestants. Members of both these groups came to Stafford. Did their higher status guarantee access to the local elite and diminish the stresses of transition to life in England? They can be expected to show evidence of a superficially 'respectable' lifestyle based on clear gender divisions and the male-breadwinner norm, but we must be on the look-out for family tensions reflecting both elite expectations and individual personalities. We need to assess the attitudes and behaviour they displayed towards their mostly Catholic Irish compatriots. To what extent, if at all, did these families act as culture brokers between the Irish and the host society in ways that have been documented by O'Leary in Wales and Belchem in Liverpool?[3] In Stafford the religious difference placed inherent limitations on this role but did not necessarily negate it. Shared national origins and identity might still be significant. These families aspired, nevertheless, to be part of the English ruling class, and the ways in which they acted out their class role were likely to be the major determinant of their local significance.

Stafford's professional and entrepreneurial Irish families may all have been Protestant but they showed considerable diversity in other ways. Five out of nine families emerged before the Famine and reflect the extensive emigration of supposedly dynamic Protestants, particularly from Ulster, in that period. The emergence of the other four was strung out between 1851 and the 1880s. Three families were from Ulster, but in the end they were marginally outnumbered by the four from Leinster. The origin of the other two families has not been traced. In five cases nuclear units were established in Britain by the marriage of an Irish male to an English woman, a clear case of ambitious lone emigrants forming liaisons as they became established in English society. Three families did, nevertheless, emigrate as pre-existing nuclear units, one of which was that of John Hayes Hatton, Staffordshire's Chief Constable, whom we met in relation to the Giltrap family (Chapter 7). The other family, the Twiggs, arrived in the late 1880s. He was an English bank accountant who had presumably worked in Ireland and married an Irish woman there.

Although all these high-status families became fully involved in Stafford society in the short term, only two went on to integrate more deeply in the long term. In one case that integration was vestigial and did not last beyond the Second World War. Five proved to be long-term transients. This repeats the pattern that skilled and higher-status families and their descendants were *more* mobile than the unskilled. Two families died out in Stafford. One was Cooper Crawford, a medical doctor who never married, whilst the other family, the Maynes, produced no children.

Two case studies have been chosen to reflect the range of these families:

• Gibson: a shoe entrepreneur's family who became major political players in the local community;
• Clendinnen: Stafford's first Medical Officer of Health but with a family life that brought suffering and division.

There is another group of Irish 'professionals' who must also be considered, namely the Irish Catholic priests who at various times served in Stafford. The two most significant, Michael O'Sullivan and James O'Hanlon, are studied to see the roles they played and whether there were tensions amongst their ethnic background, their relationship with Irish compatriots and their work in a Church with roots in the English Catholic community.

The Gibson family: from Ulster to the mayoral chamber

Hugh Woods Gibson was the most 'successful' Irish immigrant to settle in nineteenth-century Stafford. His case demonstrates that religious links between Ulster and England could play a significant role in establishing Protestant immigrants in the host economy, but it also cautions against making simple assumptions about the attitudes and behaviour patterns inculcated by an Ulster Presbyterian background. Gibson and his family demonstrated a flexible response to the opportunities in England and Stafford. His case is at the opposite end of the spectrum from Lambert Disney's (Chapter 8).

Arrival in Stafford

On 29 October 1840 an 'H. Gibson' was admitted to membership of Stafford's Zion (Congregational) Chapel. He was recommended 'by letter from the pastor of the Presbyterian Church Bangor.'[4] This was Hugh

Woods Gibson. He had been born in 1821 and was just nineteen years old. His father, William Gibson, was a farmer, probably at Ballymullin in the vicinity of Bangor, Co. Down, who possibly had other interests in Belfast and was a man of some substance.[5] The Gibsons were staunch Presbyterians, and William named his son after Hugh Woods, who was minister at their chapel in Bangor from 1808 to 1856.[6] Hugh Gibson may have come to Stafford with his brother William, a tailor, because a William Gibson was also admitted to the chapel 'by a letter of dismission from a church at Belfast' in September 1839.[7] Alternatively, 'William' may have been Hugh's father and was there to set his son up in Stafford's main trade by seeking sponsorship from shoe manufacturers in the Zion Chapel and other Protestant congregations. Whatever the circumstances, the tactic paid off, and in 1840 Hugh Gibson got a job with one of the principal manufacturers, Thomas Benson Elley. He was now on the path to advancement. Hugh's brother William did also move to England and was successful. He established a tailoring business in Wokingham, Berkshire, and ultimately owned land in the area. Hugh was to meet his wife through him.

William and Hugh Gibson's choice to join the Congregational Chapel in Stafford was a prudent strategy to make business contacts, and for Hugh it was a significant act in jettisoning his roots. They could have joined the long-established Presbyterian congregation in the town, but it was small and in 1838 its minister had been dismissed for heresy.[8] He took most of the congregation with him to set up a branch of the Exclusive Brethren. The schism did cause Hugh Gibson to have a religious wobble, because records show he 'joined the Brethren' some time between 1840 and 1843.[9] He rejoined the Congregationalists later, however.

Although described as a 'cordwainer' in the 1841 Census, Gibson was no humble shoemaker. Elley ran a substantial business in leather goods involving a tannery, curriers and shoemakers in Stafford, Stone, Northampton and Kettering.[10] Elley 'was not long in discerning the business ability of his young assistant' and Gibson became an indispensable part of the firm. In 1848 he was sent to represent Elley's in London.[11] Three years later he married Ellen Cleare Targett in Wokingham, a connection clearly made through his brother William. She was a Baptist but her background is otherwise obscure.[12] Gibson's success in promoting the business in London earned him a place in Elley's top management, and in 1854 the couple relocated back to Stafford.[13] Tragedy struck, however. On 18 March 1857 Ellen died after giving birth to the couple's first child, also Ellen.[14] Despite this blow, Hugh Gibson's faith and ambition drove him on. Elley died in 1860 and Gibson became one of the partners of the reconstructed business along with Elley's widow and William Francis Woolley, another Stafford shoe manufacturer.[15] Gibson and Woolley were close associates at the Congregational Chapel, partly because both suffered bereavement in February/March 1857, and they were elected deacons in June 1860.[16] In 1862 Gibson remarried. His new wife, Sarah Payne, was the daughter of a china merchant from Southampton who in 1861 was living as a 'fundholder' on inherited wealth. He probably met her or her father whilst in London. Gibson was so happy with his marriage that he threw a party and dance for around 100 of his workpeople at the Vine Inn.[17] Sarah was already thirty-five and the couple were to have only one child, Henry Payne Gibson, who was born in 1863.

The public figure

Gibson's public celebration of his marriage is one of many incidents that demonstrate how he assiduously courted public opinion in Stafford to further his interests. His next step was to get elected to the Borough Council, which he achieved in November 1864.[18] He was a Liberal and rose to be chairman of the local party by the time of the 1868 election. He strongly backed Gladstone's policy of Irish Church disestablishment and publicly sought the support of local Catholics for the Liberal candidate, H. D. Pochin, later unseated for electoral malfeasance. John Fanning, the priest at St Austin's, sat alongside him on the platform at an election meeting attended by 'nearly a thousand' people.[19] Gibson rejected Protestant criticism of doing this, stating that:

> It had been said that he [Mr Gibson] and some of those around him had stood together on a platform with Roman Catholics prepared to join with them – first in destroying the Irish Church and then destroying the English Church. There was no truth in that representation ... For his part he was perfectly satisfied to leave the cause of Protestantism, to which he was deeply attached, to contend on terms of perfect equality and had no fear of the result.[20]

The 1868 election in Stafford was notoriously violent and corrupt, and it was alleged that Tory employees at Elley, Gibson and Woolley had been intimidated, a charge denied by Gibson.[21] His local influence ensured that no mud stuck and in 1871 he was elected mayor. At the nomination it was said that 'From the time he came to Stafford ... he had always displayed indomitable energy, perseverance and uprightness of conduct, qualities which had earned him the position of one of the largest manufacturers in the town.'[22] This quotation emphasises how Gibson, an in-migrant, personified the expansion of the Stafford shoe trade to its peak in the 1860s and 1870s. That was, however, prosperity based partly on ruthless exploitation of workers and a disregard for the environmental costs. In 1871 the firm was summoned on four counts of employing under-age children, two of whom, Emma Farrell and Ellen Carroll, were second-generation Irish.[23] The firm's tanyard was also channelling its noisome effluent into a ditch running to the River Sow.[24]

Gibson then demonstrated his shrewdness, however. He got out of the shoe trade because it had reached its peak and problems like these were being publicised. T. B. Elley's son was now old enough to take over management of the firm and Gibson severed his connection with it in 1873.[25] He diversified into land development and finance, as well as the coal and iron trades. By the 1880s he was, amongst other things, a director of the Sheepbridge Coal and Iron Company, Sheffield, and colliery firms in Nottinghamshire and Cannock Chase.[26] Gibson continued, nevertheless, his political and public activities in Stafford, and he gathered the range of posts common to influential small-town business people in the nineteenth century. He was a magistrate, school governor, hospital governor, trustee of local building societies and charities, a director of the gas company, Poor Law Guardian, and more besides. He was also elected Mayor for a second time in 1876 after the sudden death of the newly installed incumbent, and was recalled partly because he had got H. D. Pochin, the industrialist and unseated MP of the 1868 election, to donate money for the new Borough Hall.[27] It opened in 1877 and is today the town's main arts venue.[28] Gibson's involvement with Pochin underlines how his business affairs were now national, not local. Overall, his political stance was broadly progressive and this reflected both his Liberal politics and religious beliefs. He remained closely involved in the affairs of the Congregational Chapel and was inevitably part of the temperance movement. In 1877 gave his views to a public meeting:

> If they convinced the reading and intelligent portion of the community they had then something with which to work on the lower classes ... He was afraid, however, that ... the vice of drunkenness had been on the increase among the poorer classes. He was speaking now as a magistrate of the Borough ... He was convinced, however, that punishment would never make a man temperate. They had the same offenders time after time before them for the same offence. ... He was sorry that drinking was not confined to men, but he feared that in women especially it was very much on the increase. It was a very sad thing to see mothers of children coming before the magistrate again and again and fined for drunkenness.[29]

His vision was simply of a society divided between the enlightened middle and upper classes and a residuum of the poor mired in the problems of drink. He had no solution but temperance to offer, but his attitudes demonstrated pity and concern rather than fruitless censure.

The Protestant businessman and his family

In 1883 the Gibson family left Stafford and retired to Edgbaston in Birmingham. Hugh Gibson gave up all his local offices. The decision to leave was sudden and came as 'a painful surprise' to their associates at the Congregational Church. A letter from the pastor made reference to a personal bereavement, though who had died has not been positively identified.[30] The swiftness of their departure shows Gibson's single-mindedness. He would not let sentimental attachments stand in his way. Although he came from the Presbyterian business class of Ulster, neither he nor his parents conformed to any stereotype of inward-looking, embittered Orangeism. Gibson's sense of self had evolved to view the world confidently with an outward-looking and opportunistic mindset. His Nonconformist religion played a significant role in deter-mining his political Liberalism and generally progressive attitudes, but at root Gibson retained a fundamentally conservative class perspec-tive on British society. His beliefs were doubtless sincerely held but his switch to the Congregationalists and his deep involvement with that sect in Stafford brought social and material benefits as well as spirit-ual ones. Even so, his decision to leave the Presbyterians was ultim-ately irrelevant because Stafford's Nonconformist business class did not let sectarian squabbles interfere with its economic self-interest. The relatively open environment of Stafford was ideal for Gibson's advancement.

Gibson's family life was damaged by the early death of his first wife. His speedy second marriage to someone he knew already suggests a desire for love and family bonds, but also that he wanted someone to carry out wifely duties looking after his orphaned child and making a home fit for a prosperous and influential businessman. We know little of Sarah Payne-Gibson; she stayed in the background and superficially accepted the gender role assigned to her. She certainly had increasingly nice houses to manage as the family moved from the town centre to Burton Villa in the country outside Stafford and then to leafy Edgbaston. Even so, Sarah may not have totally accepted her maternal role in rela-tion to step-daughter Ellen. How else do we explain the fact that in 1871 Ellen, then fourteen, had been sent as a boarder to a private school in Rowley Park, only a mile from her family home? Ten years later she had left Stafford altogether and had moved in with her uncle William Gibson in Wokingham. These facts suggest she was estranged from her step-mother.

Sarah Gibson probably favoured and spoilt her own child, Henry Payne (b. 1863). Hugh Gibson probably did the same, since he now had a male heir to carry on the family business. Henry failed in the task, how-ever. After the family moved to Birmingham Henry married the daughter of a button manufacturer and the couple speedily had three children. His father set him up as a coal merchant and as agent to one of his collieries, and that got him a nice house in Edgbaston five minutes away from his father. By 1901 Henry had, however, sunk to being an agent in colliery ropes and the family had moved in with Hugh Gibson. Henry died five years later in 1906, aged only forty-three.[31] Also in Edgbaston in 1901 was daughter Ellen. Her step-mother had died in 1893 and, tensions removed, she had gone home to play the matriarchal role looking after her ailing father.[32] Hugh Woods Gibson died on 19 December 1901 aged eighty. He left a fortune of £82,677, worth around £8.3 million at 2012 prices.

Gibson was an extreme example of a young Irish immigrant determined to conform to the mores of the dominant culture in order to get on. In his recorded public utterances later in life he made no reference to his origins but neither did he hide them. His obituary pointed out that he came to Stafford 'from the north of Ireland' but we have seen that he carried little baggage of Protestant sectarianism and none of Orangeism. He slid easily into the English business class and his mixed-ethnicity family were defined by their class position and their Nonconformity, not by any residual Ulster identity. Stafford was a benign environment for such people to prosper, but when the Gibsons left the town they were also saying it was too small and provincial to satisfy them. Despite their deep involvement with Stafford society, they had still proved to be long-term transients in the town.

A violent doctor: the problematic Clendinnen family

The Clendinnen family arrived in Stafford in 1874 because William Ellis Clendinnen had been appointed the borough's first Medical Officer of Health (MOH). They settled in St Mary's Grove in the town centre and on the surface seemed to be a respectable professional family. There was a darker side, however, and the family's problems epitomise Victorian debates about male authority and women's rights in marriage. Clendinnen ultimately resigned his post in 1884 and emigrated to Australia. A descendant of his residual family nevertheless stayed on in Stafford and remained in the town for over fifty years. This family highlights how the structural forces behind Irish emigration and settlement always worked through circumstances that were specific to the emigrants themselves.

A superfluity of Irish doctors

In the nineteenth century an Irish doctor was more likely to emigrate than an Irish labourer. More than half the doctors who trained in Ireland between 1860 and 1905 subsequently left the country. Of those who emigrated just over half ended up practising in Britain and another quarter were in the British military.[33] William Ellis Clendinnen was, therefore, part of a massive outflow of members of the medical profession in Ireland. It was caused by complementary forces. The first was the substantial increase in the output of Irish medical schools caused by the establishment in 1845 of the Queen's University with colleges in Belfast, Cork and Galway. They offered medical education to a wider spectrum of applicants, particularly Catholics, than Trinity and the Royal Colleges, which had an Anglo-Irish Protestant bias.[34] The second factor was, however, the chronic lack of openings for doctors in Ireland. The poverty of the country meant that incomes from private practice were low. Openings in the Poor Law and dispensaries were limited and the pay very poor. There were, in other words, strong 'push' factors encouraging Irish doctors to leave. On the 'pull' side of the equation, opportunities were increasing abroad because of population growth; the development of public, charity and contract medical services in industrial areas; and the expansion of the British empire.[35]

Despite the apparent opportunities available in Britain, it was not easy for Irish doctors to establish themselves there. The profession was snobbish and nakedly competitive. Outsiders in search of positions were seen as a threat and could encounter prejudice, particularly in England.[36] Immigrant doctors often lacked both the money and the contacts to obtain lucrative private practices, whilst jobs were limited in the small public sector and in contract work, and the salaries mediocre. Catholic doctors trained at the unfashionable Irish colleges found it particularly difficult to get work in England, and Miskell has shown how this situation steered them towards industrial Wales.[37]

William Ellis Clendinnen's career illustrates many of the general points made above. A forbear, James Clendinnen, had moved from Dumfriesshire to Co. Down in the mid-eighteenth century, but his son, John Clendinnen, a Wesleyan minister, had been sent to Co. Cork and subsequently to Co. Carlow. William Ellis's father, also called William, became a doctor and practised at Hackettstown, Co. Carlow.[38] He married Lydia Deaker, a Wexford woman. The couple had at least twelve children, though only about half survived to adulthood. One was William Ellis Clendinnen who was born in 1838. Although the Clendinnens' background was Ulster-Scots, by the 1830s the family was more characteristic of the Anglo-Irish Ascendancy with their apparently secure medical practice, country dwelling at Clonmore Lodge and a religious switch to the Church of Ireland.[39] William Ellis's sense of self was gained in these surroundings and they seem to have produced a self-confident, domineering man. He trained mostly under his father and in 1865 received the Licentiate of Apothecaries' Hall in Dublin. In the same year he won the more prestigious Licentiate of the Royal College of Surgeons in Edinburgh.[40] At that point he, like many other doctors, took the decision to leave Ireland.

Rape

Clendinnen came to England around 1865. The first we know of his arrival is when he got married in Birmingham on 20 September 1866 to Sarah Pritchard, a twenty-eight-year-old woman of independent means. We do not know why Clendinnen went to the Midlands or how he met Sarah. His father may have had contacts in the area or perhaps it was a convenient and less competitive destination where he could get his foot in the door by doing locum work. All we do know is that by 1867 the couple had arrived in Cheswardine, a village about three miles from Market Drayton and deep in the Shropshire countryside.[41] William had managed to buy a small country practice there, but their income was probably no more than £300 a year.[42]

Superficially it seemed as though Dr and Mrs Clendinnen were establishing themselves well. Their first child, Evelyn Lydia, arrived in 1868 and Sarah became pregnant with Bertram William in 1869. William's aberrant behaviour then became apparent. His sex drive was probably frustrated by her pregnancy and he saw women as bodies to be exploited. On 29 September 1869 he was arrested and charged with raping Margaret Turnbull in his surgery. She was the twenty-one-year-old daughter of a local publican and builder who, it was said at the initial hearing, could 'almost be called half-witted'.[43] Clendinnen was sent for trial at the Shropshire Spring Assizes and the defence did not contest that sexual intercourse had taken place. It was alleged that the girl had said she must 'tell them at home' to which his response had been 'For God's sake don't. If there is anything the matter I will make it alright with you afterwards', a clear reference to performing an abortion. Clendinnen's defence was that the sex had been consensual and, although the judge pointed out Margaret's low intellect raised 'peculiar circumstances', the jury accepted Clendinnen's argument and found him not guilty, 'at which there was considerable applause in a crowded Court'.[44] The verdict was a clear miscarriage of justice. The whole incident demonstrated the domineering and manipulative side of Clendinnen's character.

Medical Officer of Health in Stafford

Despite his acquittal, Clendinnen's reputation in Cheswardine must have been tainted by the case, and the situation was demeaning for Sarah. He needed to find another job and was helped by the passing of the 1872 Public Health Act. This set up sanitary districts and stipulated that they appoint an MoH. Stafford certainly needed one, but the Borough Council was dilatory and only made an appointment in August 1874. One of the councillors still 'questioned whether the appointment would be of practical use in the town', but William Ellis Clendinnen was appointed. His salary was just £50 a year, a miserable sum that emphasises the unattractive nature of such appointments and why Irish doctors desperate for jobs would take them.[45] His brother Joseph George Clendinnen took the same route and became MoH for the Sedgley Local Board in the Black Country.[46] His family became well established in the Midlands.

William Clendinnen's small salary as MoH – later increased to £100 – meant he had to supplement it where he could. He established his own practice but found it difficult to break into the market for lucrative clients. Work amongst the poor was mainly his lot, a recorded example being when he was summoned to a filthy house in Appleyard Court to find twin babies dead, one stillborn and one from neglect. The mother was said to be 'a drunken woman'.[47] He was elected as a Church of England candidate to the School Board and in 1883 was thanked for making no charge for certificates of ill health needed by parents too poor to pay.[48] He also earned some money as surgeon to the 25th Staffordshire Rifle Volunteers and as medical officer to the new fire brigade.[49] The suspicion must be, however, that the family survived partly on Sarah Pritchard-Clendinnen's private means.

Clendinnen did prove to be a vigorous MoH, though the committee he served often proved reluctant to carry out his recommendations if they penalised landlords and demanded the closure of their properties.[50] Within a month of his appointment he had done a house-to-house survey of sanitary conditions and found a 'truly deplorable state of things'. His first annual report chronicled a 'wretched state of things' with 'ashpits full to overflowing … impurity of water' and water having to be carried half a mile to houses in Eastgate Street. There was appalling pollution by sewage.[51] He immediately and successfully set about replacing 'the foul middens and reeking cess-pools' by the Rochdale pail-privy system, in which excreta were removed in sealed tubs to a sanitary depot outside the Eastgate.[52] We saw that this was the work Martin McDermott was doing when he died in 1877 (Chapter 6). Clendinnen felt this system was preferable to water closets and advocated it to his professional colleagues in the Midlands.[53] A mains drainage system was begun, though it was not completed until well after Clendinnen's time.

A battered wife

Though his salary was poor, Clendinnen's work put him in the public eye and he established his position in the social elite of the town. He was one of Hugh Gibson's associates in the Liberal Party.[54] All of this hid, however, a family life that was broken and violent. It came to a head on 30 May 1884. William Clendinnen:

came home at about three o'clock in the p.m. He struck [his wife Sarah] several times and kicked her on the back and attempted to strike her with the handle of a broom, but the servant threw herself in the way and succeeded in getting possession of it. In consequence of his harsh treatment on that occasion, and during the last eighteen years, she was afraid of the defendant and prayed for a judicial separation and that she might have custody of the children.[55]

That statement in the magistrate's court laid bare William Clendinnen's behaviour towards his wife since their marriage in 1866. He made no attempt to contest the allegations and acceded to the judicial separation as well as her custody of the children. Coupled with the rape of Margaret Turnbull in 1869, we see a violent and oppressive man, the ultimate in Victorian male domination. He probably married Sarah for her money and despised, battered and degraded her. He primarily used women as sexual objects. The children had been battered as well – a charge of assault against his daughter Evelyn was withdrawn at the same hearing. But why did Sarah dramatically expose matters in 1884 and demand separation? There are two likely reasons. One was that three of her children were now in their teens and were able to give Sarah backing finally to make the break. Friends at church may also have given her support. The other reason was the passage of the Married Women's Property Act of 1882. Until 1883 the law had given William Clendinnen, as husband, absolute ownership and control of his wife's assets, even those acquired before marriage.[56] Sarah's independent means were vital to the couple's domestic economy and if she had tried to get out of the marriage earlier she would have been left penniless. Under the 1882 Act she regained ownership and control of her assets and could realistically set up an independent home for her children.

We cannot know the origins of William Clendinnen's character and behaviour. They may have been inherently pathological. He does seem to have related effectively to outsiders in his public and professional life, and as MoH he successfully convinced the councillors to implement his policies. He may nevertheless have identified with his family's adopted and supposedly superior Anglo-Irish attitudes, and they would have left him embittered that his achievements in England were poorly paid jobs in obscure parts of the Midlands. It is an outlook redolent of Lambert Disney (Chapter 8). It shows again that a favoured Protestant background in Ireland was no guarantee of smooth integration into English society. What we do know is that the revelations of 1884 ended his career in Stafford. The change was not immediate – he continued to carry out public functions for some months and in November 1884 even proposed a toast at the mayoral banquet.[57] Given the circumstances, he must have had a thick skin, but it does show there was a residue of respect for him amongst the social elite. He finally resigned from his post as MoH in the same month, however. It was said that he had discharged his duties 'most efficiently', although one councillor said his final salary of £100 was 'exceedingly high'.[58] He left Stafford early in 1885 and went to Australia, where he did insurance medicals in Perth. That lasted no more than a year because in May 1886 he went on a kangaroo hunt and fell from his horse, sustaining fatal injuries. He died a poor man – his personal estate was just £5.[59]

The aftermath: a scattered family

Sarah Clendinnen's misfortune might have led her to desert Stafford, but she had in fact put down roots and remained in the town for a number of years after William's departure and death. Her children were reaching adulthood in the late 1880s and early 1890s, and their careers diverged markedly. None entered the medical profession, a clear rejection of their father's path. Evelyn, the first born, emigrated to Southern Rhodesia and married the editor of the *Bulawayo Chronicle*.[60] Bertram also left Britain and had an adventurous career in Canada and the USA. He died in San Diego, California, in 1942.[61] It is clear, then, that two of Clendinnen's children wanted to escape from Stafford. It was otherwise with Alfred Clendinnen (b. 1875). He remained at home to support his mother and trained as a pharmaceutical chemist. In the 1890s he found work on Merseyside and mother and son moved to Seacombe on the Wirral. They lived in that area for the rest of their lives, Sarah dying in 1930, and Alfred, who ultimately married, in 1943.[62]

The connection between Stafford and all but one of the Clendinnen family lasted for about twenty years before they moved elsewhere. That pattern would have rendered the family 'long-term transients' if it were not for Sarah's third child, Ernest (b. 1872). He remained at home during the 1890s and became a post office clerk and telegraphist. When Alfred and Sarah moved to Merseyside, Ernest stayed in Stafford. In the 1890s and 1900s he was a keen sportsman and involved in running various sports clubs. He integrated into Stafford social life.[63] More interestingly, he also shows evidence of rejecting key aspects of his father's identity. On 18 January 1896 he attended the County Conservative Ball in the Borough Hall. It was attended by many of the town's Catholic elite. A week later he was at the Catholic 'Cinderella Dance' at the same venue, hobnobbing again with many of the elite from St Austin's Church. Although these events were attended by non-Catholics, it does show Ernest Clendinnen was happy to associate with both Tories and Catholics, a radical and conscious break with his father's Liberal and Anglican position. In 1904 he married Alice Matilda Jones, the daughter of a farmer from Dawley in Shropshire. The couple had one child, Ernest Bertram, born in 1907.[64]

Ernest lived in Stafford until the 1930s and married a Stafford woman in 1936, but the couple subsequently emigrated to Australia.[65] His father served with the Royal Engineers during the Great War but the couple later moved back to Alice Matilda's home base in Shropshire. Many years later, in 1954, they went to Australia to live with their son and daughter-in-law.[66] All trace of the Clendinnen family had finally disappeared from Stafford.

Origins, gender conflicts and identity

Like Lambert Disney, William Ellis Clendinnen was brought up in a family that appeared securely part of the lower reaches of the Ascendancy, but his youth coincided with the Ascendancy's increasing loss of self-confidence following Catholic Emancipation.[67] Clendinnen came of age in the troubled aftermath of the Famine. His life choices were conditioned both by the general uncertainty latent in his social class and the specific difficulties faced by newly trained doctors in Ireland. His choice was to leave but, like Disney's, it was probably a reluctant, perhaps embittered, departure. He faced major problems becoming established in England and his marriage to Sarah Pritchard was one of convenience to secure his income.

Clendinnen's marriage exposes how male domination, control and even violence were reinforced by the law in Victorian England. Reform of the situation to help people like Sarah Clendinnen was no foregone conclusion. Many MPs supported the changes brought by the 1882 Act only because they saw marital violence and abuse of property as an affliction of the poor caused mostly by drink.[68] The Clendinnen case demonstrates the essential truth that such behaviour also occurred amongst the middle and upper classes. Although Sarah was initially a secure, probably confident, middle-class English woman, she was trapped in her marriage and the victim of William's personal, social and professional frustrations. He would have resented depending on his wife's income because he saw it degrading his masculinity. Perhaps Sarah harped on about it. The superficial trappings of middle-class respectability hid a household so dominated by enmity and violence that it must have been traumatic for the children. In this situation, the mixed ethnic character of William and Sarah's family unit held little significance for the identity of their children. They can have had little pride or even interest in their father's heritage – indeed, their identity was probably formed partly in opposition to what and where he represented. The history of the Clendinnen family demonstrates how the trajectories of even apparently favoured Irish immigrants were unpredictable and the results complex.

Professionals and entrepreneurs

The professional and entrepreneurial Irish who settled in Stafford were unified by their Protestant religion but by little else. These families might superficially slot easily into Stafford's social and business scene, but the two case studies have demonstrated that appearances could be deceptive. Such families could be undermined by gender conflicts and premature mortality, and they also had little ultimate commitment to the local society in which they settled. It was an instrument in their life's ambitions and all proved to be transient. Because of the religious divide, we see no evidence that these elite families performed any brokerage role between the mass of mainly Catholic Irish and the host society. Indeed, in his role of magistrate Hugh Gibson was involved directly in imposing State sanctions on Irish men and women for their usually pathetic misdemeanours. But neither did most of the professional and entrepreneurial Protestants attempt to stoke anti-Irish or anti-Catholic prejudice in Stafford. The one exception was James Speers, a Presbyterian minister from Belfast who was in Stafford at the time of the restoration of the Catholic Hierarchy in 1850. He was vocal in the Protestant 'papal aggression' agitation that followed and was a frequent anti-Catholic speaker, although he also served on the local Famine Relief Committee alongside Edward Huddleston, the Catholic priest.[69] His impact on general sentiment in the town was minimal. The prime aim of Stafford's middle- and upper-class Irish was to secure their favoured position in local society.

Finale: two Catholic priests and their work in Stafford

Catholicism, the Church and the Irish

In 1886 Cardinal Manning commented that 'the English Catholics are few. The mass of our people are Irish and united with Ireland.'[70] Whatever the validity of this statement nationally, it was not true of nineteenth-century Stafford. For most of the nineteenth century *English* Catholics formed a majority of the Church's adherents in the town, and this unusual fact inevitably influenced the role played by Catholic priests.[71] It was never the case that the role of the Church in Stafford was 'increasingly to become an Irish mission'.[72] It was composed of a mixture of old Catholics, converts,and emergent middle- or working-class Catholics, as well as the Irish. The priests had to operate within a diverse constituency.

The role played by the Church in reinforcing, modifying or denationalising Irish identity has been subject to much research and debate.[73] Gilley has emphasised, however, that much of Irish Catholic religious life in

Britain remains hidden.[74] We still lack studies of Irish Catholic life within the missions that probe the motivations and even the beliefs of those engaged. Gilley and Mary Heimann have criticised historians for viewing the religious dimension solely, and perhaps ahistorically, in terms of modern self-interested secular motivation, an approach that undervalues the role their belief and devotion really played in people's behaviour.[75]

The relationship between Catholicism and Irishness has moved beyond seeing them as interchangeable labels. We have seen the diversity of the Irish immigrants in Stafford and the fact that identity was an evolving and contested phenomenon for individuals and families. When considering the significance of Catholic priests on Irish families, this variety and fluidity of identity must also be related to the dynamic nature of the Church itself in the same period. Whilst the arrival of the Irish greatly increased the Church's congregation, even in Stafford, the role of priests was defined by the forces that converted English Catholicism from a 'community of dissent' to a secure and disciplined Church by the First World War.[76]

Belchem has argued that in the particular circumstances of Liverpool, middle-class Catholic migrants 'constructed a self-enclosed, self-sufficient network which, to the eyes of the host population, served only to emphasise Irish-Catholic apartness.'[77] O'Leary has, by contrast, argued that in Wales the aspirant Catholic Irish created an idealised or imagined Irish community whose values and norms were viewed as respectable not only by its Irish adherents but by observers in the host society. He implies this was a key factor in the longer-term integration of the Irish and their descendants.[78] Stafford offers a third scenario. Here the Catholic Irish faced a substantial host Catholic population. This situation and the emergent identity of second- and later-generation children meant that aspirant Irish families had to seek respectability within the wider Stafford Catholic community rather than through a representation of Irishness to the host population.

Hickman has argued that 'even the most ultramontane priest, favourably disposed towards his Irish parishioners, was part of an enterprise whose ultimate aim was the incorporation and denationalisation of the Irish.'[79] This phrase implies a coherence to the Church's activities that is perhaps more apparent with hindsight than it was at the time. The arrival of the Irish caused mixed reactions. On the one hand they boosted the strength of the Church within a traditionally hostile environment, but on the other hand any militant manifestation of Irish identity threatened the Church's search for security and respectability in English life. The Church had to balance this dilemma with the danger that repression of Irish identity might alienate the Irish from it and towards either secular Irish nationalism or English secular culture and politics. Hickman has emphasised the role of Catholic schools in resolving these dilemmas in the longer term, but in the period up to 1914 the Church's direct activity with parishioners was equally significant.

The priest's work in the mission covered four potential functions. His prime role was, of course, to be the spiritual leader and guide of his flock, but his success in doing this was determined by his personal charisma, or lack of it. In practice that role merged with a second need to safeguard and enhance the strength of the Church and impose its discipline, particularly as concerns about secularisation and 'leakage' increased in the later nineteenth century. This demanded action to involve the laity in building up a strong parish community. Thirdly, in his parish and community work the priest could open up – or deny – opportunities for social advancement to those amongst the Irish who aspired to it. His willingness to do so would be conditioned by his own class attitudes and the power wielded by the existing elites. Finally, the priest faced demands to act as a social worker, responding to problems of family stress. His willingness and effectiveness to act in this way were determined by both his previous experience and his ability to empathise with their difficulties. We can, therefore, assess how Stafford's priests ministered to their Irish flock in relation to this range of functions.

Stafford's Catholic priests

In the nineteenth century St Austin's in Stafford was a plum posting for Catholic priests. It was a well-established church in a nice area with many rich and well-connected adherents. Between 1791 and 1920 it was served by thirteen parish priests of whom eight were English, one was French and four were Irish or Irish-descended. As the mission expanded with the arrival of the Famine Irish and its own internal growth, curates and assistants were drafted in to support the parish priest. Of the sixteen known, seven were English and nine were Irish.[80] The Irish priests formed, therefore, a small but significant cohort amongst Stafford's immigrants.

Catholic priests were, by definition, lone migrants, but that is not to say that their family circumstances were immaterial. They usually lived in a quasi-family situation in the presbytery and, more importantly, their family background influenced their route into the priesthood and their progression within it. We have already seen one instance in the case of Charles Cronin (Chapter 8). The pattern is repeated in the two Irish priests examined here. Although neither conforms to the strict definition of a 'settled family' used in this book – because one only stayed in Stafford for seven years, whilst the other was not Irish-born but the first-generation child of immigrants – they were the most significant Irish priests in the town. Michael O'Sullivan was at St Austin's between 1859 and 1866 whilst James O'Hanlon came to the church as a curate in 1884 and in 1895 was appointed the first priest at St Patrick's.

Michael O'Sullivan: 'the *beau ideal* of the Soggarth Aroon'?[81]

Michael O'Sullivan was Stafford's first Irish priest. He came from Co. Limerick and was born in 1823. His origin was typical of many who entered the priesthood in Ireland at that time in that he was the son of a middle-class farmer.[82] His father died when he was three months old but he was supported by an uncle with the means to pay for his education and was sent to England to be a boarder at Sedgley Park, an exclusive Catholic school near Wolverhampton. That meant that O'Sullivan moved into a largely upper-class English Catholic environment at an early age, and his sense of self and identity was determined more by that than by his broken family circumstances in Ireland. From Sedgley Park he moved, in 1837, to the seminary at St Mary's College, Oscott, near Birmingham, which trained priests for the Midlands and farther afield.[83] Oscott's predominantly upper- and middle-class alumni formed an elite network of mutual influence and support, and Michael O'Sullivan was to move smoothly into that network. He did further study in Rome and was ordained in 1848. He typified the highly trained and disciplined clerics who received promotion in the mid-century Church.[84]

O'Sullivan began his ministry in 1848 as an assistant priest at St Peter's in Birmingham. That was a significant posting because the church's previously English Catholic congregation had migrated to the new St Chad's Cathedral during the 1840s and been replaced by the poor Irish of the city.[85] O'Sullivan arrived at the same time as the Famine influx and he was thrown into working with destitute compatriots very different from his own social background. It must have been a character-building experience, but it only lasted three years before he was moved to the more favoured environment of the Cathedral. He was there until 1857 and was then posted to the rural Catholic community of Brewood in Staffordshire. He moved to Stafford in December 1859.

Michael O'Sullivan's ministry

O'Sullivan faced three challenges in his new mission. The first was to provide a new church to cope with the doubling of the Catholic population that took place in the 1850s. Money began to be raised in 1856, and most of the funds came from wealthy patrons amongst the old families and the farming, commercial and professional classes. O'Sullivan pursued the project vigorously but this meant his priority was to cultivate the goodwill and generosity of the better-off English part of his congregation. The poor Irish were not welcome at the new church's opening on 2 July 1862:

> Shortly before eleven the doors were opened and the church was soon moderately filled by a congregation, the majority of whom appeared to be of the middle class. The fact of a considerable number attending is the more to be remarked as the prices charged for admission were comparatively high.[86]

The aim was a decorous event with no danger of the unwashed hordes embarrassing the eminent clerics and benefactors present. At the dinner following the opening O'Sullivan gave his view of the position of Catholics in England:

> It was an ordinary objection made to Catholics that their religion tended to denationalise them; but the truth was that with them devotion to religion and devotedness to the true interests of their country were not contradictory but correlative principles; and the real Catholic was not only a sincere friend to his faith but the sincerely loyal subject to his sovereign. Their motto was, first, 'to fear God' and next 'to honour the King'. (*Cheers*)[87]

There could be no clearer statement of the Church's desire to gain a foothold in the respectable English establishment, and it demonstrates O'Sullivan's second challenge in Stafford: the need to secure the Church's position in local society and combat anti-Catholicism. This was done partly by hobnobbing with the elite and also by promoting public events such as fêtes and balls open to non-Catholics.[88] O'Sullivan also became involved in local activities, for example as a governor of the infirmary and a patron of the local 'Lancashire Relief Fund' during the Cotton Famine.[89] He took a more combative approach to the issue of a Catholic chaplain at the gaol. In 1863 a new Government provision for salaried prison chaplains, including Catholics, aroused the opposition of the anti-Catholic vicar of Christ Church, Thomas Harrison. A lengthy newspaper correspondence broke out amongst him, Michael O'Sullivan and other protagonists. O'Sullivan accused the vicar of 'warming up a dish of the old anti-Catholic hash' and went on to demonstrate a thoughtful, confident and muscular stance on behalf of the Church. Neutral opinion seemed to think the priest got the better of the exchange. Nevertheless, there was another round of controversy before, in 1866, the magistrates voted to appoint a Catholic chaplain.[90]

O'Sullivan's third challenge was to minister to his parishioners – particularly those, like many of the Irish, in both spiritual and material poverty. In 1863 he made an oblique comment on the poverty of many of his parishioners by saying that 'Though, like the Christians of old, the Roman Catholics had not many rich, not many noble among them, still union was strength and their united efforts would do much.'[91] More concrete action on poverty followed with the establishment of the local Society of St Vincent de Paul 'for the purpose of collecting and distributing to the most poor and needy people about them – not solely Catholics.'[92] We have, however, no direct evidence of how, and to what extent, O'Sullivan ministered directly to the needs of his Irish flock. We do know that at least one Irish person had no love for him in particular or the Church in general. In May 1862 Mary McDermott, a twenty-three-year-old char-woman from Dottell Street, was sent to the house of correction for break-ing seven panes of glass in the priest's house. She said 'she would have done even more damage if she had not been prevented.' The reason for her anger was not stated, but it may have been resentment at the priest's upper-class persona, as well as lingering hostility to the Catholic clergy and their fees amongst the rural poor of the west of Ireland.[93] In practice, much of the work amongst people like Mary McDermott was done by young assistant priests, but there is no evidence that O'Sullivan had any interest in acting as a 'culture broker' or voice for his Irish parishioners.

Even so, he was aware of the danger of losing contact with the Catholics of the north end, many of whom were Irish. In 1862 he said that:

> Stafford reminded him of a definition of a line in Euclid – it was 'length without breadth' – and as their church stood at one end, it was with some difficulty that they reached the large Catholic population at the other. They found it hard, in fact, 'to make both ends meet'. (*Laughter*) He hoped that in time, however, they would be able to raise a building at the opposite extremity where the holy sacrifice might be offered and the children of the poorer people taught. (*Hear, hear*)[94]

He was pointing to the need for a new church but also he was also identi-fying how the new church's mainly working-class and – he hinted – partly Irish congregation would be separated from the predominantly English and respectable clientele of St Austin's. It was left to his successor, James O'Hanlon, to bring this about.

A beloved priest?

In 1866 O'Sullivan was summoned back to St Chad's Cathedral and promoted to Vicar-General of the Birmingham Diocese. He finished his career in another wealthy parish, St Augustine's, Solihull. When he left Stafford he was presented with twenty-five sovereigns collected by Protestants in the town and there were public statements praising his 'gentlemanly, courteous, bearing, genial humour … and straightforward-ness.'[95] O'Sullivan had successfully furthered the Church's aim of estab-lishing a secure position within respectable English society. When he

Figure 10.2 Canon Michael O'Sullivan, c. 1880. Stafford's first Irish Catholic priest

died in 1892 it was said that 'He loved his Irish fatherland with intensity, and was never so proud as when his audience consisted of the sons and daughters of the Emerald Isle; indeed, he was the *beau ideal* of the Soggarth Aroon.'[96] We must, however, cast a jaundiced eye on this statement. O'Sullivan's relationship with his fatherland had been distant since he was a child, and his love of the country was probably a romantic conception of his birthplace common to those in adult life. It is, furthermore, likely that his pride in 'an audience of the sons and daughters of the Emerald Isle' was primarily when socialising with the Irish who had 'made it' in Birmingham and Solihull: 'No man was more welcome at a dinner party and no man, while freely contributing by his wit to the pleasure of his companions, knew better how to maintain the dignity of his clerical character, or to secure personal respect.'[97] We see a confident man most at home in the elite circles of Oscott alumni, English Catholic clerics and the better-off laity of Midland society (Figure 10.2). He was also active in the world of mammon and amassed a significant fortune. When he died his estate was valued at £2,249, worth around £225,000 at 2012 prices. He left 80 per cent of it to his half-brother's family but he did remember Stafford with a bequest of £50 to St Patrick's mission.[98] It was hardly a generous gift: under one-tenth of the £550 the new church cost in 1895.[99]

During his sojourn in Stafford Michael O'Sullivan had mobilised his financial and organisational skills effectively to build the new St Austin's, galvanise parish life and promote the church's position in the town. All the Irish, if and when they went to Mass, now at least had pews rather than having to mill around the walls and doors whilst their Staffordian co-religionists sat in the body of the church. The aspirant Irish could benefit but only as long as they accepted the dominant English social milieu of the Stafford church. Michael O'Sullivan clearly conforms to those Irish priests in England who had no interest in fostering Irish identity or acting as a culture broker between the Irish and the host community. He was furthered the interests of the English Church and the Irish had to fit in as best they could.

James O'Hanlon: St Patrick's priest

James O'Hanlon was the priest who realised O'Sullivan's dream of a church to serve the working-class north end of Stafford. It took thirty-three years to achieve but O'Hanlon played a major role in helping the new mission to develop a strong parish community. The extent to which he encouraged that community to express the Irish heritage of many of its members is more open to question.

A working-class priest with connections

James O'Hanlon was born in 1859 in Denny, Stirlingshire. His parents, Francis and Bridget, came to Scotland in the early 1850s as Famine emigrants and lived first in Airdrie before his father found work as an iron miner in Denny. James O'Hanlon's background was, therefore, that of classically poor Irish immigrants, and things got worse when his father died in the late1860s.[100] In 1871 he was living with his uncle's family in Denny, although his Uncle Michael, an iron miner in 1861, was also by then dead. Such impoverished circumstances made James's future look bleak. He benefited, however, from family connections back in Ireland.

The O'Hanlons came from the Ballymoyer-Loughgilly district of Co. Armagh, north-west of Newry. This was the historical heartland of the O'Hanlons, some of whom had survived on their lands after the Plantation of Ulster in 1609. By the nineteenth century there were multifarious branches of the family in the area and among them was another James O'Hanlon who had been born in 1839 in Loughgilly. He was probably James Jr's uncle. He got support from the family's network and its residual wealth to move to England in 1861 and enter Oscott College. He was ordained in 1865, joined the charmed circle of Oscott alumni and went on to become an eminent cleric in the Birmingham diocese.[101] James Jr benefited in turn from his uncle's patronage. He came to Oscott in September 1880 and was ordained in December 1883, after which he was sent as a curate to St Austin's, Stafford.[102]

Both O'Hanlon's family background and his education conditioned his sense of self and identity. He grew up in impoverished surroundings with parents forced to emigrate because of the Famine, but with continuing links to the family back in Co. Armagh. This softened the blow of exile but transmitted feelings of romantic attachment to the family's home-land that were passed on to those, like James, born in Scotland. The loss of both his father and uncle forced him to be self-reliant within a family where the women had to take the leading role. Family obligations were strong and James was clearly encouraged to get a good basic education in Scotland before finding backing to go to Oscott. He must have entered the priesthood with a sense of loyalty to his background and gratitude for the support he had received. He had no inclination to deviate from the Church's conservative and integrationist strategy and he was well-fitted to take its message to working-class peers who were in danger of lapsing from the faith. That was to be his role in Stafford.

Building the working-class parish community

Two years after O'Sullivan's departure from Stafford the first tangible step to bolstering the Church's presence in the north end came with the opening in 1868 of St Patrick's School at the corner of the new street in Foregate that was named after the saint. The choice of patron saint was significant and fits the trend at this time of adopting patriotic sym-bols to strengthen the Church's appeal amongst the potentially errant Irish.[103] By 1873 the school had 136 children on the books but only 84 were Catholic; the rest were (perhaps nominal) Protestants.[104] With the coming of compulsory primary education the numbers increased, and between one-third and a half of the children enrolled at the school from 1884 to 1913 came from Irish or Irish-related families.[105] The school pro-vided a physical base for the Church but it still needed more of an active presence. From 1884 James O'Hanlon provided it, being charged by Canon Hawksford with special responsibility for the area.[106] He immedi-ately started a Mass centre on the first floor of the school.[107] For the next ten years he waged a campaign for a separate mission in the Foregate, but Canon Acton, who took over at St Austin's in 1885, opposed him since it would reduce his congregation by 60 per cent and cause problems for his still-indebted church. He also feared the local Catholic population was too poor to support a new mission, but he had to balance this against the threat that north end Catholics would be lost to the Church altogether. O'Hanlon, working with notable lay people like Bartholomew Corcoran, persisted, and Acton finally agreed to back the scheme in the early 1890s. A major reason was concern about the increasing 'leakage' of Catholics who had contracted mixed marriages. In 1888 Acton reported to the

Figure 10.3 Fr James O'Hanlon's legacy: the interior of St Patrick's 'Iron Church', erected in 1895 (image courtesy of Mary Mitchell and the late Roy Mitchell)

Bishop that in the past ten years 58 out of 108 marriages in Stafford had been mixed. Most were amongst the working-class Catholics of the north end.[108] Acton rewarded O'Hanlon by recommending that the Bishop appoint him as priest in the new parish.[109] On Christmas morning 1893 it opened to serve an estimated 700 parishioners, about half of whom were Irish or Irish-related.[110] Initially services continued to be held in the school, but in 1895 the new pre-fabricated building was erected adjacent to the school. This 'temporary iron church' was to last for thirty-five years (Figure 10.3).[111]

James O'Hanlon proved to be a vigorous and well-liked priest who was involved in many parish activities. His first act in 1884 to reclaim 'at risk' Catholics was to set up St Patrick's Young Men's Association. Michael O'Sullivan was invited back to chair its inaugural meeting.[112] There was also a more general Catholic Club in Broad Street 'to provide a social centre for the Catholic men of the area' as a counterweight to the pubs.[113] Three years later O'Hanlon was stage manager for 'The Roman Martyrs', a drama at St Patrick's School designed to instil pride in the sufferings endured by the early Catholics. He went on Sunday School trips to Milford and in August 1888 helped organise games for the 240 children present.[114] Outside missioners were brought to Stafford 1889 and 1895. The latter mission, by two Franciscan fathers, was 'to urge more earnest observance of religious duties' and was 'well-attended'.[115] O'Hanlon also went to the social soirées. These fund-raising events had been a feature of St Austin's social calendar since the early 1870s, and once St Patrick's parish was established its annual soirées at the Borough Hall also became a feature of Stafford's social scene. We have seen already how they were attended by members of aspirant Irish families like the Corcorans, Mitchells and Mulrooneys, as well as by English Catholics and non-Catholics. O'Hanlon trained and accompanied the choir that performed at the 1897 soirée, so he had musical talents to offer his parishioners. He was not, however, seen at the Catholic balls held in this period, and he failed to hobnob with rich society figures. He avoided wining and dining in the elite social circles so enjoyed by Michael O'Sullivan. This unfortunately means we have no surviving record of his views expressed in public. The impression is of a humble man for whom material considerations and prestige among the upper classes were unimportant. He was more at home amongst the working-class people of the Foregate. O'Hanlon's local standing saw him elected to the School Board and the Poor Law Guardians after Canon Acton died in 1899.[116]

What was his relationship with his Irish and Irish-descended parishioners? As with O'Sullivan, we have one case where he aroused someone's ire. In September 1897 Margaret McGann was arrested for being drunk and disorderly and creating a scene outside the presbytery. O'Hanlon had agreed to receive money sent by McGann's brother in India, and she claimed she had not got what she expected. She was penniless. The Mayor gave her seven days' imprisonment for her outburst, which he described as 'very ungrateful conduct'.[117] The incident is significant for shedding a ray of light on the important work done by the priest in his role as social worker amongst his impoverished community. It is clear, however, that O'Hanlon toed the Church's line on deflecting any latent Irish nationalism amongst his flock into 'safe' channels. There are but two surviving examples of his involvement in specifically Irish activities. In November 1886 he gave a magic lantern show entitled *A Tour in Ireland* that had 'views of the scenery and humorous anecdotes'.[118] Ten years later he presided at St Patrick's Day celebrations in the schoolroom when a lecture was given on the Young Ireland movement.[119] Most of the evening was, however, given over to Irish songs, two by the priest himself. This was scarcely radical stuff and it is clear that O'Hanlon pursued the Church's stance of encouraging a romantic view of Ireland and the Irish heritage but actively promoting the development of a community of English Catholics. We have, however, argued already that such a perspective coincided with the apparent wishes of almost all of Stafford's settled Irish families.

James O'Hanlon and his legacy

Fifteen years' work building up the Catholic presence in the north end left O'Hanlon drained, and in 1899 the Church authorities decided he needed a rest. He was sent to the quiet chaplaincy at Stonor in rural Oxfordshire but was later brought back to St Michael's Church in inner-city Birmingham.[120] He finished his career at SS. Joseph and Helen in King's Norton and died in June 1925.[121] His effects were worth a mere £50 (£2,500 at 2012 prices), a huge contrast to Michael O'Sullivan's wealth. His work in Stafford had left his congregation 'devoted to their first Rector'. They would miss 'his genial presence' and they decided to offer him a farewell gift. He chose a telescope because his main non-clerical interest was astronomy, but they also gave him 'a purse of gold'. He clearly did not use it to make his fortune.[122]

We see in James O'Hanlon a man who had pursued his ministry with little apparent thought of material reward. The parish community built up at St Patrick's was active and inclusive, and interviewees for this research who grew up in the parish in the interwar period emphasised this even though at least one of the subsequent priests had less of O'Hanlon's 'genial presence'. His ministry encouraged aspirant people from all backgrounds but the context he created was that of an English Church with only gestures to romantic Irishness. Despite its name, St Patrick's Church and School played a significant role in 'denationalising' the Irish but, in saying this, we must remember three things. Firstly, by the time St Patrick's was established many of Stafford's Irish families were into their second or even third generation. 'Ethnic fade' was inevitably occurring and this was encouraged by a second factor, the high rate of inter-ethnic and mixed-faith marriages. By Edwardian times the vast majority of the church's marriages were inter-ethnic and around half were mixed-faith.[123] We have seen much evidence of this in the families studied in this book, and we have also seen evidence of the final point – that most of Stafford's 'Irish' families positively decided to integrate into the local community rather that retain a relict Irish identity. The environment created by James O'Hanlon's ministry played its part in that process.

The role of the priests

This study of Michael O'Sullivan and James O'Hanlon has been a small contribution to Gilley's call for more investigation of Irish Catholic life in the missions of England.[124] Stafford's priests had to deal with a congregation whose ethnicity was always, apart from the immediate Famine years, tilted towards the English Catholics. The Catholics in both ethnic groups were socially diverse, however, and differences in class were at least as important as contrasts in ethnicity. Within this context we can see the priests carried out their four functions with varying degrees of effectiveness in relation to the Catholics with an Irish heritage. By definition, they fulfilled the function of religious leader and guide but there were contrasts in the degree of spiritual inspiration they offered. They clearly strengthened the 'political' position of the Church in Stafford and implemented its codes of discipline, but the priority they gave to social work amongst the Irish varied. The priests fostered the development of a parish community but St Austin's long-term ethos remained that of a respectable, primarily English and somewhat snobby parish. The poor – both English and Irish – could feel out of place there, a situation that continued into the twentieth century and was reported by people interviewed for this work. St Patrick's developed a more inclusive community. It is clear, however, that in Stafford the Church made no attempt to bolster Irish identity or Irish nationalism, and there was no process of setting Irish Catholics apart from the host society. This contrasts with the role of the Church amongst the Irish in the north of England as documented by Belchem, Lowe and MacRaild.[125] In Stafford Irish Catholics had to make the best of a strongly English Church, but the rewards for those who did so were substantial.

Notes

1 N. H. Carrier and J. R. Jeffery, *External Migration: A Study of the Available Statistics* (London: Her Majesty's Stationery Office, 1953), derived from Table X, occupational distribution of emigrants from Ireland, 1877–1920.

2 The data on Figure 10.1 has been obtained from the following sources. Northallerton and Consett: unpublished data kindly provided by John Perkins; Liverpool and Lancaster: C. Pooley, 'Segregation or integration? The residential experience of the Irish in mid-Victorian Britain' in Swift and Gilley, *The Irish in Britain*, Table 2.4; Lees, *Exiles of Erin*, Table A2; York: F. Finnegan, *Poverty and Prejudice: A Study of Irish Immigrants in York, 1840–75* (Cork: Cork University Press, 1982), Table 28; Camborne and Tredegar: L. Miskell, 'Custom, conflict and community: A study of the Irish in South Wales and Cornwall, 1861–91' (Ph.D. thesis, University of Wales, Aberystwyth, 1996), Figures 7 and 8; Cleator Moor and Barrow-in-Furness: MacRaild, *Culture, Conflict and Migration*, Tables 3.4 and 3.5; Widnes: unpublished data kindly provided by Joanne Hicks. Some percentages do not total 100 owing to the different classifications used.

3 O'Leary, *Immigration and Integration*, esp. pp. 187 and 203; J. Belchem, 'Class, creed and country: The Irish middle class in Victorian Liverpool' in Swift and Gilley, *Irish in Victorian Britain*, pp. 190–211.

4 SRO D4800/2/8/1, Congregational Church, Stafford, Roll of Members, 1798–1901.

5 Public Record Office of Northern Ireland (PRONI), MIC 1P/23/1, First Presbyterian Church, Bangor, marriages, 1808–45. Hugh Gibson stated that his father was William, a farmer, on his marriage certificate in 1862. There were many Gibsons in this part of Northern Ireland, and it has proved impossible definitively to identify this William Gibson, though the William who married Jane Johnson in Bangor in 1818 seems the most likely.

6 The Revd Jas. McConnell, *History of the First Presbyterian Chapel, Bangor* (n.d. [c. 1915]), copy on PRONI microfilm MIC 1P/23/2.

7 SRO D4800/2/8/1.

8 *VCH Stafford*, Vol. 6, p. 255.

9 SRO D4800/2/8/1.

10 A. M. Harrison, 'Elleys of Stafford', *Journal of the Staffordshire Industrial Archaeology Society*, 8 (1978), pp. 50–65.

11 Obituary of Hugh Woods Gibson, *SA*, 21 December 1901. In 1851 his brother Robert, described as a tailor, was living with him on the edge of the City of London but nothing more is known of his life.

12 Wokingham RD, Marriages, October–December 1854, 2c/741. She was born outside Berkshire around 1830 and was at boarding school in Wokingham in 1841 but she has not been traced in the 1851 Census.

13 SRO D4800/2/8/1, 1 May 1856: Hugh Gibson 'transferred from the Tabernacle, London' and Ellen Gibson 'transferred from the Baptist Church at Wokingham'.

14 *Ibid.*, note of Ellen Gibson Sr's death.

15 Harrison, 'Elleys of Stafford', p. 59.

16 SRO D4800/2/8/1. Woolley's mother died on 4 February 1857.

17 *SA*, 5 April 1862.

18 *Ibid.*, 5 November 1864.

19 *Ibid.*, 15 August 1868.

20 *Ibid.*, 17 October 1868.

21 *Ibid.*, 15 June 1869.

22 *Ibid.*, 11 November 1871.

23 *Ibid.*, 12 August 1871.

24 *Ibid.*, 20 May 1871.

25 Harrison, 'Elleys of Stafford', p. 61.

26 Obituary, *SA*, 21 December 1901.

27 *Ibid.*, 16 December 1876.

28 *Ibid.*, 4 July 1877, 5 August 1875, 23 June 1877 and *passim*. Also obituary, 21 December 1901.

29 *Ibid.*, 12 May 1877.

30 SRO D4800/2/8/1, letter to H. W. Gibson from S. B. Handley, 18 September 1882. Gibson's first wife's brother, Edward Cleare Targett, died early in 1882, though the connection seems somewhat remote. Reading RD, Deaths, January–March 1882, 2c/256: Edward Cleare Targett.

31 Cannock RD, Deaths, April–June 1906, 6b/283: Henry Payne Gibson.

32 Obituary, *SA*, 21 December 1901. Ellen never married, and died in Oxton, Birkenhead, in 1918. She left effects of £53,649, worth about £3.1 million today. England and Wales National Probate Calendar (Index of Wills and Administrations), 1856–1966: Ellen Mary Gibson of Oxton, Ches., died 11 September 1918; *Ancestry* (accessed 7 June 2013).

33 G. Jones, '"Strike out boldly for the prizes that are available to you": Medical emigration from Ireland, 1860–1905', *Medical History*, 54 (2010), pp. 57–74 (pp. 57–60), and Tables 1 and 2. A total of 53 per cent emigrated, and 52.3 per cent of those emigrating went to Britain with 25.8 per cent into the military.

34 L. M. Geary, 'Australia *felix*: Irish doctors in nineteenth-century Victoria' in O'Sullivan, *The Irish World Wide*, Vol. 2, pp. 162–79 (pp. 166–7).

35 L. Miskell, '"The heroic Irish doctor"? Irish immigrants in the medical profession in nineteenth-century Wales' in Walsh, *Ireland Abroad*, pp. 82–94.

36 Geary, 'Australia *felix*', p. 163.

37 Miskell, '"Heroic Irish doctor"?', p. 85.

38 General Medical Council, *UK Medical Registers*, 1867/1871/1879/1883/1887; *Ancestry* (accessed 10 March 2013). In 1867 and 1871 both William and his father gave their address as Clonmore Lodge, Baltinglass, Co. Wicklow, but Baltinglass was presumably the post town because Clonmore is closer to Hackettstown. The 1883 entry merely reads Hackettstown, Co. Carlow.

39 The marriage of William's daughter Charlotte took place on 22 October 1856 at the Church of Ireland church in Clonmore.

40 General Medical Council, *UK Medical Register*, 1883.

41 *The Times*, 19 August 1867; Clendinnen of Cheswardine, Salop, reported as having passed the examination of Apothecaries' Hall in London and received a certificate to practice.

42 A. Digby, *Making a Medical Living: Doctors and Patients in the English Market for Medicine, 1720–1911* (Cambridge: Cambridge University Press, 1994), Table 5.2, p. 144.

43 *Liverpool Mercury*, 14 October 1869.

44 *Birmingham Daily Post*, 24 March 1870.

45 *SA*, 8 August 1874.

46 See *Birmingham Daily Post*, 7 December 1882; and *Reynold's Newspaper*, 6 January 1884.

47 *SA*, 9 June 1877.

48 *Ibid.*, 13 March 1880 and 6 January 1883.

49 *Ibid.*, 10 October 1874, 13 July 1878, 1 February 1879.

50 SRO D1323/B/4, SBC Sub-Sanitary Committee minutes, 31 December 1872–9 March 1875 (10 September 1874); D1323/C/4/1, 17/28 November 1876, 31 December 1876, 9 January 1877.

51 *SA*, 6 February 1875.

52 *VCH Stafford*, Vol. 6, p. 232; G. Timmins, 'Work in progress. Back passages and excreta tubs: Improvements to the conservancy system of sanitation in Victorian Lancashire', *Transactions of the Historic Society of Lancashire and Cheshire*, 161 (2012), pp. 47–63 (pp. 60–1).

53 *Birmingham Daily Post*, 7 July 1876: Birmingham and Midland Association of Medical Officers meeting.

54 *SA*, 23 October 1880 and 22 November 1881.

55 *Ibid.*, 19 July 1884.

56 A. Hudson, *Equity and Trusts*, 6th edn (London: Routledge–Cavendish, 2010), p. 711.

57 *SA*, 8 November 1884.

58 *Ibid.*, 15 November 1884.

59 'A sad end', *Ancestry*, 085mm, submitted by PBird4881, 9 November 2010 (accessed 9 May 2013). The source is not stated. England and Wales, National Probate Calendar (Index of Wills and Administration, 1858–1966), Personal Estate of William Ellis Clendinnen: administration granted to Sarah Clendinnen, 29 February 1888; *Ancestry* (accessed 17 March 2013).

60 *SA*, 25 May 1895.
61 US Army Register of Enlistments, 16 November 1895: discharged 15 November 1898; *Ancestry* (accessed 28 May 2013). Canada: Soldiers of the First World War, 1914–18; attestation 23 September 1914. *SA*, 27 March 1915; *Ancestry* (accessed 28 May 2013). California Death Index 1940–97: Bertram William Clendinnen, San Diego, 12 October 1942; *Ancestry* (accessed 28 May 2013).
62 England and Wales Probate Calendar (Index of Wills and Administration): deaths of Sarah Clendinnen, 28 May 1930, and Alfred Ellis Clendinnen, 20 February 1943; *Ancestry* (accessed 9 May 2013).
63 *SA, passim*, e.g. 24 March 1894, 1 October 1898 and 15 March 1902.
64 Madeley RD, Marriages, January–March 1904, 6a/898: E. C. A. Clendinnen and Alice Matilda Jones; Stafford RD, Births, July–September 1907, 6b/19: Ernest Bertram Clendinnen.
65 Stafford RD, Marriages, October–December 1936, 6b/63: Ernest B. Clendinnen and Sheila Carridge.
66 *Stafford's Roll of Service in the Great War* (Stafford: J. and C. Mort, 1920).
67 R. F. Foster, *Modern Ireland, 1600–1972* (Harmondsworth: Penguin, 1989), pp. 306–7.
68 B. Griffin, 'Class, gender and Liberalism in Parliament, 1868–1882: The case of the Married Women's Property Acts', *The Historical Journal*, 46:1 (March 2003), pp. 59–87.
69 *SA*, 7 December 1850, 1 February 1851, 29 April 1854, 16 January 1847.
70 Letter, 25 February 1886, quoted in S. Leslie, *Henry Edward Manning: His Life and Labours* (London: Burns, Oates and Washbourne, 1921), p. 415.
71 Herson, 'The English, the Irish and the Catholic Church in Stafford', p. 46, table. Only between 1851 and 1861 did the Irish and mixed-family Catholics achieve a bare majority: 51 per cent. By 1891 the Irish proportion had dropped to 43 per cent.
72 D. M. MacRaild, *The Irish Diaspora in Britain, 1870–1939*, 2nd edn (Basingstoke: Palgrave Macmillan, 2011), p. 54; W. Lowe, *The Irish in Mid-Victorian Lancashire: The Shaping of a Working Class Community* (New York: Peter Lang Publishing, 1989), Chapter 4.
73 For example B. Aspinwall, 'Catholic devotion in Scotland' in Mitchell, *New Perspectives*, pp. 31–43; Hickman, *Religion, Class and Identity*; Fielding, *Class and Ethnicity*; P. O'Leary, 'From the cradle to the grave: Popular Catholicism among the Irish in Wales' in P. O'Sullivan (ed.), *The Irish Worldwide*, Vol. 5: *Religion and Identity* (Leicester: Leicester University Press, 2000), pp. 183–95.
74 S. Gilley, 'Roman Catholicism and the Irish in England', *Immigrants and Minorities*, 18:2/3 (July/November 1999), pp. 146–67.
75 *Ibid.*, pp. 148–9; M. Heimann, 'Devotional stereotypes in English Catholicism, 1850–1914' in F. Tallett and N. Atkin (eds), *Catholicism in Britain and France since 1789* (London: The Hambledon Press, 1996), pp. 13–26.
76 J. Bossy, *The English Catholic Community, 1570–1850* (London: Darton, Longman and Todd, 1975), pp. 396–401; E. Norman, *The English Catholic Church in the Nineteenth Century* (Oxford: Clarendon Press, 1984).
77 J. Belchem, 'The Liverpool-Irish enclave', *Immigrants and Minorities*, 18:2/3 (July/November 1999), pp. 128–46 (pp. 142–3).

78 O'Leary, 'The cult of respectability', pp. 134–5.

79 Hickman, *Religion Class and Identity*, p. 111.

80 J. Gillow, *St Thomas's Priory; or, The Story of St Austin's, Stafford* (Stafford: locally published, [c. 1892–94]); Greenslade, *St Austin's, Stafford*, pp. 28 and 99; miscellaneous evidence, notably priests conducting burials at the Stafford Borough Cemetery.

81 Panegyric by The Revd Dr M'Cave, Birmingham, quoted in Gillow, *St Thomas's Priory*, p. 132. 'Soggarth Aroon' is anglicised Irish for 'beloved priest'.

82 Foster, *Modern Ireland*, p. 338.

83 Gillow, *St Thomas's Priory*, pp. 121–2.

84 *Ibid.*, pp. 114–18.

85 MacRaild, *The Irish Diaspora*, p. 75.

86 *SA*, 19 July 1862.

87 *Ibid.*

88 E.g. *ibid.*, 11 August 1860.

89 *Ibid.*, 11 April 1863 and 22 November 1862.

90 *Ibid.*, 16 January–6 February 1864; 31 March–14 April 1866.

91 *Ibid.*, 21 February 1863.

92 *Ibid.*, 22 April 1865.

93 *Ibid.*, 10 May 1862; S. J. Connolly, *Priests and People in Pre-Famine Ireland, 1780–1845* (Dublin: Four Courts Press, 2001), pp. 225–38.

94 *SA*, 19 July 1862.

95 *Ibid.*, 10 November and 1 December 1866.

96 Panegyric by M'Cave, quoted in Gillow, *St Thomas's Priory*, p. 132.

97 *Ibid.*, p. 131.

98 HM Courts and Tribunals Services, Probate Service, Will of The Revd Michael O'Sullivan, died 12 January 1892 in Solihull, probate granted Birmingham, 12 March 1892, resworn March 1894.

99 P. E. Donnelly, *St Patrick's, Stafford, 1895–1945: Recollections of a Parishioner*, part of *Souvenir of the Golden Jubilee of St Patrick's*, p. 3.

100 His death has not been located in Scotland but their last child was born in 1867.

101 McInally, *Edward Ilsley*, pp. xx–xxi and *passim*.

102 Oscott College, *List of Superiors, Masters and Students 1794–1889*, www.oscott.net/uploads/1/3/6/.../listofsuperiorsmastersandstudents_1.pdf (accessed 22 May 2013).

103 Hickman, *Religion, Class and Identity*, p. 114.

104 BAA P255/5/1, Stafford, St Austin's, Mission Book, 1873–95: returns ordered by the Bishop, 31 May 1873.

105 St. Patrick's Roman Catholic School, Stafford, admission books. I am indebted to the late Roy Mitchell for his work on the registers.

106 Donnelly, *Recollections of a Parishioner*, p. 1.

107 Greenslade, *St Austin's, Stafford*, p. 17.

108 BAA, P255/5/1, copy of return to the Bishop of the Diocese on mixed marriages for ten years ending 31 October 1888.

109 BAA Z6/6/1/2/3, Ilsley Papers, 30 October 1893: letter from The Very Revd Canon Acton to The Rt Revd Edward Ilsley.

110 *SA*, 30 December 1893.
111 Donnelly, *Recollections of a Parishioner*, pp. 1–5.
112 *SA*, 23 February 1884.
113 Greenslade, *St Austin's, Stafford*, p. 25; *SA*, 29 December 1888.
114 *SA*, 25 August 1888.
115 *Ibid.*, 6 April 1889, 7 December 1895.
116 *Ibid.*, 11 March and 29 April 1899.
117 *Ibid.*, 25 September 1897.
118 *Ibid.*, 27 November 1886.
119 *Ibid.*, 21 March 1896.
120 *Ibid.*, 18 November 1899; 1901 census return; *Kelly's Directory of Birmingham*, 1908.
121 England and Wales National Probate Calendar (Index of Wills and Administrations), 1856–1966: The Revd James O'Hanlon, 'clerk', died 28 June 1925; *Ancestry* (accessed 5 June 2013).
122 Donnelly, *Recollections of a Parishioner*, p. 3.
123 J. Herson, 'Migration, "community" or integration?', pp. 172–3, and Figures 2 and 3.
124 Gilley, 'Roman Catholicism and the Irish in England', pp. 146–67.
125 Belchem, *Irish, Catholic and Scouse*, pp. 18–19; W. Lowe, 'The Lancashire Irish and the Catholic Church, 1846–71: The social dimension', *Irish Historical Studies*, 20:78 (September 1976), pp. 105–55; MacRaild, *Culture, Conflict and Migration*, pp. 122–4.

Divergent paths: the conclusions to be drawn

By the 1920s descendants of Stafford's nineteenth-century Irish immigrants formed an integral part of the town's society. The many families with an Irish heritage constituted the positive legacy that remained after processes of attrition had removed others through generational failure or dispersal to places elsewhere. The surviving families were not a readily identifiable body of people. The diversity of the initial immigrants, their relatively small absolute numbers and the social pressures towards integration ensured that their Irish heritage was a constituent part in their family identities rather than a prime determinant of it. There was no relict Irish 'community' in 1920s Stafford.

This book has presented the histories of twenty-two families and an overview of all 206 Irish families who settled long-term in Stafford in the nineteenth century. They were ordinary families united only by a common origin in Ireland. We now turn to what can be drawn from this evidence, but we need firstly to identify what the family-history approach was able to reveal successfully and where it proved less effective.

Revealing lives through family history

It was said in Chapter 1 that the work intended to offer neither fiction nor 'faction' but to rest on what can reasonably be inferred from known historical facts. The case studies have demonstrated that it is indeed possible to write a plausible history of any family. Reconstruction of a family's genealogy and its households provides the skeleton on which to hang a family's history, but after that the degree of detail varies. The historian is the prisoner of his or her sources. Some families left copious evidence in the documentary record, through inherited knowledge and through oral history, whilst others, like Margaret Carr, left very little. Even she, however, offered enough clues to allow us to form an overall picture of her sad life in Stafford. It has proved possible to form a view of the nature of blood and non-blood relationships in a family; the patterns of kinship; and also something of the relative balance amongst contract, power and intimacy in a family's practices. The evidence has permitted reasonable speculation about household conditions and the extent to which there was a nurturing home. This has intrinsically raised questions about gender roles. The relative balance of gender power and influence has been a theme running through the case studies, and in a number of cases it has been linked to the question of whether there was a conscious family strategy and who might have generated it.

The senses of self and the identities present in members of a family and across families as a whole have been more problematic issues. We have frequently been left to speculate on how people's backgrounds, especially in Ireland, shaped their sense of self. With identity we have been on firmer ground because revealed behaviour and some surviving testimony have provided evidence to make conclusions on identities and their mutation. The distinction between a family having an Irish identity and an Irish heritage has been stressed. Perhaps the most problematic area has been diasporic or transnational relations. We have frequently identified individuals and families who probably emigrated, but in only a limited number of cases do we know where they went or whether they continued to have links with the family in England. It has therefore proved difficult to estimate the influence of diasporic links on the history of families in Stafford, but overall conclusions in this area are discussed later.

Having assembled each family's history, it has proved possible to identify broadly what its overall trajectory or 'fate' was, and the book rests on the tripartite division between long-term transient, integrating and terminal families. Because every family's history was unique they did not all fit neatly into one or other category. They could show elements of more than one trajectory, and for some families more than one allocation was possible. Each category can therefore be visualised as having a substantial core of families conforming to the trajectory but a penumbra of families who had more mixed characteristics.

In sum, the use of collective family biography (or 'family prosopography') has provided a picture of the lives of a cross-section of ordinary families in Victorian England. It helps to bridge the gap between academic social history and antiquarian family history, to the benefit of both, and it needs to be adopted elsewhere to provide comparative evidence. It is, however, important to generalise from the particular. What does all this detailed evidence suggest generally about these families, and what are the implications for historical studies of both Irish migration and the family more generally?

Table 11.1 Family fate by occupational group (%)

	Labouring	CC&S	Military	Boot/ shoe	Ent. and Prof.	**Total**
LTT	34.0	39.3	25.0	26.3	55.6	**35.0**
Integrating	43.4	42.9	62.5	68.4	22.2	**46.1**
Terminal	22.6	17.9	12.5	5.3	22.2	**18.9**
Total no. of families	**106**	**56**	**16**	**19**	**9**	**206**

LTT = long-term transient families.
CC&S = craft, clerical and service families.
Ent. and prof. = entrepreneurial and professional families.

The divergent families

We have seen that the fates of families with initially similar characteristics often diverged and, conversely, that many contrasting families ultimately shared the same fate. It is necessary, therefore, to summarise the characteristics common to families with the same fate, and to do this we need to consider answers to the three questions posed in Chapter 1:

- How was family life amongst the Irish affected by the specific experience of emigration and settlement? This question also covers the senses of self engendered by their earlier lives in Ireland. It is summarised below as 'heritage and migration'.
- How did Irish families operate and evolve as social entities? This is summarised as 'family relationships'.
- How did the Irish families interact with the wider social and economic environment?

Table 11.1 gives the proportion of families in each occupational group who experienced the three different fates. It shows that in all but one of the occupational groups families followed a similar pattern, in that integrating families were always the biggest single category. They formed an absolute majority of the ex-military and shoe-trade families. Only the small group of entrepreneurs and professionals was exceptional in having a minority of integrating families. Long-term transients were always the large minority amongst the other occupational groups whilst a smaller but significant residue always proved to be terminal families. Thus, although we have seen big differences in family circumstances, it seems long-term forces *tended* to produce a similar distribution of outcomes. Families following each trajectory exhibited a distinct range of characteristics but, as the case studies have shown, the causal connections amongst family background, family dynamics and the wider context were complex. The following section outlines an 'ideal-typical' picture of the characteristics of the three classes of family, but it must not be assumed that they applied in total to every family. Each family's history was unique and the variation across them was infinite.

The long-term transient families

Heritage and migration

What characteristics did the long-term transient families display in terms of the Irish heritage they brought with them and the specific impact of migration? These families seem to have had harsh circumstances in Ireland either in terms of their formative younger years, the reasons why they left, or both. The Catholic labourers and, to some extent, the transient craft, clerical and service families often had an ethos of suspicion of or even hostility to outsiders and authority. They had grown up in a society at political or actual war with the landlord class and the British State. The post-1846 emigrants had been seared by the Famine and the extra suffering it had brought. These people had had to fight to survive in a harsh world of land hunger and political oppression. Their ties of blood and kinship were defensive and immediate contractual obligations were strongly enforced. They were alienated from the existing power structures in Ireland and carried these attitudes with them when they emigrated. Britain and Stafford were potentially hostile worlds against which a defensive wall had to be erected. In the case of the Walsh family, who arrived in the 1860s, these attitudes were expressed in fairly conventional quasi-nationalist terms, whereas families like the Kearnses and Kellys had a more inchoate hostility to outsiders, including some other Irish people. The stance of many of these families towards the outside world had not been obviously mediated by the Catholic Church, and their spiritual base was often weak or nonexistent. They were not susceptible to inclusion in the Catholic life of Stafford. Many unconsciously sought a defensive Irish community, and in Stafford the small size of the Irish population meant that community only existed weakly. Furthermore, the stresses of migration and settlement appeared to undermine or destroy any positive Irish ethos. Such families typically ended up in a state of apparent anomie demonstrated by drink and household stress.

The Protestant transient families generally had a less troubled background but one that could, nevertheless, leave a mixed legacy. Although the Giltraps benefited from their origins and were able to move smoothly into English society, the Disney family demonstrates how some

Protestants were unable to reconcile the conflict of their privileged sta-
tus in Ireland with the circumstances of emigration and settlement in
England. Though they proved to be nominally 'integrating' families, the
Hamiltons and Clendinnens showed many of the same characteristics.

Family relationships

In the long-term transient group internal processes split between those,
in a minority of cases, that enhanced family cohesion and those in the
majority that promoted family break-up. Some, like the Walshes, Giltraps
and Gibsons, were generally cohesive families in which husbands and
wives set out to achieve specific objectives that ultimately led to their
departure from Stafford. The other families indicate a more usual feature
of long-term transience: family atomisation. We see a common pattern.
There was often marital stress or breakdown. The domestic environment
was unstable, and nurturing home support deficient. These problems
could be made worse by traumatic life events, notably the premature
death of parents or children. The parents, and particularly the mothers,
sometimes led unstructured and even deviant lives, and the children who
survived were neglected. They often grew up within an inward-looking
milieu and had problematic contacts with the host community. There
was intergenerational tension, and the children tended, on reaching
maturity, to reject both their parents and the Stafford environment in
which they had grown up. The flight of children from the town was a
frequent cause of long-term family transience even when the immigrant
generation stayed in Stafford.

Interaction with the environment

Although families like the Giltraps and Gibsons left mainly for occupational reasons, the long-term transient families' relationship with the
changing Stafford environment was often problematic. They provide
evidence of how the forces of global capitalism dislocated many 'traditional' Irish families and forced their members into the reserve army of
labour with dysfunctional results on family life. For the manual workers' families the Victorian economy meant poverty and insecurity, and
it often provoked a reaction in drunkenness, casual violence and petty
criminality. These forces acted on families already damaged by migration
and disrupted relationships. In modern terms they could show symptoms of transmitted deprivation. Up to 1871 the children received little
or no schooling, and even after that date they tended, like the Shiel or
some of the Larkin children, to be alienated from school. They made few

useful contacts and learned few skills. Both parents and children failed to find jobs in the growth areas of the economy, and although they might get jobs in the shoe trade, such employment was always insecure and worsened as the industry began to decline. Although many were nominal Catholics, they were unable – and probably did not wish – to find useful social contacts in the respectable Catholic population. All of these factors tended to mean that individuals from transient families failed to find marriage partners in either the Irish or the host community. There was little to keep them in Stafford. Their chances might be better if they joined the forces; moved to bigger towns like Walsall, the Potteries or Birmingham; or joined the waves of English and Irish emigrants to North America and Australasia. These processes took years, often decades, to work through but they explain why a substantial proportion of Stafford's settled Irish families ultimately disappeared.

There was an alternative scenario amongst the more skilled and non-manual families, and that was transience provoked by economic and employment opportunities. In Chapter 8 we saw that shoemakers often moved amongst the various shoe towns, and it was similarly the case with railway and public-service workers and those with other saleable manual or professional skills. The reasons for moves were not always positive, however. Two substantial Protestant entrepreneurial families left Stafford because their businesses went bankrupt.

The integrating families

Heritage and migration

The integrating families had experienced many of the same influences as the long-term transients in their earlier lives in Ireland, and their initial environment in Stafford was often similar to, and alongside, that of their transient compatriots. The case-study evidence suggests, however, that the personalities of members of these families had been less damaged by the disrupted economy and society of pre-Famine and Famine Ireland. They overcame the drastic challenge of emigration and settlement in a positive manner and showed fewer symptoms of stress like drunkenness and family conflict. One reason for this was, in the case of Catholics, that their adherence to the Church was stronger than amongst the transient families. They had probably developed a stronger spiritual commitment during their childhood in Ireland and they were open to the social opportunities offered by the Church in Stafford as well as its spiritual security. Even so, some survivor families had apparently weak spirituality, and prior loyalty to the Church was not a universal force leading to integration.

Although there are these suggestive characteristics, the known factors in the integrating families' Irish previous heritage did not clearly predispose them to stay in Stafford. We have seen, in fact, that in a number of cases 'integration' was a close-run thing and depended on the survival of perhaps one or two individuals when other family members died out or left.

Family relationships

Heritage and emigration provided a framework of founding experiences and attitudes, but their actual influence was conditioned by the character of individuals, the nature of family relationships and the family's inter-action with the changing environment. We can point to certain traits in integrating families. Key individuals, especially women, often played a vital role in holding the family together and defining its ethos, aspira-tions and objectives. Such families tended to show strong kinship links and they fulfilled their mutual obligations. The integrating families gener-ally created a nurturing 'home base' free, as far as possible, from transient lodgers and other unsettling forces. Although many were poor, over time and down the generations they aspired to improve their jobs and housing and also to extend their social contacts into Stafford society. Some fam-ilies achieved clear respectability in the second generation but for others the process was slower and only came to fruition after a number of gen-erations. The result was that families lost their Irish identity, and we have seen certain cases where this 'ethnic fade' resulted from decisions to reject or at least obscure ethnic origins. In most cases, however, the replace-ment of Irish identity by a more neutral Irish heritage was the inevitable result of intermarriage, generational succession and the need to make the best of day-to-day opportunities. The 'denationalising' role of the Catholic Church also played a part but it has been argued that the case-study fam-ilies were conscious and willing participants in this process. The loss of knowledge revealed by oral-history evidence suggests that, in many fam-ilies, memories of Ireland and the traumas of emigration and settlement were consciously expunged by the second generation born in Stafford.[1] The Irish heritage of these families dwindled in significance once the Irish-born immigrants had died. It is important to remember, too, that the integrating Protestant families similarly lost – or rejected – any distinctive identity. There were no Orange mobs to recruit them here.

Interaction with the environment

The ethos and objectives of the integrating families helped them to exploit the opportunities in Stafford. Over time and down the generations they showed the flexible responses demanded by an evolving capitalist economy. As the town's employment base widened members of these families were able to exploit the trend by getting better jobs in the growth sectors. In these circumstances they were alongside local people and became part of the local work community. They became pre-eminently members of their peer class group rather than an ethnic stratum parallel to it. As primary education took hold, children growing up in Stafford were increasingly likely to go to school and to find friends and contacts amongst their local peers. Although many integrating families initially lived close to other Irish immigrants, Stafford had no Irish ghettos, and integrating families inevitably interacted with neighbours from the host population. They tended to stay in the same area – and sometimes the same house – for long periods, and thus became part of the local community, whatever its stresses. In a supportive family environment their children were resilient and flexible – they learned and adapted. Migration had opened up opportunities for the children and they could play a role as 'culture brokers' between their parents and the host society. Poverty meant that some families were forced to take lodgers, and even run lodging houses, in their early decades in the town. This initially tended to reinforce the Irish environment of such families, and for some this way of life continued into the 1900s. It could be associated with the symptoms of social stress – drunkenness, 'Irish Rows' and petty criminality. Even so, most integrating families avoided the worst of drink and degradation, and some actively sought respectability. For Catholics, contacts in the Church were central to this process, but by the 1900s they were also participating in other social activities. These contacts – through housing, work, Church and community involvement – gave individuals more chances to meet possible marriage partners. The history of the integrating families shows the importance of intermarriage with people from the host population. By the 1900s most marriages took place across the ethnic boundary and, in many cases, across the religious ones as well. The Irish identity and heritage of these families were diluted remorselessly.

The terminal families

Heritage and migration

The terminal families can be seen as intermediate between the transients and the integrators. They showed features of both. On the one hand, like the integrators their members stayed on in Stafford rather than leaving, and they showed some commitment to life there. On the other hand, like the transients their settlement was ultimately insecure and their involvement in local society limited. What differentiates them from the other two categories? The key factor was that most were nuclear families, childless couples or lone individuals. For many, their wider family links had already been lost, damaged or destroyed, particularly during the Famine, and they arrived in Stafford alone and isolated. Many arrived in middle age and most of their children, if any, had left home or died before they emigrated. Their adaptability was poor and their confidence was probably low. There is little evidence that Catholic families had any significant tradition of sustenance from faith or the Church.

Family relationships

Having settled in Stafford, there were three distinctive features about the family relationships of terminal families. The first was that they were poor and often old. Their earnings often depended on casual jobs on the social margins and many were forced to lodge with other families or in lodging houses. Some were themselves forced to keep lodging houses at the bottom of the market. These conditions inevitably stressed family or quasi-family relations. Secondly, they were vulnerable to trauma, particularly through the premature death of key individuals. Both the Jordan family and Jane Duffy, for example, suffered devastating events in Stafford that undermined their future as effective family units. The final feature was a more indefinable passivity that was the outcome of the disruption and possible traumas they had suffered in Ireland, during migration and in Stafford itself. These families had no other kin in the area and were unable to call on family support obligations. They often seem to have lacked the social skills to build effective relationships. They also lacked the ability to move on mentally and, if necessary, away. Even if they did, in some cases they failed to succeed elsewhere and were forced to return to Stafford.

Interaction with the environment

The terminal families lived in a twilight world where they could not respond effectively to either the local or the wider environment. Most were stuck in insecure, poorly paid and declining occupations, and because of this they were stranded in poverty. Social isolation was the result. They could not benefit from useful contacts amongst either the Irish or local people. The children growing up in Stafford in such families failed to carry out any obvious role as culture brokers and often died prematurely. Their low status, and lack of social integration and confidence, meant the children frequently failed to marry and these families had a fundamental inability to reproduce themselves. They just wasted away as the initial immigrants and their children died out. These families were the particular victims of the disruption brought about by the Famine, and by global economic forces that had their impacts even on a small town like Stafford.

The problem of symptoms and causes

Although it is argued that families who followed each of the three trajectories exhibited the characteristics described above, there is an uneasy relationship between apparent symptoms of family behaviour and their underlying causes. The Irish heritage of families provoked varied symptoms of behaviour in Stafford but this behaviour in turn caused varied outcomes in the overall trajectories that families followed. For the moment this fundamental problem of causality will be 'parked' in favour of discussion of the Irish dimension to the study, but we shall return to it at the end of the book.

Irish migration and the family perspective

Chapter 1 outlined a number of issues in Irish migration studies that might be enlightened by a family-history approach, and we are now in a position to make some conclusions on these issues. Firstly, the study has drawn out the *long profile* of Stafford's Irish families and has therefore contributed to the growing literature on the Irish migrant experience in the seven or more decades after the Famine. The different adjustments made by immigrant families as they evolved demonstrate a transition from raw immigrants to families who had reached varying degrees of accommodation and integration with the host society, be it in Stafford or elsewhere. The picture is one of great diversity, and the case studies have provided evidence of how each family went through that transition.

The responses were conditioned partly by the families' *ethnicity*. The study has answered the question 'Who were the Irish?' in relation to this particular town, and it reveals a complex picture that contrasts with the often monochrome perspective of more general studies. Stafford's immigrants proved to be a sample from almost the complete range of Irish society, so much so that the case studies could not encompass their full breadth of origins. Although there was the large group of Catholic Irish from the Castlerea area, even they exhibited some social diversity, and the rest came from all parts of Ireland, all classes, all religious persuasions and all the country's historic ethnic groups. The absolute numbers of Irish were always too small and too diverse to sustain purely 'Irish' social or economic agencies, however. There was never a single Irish 'ethnic

community' in Stafford and, indeed, neither were there 'ethnic communities' or 'ethnic associations', in Don Handelman's definitions as bodies
of people either occupying territory with boundaries, or at least having
social organisations actively to further the group's interests.[2] At most the
Castlerea Irish and their associates formed a transitory 'ethnic network'
whose value declined rapidly once second-generation children interacted
with or moved into the host society. To endure, ethnic consciousness
needed to be reinforced continuously by reference to an external threatening and discriminatory 'other', but such forces were feeble in Stafford.
The life chances of the Irish were determined more by their class position
and their family circumstances than by their ethnicity per se.

This had big implications for *identity*. It is impossible to generalise
about the identity of 'the Irish' in Stafford. Immigrants arrived with a large
range of identities, conscious and unconscious, and these were modified
by their experiences in the town and by generational succession. To continue to be meaningful, any form of 'Irish' identity had to be sustained by
reaction to an oppositional 'other' identity or social force. The evidence
from Stafford is that even members of the long-term transient families
were not reacting to such a force, though they may have found the town
claustrophobic and unrewarding in other ways. This book has argued that
the family was the main conduit of identity formation, and it is clear that
'Irish' identities amongst settled families with an Irish origin mutated or
dissolved within one or two generations. Those who integrated decided –
implicitly or explicitly – that their future lay in broadly conforming to the
norms, values and identities they found in Stafford's peer class and status
communities. Families retained an objective and sometimes conscious
Irish *heritage* but there was no utility in retaining an Irish *identity*.

The need to respond to circumstances raises the question of who
determined these responses, and particularly the *gender relations*
involved. Stafford's employment base was skewed towards male jobs, at
least for the initial immigrants, and many women, though not all, were
superficially 'tied migrants' 'trailing' behind their partners.[3] This might
imply that women took a passive, male-dominated role in adapting to the
new environment. The family histories have shown otherwise. Though
there was evidence of stereotypical oppressive male behaviour, we have
seen 'strong' women who dominated their households, and also that
the fortunes of many families were strongly influenced, or even determined, by the positive roles taken by women. Catholic families from the
Castlerea area particularly showed these qualities, and they suggest that
Polly Radosh's picture of relative gender equality within traditional rural
Irish families was exported amongst many emigrants from this group.[4]
More predictably, women took a leading role in seeking respectability
through involvement in Catholic Church activities. As families moved,
however, into the second and third generation, and the Church asserted

its discipline in the face of 'leakage', increasing integration into English society imposed its model of dominant patriarchal power. The Protestant and mixed-ethnicity families had shown this pattern all along.

Were the Irish families revealed to be *exiles* or *opportunists* in terms of the Miller/Akenson debates? The evidence is inevitably mixed. A family's origin and earlier experiences in Ireland were no sure guide to its subsequent trajectory. We have seen that some families did demonstrate features conforming to the picture of Catholic emigrants painted by Miller and summarised by Akenson's critical phrase, 'Gaelic-Catholic disability variable'.[5] This was particularly so amongst the terminal and long-term transient families. Even so, the case studies have intrinsically identified the family practices that enabled families to deal positively with the challenges facing them.[6] The evidence has not supported the perspective that the Irish families were passive victims of exile but rather that they were opportunists who reacted to, and exploited, the situation as they perceived it, whatever their initial traumas or disadvantages. They weighed up the advantages or disadvantages of staying in Stafford with those potentially present elsewhere in the Irish Diaspora, and we have seen the results of those decisions in the different fates of families.

This brings us to the last issues we identified in Irish migration studies, the relationship between the *local environment* and the *Diaspora*. Kevin Kenny has called for historical enquiry into 'how the diasporic sensibilities of the Irish vary according to the places where they reside'.[7] Hard evidence for diasporic sensibilities amongst the Irish in Stafford is difficult to pinpoint. Documentary testimony is lacking but we have seen occasional evidence of contacts between family members in Stafford and relatives elsewhere in Britain and overseas. Although many people left Stafford simply to get better jobs or to join the forces, some of the emigrants would have been influenced by diasporic sensibility and would have benefited from diasporic connections. Families that proved to be long-term transient probably operated at various levels of a national and transnational diasporic network. Those that ultimately integrated or were terminal were less likely to have significant diasporic links, and oral-history evidence suggests that little or no diasporic consciousness was transmitted down the surviving Irish-descended families.[8] Stafford's nineteenth-century Irish families therefore demonstrate conformity to Cohen's criteria for a diasporic people to only a limited degree.[9] Many did experience traumatic dispersal but the families that integrated largely lost any collective memory, myth or idealisation of the homeland. They did not retain a strong ethnic consciousness. The picture amongst the terminal and transient families is less clear. One family, the Walshes, almost certainly did have these features, but generally the Irish presence in Stafford was too weak and fragmented to sustain a diasporic consciousness, even amongst those families who proved to have little ultimate commitment to the town. We have seen, too, that there were no community leaders who wished to articulate such a consciousness.

Many writers have described the Irish as 'outcasts' from the host society in various localities where they settled in Britain. They experienced hostility and discrimination from the local population. Stafford presents a more complex picture. Overt prejudice, hostility and discrimination were rare here, yet some families or individual members remained apparently alienated from the host society and ultimately moved on. The evidence suggests this reflected the senses of self they brought from the fractured society of quasi-colonial Ireland and the often damaged family relationships they suffered in Britain. For many, though not for all, these problems were compounded by the stresses of poverty and deprivation. Stafford's social and economic environment was, nevertheless, relatively benign in comparison with many other places, and its economic diversification offered widening opportunities to the families that stayed and integrated. There are implications here for the wider issue of immigration and multiculturalism. Stafford's experience of Irish immigration, and also that of many of its immigrant families, was 'successful' in the sense that over time and down the generations a substantial proportion of the immigrant families integrated into the town's society with little social disruption. A major reason was that their numbers and proportion in relation to the town's population were relatively small. They were, furthermore, diverse in origins and skill, and they were never segregated into a 'ghetto community' or enclave. They were, of course, white and they spoke English from the start. Their descendants were visually and orally indistinguishable from the host population and the triggers for discrimination or abuse became weaker. These were decisive advantages in comparison with the problems faced by many of Britain's immigrants in the twentieth century and more recently. Those coming from rural Ireland bore psychological burdens in moving to an English town, but for many the transition was ameliorated by previous experience through migrant work and by the continuing possibilities for familiar work on the farms. It was their children who gained most from their parents' sacrifice and we have seen the processes by which this occurred in many families.

The picture of Irish immigration that emerges from this book runs counter to that documented in the big cities and the industrial areas of Britain that dominate the academic literature on the subject. It may nevertheless characterise the experience of many of the Irish who settled in the smaller towns and areas of dispersed population. In Chapter 1 Macraild's questioning of the 'typicality' of Stafford was quoted and it was asked what defines the 'exceptional' or the 'typical'? The answer has to be that more studies of collective family biography are needed in other places to explore the responses made by real people, as opposed to generalised constructs of the Irish population. Only through this type of work will we begin to know what was 'typical' and 'exceptional'.

Families, households and their context

It remains to make brief comments on some of the implications of the Stafford Irish for the wider field of family studies. The approach has demonstrated that, whatever the conceptual problems at the margins, *identifiable and functioning families* existed, can be identified, and have histories amenable to documentation and analysis. The history of these families has captured something of the web of relations and generational transitions they experienced, together with the forces that moulded them.[10] The empirical evidence suggests conclusions in five particular areas of family studies.

Firstly, by its nature the family-history approach emphasises a family's genealogy and its dynamic relationships, but the work has particularly demonstrated the complexity of individuals' relationships with their wider families, quasi-families and social networks. Following the trajectories of families reveals the poverty of the *individualization thesis*'s one-dimensional approach to personal motivation and interpersonal relations. Though the detailed interchanges amongst family members are largely lost to us, the results in terms of the development of self in childhood, of the significance of religious belief and commitment, of gender roles and fulfilment, or otherwise of kinship obligations, are all apparent in the rich pattern of family behaviour revealed over time. People were not free-floating individuals making purely instrumental choices but members of open and dynamic entities that provided webs of both constraint and support.

Secondly, if individuals were socially constrained in their decisions, to what extent did families adopt a similarly constrained but nevertheless coherent approach to the challenges they faced? In other words, did they adopt a *family strategy*? By definition, all the families and lone individuals who settled in Stafford had already taken one strategic life-course decision – to emigrate. The degree of freedom in that choice clearly varied, but all had had to make the drastic shift to a place and a life different from where they had grown up. We have seen that their ability to do this successfully varied, but it has been argued that the behaviour of some families suggests they did pursue a more or less conscious and coherent strategy. This was reflected in the ethos that socialised its members as they grew up within it or came in from the outside through marriage, adoption or association. Women frequently played a major – even central – role in defining and pursuing family strategies. In 'successful', aspirant families the strategy had to be mutually accepted by both dominant males and females. We have, however, seen cases where the ethos was more destructive, and men and women who were outside it were marginalised or bullied.

The study has provided evidence that undermines yet further the supposed *transition to the nuclear family* during industrialisation and urbanisation. Superficially it might be thought that the migrant Irish would demonstrate the clear dichotomy between the pre-industrial extended family and the flexible nuclear unit demanded by capitalist production, but we have seen that in practice there was no such simple transformation. There were certainly complex families in Stafford based on kinship links from rural Ireland, but there were also nuclear and smaller units from such a background and, conversely, complex families that developed in Stafford itself. Family evolution or decline were affected by the character of key individuals and a family's openness to network links. Siblings – brother/sister, aunt/uncle, cousin and beyond – were important in developing contacts and interlinkages, and they vindicate in working-class families as well as middle-class ones Davidoff's emphasis on their significance. The extent of these kinship links could vary but some families demonstrated a 'penumbra' of blood relationships that were significant for key life-course opportunities.[11] The evidence suggests that it was the extended families that were most 'successful' and whose members proved best able to respond flexibly to the changing nature of the economy. Nuclear families and lone individuals were particularly vulnerable to unemployment, poverty, illness and death, and the evidence is that such units proved *less adaptable* to changes in their external environment, rather than more so, as postulated by the original theorists. Their fate was either to be terminal or to be ultimately transient through the attrition of collective or individual out-migration.

The nature of *home and household* both expressed but also influenced the trajectories followed by families. The case studies covered families crowded into Stafford's worst slums, those who lived in middle-class villas and those somewhere in between. The slum-dwellers often had to live not just in poor houses but in households with a shifting cast of kin and lodgers that created anomic conditions for children and stress for adults. There was little chance here to create the model Victorian 'home', and for some families these circumstances were repeated down the generations. Things were not necessarily better in the more superior houses, however, because we have seen how family dynamics could make the house either a nurturing home or a den of oppression and conflict. In general terms women were the key home-makers but their ability to do this was either enhanced or destroyed by the character of the resident males. Cases of reversal of stereotypical gendered household roles were, however, revealed, and emphasise how every family's history was unique. There was, furthermore, no obvious evidence to support Gillis's assertion that

Catholics were 'slower to attribute a sacred quality to domestic space.'[12] If they could afford it, Catholic families sought domestic heaven as much as Protestants.

Finally, we have to return to perhaps the most problematic issue of all – what really determined the trajectories that families followed? This is in essence the *nature vs nurture*, or heredity and environment, debate. We have seen that the trajectories followed by Stafford's Irish families could not be predicted purely by their superficial characteristics. Complex forces were at work. There was, firstly, the genealogical 'family', a body of genetic kin that provided the raw material of physiological inheritance to its members but was modified in each generation by usually unrelated genes from outside. This genetic reservoir both favoured and disadvantaged a range of physical, intellectual and emotional traits amongst those contained in it, but it is impossible to disentangle this inheritance from the influence of the second factor: the practices of family members in terms of interpersonal relationships, child-rearing behaviour, religious beliefs and so on. These produced an inherited family culture infused, in each generation, by influences from non-blood partners.

Emphasising relationships within families runs the risk, however, of overlooking the third factor, the impact of the wider community, society and economy. The Irish families examined in this book were particularly exposed to the massive economic and social changes of the Victorian period and the early twentieth century. Their responses did not follow the simple predictions of Marx, Engels or the functionalist sociologists, but that is not to say they were free agents in the capitalist economy and its superstructure. The division between 'home' and outside waged work became more rigid, even if it came relatively late in this shoe town. That process tended to sharpen gender divisions and undermine the power of women in the family. Even so, the continuing strength of extended families and kinship relationships provided flexibility and support to family members and could in part have been a response to the demands of the economic system. Overall, the history of these Irish families offers some sustenance to the Marxist feminist perspective that sees the family in part as an ideological construct whose role was to keep people functioning and reproducing in spite of the stresses in the external environment.[13] Continuing family obligations and collective family values were an essential part of that process.

The histories of Stafford's Irish families were specific to that place and that period. Its changing environment offered families varying amounts of room for manouevre and it was argued earlier that the environment here was perhaps more benign than other places. This provokes a final and counterfactual point. If many of Stafford's Irish had gone to other places their family trajectories would have been different not just in terms of superficialities – jobs, housing etc. – but probably in their fundamental nature. Their fates would have been different. We therefore need other studies to examine the experiences of representative families elsewhere.

Notes

1 Herson, 'Family history and memory', p. 220.
2 D. Handelman, 'The organisation of ethnicity', *Ethnic Groups*, 1 (1977), pp. 187–200.
3 Halfacree, 'Household migration and the structuration of patriarchy: Evidence from the USA', *Progress in Human Geography*, 19:2 (2005), pp. 159–82.
4 Radosh, 'Colonial oppression', p. 272.
5 Miller, *Emigrants and Exiles*, esp. pp. 259 and 277; D. H. Akenson, 'The Irish in the United States' in O'Sullivan, *The Irish World Wide*, Vol. 2, p. 117.
6 Morgan, *Family Connections*, pp. 188–99.
7 Kenny, 'Diaspora and comparison', p. 162.
8 Herson, 'Family history and memory', p. 220.
9 Cohen, *Global Diasporas*, pp. 180–7.
10 Smart, *Personal Life*, pp. 38–45 and 81–93.
11 Davidoff, *Thicker than Water*, esp. Chapter 7.
12 Gillis, *World of Their Own Making*, p. 126.
13 R. Rapp, E. Ross and R. Bridenthal, 'Examining family history' in Newton, Ryan and Walkowitz, *Sex and Class*, pp. 232–58.

Bibliography

Primary sources

Birmingham Archdiocesan Archives (BAA)

P255/1/1, Stafford, St Austin's, Register of Baptisms, 1804–31.
P255/1/2, Stafford, St Austin's, Register of Baptisms, 1831–58.
P255/1/3, Stafford, St Austin's, Register of Baptisms, 1858–70.
P255/1/4, Stafford, St Austin's, Register of Baptisms, 1870–83.
P255/1/5, Stafford, St Austin's, Register of Baptisms, 1883–90.
P255/2/1, Stafford, St Austin's, Register of Confirmations, Marriages and Burials, Vol. 7: 1828–57.
P255/3/1, Stafford, St Austin's, Register of Marriages, 1858–80.
P255/4/1, Stafford, St Austin's, Register of Burials, 1858–74.
P255/4/2, Stafford, St Austin's, Register of Burials, 1875–93.
P255/5/1, Stafford, St Austin's, Mission Book, 1873–95.
Z6/6/1/2/3, Ilsley Papers.

*British Library of Political and Economic Science (now LSE Library),
London School of Economics*

Webb Trade Union Collection

Vol. 4, letters from F. Evans, Stafford Trades Council.
Vol. 15, hand shoemakers.
Vol. 24, leather trades and National Union of Boot and Shoe Operatives.

National Archives of Ireland (NAI)

Distress Papers, Vols 1/2, CSOCR 77/8, 1847, box nos. 1471–81.
Famine Relief Commission Papers, 1844–47, series RLFC3/2, Cos Galway, Mayo and Roscommon.
Outrage Reports, 1845, Co. Roscommon, documents in the series 25/1147–23909.

National Library of Ireland (NLI)

Roman Catholic Parish Records (microfilm)

P4211, Boyounagh, Co. Galway, baptisms and marriages, 1838–65.
P4211, Dunmore, Co. Galway, baptisms and marriages, 1833–59.
P4617, Lough Glynn, Co. Roscommon, baptisms and marriages, 1835–40.
P4618, Ballinakill and Kilcrone, Co. Roscommon, baptisms and marriages, 1831–63
P4619, Kilkeevin, Co. Roscommon, baptisms and marriages, 1826–60.
P6955, Tibohine, Co. Roscommon, baptisms, 1833–64.

Tithe Applotment Books (TAB)

11/11, film 37, Dunmore, Co. Galway (1824).
11/15, film 38, Templetogher, Co. Galway (1828).
11/16, film 38, Kilcroan, Co. Galway (1833).
11/18, film 38, Boyounagh, Co. Galway (1831–34).
11/20, film 38, Kilbegnet, Co. Galway (1833).
11/40, film 39, Moylough, Co. Galway (1837)
25/10, film 87, Tibohine, Co. Roscommon (1825).
25/15, film 88, Kilkeevin, Co. Roscommon (1832).
25/17, film 88, Kiltullagh, Co. Roscommon (1833).
25/18, film 88, Balintober, Co. Roscommon (1832).

Parish of St Austin, Stafford

Register of Marriages, 1881–1910.

Probate Offices, England

England and Wales National Probate Registry, Will of the Revd Michael O'Sullivan, died 12 January 1892 in Solihull, probate granted Birmingham, 12 March 1892.
Probate Registry, London, will of Bartholomew Corcoran, died 3 June 1908, probate granted 17 July 1908.

Public Record Office of Northern Ireland (PRONI)

MIC 1P/23/1, First Presbyterian Church, Bangor, marriages, 1808–45.
The Revd Jas. McConnell, *History of the First Presbyterian Chapel, Bangor* (n.d. [c. 1915]), copy on PRONI microfilm MIC 1P/23/2.

St Patrick's Church, Stafford

Liber matrimonium, 26 March 1894–1 February 1940.

St Patrick's Roman Catholic School, Stafford

Admission books.

Stafford Borough Council (SBC)

Environmental, Health and Housing Department, Register of Houses in Clearance
Areas, Housing Acts 1936 and 1957.
Stafford Borough Council Burial Registers, 1856–1921.

Staffordshire Record Office (SRO)

C/PC/1/6/1, Staffordshire Police Force Register, 1842–63.
C/PC/1/6/2, Staffordshire Police Personnel Register, 1863–94.
C/PC/5/39, List of Cases, Stafford Borough Petty Sessions, 1884–88.
D240/E/F/4/7, Ingestre General Estate Wages Book, 1848–55.
D659/1/4/7–8, Stafford Poor Law Union: Workhouse Admissions, 1847–48.
D659/1/4/52, Stafford Poor Law Union Indoor Relief List, 1882/83.
D659/8a/4–5, Stafford Poor Law Union, Board of Guardians Minute Book, 25
    May 1844–3 February 1848.
D1174/3/1/1, Stafford Wesleyan Chapel, Trustees' Minutes and Accounts,
    1850–83.
D1174/3/3/1, Stafford Wesleyan Sunday School, Teachers' Meeting and
    Committee Minutes, 1820–47.
D1225, LNWR Staff Register, Stafford, 1898–1927.
D1323/B/1/1, Stafford Borough Watch Committee, Minutes 1836–42 and
    1850–54.
D1323/B/4, Stafford B[orough] C[ouncil] Sub-Sanitary Committee Minutes, 31
    December 1872–9 March 1875.
D1323/C/4/1–2, Stafford Borough Council Public Health Committee Minutes,
    9 March 1875–27 January 1880 and 24 February 1880–25 September
    1888.
D1323/C/4/5, Stafford Borough Council, Public Health Committee
    Minutes, 1911.
D1419/4/5, Stafford Borough Council General Rate Book, 1914.
D3180/1, Corporation of Stafford Year Book, 1899–1900 and 1901.
D3704, Stafford Borough Council, Register of Common Lodging Houses,
    1878–1940.
D4338/D/1/1, Stafford Shoe Manufacturers' Association, Minute Book,
    1877–80.
D4338/E/1/5 Stafford and District Humane Burial Society Register, 1876–1930s.
D4800/1, Presbyterian Church Records, Stafford.
D4800/2, Congregational Church Records, Stafford.
D4800/2/8/1, Congregational Church, Stafford, Roll of Members, 1798–1901.
D5008/2/7/11/1, Borough of Stafford Poll Book, Elections of 1868 and 1869.
D6117/1/4, Stafford Borough Council, Medical Officer of Health Annual Reports,
    1904–13.

Census Enumeration Returns, 1841–1901 (microfilms).
Church of England Marriage Registers, microfiches for Stafford St Mary's, St Chad's, St Thomas's and Christ Church.

William Salt Library, Stafford

Gillow, J., *St Thomas's Priory; or, The Story of St Austin's, Stafford* (Stafford: locally published, [c. 1892–94]).
Halden, J. *Stafford and District Directory and Almanack* (Stafford: Halden & Co., 1891–1907).
Jones Collection, 7/00/165, C. H. Gillard, auctioneers, sale catalogues, property in slum areas, 1860–89.
Staffordshire Advertiser, 1825–1922 (*SA*)

Official publications

Census, 1821–1921: Tables of Population and Houses, Staffordshire.
Census, 1841: County of Stafford. Occupations, Stafford Borough.
Census, 1871: Occupations of Males and Females in Principal Towns. Stafford Borough.
Census, 1871: Tables of Birthplaces of the People in Principal Towns in England and Wales. General Table VIII: Population of Cities and Boroughs Having Defined Municipal or Parliamentary Limits.
Census of Ireland, 1821, 1831, 1841, 1851, 1861: Population Tables for Cos Galway, Mayo and Roscommon, Baronies, Parishes and Townlands.
Census of Ireland, 1841: General Summary and County Tables. Table VI, Table of Occupations.
Census of Ireland, 1861, Part 4, Vol. 2: Occupations.
Census of Ireland, 1881: Occupations, Tables 18/19.
Census of Ireland, 1911: Occupations, Table 20, Occupations of Males and Females by Ages, Religious Persuasion and Education.
Ordnance Survey, 1:500 Plans, Stafford Borough (surveyed 1880; published 1881).
Parliamentary Papers, 1842 (007): Commission on the Sanitary Condition of the Labouring Population of Great Britain. Local Reports on England, No. 15: E. Knight, 'On the Sanitary State of the Town of Stafford.'
Parliamentary Papers, 1865, XX: Children's Employment Commission, 1862, 4th Report; Report on Bootmakers, Tailors, Hatters, Glovers etc.
Parliamentary Papers, House of Commons, Select Committee on Corrupt Practices at the Last Election for Stafford Borough: Report and Minutes of Evidence, 1833 (537).
Parliamentary Papers, Papers Relating to Proceedings for the Relief of Distress, and State of Unions and Workhouses in Ireland, 1848 and 1849 (particularly Castlerea Union).
Royal Commission of Inquiry into the State of the Law and Practice in Respect of the Occupation of Land in Ireland (Devon Commission), Minutes of Evidence,

Pts II and III, 1845 (evidence relating to parishes in Cos. Galway, Mayo and Roscommon).
Royal Commission on the Condition of the Poorer Classes in Ireland (1836).

Newspapers

Birmingham Daily Post
Caledonian Mercury
Catholic Herald
Daily News
Daily Sketch
Express and Star (Wolverhampton)
Freeman's Journal
Liverpool Mercury
Morning Chronicle
Preston Guardian
Reynold's Newspaper
Roscommon Journal
Staffordshire Advertiser (SA)
Stafford Mercury
The Times
Tuam Herald

Unpublished dissertations

Dolan, R., 'The Great Famine in the Barony of Roscommon, 1845 to 1850' (M.A. thesis, University College, Galway, 1999).

Herson, J. D., 'Why the Irish went to Stafford: A case study of Irish settlement in England, 1830–71' (M.Sc. thesis, London School of Economics and Political Science, University of London, 1986).

Huggins, M. J., 'Agrarian conflict in pre-famine County Roscommon' (D.Phil. thesis, University of Liverpool, 2000).

Lawton, R., 'Population migration to and from Warwickshire and Staffordshire, 1841–91' (M.A. thesis, University of Liverpool, n.d.) (copy of Staffordshire section in William Salt Library, Stafford, TH48).

Letford, L., 'Irish and non-Irish women living in their households in nineteenth-century Liverpool: Issues of class, gender, religion and birthplace' (Ph.D. thesis, University of Lancaster, 1999).

Melvin, P., 'The landed gentry of Galway, 1820–1880' (Ph.D. thesis, Trinity College Dublin, 1991).

Miskell, L., 'Custom, conflict and community: A study of the Irish in South Wales and Cornwall, 1861–91' (Ph.D. thesis, University of Wales, Aberystwyth, 1996).

Secondary sources

Aalen, F. H. A., K. Whelan and M. Stout, *Atlas of the Irish Rural Landscape* (Cork: Cork University Press, 1998).

Accampo, E., *Industrialization, Family Life and Class Relations: Saint Chamond, 1815–1914* (Berkeley: University of California Press, 1989).

Akenson, D. H., *The Irish Diaspora: A Primer* (Toronto: P. D. Meany, 1993).

American Psychiatric Association, *Diagnostic and Statistical Manual of Mental Disorders IV (Text Revision)*, 4th edn (Washington, DC: American Psychiatric Publishing, 2011).

Anderson, M., *Approaches to the History of the Western Family, 1500–1914* (London: Macmillan, 1980).

Anderson, M., *Family Structure in 19th Century Lancashire* (Cambridge: Cambridge University Press, 1971).

Anslow, J. and T. Randall, *Around Stafford in Old Photographs* (Stroud: Alan Sutton, 1991).

Anslow, J. and T. Randall, *Stafford in Old Photographs* (Stroud: Alan Sutton, 1994).

Ariès, P., *Centuries of Childhood: A Social History of Family Life* (New York, Jonathan Cape, 1962).

Banister, R., *Brain's Clinical Neurology*, 5th edn (Oxford: Oxford University Press, 1978).

Bartlett, T. and K. Jeffery (eds), *A Military History of Ireland* (Cambridge: Cambridge University Press, 1996).

Beckett, I. F. W., 'War, identity and memory in Ireland', *Irish Economic and Social History*, 36 (2009), pp. 63–84.

Belchem, J. 'Class, creed and country: The Irish middle class in Victorian Liverpool' in R. Swift and S. Gilley (eds), *The Irish in Victorian Britain: The Local Dimension* (Dublin: Four Courts Press, 1999), pp. 190–211.

Belchem, J., *Irish, Catholic and Scouse: The History of the Liverpool Irish, 1800– 1939* (Liverpool: Liverpool University Press, 2007).

Belchem, J., 'The Liverpool-Irish enclave', *Immigrants and Minorities*, 18:2/3 (July/November 1999), pp. 128–46.

Belchem, J., *Merseypride: Essays in Liverpool Exceptionalism* (Liverpool: Liverpool University Press, 2000).

Belchem, J. and K. Tenfelde (eds), *Irish and Polish Migration in Comparative Perspective* (Essen: Klartext, 2003)

Bew, P., *Ireland: The Politics of Enmity* (Oxford: Oxford University Press, 2007).

Bielenberg, A., 'What happened to Irish industry after the British industrial revolution? Some evidence from the first UK Census of Production, 1907', *Economic History Review*, 61:4 (November 2008), pp. 820–41.

Bielenberg, A., *Ireland and the Industrial Revolution: The Impact of the Industrial Revolution on Irish Industry, 1801–1922* (London: Routledge, 2009).

Bielenberg, A. (ed.), *The Irish Diaspora* (Harlow: Pearson Education, 2000).

Bossy, J., *The English Catholic Community, 1570–1850* (London: Darton, Longman and Todd, 1975).

Bradley, W. J., *Gallon: The History of Three Townlands in County Tyrone from the Earliest Times to the Present Day* (Derry: Guildhall Press, 2000).

Buckland, P., *Irish Unionism I: The Anglo-Irish and the New Ireland, 1885–1922* (Dublin: Gill and Macmillan, 1972).

Butters, P., *Yesterday's Town: Stafford* (Buckingham: Barracuda Books, 1984).

Butters, R. and N. Thomas, *Stafford: A History and Celebration* (Salisbury: Francis Frith Collection, 2005).

Calhoun, C. J., 'Community: Toward a variable conceptualisation for comparative research', *Social History*, 5:1 (January 1980), pp. 105–29.

Campbell, M., *Ireland's New Worlds: Immigrants, Politics and Society in the United States and Australia, 1815–1922* (Madison: University of Wisconsin Press, 2008).

Carrier, N. H. and J. R. Jeffery, *External Migration: A Study of the Available Statistics* (London: Her Majesty's Stationery Office, 1953).

Chamberlain, M., *Family Love in the Diaspora: Migration and the Anglo-Caribbean Experience* (London: Transaction, 2006).

Chinn, C., *Birmingham Irish: Making Our Mark* (Birmingham: Birmingham Library Services, 2003).

Christiansen, R., *A Regional History of the Railways of Great Britain*, Vol. 7: *The West Midlands* (Newton Abbot: David and Charles, 1973).

Clapham, J. H., 'Irish immigration into Great Britain in the nineteenth century', *Bulletin of the International Committee of Historical Sciences*, 20 (July 1933), pp. 596–605.

Clarke, J., *Christopher Dillon Bellew and His Galway Estates, 1763–1826*, Maynooth Studies in Local History, 49 (Dublin: Four Courts Press, 2003).

Cohen, R., *Global Diasporas* (London: University College London Press, 1997).

Coleman, A., *Riotous Roscommon: Social Unrest in the 1840s*, Maynooth Studies in Local History, 27 (Dublin: Irish Academic Press, 1999).

Collier, P., *Exodus: Immigration and Multiculturalism in the 21st Century* (London: Allen Lane, 2013).

Connolly, S. J., *Priests and People in Pre-Famine Ireland, 1780–1845* (Dublin: Four Courts Press, 2001).

Cooke, T. J., 'Migration in a family way', *Population, Space and Place*, 14 (2008), pp. 255–65.

Cooper, D., *The Staffordshire Regiments: Imperial, Regular and Volunteer Regiments, 1705–1919* (Leek: Churnet Valley Books, 2003).

Cousens, S. H. 'The regional pattern of emigration during the Great Irish Famine, 1846–51', *Transactions of the Institute of British Geographers*, Second Series, 28 (1960), pp. 119–34.

Cousens, S. H., 'The regional variation in emigration from Ireland between 1821 and 1841', *Transactions of the Institute of British Geographers*, 37 (1965), pp. 15–30.

Cronin, C. 'The English College, in Rome', in *The Catholic Encyclopedia* (New York: Robert Appleton, 1909), http://paperspast. natlib. govt. nz/cgi/papers.

Cullen, L. M., *An Economic History of Ireland since 1660* (London: B. T. Batsford, 1972).

Davidoff, L., 'Kinship as a categorical concept: A case study of nineteenth century English siblings', *Journal of Social History*, 39:2 (Winter 2005), pp. 411–13.

Davidoff, L., *Thicker than Water: Siblings and Their Relations, 1780–1920* (Oxford: Oxford University Press, 2012).

Davidoff, L., M. Doolittle, J. Fink and K. Holden, *The Family Story: Blood, Contract and Intimacy, 1830–1960* (Harlow: Addison Wesley, Longman, 1999).

Davies, S., *Liverpool Labour: Social and Political Influences on the Development of the Labour Party in Liverpool, 1900–1939* (Keele: Keele University Press, 1996).

Deacon, B. and M. Donald, 'In search of community history', *Family and Community History*, 7:1 (May 2004), pp. 13–18.

Delaney, E., *The Irish in Post-War Britain* (Oxford: Oxford University Press, 2007).

Denley, P., S. Fogelvik and C. Harvey (eds), *History and Computing II* (Manchester: Manchester University Press, 1989).

Denvir, J., *The Irish in Britain from the Earliest Times to the Fall and Death of Parnell* (London: Kegan Paul, Trench, Trübner, 1892).

Dickens, C., 'A plated article', *Household Words*, 24 April 1852.

Digby, A., *Making a Medical Living: Doctors and Patients in the English Market for Medicine, 1720–1911* (Cambridge: Cambridge University Press, 1994).

Donnelly, J. S., Jr, *The Great Irish Potato Famine* (Stroud: Sutton, 2001).

Donnelly, P. E., *St Patrick's, Stafford, 1895–1945: Recollections of a Parishioner*, part of *Souvenir of the Golden Jubilee of St Patrick's, Stafford, with the History of the Parish* (Stafford: St Patrick's Church, 1945).

Drake, M. (ed.), *Time, Family and Community: Perspectives on Family and Community History* (Oxford: Blackwell, 1994).

Dunnigan, D., *A South Roscommon Emigrant: Emigration and Return, 1890–1920*, Maynooth Studies in Local History, 73 (Dublin: Four Courts Press, 2007).

Dupree, M. W., *Family Structure in the Staffordshire Potteries, 1840–1880* (Oxford: Clarendon Press, 1995).

Elliott, B. S., *Irish Migrants in the Canadas: A New Approach* (Kingston, ON: McGill-Queen's University Press, 1988).

Engels, F., *The Origin of the Family, Private Property and the State* (London: Lawrence and Wishart, 1977).

Fielding, S., *Class and Ethnicity: Irish Catholics in England, 1880–1939* (Buckingham: Open University Press, 1993).

Finch, J., *Family Obligations and Social Change* (Cambridge: Polity Press, 1989).

Finnegan, F., *Poverty and Prejudice: A Study of Irish Immigrants in York, 1840–75* (Cork: Cork University Press, 1982).

Finnegan, R. and M. Drake (eds), *From Family Tree to Family History* (Cambridge: Cambridge University Press, 1994).

Fisher, M. J., *Staffordshire and the Gothic Revival* (Ashbourne: Landmark Publishing, 2006).

Fisher, M. J. and A. Baker, *Stafford's Hidden Gem: St Chad's Church, Greengate Street. A History and Guide* (Stafford: St Chad's Church, 2000).

Fitzgerald, P. and B. Lambkin, *Migration in Irish History, 1607–2007* (Basingstoke: Palgrave Macmillan, 2008).

Fitzpatrick, D., *Oceans of Consolation: Personal Accounts of Irish Migration to Australia* (Cork: Cork University Press, 1994).

Flynn, J. S., *Ballymacward: The Story of a Galway Parish* (n.p.: J. S. Flynn, 1991).

Foster, R. F., *Modern Ireland, 1600–1972* (Harmondsworth: Penguin, 1989).

Foster, R. F., *Paddy and Mr Punch: Connections in Irish and English History* (Harmondsworth: Penguin, 1995).

Fox, A., *A History of the National Union of Boot and Shoe Operatives, 1874–1957* (Oxford: Basil Blackwell, 1958).

Frankenberg, R., *Communities in Britain: Social Life in Town and Country* (Harmondsworth, Penguin, 1966).

Freeman, T. W., *Ireland: A General and Regional Geography*, 3rd edn (London, Methuen, 1965).

Frost, G., *Living in Sin: Husbands and Wives in Nineteenth Century England* (Manchester: Manchester University Press, 2008).

Geary, F., 'Deindustrialisation in Ireland to 1851: Some evidence from the census', *Economic History Review*, 51:3 (August 1998), pp. 512–41.

Geary, L. M. 'Australia *felix*: Irish doctors in nineteenth-century Victoria' in P. O'Sullivan (ed.), *The Irish World Wide*, Vol. 2: *The Irish in the New Communities* (Leicester: Leicester University Press, 1992), pp. 162–79.

Gibbon, S., *The Recollections of Skeffington Gibbon from 1796 to the Present Year* (Dublin: James Blundell, 1829).

Gillis, J. R., *A World of Their Own Making: Myth, Ritual and the Quest for Family Values* (Cambridge, MA: Harvard University Press, 1996).

Gilley, S., 'Roman Catholicism and the Irish in England', *Immigrants and Minorities*, 18:2/3 (July/November 1999), pp. 147–67.

Greaney, J., *Dunmore* (n.p.: J. Greaney, 1984).

Greenslade, M. W., *Catholic Staffordshire* (Leominster: Gracewing, 2006).

Greenslade, M. W., *St Austin's, Stafford, 1791–1991* (Birmingham: Archdiocese of Birmingham Historical Commission, 1991).

Greenslade, M. W., D. A. Johnson and C. R. J. Currie, *A History of Stafford* (extract from Greenslade, Johnson and Currie, *The Victoria History of the County of Stafford*, Vol. 6 (Stafford: Staffordshire County Library, 1982) (*VCH Stafford*).

Greenslade, M. W., D. A. Johnson and C. R. J. Currie, *The Victoria History of the County of Stafford*, Vol. 6 (Oxford: Oxford University Press for the Institute of Historical Research, University of London, 1979).

Griffin, B., 'Class, gender and Liberalism in Parliament, 1868–1882: The case of the Married Women's Property Acts', *The Historical Journal*, 46:1 (March 2003), pp. 59–87.

Gritt, A. (ed.), *Family History in Lancashire: Issues and Approaches* (Newcastle-upon-Tyne: Cambridge Scholars Publishing, 2009).

Hafford, C., 'Sibling caretaking in immigrant families: Understanding cultural practices to inform child welfare practice and evaluation', *Evaluation and Program Planning*, 33 (2010), pp. 294–302.

Halfacree, K. H., 'Household migration and the structuration of patriarchy: Evidence from the USA', *Progress in Human Geography*, 19:2 (2005), pp. 159–82.

Handelman, D., 'The organisation of ethnicity', *Ethnic Groups*, 1 (1977), pp. 187–200.

Hareven, T., *Family Time and Industrial Time: The Relationship between Family and Work in a Planned Corporation Town, 1900–1924* (Cambridge: Cambridge University Press, 1982).

Harrison, A. M., 'The development of boot and shoe manufacturing in Stafford, 1850–1880', *Journal of the Staffordshire Industrial Archaeology Society*, 10 (1981), pp. 1–80.

Harrison, A. M., 'Elleys of Stafford', *Journal of the Staffordshire Industrial Archaeology Society*, 8 (1978), pp. 50–65.

Heinrick, H., *A Survey of the Irish in England (1872)*, ed. A. O'Day (London: The Hambledon Press, 1990).

Herson, J. D., 'The English, the Irish and the Catholic Church in Stafford, 1791–1923', *Midland Catholic History*, 14 (2007), pp. 23–46.

Herson, J. D., 'Family history and memory in Irish immigrant families' in K. Burrell and P. Panayi (eds), *Histories and Memories: Migrants and Their History in Britain* (London: Tauris Academic Studies, 2006), pp. 210–33.

Herson, J. D., 'Irish immigrant families in the English West Midlands: A long-term view, 1830–1914' in J. Belchem and K. Tenfelde (eds), *Irish and Polish Migration in Comparative Perspective* (Essen: Klartext Verlag, 2003), pp. 93–108.

Herson, J. D., 'Irish migration and settlement in Victorian England: A small town perspective' in R. Swift and S. Gilley (eds), *The Irish in Britain, 1815–1939* (London: Pinter Press, 1989), pp. 84–103.

Herson, J. D., 'Migration, "community" or integration? Irish families in Victorian Stafford' in R. Swift and S. Gilley (eds), *The Irish in Victorian Britain: The Local Dimension* (Dublin: Four Courts Press, 1999), pp. 156–89.

Herson, J. D., 'Why the Irish went to Stafford: A case study of Irish settlement in England, 1830–71', *Liverpool Polytechnic Papers in Social Studies*, 1 (April 1988).

Hickman, M. J., 'Census ethnic categories and second-generation identities: A study of the Irish in England and Wales', *Journal of Ethnic and Migration Studies*, 37:1 (January 2011), pp. 79–97.

Hickman, M. J., *Religion, Class and Identity: The State, the Catholic Church and the Education of the Irish in Britain* (Aldershot, Ashgate, 1995).

Hobsbawm, E. J., *Labouring Men: Studies in the History of Labour* (London: Weidenfeld and Nicolson, 1968).

Hobsbawm, E. J. (ed.), *Worlds of Labour* (London: Weidenfeld and Nicolson, 1984).

Hudson, A., *Equity and Trusts*, 6th edn (London: Routledge–Cavendish, 2010).

Hunt, E. H., *British Labour History, 1815–1914* (London: Weidenfeld and Nicolson, 1981).

Hutchinson, J. and A. D. Smith, *Ethnicity* (Oxford: Oxford University Press, 1996).

Jagger, P. J. (ed.), *Gladstone* (London: The Hambledon Press, 1998).

Jenkins, R., *Rethinking Ethnicity: Arguments and Explanations* (London: Sage, 1997).

Jenkins, R., *Gladstone* (London: Pan Macmillan, 2002).

Jenkins, W., 'In search of the lace curtain: Residential mobility, class transformation and everyday practice among Buffalo's Irish, 1880–1910', *Journal of Urban History*, 35:7 (2009), pp. 970–97.

Johnson, J. H., 'Harvest migration from nineteenth-century Ireland', *Transactions of the Institute of British Geographers*, 41 (June 1967), pp. 97–103.

Jones, G., '"Strike out boldly for the prizes that are available to you": Medical emigration from Ireland, 1860–1905', *Medical History*, 54 (2010), pp. 55–74.

Jong, G. F. de and D. R. Graefe, 'Family life course transitions and the economic consequences of internal migration', *Population, Space and Place*, 14 (2008), pp. 267–82.

Jordan, T. E., 'Queen Victoria's Irish soldiers: Quality of life and social origins of the thin *green* line', *Social Indicators Research*, 57 (2002), pp. 73–88.

Karsten, P., 'Irish soldiers in the British army, 1792–1922: Suborned or subordinate?', *Journal of Social History*, 17 (Autumn 1983), pp. 31–64.

Keen, H., P. Martin and S. J. Morgan, *Seeing History: Public History in Britain Now* (London: Francis Boutle, 2000).

Kemp, J., *The Freemen of Stafford Borough, 1100 to 1997* (Stafford, J. Kemp, 1998).

Kenny, K., 'Diaspora and comparison: The global Irish as a case study', *Journal of American History*, 90:1 (June 2003), pp. 134–62.

Kenny, K. (ed.), *Ireland and the British Empire* (Oxford: Oxford University Press, 2004).

Kertzer, D. I. and M. Barbagli (eds), *Family Life in the Long Nineteenth Century* (New Haven: Yale University Press, 2002).

Khan, V. S. (ed.), *Minority Families in Britain: Support and Stress* (London: Macmillan, 1979).

Kinealy, C., *This Great Calamity: The Irish Famine, 1845–52* (Dublin: Gill and Macmillan, 1994).

Kofman, E., 'Family-related migration: A critical review of European studies', *Journal of Ethnic and Migration Studies*, 30:2 (March 2004), pp. 243–62.

Larkin, E., 'The devotional revolution in Ireland, 1850–75', *American Historical Review*, 77:3 (June 1972), pp. 625–52.

Leavey, G., S. Sembhi and G. Livingston, 'Older Irish migrants living in London: Identity, loss and return', *Journal of Ethnic and Migration Studies*, 30:4 (July 2004), pp. 763–79.

Lees, L. H., *Exiles of Erin: Irish Migrants in Victorian London* (Manchester: Manchester University Press, 1979).

Leslie, S., *Henry Edward Manning: His Life and Labours* (London: Burns, Oates and Washbourne, 1921).

Lewis, R., *Around Stafford* (Stroud: Tempus, 1999).

Lewis, R., *Stafford Past: An Illustrated History* (Chichester: Phillimore, 1997).

Lewis, R., *Stafford and District* (Wilmslow: Sigma Press, 1998).

Lewis, R. and J. Anslow, *Stafford as It Was* (Nelson: Hendon, 1980).

Lewis, R. and J. Anslow, *Stafford in Old Picture Postcards* (Zaltbommel: European Library, 1984).

Lewis, S., *A Topographical Dictionary of Ireland* (London: S. Lewis, 1839).

Lowe, W., *The Irish in Mid-Victorian Lancashire: The Shaping of a Working Class Community* (New York: Peter Lang, 1989).

Lowe, W., 'The Lancashire Irish and the Catholic Church, 1846–71: The social dimension', *Irish Historical Studies*, 20:78 (September 1976), pp. 105–55.

MacRaild, D. M., *Culture, Conflict and Migration: The Irish in Victorian Cumbria* (Liverpool: Liverpool University Press, 1998).

MacRaild, D. M., *Faith, Fraternity and Fighting: The Orange Order and Irish Migrants in Northern England, c. 1817–1920* (Liverpool: Liverpool University Press, 2005).

MacRaild, D. M. (ed.), *The Great Famine and Beyond: Irish Migrants in Britain in the Nineteenth and Twentieth Centuries* (Dublin: Irish Academic Press, 2000).

MacRaild, D. M., *The Irish Diaspora in Britain, 1750–1939*, 2nd edn (Basingstoke: Palgrave Macmillan, 2011).

Marx, K., *Capital*, Vol. 1 (London: Lawrence and Wishart, 1974).

Marx, K. and F. Engels, *The Manifesto of the Communist Party* (London: CRW, 2004).

McBride, L. W. (ed.), *The Reynolds Letters: An Irish Emigrant Family in Late Victorian Manchester* (Cork: Cork University Press, 1999).

McElwee, W., *The Art of War: Waterloo to Mons* (London: Purnell, 1974).

McInally, M., *Edward Ilsley: Bishop of Birmingham, 1888–1911; Archbishop,1911–1921* (London: Burns and Oates, 2002).

Middlefell, A., *The Ancient Town of Stafford from the Eighth to the Twentieth Century* (Stafford: A. Middlefell, 2000).

Midgley, L. M. (ed.), *The Victoria History of the County of Stafford*, Vol. 5: *East Cuttlestone Hundred* (1959), at www.british-history.ac. uk/report/aspx?compid=53393&strquery.

Miller, K. A., *Emigrants and Exiles: Ireland and the Irish Exodus to North America* (New York: Oxford University Press, 1985).

Miller, K. A., D. N. Doyle, B. Boling and A. Schrier, *Irish Immigrants in the Land of Canaan: Letters and Memoirs from Colonial and Revolutionary America, 1675–1815* (Oxford: Oxford University Press, 2003).

Miskell, L., '"The heroic Irish doctor"? Irish immigrants in the medical profession in nineteenth-century Wales' in O. Walsh (ed.), *Ireland Abroad: Politics and Professions in the Nineteenth Century* (Dublin: Four Courts Press, 2003), pp. 82–94.

Miskell, L., 'Informal arrangements: Irish associational culture and the immigrant household in industrial South Wales' in J. Belchem and K. Tenfelde (eds), *Irish and Polish Migration in Comparative Perspective* (Essen: Klartext, 2003), pp. 111–12.

Mitchell, M. J. (ed.), *New Perspectives on the Irish in Scotland* (Edinburgh: John Donald, 2008).

Mokyr, J., *Why Ireland Starved: A Quantitative and Analytical History of the Irish Economy, 1800–1850* (London: George Allen and Unwin, 1985).

Morgan, D. H. J., *Family Connections: An Introduction to Family Studies* (Cambridge: Polity Press, 1996).

Morley, J., *The Life of William Ewart Gladstone*, Vol. 2 (London: Macmillan, 1903).

Myers, S. M., 'Childhood migration and social integration in adulthood', *Journal of Marriage and the Family*, 61 (August 1999), pp. 774–89.

Namier, L. B., *The Structure of Politics at the Accession of George III* (London: Macmillan, 1927).

Neal, F., *Black '47: Britain and the Famine Irish* (Liverpool: Newsham Press, 2003).

Newton, J. L., M. P. Ryan and J. R. Walkowitz (eds), *Sex and Class in Women's History* (London: Routledge and Kegan Paul, 1983).

Nolan, J., *Ourselves Alone: Women's Emigration from Ireland, 1885–1920* (Lexington: University Press of Kentucky, 1989).

Norman, E., *The English Catholic Church in the Nineteenth Century* (Oxford: Clarendon Press, 1984).

Ó Catháin, M. '"Dying Irish": Eulogising the Irish in Scotland in *Glasgow Observer* Obituaries', *The Innes Review*, 61:1 (2010), pp. 76–91.

O'Day, A., 'A conundrum of Irish diasporic identity: Mutative ethnicity', *Immigrants and Minorities*, 27:2/3 (July/November 2009), pp. 317–39.

O'Day, A., 'The political behaviour of the Irish in Great Britain in the later nineteenth and early twentieth centuries', in J. Belchem and K. Tenfelde (eds), *Irish and Polish Migration in Comparative Perspective* (Essen: Klartext, 2003), pp. 93–108.

O'Dowd, A., *Spalpeens and Tatty Hokers: History and Folklore of the Irish Migratory Agricultural Worker in Ireland and Britain* (Blackrock: Irish Academic Press, 1991).

O'Farrell, P., *Letters from Irish Australia, 1825–1925* (Sydney: New South Wales University Press, 1989).

Ó Gráda, C., 'Did Ireland "under"-industrialise?', *Irish Economic and Social History*, 37 (2010), pp. 117–23.

Ó Gráda, C., *Ireland: A New Economic History, 1780–1939* (Oxford: Clarendon Press, 1995).

O'Leary, P., 'The cult of respectability and the Irish in mid-nineteenth century Wales' in O'Leary (ed.), *Irish Migrants in Modern Wales* (Liverpool: Liverpool University Press, 2004), pp. 109–40.

O'Leary, P., *Immigration and Integration: The Irish in Wales, 1798–1922* (Cardiff: University of Wales Press, 2000).

O'Leary, P. (ed.), *Irish Migrants in Modern Wales* (Liverpool: Liverpool University Press, 2004).

O'Leary, P., 'Networking respectability: Class, gender and ethnicity among the Irish in South Wales, 1845–1914', *Immigrants and Minorities*, 23:2/3 (July/November 2005), pp. 255–75.

O'Sullivan, P. (ed.), *The Irish World Wide*, Vol. 2: *The Irish in the New Communities* (Leicester: Leicester University Press, 1992).

O'Sullivan, P. (ed.), *The Irish World Wide*, Vol. 5: *Religion and Identity* (Leicester: Leicester University Press, 2000).

Osgood, D., 'The Irish in Ashton-under-Lyne in the 1860s', *Transactions of the Historic Society of Lancashire and Cheshire*, 149 (2000), pp. 145–71.

Parkin, R., *Kinship: An Introduction to the Basic Concepts* (Oxford: Blackwell, 1997).

Porter, A. (ed.), *The Oxford History of the British Empire*, Vol. 3: *The Nineteenth Century* (Oxford: Oxford University Press, 1999).

Poulton-Smith, A., *Bloody British History: Stafford* (Stroud: The History Press, 2013).

Press, J., *The Footwear Industry in Ireland, 1922–1973* (Dublin: Irish Academic Press, 1989).

Press, J., 'Protectionism and the Irish footwear industry', *Irish Economic and Social History*, 13 (1986), pp. 74–89.

Pryce, W. T. R. (ed.), *From Family History to Community History* (Cambridge: Cambridge University Press, 1994).

Quinlivan, P. and P. Rose, *The Fenians in England, 1865–72: A Sense of Insecurity* (London: John Calder Press, 1982).

Radosh, P., 'Colonial oppression, gender and women in the Irish diaspora', *Journal of Historical Sociology*, 22:2 (June 2009), pp. 269–89.

Reed, M. C., *The London and North Western Railway: A History* (Penryn: Atlantic Transport, 1996).

Reid, D. A., 'The decline of St Monday, 1766–1876', *Past & Present*, 71 (1976), pp. 76–101.

Roberts, E., *A Woman's Place: An Oral History of Working-Class Women, 1890–1940* (Oxford: Basil Blackwell, 1984).

Roberts, F. and N. Henshaw, *A History of Sedgley Park and Cotton College* (Preston: T. Snape, 1985).

Rowe, D. M., 'Binding Prometheus: How the nineteenth century expansion of trade impeded Britain's ability to raise an army', *International Studies Quarterly*, 46:4 (December 2002), pp. 551–78.

Ryan, L., R. Sales, M. Tilki and B. Siara, 'Family strategies and transnational migration: Recent Polish migrants in London', *Journal of Ethnic and Migration Studies*, 35:1 (January 2009), pp. 61–77.

Scally, R. J., *The End of Hidden Ireland: Rebellion, Famine and Emigration* (Oxford: Oxford University Press, 1995).

Shorter, E., *The Making of the Modern Family* (New York: Basic Books, 1975).

Smart, C., *Personal Life: New Directions in Sociological Thinking* (Cambridge: Polity Press, 2007).

Smelser, N., *Social Change in the Industrial Revolution: An Application of Theory in the Lancashire Cotton Industry, 1770–1840* (London: Routledge and Kegan Paul, 1959).

Smith, D. P., 'An "untied" research agenda for family migration: Loosening the "shackles" of the past', *Journal of Ethnic and Migration Studies*, 30:2 (March 2004), pp. 263–82.

Smith, D. S., 'Family strategy: More than a metaphor?', *Historical Methods*, 20:3 (Summer 1987), pp. 118–20.

Smith, M. T. and D. M. MacRaild, 'Paddy and Biddy no more: An evolutionary analysis of the decline in Irish Catholic forenames among descendants of 19th century Irish migrants to Britain', *Annals of Human Biology*, 36:5 (September/October 2009), pp. 595–608.

Soanes, C. and Stevenson, A. (eds), *Concise Oxford English Dictionary*, 11th edn (Oxford: Oxford University Press, 2004).

Solomos, J., 'Beyond racism and multiculturalism', *Patterns of Prejudice*, 32:4 (1998), pp. 45–62.

Souvenir of the Golden Jubilee of St Patrick's, Stafford, with the History of the Parish (Stafford: St Patrick's Church, 1945).

Speirs, E. M., 'Army organisation in the nineteenth century' in T. Bartlett and K. Jeffery (eds), *A Military History of Ireland* (Cambridge: Cambridge University Press, 1996), pp. 335–57.

Stafford's Roll of Service in the Great War (Stafford: J. and C. Mort, 1920).

Staffordshire County Council, *Stafford Maps*, Local History Source Book L3 (Stafford: Staffordshire County Council Education Department, 1969).

Staffordshire Industrial Archaeology Society, *100 Years of Business in Stafford, 1900–2000* (Stafford: SIAS, 2000).

Steedman, C., *Policing the Victorian Community: The Formation of the English Provincial Police Forces, 1856–80* (London: Routledge and Kegan Paul, 1984).

Stobart, J. and N. Raven, *Towns, Regions and Industries: Urban and Industrial Change in the Midlands, c. 1700–1840* (Manchester: Manchester University Press, 2005).

Stone, L., *Family, Sex and Marriage in England, 1500–1800* (London: Weidenfeld and Nicolson, 1977).

Stone, L., 'Prosopography', *Daedalus*, 100:1 (Winter 1971), pp. 46–79.

Stone, L., *Road to Divorce: England, 1530–1987* (Oxford: Oxford University Press, 1990).

Swift, R., 'Identifying the Irish in Victorian Britain: Recent trends in historiography', *Immigrants and Minorities*, 27:2/3 (July/November 2009), pp. 134–51.

Swift, R. and S. Gilley (eds), *The Irish in Britain, 1815–1939* (London: Pinter Press, 1989).

Swift, R. and S. Gilley (eds), *The Irish in Victorian Britain: The Local Dimension* (Dublin: Four Courts Press, 1999).

Swords, L., *In Their Own Words: The Famine in North Connacht, 1845–9* (Blackrock: The Columba Press, 1999).

Syme, R., *The Roman Revolution* (Oxford: Clarendon Press, 1939).

Talbot, E., *Railways in and around Stafford* (Stockport: Foxline, 1994).

Tallett, F. and N. Atkin (eds), *Catholicism in Britain and France since 1789* (London: The Hambledon Press, 1996).

Tilly, L. A., 'Beyond family strategies, what?', *Historical Methods*, 20:3 (Summer 1987), pp. 123–5.

Timmins, G., 'Work in progress. Back passages and excreta tubs: Improvements to the conservancy system of sanitation in Victorian Lancashire', *Transactions of the Historic Society of Lancashire and Cheshire*, 161 (2012), pp. 47–63.

Trew, J. D., 'Reluctant diasporas of Northern Ireland: Migrant narratives of home, conflict, difference', *Journal of Ethnic and Migration Studies*, 36:4 (April 2010), pp. 541–60.

Turnbull, G., *Trauma* (London: Bantam Press, 2011).

Vaughan, W. E. (ed.), *A New History of Ireland*, Volume 5: *Ireland under the Union, 1801–70* (Oxford: Clarendon Press, 1989).

Vaughan, W. E. and A. J. Fitzpatrick, *Irish Historical Statistics: Population 1821–1971* (Dublin: Royal Irish Academy, 1978).

Vertovec, S., 'Conceiving and researching transnationalism', *Ethnic and Racial Studies*, 22:2 (1999), pp. 447–62.

Vertovec, S., 'Transnationalism and identity', *Journal of Ethnic and Migration Studies*, 27:4 (October 2001), pp. 573–82.

Waller, P. J., *Democracy and Sectarianism: A Political and Social History of Liverpool, 1868–1939* (Liverpool: Liverpool University Press, 1981).

Walsh, O. (ed.), *Ireland Abroad: Politics and Professions in the Nineteenth Century* (Dublin: Four Courts Press, 2003).

Walton, J. K., *Lancashire: A Social History, 1558–1939* (Manchester: Manchester University Press, 1987).

Watts, J., *The Facts of the Cotton Famine* (London: Frank Cass, 1968 [1866]).

Weld, I., *Statistical Survey of the County of Roscommon* (Dublin: R. Graisterry, 1832).

Weller, T. (ed.), *History in the Digital Age* (Abingdon: Routledge, 2013).

Williams, M. E., *Oscott College in the Twentieth Century* (Leominster: Gracewing, 2001).

Wylie, M. S., 'The long shadow of trauma', *Psychotherapy Networker*, 13 April 2010, www.psychotherapynetworker.org/magazine/recentissues/2010-marapr /item/810-the-long-shadow-of-trauma.

Young, M. and P. Willmott, *The Symmetrical Family: A Study of Work and Leisure in the London Region* (Harmondsworth: Penguin, 1975).

Websites

Cotton College, Staffordshire, www.freewebs.com/cottoncollege/.

Diaspora Connections, www.staff.ljmu.ac.uk/socjhers/stafford/index.html.

Douai Abbey, http://douaiabbey.org.uk/.

Griffith's Valuation data, www.leitrim-roscommon.com/GRIFFITH/.

Ireland.com (Irish Times), Irish Ancestors (surname distributions), www.irish-times.com/ancestor/surname/.

Leitrim-Roscommon Griffith's Display, www.leitrim-roscommon.com/GRIFFITH/.

Oscott College, *List of Superiors, Masters and Students 1794–1889*, www.oscott. net/uploads/1/3/6/.../listofsuperiorsmastersandstudents_1.pdf

World War I casualty lists of the Royal Navy and Dominion Navy, www.naval-history.net.

Online resources

Ancestry, www.ancestry.co.ukCalifornia Death Index 1940–97.

Canada: Soldiers of the First World War, 1914–18.

Canadian Passenger Lists, 1865–1935.

Census of England and Wales, Census of Scotland, Enumeration Returns 1841–1901.

Census of England and Wales, Census Schedules, 1911.

Indices of Births, Marriages and Deaths, England and Wales, 1835–1915 and 1915–2000.

England and Wales National Probate Calendar (Index of Wills and Administrations), 1858–1966.

General Medical Council, *UK Medical Registers*, 1867/1871/1879/1883/1887.

Kelly's Directory of Birmingham, 1908.

Kelly's Directory of Birmingham, Staffordshire, Worcestershire and Warwickshire, Part 2: *Staffordshire* (London: Kelly, 1872).

London Metropolitan Archive and Guildhall Library, UK Poll Books and Electoral Registers, 1865.

National Archives, WO363, British Army World War I Service Records, 1914–1920.

National Archives, RAIL410, Staff Registers of the London and North Western Railway.

New York Passenger Lists, 1820–1957.

Parish Registers, St Andrew's Church, Ancoats, Manchester.

Primary Valuation of Ireland (Griffith's Valuation), 1848–64; (available in numerous online and archive locations).

Reakes, J. (compiler), *Ireland: The Royal Irish Constabulary, 1816–1921*.

US Army Register of Enlistments.

US Census Returns, 1880 and 1910.

White's Historical Gazetteer and Directory for Staffordshire, 1851.

FindMyPast, www.findmypast.co.ukBritish Army Service Records, National Archives, WO97 Chelsea.

Staffordshire Name Indexes, www.staffsnameindexes.org.ukD659/1/4/10, Stafford Poor Law Union, Workhouse Admission Book, 1836–1900.

Author's database (see pp. 23–4)

The main tables in the database are listed below. Those marked * are part of the relational database.

Burials – adult Irish burials at St Austin's RC Church, Stafford, 1832–93: 7 fields, 356 records.

*Dwellings** – details of dwellings occupied by Irish families at some date, 1841–1901: 6 fields, 995 records.

*EDs** – population and housing data for Stafford and district enumeration districts, 1841–1901: 12 fields, 307 records.

*Families** – settled Irish families and known Stafford Catholic families: 34 fields, 369 records.

*Households** – addresses and household data on all Irish households, 1841–1901: 11 fields, 1,367 records.

*Incidents** – summary details of incidents in Stafford relating to or relevant to the Irish, 1767–1956: 5 fields, 3,143 records.

*Marriages** – marriage details involving at least one Irish or Irish-descended partner at St Austin's and St Patrick's RC Churches, 1835–1919: 25 fields, 388 records.

*Military** – First World War military service of Irish or Irish-descended men in Stafford: 12 fields, 196 records. (From *Stafford's Roll of Service in the Great War* (Stafford: J. and C. Mort, 1920)).

*Olims** – selected baptism records of Irish Catholic families, 1812–1894, to trace mother's maiden name ('olim'): 13 fields, 275 records.

*Priests** – details of Catholic and some other priests in Stafford, 1784–1938: 11 fields, 115 records.

*Pubs** – pubs and beer houses operating in Stafford, c. 1885: 9 fields, 145 records.

*SBCBurials** – burials of Irish or Irish-descended people at the Stafford Borough Council Cemetery, 1856–1921: 15 fields, 954 records.

*Staffdirish** – census enumeration data for all individuals living in a household containing at least one Irish person, 1841–1901: 16 fields, 8,146 records.

StPatRegisters – school roll details of Irish or Irish-descended pupils at St Patrick's School, 1884–1944: 10 fields, 414 records. (Data collected by the late Roy Mitchell.)

Index

Note: 'n' after a page reference indicates the number of a note on that page.

women
  roles in families, 5, 11, 13–14, 16,
    38, 92–3, 95, 112–3, 119–42
    passim, 166, 169, 191, 206, 246,
    261, 275, 288, 304, 308
  as 'tied migrants', 17, 308

Woolley, William Francis, shoe
  manufacturer 269, 270
workhouse *see* Stafford

Young, Michael and Willmott,
  Peter 37

LIBRARY, UNIVERSITY OF CHESTER